# Alaska Adventure
# 55 WAYS

# Alaska Adventure

## 55 WAYS

## SOUTHCENTRAL WILDERNESS EXPLORATIONS

**John Wolfe Jr. &**
**Rebecca Wolfe**

Foreword by
Helen D. Nienhueser

MOUNTAINEERS
BOOKS

**MOUNTAINEERS BOOKS** is dedicated to the exploration, preservation, and enjoyment of outdoor and wilderness areas.

1001 SW Klickitat Way, Suite 201, Seattle, WA 98134
800-553-4453, www.mountaineersbooks.org



Printed in China
Distributed in the United Kingdom by Cordee, www.cordee.co.uk

First edition, 2022
Previously published in different form as *55 Ways to the Wilderness in Southcentral Alaska*: 1972, 1978, 1985, 1994, and 2002.

Copyeditor: Jennifer Kepler
Design and layout: McKenzie Long
Cartographer: Pease Press
All photographs by the authors unless credited otherwise
Cover photographs: Front: *Lower Reed Lake, Trip 43, in the Talkeetna Mountains* (Photo by Shawn Horning); Back, left to right: *cycling on the beach (Trip 3), on the trail to Crescent Lake (Trip 14), and skiing on the Peters Creek Trail (Trip 36)*
Frontispiece: *Alpine meadows on a terrace at Thompson Pass, Trip 53, in early July*

The background maps for this book were produced using CalTopo. For more information, visit caltopo.com.

Library of Congress Cataloging-in-Publication Data is on file for this title at https://lccn.loc.gov/2021041451. LC ebook record is available at https://lccn.loc.gov/2021041452.

Mountaineers Books titles may be purchased for corporate, educational, or other promotional sales, and our authors are available for a wide range of events. For information on special discounts or booking an author, contact our customer service at 800-553-4453 or mbooks@mountaineersbooks.org.

Printed on FSC-certified materials

MIX
Paper from responsible sources
FSC® C008047

ISBN (paperback): 978-1-68051-542-8
ISBN (ebook): 978-1-68051-543-5

***An independent nonprofit publisher since 1960***

## To Nancy, Hans, and Helen

This guidebook originated more than five decades ago. Its various editions have always been dedicated to Hans Van der Laan, the book's first mapmaker, "who lives in the hearts of his family and friends and who, through his part in this book, shares with others his love of Alaska's mountains and valleys"—sentiments we renew here. Hans died at age thirty-three in an avalanche near Eklutna Glacier before that first edition was released in 1972.

We now also dedicate this guide to Nancy Simmerman, professional photographer, who created high-quality images for the first edition, went on to coauthor two more editions, and devoted untold hours to the book.

Finally, we dedicate this edition to Helen D. Nienhueser, the book's original author and coauthor of four later editions. She is our mom and grandma, who has always made sure that the book, trails, peaks, and preservation of a healthy and beautiful environment are part of our lives.

*The original team: Nancy (left), Hans, and Helen*

Trip Locator
ALASKA RANGE
Alaska Hwy
Tok
Denali National Park and Preserve
Denali
20,310'
Parks Hwy
Richardson Hwy
Copper Basin
Denali State Park
Mat-Su
Slana
MENTASTA MOUNTAINS
Tok Cutoff
Copper River
Nabesna
Yentna River
SUSITNA VALLEY
Talkeetna
TALKEETNA MOUNTAINS
Glennallen
Wrangell-St. Elias National Park and Preserve
WRANGELL MOUNTAINS
Glenn Hwy
MATANUSKA VALLEY
Matanuska River
Willow
Wasilla
Palmer
Susitna
Chugach State Park
CHUGACH MOUNTAINS
Chitina
Strelna
Kennicott
McCarthy
Chugach National Forest
Kenai
Anchorage
Valdez
Girdwood
Hope
Cook Inlet
Whittier
Prince William Sound
Nikiski
Sterling
Cordova
Soldotna
KENAI MOUNTAINS
Seward Hwy
Seward
Kenai National Wildlife Refuge
Sterling Hwy
Homer
Kenai Fjords National Park
Gulf of Alaska
Seldovia
Kachemak Bay State Park
Kachemak Bay State Wilderness Park
Little Susitna River
Knik Arm
Eagle River
Turnagain Arm
Seward Hwy
55 Trip Number
State or National Park
Wildlife Refuge
National Forest
Regional Boundary
Highway or Road
Community
0 20 40 MILES
0 20 40 KM
0 5 10 MILES
0 10 KM
For trip map legend, see page 55.

# Contents



## KENAI



## ANCHORAGE

## MAT-SU



## COPPER BASIN



OPPOSITE: *A misty July morning at one of the upper-elevation Williwaw lakes,Trip 29* (Photo by Hannah Leigh Pratt)

# Foreword

**It gives me great pleasure that my son and granddaughter are the coauthors of this new** incarnation of *55 Ways*, thus continuing what has become a family project for more than fifty years. We share the pleasure of guiding you into the places we love and ask that you join us in becoming stewards of these lands, taking care of them as you use them, and leaving no trace.

Alaska and Alaskans have changed greatly in the fifty years since the original version of this guide was published. Alaska is still a place of great beauty and abundant wilderness and wildlife. But our population has more than doubled; many Alaskans today are avid hikers, and trailheads near Anchorage are crowded on sunny summer days. Sixty years ago only hunters and mountain climbers braved the wilderness. When I started working on the first book in the late '60s, there were few protected areas in Southcentral Alaska, exceptions being the Chugach National Forest and the Kenai Moose Range—now the Kenai National Wildlife Refuge.

Big changes came to Alaska following the discovery of oil at Prudhoe Bay on the North Slope in 1968. An important change happened before the publication of our first edition: the Alaska legislature created Chugach State Park, near Anchorage, in 1970, thanks to a citizen initiative. Other changes came as a result of the need to settle land status before an 800-mile-long pipeline could be built to carry oil across Alaska to a year-round, ice-free port in Valdez. The change most relevant to hikers is the Alaska National Interest Lands Conservation Act (ANILCA), passed by Congress in 1980, which added 106 million acres of Alaska land as national parks, wildlife refuges, and other protected federal lands that belong to all of us (resulting in a total of 137 million acres of federal conservation land). One example of ANILCA-protected land in this book is Wrangell–St. Elias National Park and Preserve, the largest national park in the nation.

The promise of oil and construction of the pipeline led to a surge in population. It also led conservationists, worried about some of the changes, to become active in Southcentral Alaska. Local conservationists established offices in Anchorage, Fairbanks, and Juneau, physical places where a conservationist could be found, and the national Sierra Club opened an office in Anchorage. Not everyone saw active conservationists as a good thing: developers saw them as the enemy, and polarization between the two groups became significant. For example, the Sierra Club's membership list was top secret to protect its members from losing their jobs. When I was a volunteer director at the Alaska Center for the Environment, more than one whistleblower anonymously reported problems they had seen during

OPPOSITE: *Mount Yukla (elevation 7535 feet) in Chugach State Park from The Perch along Eagle River, Trip 25, in October*

*Helen Nienhueser, a lifelong chaser of mountain views*

work on pipeline construction. While there are traces of that polarization today, it is no longer a major sin to be a conservationist.

There is more to do. Outside Anchorage there is need for legislative protection of some areas, especially in the Talkeetna Mountains; a once-citizen-proposed Talkeetna Mountains State Park should be resurrected and considered. As in the past, securing such protection will require citizen leadership and advocacy. And Keystone Canyon, outside Valdez, needs protection.

We need more access to Chugach State Park, the third-largest state park in the country, adjacent to the largest population in the state. In particular, we need access to McHugh Peak from the west (Potter Valley); the physical access is there and has been used for years, but courts will decide whether there is legal access. Ram Valley above the Eagle River Nature Center is another place sorely in need of legal access. In itself a destination, Ram Valley also leads southeast to a key pass to the upper Peters Creek valley and Mount Rumble and northwest to a ridge walk back toward Vista Peak and the Glenn Highway.

An ongoing issue is the use of off-road vehicles in both summer and winter competing with quiet uses. Most hikers and skiers would prefer not to share trails and routes with mechanized vehicles. Progress has been made in separating these uses in the Municipality of Anchorage (including Chugach State Park), in Chugach National Forest, and in the Hatcher Pass Special Use Area in the Matanuska-Susitna Borough. Snowmachines and all-terrain vehicles (ATVs) are not allowed in the urban part of Anchorage. In Chugach State Park, snowmachines and ATVs are limited to certain areas. In most other parts of Southcentral Alaska outside of parks, off-road vehicles are generally allowed, and in Chugach National Forest in winter, snowmachines are widely allowed. We need more nonmotorized trails in these areas.

We need an organization in Southcentral Alaska that keeps watch over the whole area, taking on issues like protecting certain land, advocating for public access for outdoor recreation, and retaining areas of natural quiet across the whole area. There are many organizations that focus on specific issues or specific geographic areas such as Kachemak Bay, Kennicott, or the Susitna River. But problems and needs can go unaddressed without an organization or coalition that keeps watch over the whole area and takes action when needed. Opportunities for making a difference abound!

There are a number of groups that work on pieces of the issues related to trails and land protection in Southcentral Alaska. Among the most relevant are Great Land Trust, a nonprofit that focuses on conservation of lands for many purposes, including building trails and acquiring public access to public lands and waters; Alaska Trails, a nonprofit based in Anchorage that works statewide, providing funding ideas and sources for construction of trails as well as technical assistance, including easement acquisition; Chugach Park Fund at the Alaska Community Foundation, which raises and provides money for trail building and maintenance within Chugach State Park; Valley Mountain Bikers and Hikers, a nonprofit advocacy group for hiking and biking trails and builder of trails in the Matanuska-Susitna Borough; and Alaska Quiet Rights Coalition, which advocates for areas of natural quiet. For a full list of organizations, see the Alaska Conservation Foundation website. Most of these are membership organizations and always welcome new members and volunteers to help carry out their missions.

An alternative to a formal organization is an ad hoc group focused on a specific issue for a limited time. Such a group was responsible for the creation of Chugach State Park in 1970. It was a group of people with vision who convinced the legislature to act. We need citizen watchdogs, people who will see a need or an opportunity and pull together like-minded folk who work together as advocates for a needed park, trail, or access. Such a group is currently taking to court the issue of access to McHugh Peak from the west.

You can help take care of special places. Know what agency is responsible for management of the area, and notify the agency (or lobby the agency) when you see something that needs to be done. This book identifies the managing agency for each trip and gives contact information in the Resources section. Lobby your local assembly, state legislature, or congressional delegation for adequate funding for these agencies. Increased forest fires due to climate change are a looming threat to many of our favorite places. It is, of course, important to be careful with the use of fire. It also is critical to reduce your own carbon footprint, support renewable energy and energy-efficiency projects, and promote other government actions to reduce our collective carbon footprint; to do so is to protect these lands from unusually rapid and drastic changes.

Enjoy these special places—and protect them for our children and grandchildren to enjoy!

—Helen D. Nienhueser
Original author, *55 Ways to the Wilderness in Southcentral Alaska*

# Preface

**Our family homesteaded a plot of ground near what is now the Eagle River Nature Center. A** literal homestead, patented through the federal Homestead Act, its uphill sides abut land that became Chugach State Park. We are fortunate, privileged. We never tire of the view of rock and snow on the 6300-foot face of Eagle Peak, all jagged and imposing with a gentle rounded cap of white at the summit. Hiking the steep ridge behind the homestead is an annual rite; the view just gets bigger and broader with elevation, the forest and tall grass fall below, and you end up feeling on top of the world. This is a Southcentral Alaska mountain experience, with spruce, birch, and a wandering river laid out below, soft tundra underfoot for napping in the sun, and always more mountains above. This book helps us share these kinds of experiences with others.

Helen Nienhueser, the matriarch of our Alaska family who wrote the first version of this guide, moved to Southcentral Alaska in 1959 because of the mountains. The original *55 Ways* published in 1972 was the result of her explorations with the Mountaineering Club of Alaska, a group largely composed of other recent arrivals. We two authors, Helen's son and granddaughter, were born here and grew up admiring and sometimes living a "frontier" lifestyle—hiking, mountaineering, ski touring, paddling, picking berries, building backcountry cabins, and splitting wood to keep ourselves warm. Through these escapades, we have amassed three generations of collective memory about this land that we delight in, and we want to pass that on to you. We hope you will love this land as well, and work to protect it.

## THE LAND

Southcentral Alaska is a big place. Bounded roughly by the arc of the Alaska Range and Wrangell Mountains, the region measures almost 300 miles north to south and 350 miles east to west. Southcentral Alaska encompasses the vast drainages of the Susitna, Matanuska, and Copper Rivers. It is a land that rises up from the Pacific coast and culminates at the highest point in North America. The Chugach and Talkeetna Mountains push up almost as tall, filling out the Southcentral high ground. Between the sea and the summits lies a rich set of coastal and boreal forests, estuaries and freshwater wetlands, powerful rivers, quiet little creeks, and tundra uplands that support everything from mosquitoes and salmon to ravens and brown bears in the complex, interdependent web of life. And, not incidentally, this land supports 63 percent of the population of the state. Like the majority of Southcentral residents, our family's years here are a drop in the pond. Indigenous people have lived in Southcentral Alaska since time immemorial. With the new edition of the book, amid a rising movement toward

OPPOSITE: *Drifted snow in March creates patterns in the Placer River Valley, Trip 21.*

decolonization and equity in the outdoors, we recognize that to write a book about land necessitates acknowledging that land's first people.

## INDIGENOUS LAND ACKNOWLEDGMENT

The lands we celebrate in this book are Dena'ina, Sugpiaq (Alutiiq), and Ahtna homelands. The Dena'ina are part of a Dene (Athabascan) language group of mostly Interior peoples in Alaska and Canada (but also including Diné, sometimes referred to as Navajo, and Apache on the plains and dry mountains near the southern end of the Rockies); in parts of Southcentral Alaska, the Dena'ina are unusual among Athabascans in being a coastal people who hunt whales and fish on the ocean. The Sugpiaq (Alutiiq) people have a deep coastal tradition, living along Southcentral Alaska's shores, at the outer end of Kachemak Bay, on the southern coast of the Kenai Peninsula, and in Prince William Sound. The Ahtna are an Athabascan people centered in the Copper River watershed, whose inland territory spreads between the Alaska Range and Wrangell and Chugach Mountains and extends west at the Matanuska Valley and upper Susitna River. We acknowledge that these are the original human inhabitants of the lands in this book. These peoples reside here still, with vibrant cultures that appreciate and are deeply connected with the land of Southcentral Alaska. We are grateful for the literal and figurative trails they laid on the land. In the age of climate change, it would be wise for all of us to look to Indigenous peoples' land stewardship ethic for guidance.

Thanks to the movement for Indigenous land acknowledgment, we thought more than ever before, while hiking for this book, about the people whose lands we walk on. We are proud of our family's legacy, yet we recognize that the "frontier" ethos is one of colonialism and that this land was and still is the territory of the original people. Settlers from elsewhere intent on furs, gold, fish, timber, oil, and tourism have run rampant over the land, and the collective actions of everybody from Russian fur traders to recent homesteaders like ourselves have gravely harmed individual Alaska Natives and collective cultures.

We are finding land acknowledgment to be powerful. No matter your own cultural background, we invite you to learn more too. In this book, at the beginning of each trip entry, we provide an indication of Indigenous land: a brief acknowledgment of the people whose lands that specific trip traverses. We encourage you to check out Alaska Native Entities in the Resources section, particularly if you are not Alaska Native yourself, to learn more before you head out. Perhaps you will find out about a tribal language school you will pass to reach the trailhead or learn more about the cultural inspiration of that artist you've been following on social media.

## FULL CIRCLE

The protection of biodiversity and the effort to keep in check the outrageously fast change in climate are entirely dependent on the goodwill of the people. It is important that persons of all cultures, in their own ways, have the chance to experience the beauty and peace of the natural world and not just the disasters—floods, fires, droughts, and storms—nature can unleash. To experience firsthand the connections between plants and animals, water and soil, sun and air is to learn to love the earth. In the way that it "takes a village" to raise a child, it takes all persons and all peoples to care for the planet. We hope that this book, in its own small way, will help people of all walks of life find a way to the woods. It is time for the dominant culture that has enjoyed the Alaska concepts of "the last frontier" and "north to the future" to yield the trail to those who have been historically excluded or discouraged because of age, ability, race, size, or income and to actively support everyone's effort to enjoy the outdoors. The more that people share enjoyment and understanding of the natural world, the better chance we have of sustaining the natural network that supports us all.

—John Wolfe Jr.
and Rebecca Wolfe

# TRIPS AT A GLANCE

| | DISTANCE (MILES) | SHORTER (MILES) | TYPE | ELEVATION GAIN (FEET) | TIME | SEASON |
|---|---|---|---|---|---|---|
| **KENAI** | | | | | | |
| **1. Tutka Backdoor Trail** | 22.6 | 9 | Roundtrip | 5000 | 2–4 days | July–Sept. |
| **2. Alpine Ridge Trail and Grewingk Glacier** | 9 | 3.7 | Point to point | 2600 | Full day to 2 days | June–Oct. |
| **3. Cook Inlet Beach Bike** | 90 | 1.2 (walk) | Point to point | <500 | 3–5 days | Late May–Se |
| **4. Swan Lake Canoe System** | 13–60 | | Point to point | <500 | 2 days to 1 week | Late May–early Oct. |
| **5. Skyline Traverse** | 12.4 | 4 | Point to point | 5300 | Extended day | June–Sept |
| **6. Resurrection Pass Trail System** | 38.4 | | Point to point | 2400 | 1–2 days biking or 3–5 days hiking | June–Sept |
| **7. Russian Lakes Trail** | 21.5 | 6 | Point to point | 1600–2000 | Full day biking or 2 days hiking | June–Oct |
| **8. Caines Head** | 10–14 | | Roundtrip | 950 | 2 days | May–Sept |
| **9. Mount Marathon** | 2.5–5.2 | | Roundtrip | 2800 | Half day | Late May–O |
| **10. Harding Icefield** | 8.4 | 1 | Roundtrip | 3150 | Full day | June–Sept |
| **11. Lost Lake** | 14.8 | | Point to point | 2230–2430 | Extended day to 2 days | July–mid-Oc |
| **12. Ptarmigan and Vagt Lakes** | 10.7 | 2.8 | Point to point | 2000 | Full day to 2 days | May–Oct. |
| **13. Johnson Pass Iditarod Trail** | 23 | 4.4 | Point to point | 2000–2200 | 2 days hiking or full day biking | June–Sept |
| **14. Crescent and Carter Lakes Traverse** | 17.7 | 4.6 | Point to point | 2300 | 2–3 days | June–Oct |
| **15. Grandview Whistle Stop and Bartlett Glacier** | 6 | | Roundtrip | 750 | 2 days (train ride required) | July–mid-Se |
| **16. Manitoba Mountain** | 7.2 | 2.2 | Roundtrip | 2600 | Full day | Mid-June–Se |
| **17. Center Ridge Ski Tour** | 3.6–7 | 2 | Roundtrip | 1200 | Half day to full day | December–M |
| **18. Turnagain Pass Iditarod Trail** | 6.5 | 4.8 | Point to point | 500 | Half day to full day | Late June–Se |
| **19. Hope Coastal Walk** | Up to 6 | 1 | Roundtrip | 200 | Half day | May–Oct |
| **20. Blackstone Bay Overlook** | 6 | 1.8 | Roundtrip | 2900 | Full day | July–Sept |
| **ANCHORAGE** | | | | | | |
| **21. Skookum Glacier in Winter** | 12 | | Roundtrip | 300 | Full day | Feb.–early M |
| **22. Portage Pass in Winter** | 7.3 | 5 | Roundtrip | 480 | Full day | Feb.–Apri |
| **23. Berry Pass** | 17 | 5.5 | Roundtrip | 1900 | 2 days | June–Sep |
| **24. California Creek** | 7 | 3.7 | Point to point | 1450 | Full day | June–early O |
| **25. Crow Pass to Eagle River Traverse** | 23 | 4 | Point to point | 2800–3400 | 2–3 days | Mid-June–Se |
| **26. Penguin Peak** | 7.8 | 4 | Roundtrip | 4280 | Full day | June–Sep |
| **27. Glen Alps to Indian via Ship Lake** | 15 | 10 | Point to point | 2100–4700 | 2 days | June–mid-O |
| **28. Rabbit Creek to McHugh Creek Traverse** | 11.5 | 2.5 | Point to point | 1400 | Full day to 2 days | June–Sep |

**Notes:** A checkmark for biking, sking, or ice skating indicates that the trip is suitable for that activity. The chart specifies when only a portion may be suitable. **Shorter** is the shortest option; see each trip for details. Many trips feature ideas for extending your trip. The focus for trips for **Kids** is on children ages five to twelve; options marked with an asterisk (*) are most suitable for

| KIDS | BIKES | SKIS | SKATES | GLACIER | NEARBY SUMMITS |
|---|---|---|---|---|---|
| | | | | | |
| | | | | | |
| Glacier Lake Trail | | | | ✓ | Point 3647 |
| Short beach walks | ✓ | | | | |
| Entire trip | | ✓ | ✓ | | |
| | | | | | Point 3295; Point 3515 |
| ɔrt days on all or part of trail | ✓ | ✓ | | | |
| Part of trail, especially from west end | ✓ | ✓ | | | |
| Entire trip | | | | | |
| Part of Hiking Trail | | | | | Race Point (3022') |
| ature center trails to toe of glacier | | | | ✓ | |
| Overnight* | ✓ | ✓ | | | Mount Ascension (5710') |
| Entire trip | Iditarod Trail/ Vagt Lake | | | | |
| Center Creek bridge | ✓ | Center Creek (off-trail) | Possible | | |
| Either end to first lake | Crescent Creek Trail | Carter end to cabins | Possible | | |
| Entire trip | | | | ✓ | |
| Little Manitoba | Mills Creek Trail | ✓ | | | Manitoba Mountain (3702'); Silvertip Peak (5020') |
| See shorter options | | ✓ | | | |
| Entire trip | ✓ | Partly off-trail | | | |
| Entire trip | | | | | |
| Horsetail Falls | | | | ✓ | |
| | | | | | |
| First portion | Fat-tire bikes when conditions allow | ✓ | | ✓ | |
| Portage Lake | Fat-tire bikes when conditions allow | ✓ | ✓ | ✓ | |
| Overnight* | | | | | |
| ' and back from either end | Beaver Pond Trail (rooty) | ✓ | | | |
| Either end | | Eagle River end | | ✓ | |
| | | Bird Creek valley | | | Penguin Peak (4335') |
| | Powerline Trail | Arctic to Indian | | | The Ramp (5240'); The Wedge (4660') |
| ıke overnight from Rabbit ıke trailhead; Table Rock | Rabbit Lake Trail | Rabbit Lake Trail | Possible | | McHugh Peak (4311') |

older, more experienced children. A checkmark for **Glacier** indicates a glacier is a destination or key part of the view. The destinations in **Nearby Summits** are accessible from the route and generally mentioned in the trip descriptions.

| | DISTANCE (MILES) | SHORTER (MILES) | TYPE | ELEVATION GAIN (FEET) | TIME | SEASON |
|---|---|---|---|---|---|---|
| **29. Williwaw Lakes Loop** | 18.5 | 4 | Loop | 3800 | 2–3 days | June–Sept |
| **30. McHugh Peak** | 5.6 | 2.4 | Roundtrip | 2900 | Half day | Year-rounc |
| **31. Flattop Ridge Loops** | 6.8–8.8 | 3.2 | Loop | 2850 | Full day | Late June–ec Oct. |
| **32. Near Point and Wolverine Peak Loop** | 10.3 | 6.8 | Loop | 4265 | Full day | May–Oct. |
| **33. Anchorage Coastal Walk** | 5 | | Roundtrip | 400 | Half day | April–Oct. |
| **34. Arctic Valley Ridge Loop** | 5.6 | 4 | Loop | 2450 | Half day | May–Oct. |
| **35. South Fork Valley Trail and Ewe Valley Overlook** | 21 | 5 | Roundtrip | 3650 | 3 days | June–Sept |
| **36. Peters Creek Winter Tour** | 6.3 | | Roundtrip | 790 | Half day | Nov.–Apri |
| **37. Eklutna Lake Bikepacking** | Up to 26 miles | 17 | Roundtrip | Up to 800 | 2 days | Late May–Se |
| **38. Bold Ridge Overlook Bike to Hike** | 15.5 | | Roundtrip | 2850 | Full day | Mid-June–mid-Sept. |
| **MAT-SU** | | | | | | |
| **39. Rabbit Slough in Winter** | 10 | 4 | Roundtrip | <10 | Half day (longer if hiking) | Oct.–Marc |
| **40. Lazy Mountain Loop** | 8.5 | 5.4 | Loop | 3300 | Full day | Late May–mid-Oct. |
| **41. Hatcher Pass to Government Peak Traverse** | 7.2 | 1.3 | Point to point | 2360 | Full day | July–Sept. |
| **42. Talkeetna Mine** | 6.2 | | Roundtrip | 1800 | Half day | July–Sept |
| **43. Reed Lakes** | 9.1 | 4.7 | Roundtrip | 2100 | Full day to 2 days | July–Sept |
| **44. Nancy Lakes Canoe Loop** | 8 | 1.6 | Loop | 400 | Full day to 2 days | Mid-May–early Oct |
| **45. Peters Hills** | 15.6 | 5.4 | Roundtrip | 3100 | 2–3 days | July–Sept |
| **46. K'esugi and Curry Ridges** | 37–48 | 6 | Point to point | 6100–8300 | 3–5 days or 4–6 days | June–Sep |
| **47. Hicks Creek and Chitna Pass** | 48 | | Point to point | 5300 | 4 days or more | Late June–A |
| **48. Lion Head** | 2.3 | | Roundtrip | 1100 | Half day | June–Sep |
| **49. Belanger Pass Loop** | 17 | 5.7 | Loop | 4000 | 2–3 days | June–Sep |
| **COPPER BASIN** | | | | | | |
| **50. Mentasta Mountains Loop** | 22 | | Loop | 3050 | 3 days | June–Aug |
| **51. Dixie Pass** | 17.6 | | Roundtrip | 3730 | 3–4 days | Late June–e Sept. |
| **52. Jumbo Mine and Root Glacier Trail** | 12.1 | 4.6 | Roundtrip | 4000 | 1.5 days | June–Sep |
| **53. Moonlight Odyssey at Thompson Pass** | 6 | 2 | Roundtrip | 2000 | Half day | Late June–S |
| **54. Historic Valdez Trail** | 8.3 | 4 | Roundtrip | 2050 | Full day | Mid-May–mid |
| **55. Shoup Bay Trail** | 2 | | Roundtrip | 250 | Half day | Mid-May–C |

| KIDS | BIKES | SKIS | SKATES | GLACIER | NEARBY SUMMITS |
|---|---|---|---|---|---|
| Overnight at Williwaw Lakes* | Wolverine Bowl; Powerline Trail; Middle Fork Loop Trail in winter | Williwaw Lakes Trail; Middle Fork Loop Trail | Possible | | O'Malley Peak (5150')<br>Koktoya Peak (5148')<br>Tanaina Peak (5358')<br>West Tanaina Peak (5266')<br>Tikishla Peak (5230') |
| Ridgewalk portion | | | | | McHugh Peak (4311') |
| Out and back on Flattop<br>nnyside Trail, Powerline Trail, or Rabbit Lake Trail | Powerline Trail; Rabbit Lake Trail | Powerline Trail and Rabbit Lake Trails | | | Flattop Mountain (3510')<br>Peak 2 (3609')<br>Peak 3 (3996')<br>Flaketop Mountain (4488')<br>Ptarmigan Peak (4910') |
| latter portions; Near Point* | Near Point Trail, section on old homestead road | | | | Wolverine Peak (4491')<br>Near Point (3051')<br>Tikishla Peak (5230') |
| Entire trip | | ✓ | | | |
| Portions | | | | | Rendezvous Peak (4101')<br>Mount Gordon Lyon (4134') |
| Out-and-back day hike; overnight* | | | | | Triangle Peak (5495') |
| All or a portion* | Peters Creek Valley Trail to mile 5 only | ✓ | | | Mount Eklutna (4065') |
| Shorter portion day trip; overnight* | ✓ | ✓ | ✓ | | Pepper Peak (5415') |
| | Eklutna Lakeside Trail | | | | |
| | | | | | |
| Portion | Fat-tire bikes | ✓ | ✓ | | |
| | | Morgan Horse Trail | | | Lazy Mountain (3740')<br>Matanuska Peak (6093') |
| )ut and back to April Bowl tarns | | April Bowl (backcountry skiing) | | | Hatch Peak (4811')<br>Government Peak (4781') |
| | Archangel Road | Archangel Road (groomed) | | | |
| Overnight* | | Archangel Road (groomed); Snowbird Mine village | Possible | | |
| Entire trip | | ✓ | ✓ | | |
| Overnight(s)* | | | | | |
| Portion of full trip* | | | | | Golog (2970') |
| | ATV trails (when dry) on either end | Out and back from either trailhead | | | Mount Monarch (7108') |
| Entire trip | | | | | Lion Head (3185') |
| | ATV trails (when dry) on either end | | | | |
| | | | | | |
| Entire trip* | | | | | Noyes Mountain (8147') |
| | Nugget Creek Trail | | | | Point 5770 |
| Root Glacier Trail | | | | ✓ | |
| tter portions near trailhead | | Backcountry skiing | | | Odyssey (4539')<br>Little Odyssey (3950') |
| Portion | | | | | |
| Entire trip | | ✓ | | | |

# Introduction

**In the middle of a Southcentral Alaska summer, the sun rises slowly through the horizon and arcs** broadly for more than nineteen hours before setting just as slowly; the day is replete with light and shadows. Sunrises and sunsets last a long time compared to places farther south, and the light is richer. In midwinter, there are long nights to be sure, but the sunlight, when it comes, is syrupy gold, like the light of sunset for most of the day.

There is nothing finer than the crisp outline of deep-purple peaks silhouetted against a brightening morning sky, or the blush of alpenglow on rock and snow as the sun sinks away. And there is no place finer to observe the swell and fade of light than outdoors—deep in a wildflower meadow, high on a tundra ridge, or in the middle of a frozen lake in Southcentral Alaska.

In the following pages we present a variety of trips, focused on foot trails but including canoe trails, summer mountain bike and winter fat-bike tracks, ski routes, and even "wild skating" trips. We include multiple opportunities to adventure without any trail at all. There are quick day trips and trips that could extend to a week or more. We like to think that this book will be an all-around guide to orient visitors and new arrivals to a broad spectrum of outdoor opportunities in this part of Alaska, and to give people who have been around awhile new things to try. We hope some people will challenge themselves to undertake all 55 ways.

## IDITAROD TRAIL AND ALASKA LONG TRAIL

While this book describes short and long trips, many are on the longer side, but we have called out the shorter ways too. We encourage readers looking for day trips to find the Shorter Options section included in many trips and to check the Trips at a Glance table to determine whether a particular trip has shorter options.

Even for long trips, though, "long" is relative. Alaska is known for its long distances but not for long-distance hiking trails—nothing near the scale of the Appalachian Trail or Pacific Crest Trail, those epic routes that cross the Lower 48 with mileages in the thousands. But the Iditarod Trail, a gold rush–era winter trail from tidewater at Seward to tidewater at Nome, has captured the world's imagination, whelped a charismatic sled dog race across the state, and become formally enshrined in easements and plats. Congress designated it the Iditarod National Historic Trail. It crosses Southcentral Alaska and the Alaska Range to reach the Iditarod Mining District in the Interior before reaching the northwest coast at Nome. Yet most of its segments are winter trails only, swampish or brushy in summer and unsuitable for walking.

In Southcentral Alaska, the original author of this book found and cleared an old segment of the Iditarod Trail in Eagle River Valley with a troop of Girl

OPPOSITE: *A trail runner passes a hiker east of Berry Pass, Trip 23.* (Photo by Gretchen Nelson)

Scouts in the 1960s, and the State of Alaska reestablished the segment from there to Crow Pass as a 23-mile hiking trail after the legislature designated Chugach State Park in the early 1970s. Chugach National Forest, which has mining-era trails within its jurisdiction on the eastern Kenai Peninsula, conceived a plan to reestablish the Southern Trek of the Iditarod Trail, running from Seward to Crow Pass, as a trail that could be traversed not only in winter but also in summer. That project is taking many years but is making progress.

Now Alaska Trails, a respected nonprofit group, has picked up on an idea generated by former governor Tony Knowles for an Alaska Long Trail. It is conceived as starting with the Iditarod's Southern Trek (roughly 80 miles) and extending to and through the Talkeetna Mountains, through Denali State Park and the edge of Denali National Park and Preserve, and continuing north through Tanana Valley State Forest to Fairbanks, a total of some 500 miles connecting communities and possibly backcountry huts along the way. Given that the existing long-distance hiking trails in Alaska are the Chilkoot Trail in Southeast Alaska, at 33 miles, and the Resurrection Pass Trail on the Kenai Peninsula, at 38 miles (and getting effectively shorter due to highway rerouting), 500 miles would be no small improvement.

The Alaska Long Trail would cross the homelands of the Sugpiaq (Alutiiq), Dena'ina, Ahtna, and Tanana peoples. It would cross the Kenai, Chugach, and Talkeetna Mountains and the Alaska Range and the drainages of the Kenai, Susitna, and Yukon Rivers. It would use lands designated Chugach National Forest, Kenai Mountains–Turnagain Arm National Heritage Area, Iditarod National Historic Trail, Chugach State Park, Hatcher Pass Management Area, Denali State Park, Denali National Park and Preserve, and Tanana Valley State Forest.

Several of the trips in this book will likely be incorporated into the Alaska Long Trail or otherwise are associated with the southern Iditarod National Historic Trail system (including the main line and side trails). We identify them in the trip text. When you take one of these trips, imagine the opportunity to extend that experience for a month of 15-mile hiking days. Trail enthusiasts can keep track of trail progress: search online for "Iditarod Southern Trek" and for "Alaska Long Trail." Consider supporting the efforts of Alaska Trails (alaskatrails.org) and the Alaska Huts Association (alaskahuts.org) to bring long trails and connected backcountry huts to Alaska.

## MODES OF TRAVEL

Outdoor enthusiasts can venture into the backcountry via multiple modes, including modes suitable for summer, such as bikes and canoes, and modes better suited to winter, such as skis, fat-tire bikes, and ice skates.

### Mountain Bikes and E-Bikes

Several of these 55 ways are suited to mountain biking. There are some that may seem suitable but that we do not recommend wholeheartedly because of strong potential for conflict with hikers. Other trails are simply not good rides for most cyclists, or are closed to cyclists. See Trips at a Glance to evaluate which ones are suitable.

Those of us who ride mountain bikes tread a fine line. Cyclists are quiet, like hikers, but mechanized and fast, which can lead to safety and aesthetic conflicts with walkers. E-bikes—mountain bikes with an electric motor to assist—take these issues a step farther. It is incumbent upon those of us who value riding in the woods and mountains to ride responsibly and build goodwill to prevent severe conflicts. To this end, mountain bikers should:

*Mountain bikes and fat-tire bikes work well on several trails, as shown here on the Russian Lakes Trail, Trip 7, in September.*

- Avoid riding trails that are closed or not recommended by the land manager for bikes or e-bikes.
- Avoid wet trails, and try not to spin or skid. Seasonal trail closures for horses are a good proxy for wet-trail season.
- Never ride off a trail, to avoid damage to vegetation, unless it is a winter trail with adequate snow cover.
- Keep your speed down.

See On-Trail Etiquette later in this section for more suggestions.

When you take a trip by bike, for your own safety, carry tools and know how to use them (see Essential Gear). Regroup often with companions in case someone in the back of the group breaks down. Wear a helmet. Be careful not to overextend your trip and get so far off the road system that you would be overcome by darkness or exhaustion if you should have to walk back. Before going on overnight rides, load your bike and test its handling on a trail near home.

E-bikes are becoming more popular, largely on trails close to recharging opportunities, but backcountry trails have started to see traffic. Land managers have not settled on how to manage this user group. It is not yet clear how acceptance versus conflict among users may play out. People who have e-bikes love them because they allow extended range for less effort, they provide greater access for those with limitations, and their speed and power are fun, but others are skeptical. E-bikers should venture only where mountain biking already is an established use and not use the power boost to extend biking into backcountry areas that have not already been used by bikes, either because of distance or technical challenges.

E-bikes may extend an individual's personal range in miles, so a less experienced or less fit rider may cover the ground of a stronger mountain biker. It probably is not reasonable to use an e-bike to power through conditions that are overly difficult for most mountain bikers. To do so is to invite comparisons to motorbikes and all-terrain vehicles (ATVs) and to risk the damage to footpaths that is seen on ATV tracks. E-bikers should look up land manager guidelines about e-bikes before reaching a trailhead and should pay extra attention to cautions about trail erosion and to trail etiquette guidelines to avoid damaging trails—and relationships with other trail users.

## Canoeing

Two trips in this book describe canoeing through chains of lakes. Both present the option of combining the lakes with a river section. Lakes present few obvious dangers, but their safe appearance can lead to complacency. Even on small, apparently calm lakes, wind can kick up whitecaps in a hurry. The rivers described here are not difficult but should not be attempted without experience and training.

A plunge into Alaska's cold waters can lead to hypothermia. Know how to treat it (see Backcountry Safety later in this section) and how to administer CPR.

Follow a few basic guidelines when venturing out on the water. First, be sure you and everyone in your group knows how to swim. Always wear a life jacket. Never stand up in a canoe. Keep your weight low, and hold on to the gunwales as you shift in the boat. Move one person at a time. Leave the dog at home. On lakes, paddle close to shore. If a strong wind comes up, get off the water.

Be sure your boat will float even when full of water, and lash all gear securely. If you capsize, stay with the boat and work it to shore to ensure that your survival equipment is not lost. Have plenty of dry, warm clothes handy in a waterproof bag.

The lake trips in this book involve portaging. Lashing a stout stick across the top of a large backpack as a canoe rest can make portaging easier. Portages are high-impact areas, often with eroded or muddy trails. Try not to make trails worse. Also be especially careful to take litter with you and bury human waste more than 200 feet (100 big steps) from water.

## Winter Modes

Several of the trips in this book are best during the snow and ice season, which typically runs from November through April or early May. Other trips that are primarily summer routes are accessible in winter for those equipped for frozen conditions. There is nothing better than an outing on a blue-sky day in winter, with brilliant light on the snow and mountain peaks, and dark spruce and blue shadows creating contrast.

The winter timeline that many Southcentral Alaska residents *hope for* is as follows.

**Early winter.** A freeze-up in early winter before substantial snow has fallen can make frozen-smooth highways of lakes and some creeks, ideal for ice skates and bicycles with studded tires. Formerly muddy routes may be frozen and more pleasant for hiking. Skates and winter bikes are great when there is not yet enough snow for ski touring. Fat-tire or mountain bikes with studded tires are often at their best when trails are icy and the snow shallow.

**Midwinter.** Once snow really starts to fall, ski touring and snowshoeing are the typical choices when breaking trail is necessary. Fat-tire bikes are fun when snow trails are not too soft—that is, when packed in by continual bike use or by other users.

**Late winter.** An icy crust forms as a result of the thaw-freeze sun action on spring snow, or sometimes from the effects of rain or wind. In crust conditions, skate skiers and cyclists can move quickly over miles of terrain and are not restricted to packed trails.

The reality in Southcentral Alaska, especially closer to the coast and especially with the effects of climate change in the subarctic, is that winter conditions are variable and don't follow the hoped-for timeline. Periods of midwinter rain and warm chinook winds are not uncommon. Temperatures may vary in any winter month from above freezing to below zero Fahrenheit. Thus, outdoors people prepare for every eventuality by owning, borrowing, or renting winter gear and by paying attention to weather forecasts and online forums so they know when to do what. Has a deep freeze finally frozen the biggest lakes (e.g., Kenai and Skilak Lakes) without a snow covering, so that long-distance ice skating is possible? Has spring crust melted out at sea level but developed at higher elevations, such as Hatcher Pass and Turnagain Pass? Has a midwinter rain glazed a trail with variable ice and crust, perfect for studded bike tires but poor for much else? The idea is to take advantage of whatever nature creates, selecting from a diversity of travel modes to match conditions. See Trail and Snow Conditions in the Resources section for groups that track conditions.

*Nordic blades, which clip into skate-skiing boots, are ideal for wild skating on ice, but standard hockey skates or figure skates work too.* (Photo by Cody Priest)

### Skiing

Many people do fine without multiple pairs of skis for different purposes, but others soon find themselves collecting a quiver. Cross-country ski touring is the traditional mode for exploring summer hiking trails when they are covered in too much snow for walking. Low-angle touring packages are typically light- or medium-weight skis, often with fish scales or other no-wax traction built into the base, and midweight boots that bend at the toe.

Skate skis, the lightest and fastest skiing mode, slice across hard snow like speed skates over ice, but are suitable in the backcountry only when the surface is crusted enough to support a skier's weight. Backcountry skate skiers favor the more robust ski models, not the very lightest racing skis, because the skis should have enough strength to endure flexing through backcountry dips, and because who wants to hobble out of the backcountry on a broken ski? Skate ski boots are stiff and provide good ankle support.

The beefier option is alpine touring (AT) skis, boots, and bindings, for skiing up mountains and making fast, slick turns on the way down. An AT setup typically includes large but surprisingly light plastic boots akin to downhill ski boots, but the heel can either lock in for skiing down or release for cross-country and uphill travel, with climbing skins added on the bases for traction (skinning). The skis are wide for flotation, with good sidecut for downhill turning, and they have metal edges for icy side slopes. Their alpine co-conspirators, splitboards and telemark skis, offer more skills to master and, yes, more gear a skier could add to her quiver.

### Fat Biking

Fat-tire bikes are the chunky cousins of street bicycles, with enormously fat tires (4 to 5 inches wide) for traction and flotation on soft surfaces, and with studs in the tires to aid with steering and traction on ice. Originally developed in Alaska, fat-tire bikes have gone mainstream as designs have been refined for good performance. Such bikes usually need some kind of trail packed in by bikes or by other users—for example, the miles of snowmachine trails in the Matanuska-Susitna Borough and in parts of the Kenai Peninsula.

Bikes with studded tires, including normal mountain bikes with narrower tires, are superb on hard-packed snow and icy routes. With care, they may be suitable on smooth lake ice, but making quick turns is not recommended.

### Nordic Skating

Crisp, smooth lake ice screams for "wild skating." (Watch the short video "Wild Ice" on winterbear.com for an introduction.) Those in the know favor Nordic skates. These long-bladed skates are fast like speed skates and ride more smoothly over imperfections and cracks in backcountry ice than rink skates. Cross-country ski bindings can be mounted on Nordic skates, and skate ski boots clip in and out of the Nordic skates easily. When lakes are iced over, people can still follow the summer canoe routes (Trips 4 and 44) by skating on the ice, pulling a sled for gear if desired, and clipping in and out of the skates for the "portages." If you own hockey or figure skates, by all means, use them in the backcountry. See Traveling on Ice under Backcountry Safety later in this section.

### Winter Hiking

And what about plain old walking? Hikers certainly don't throw in the towel when the season turns cold. Summer hiking shoes are often adequate, especially for shorter hikes. Add gaiters for extra protection from snow. The gaiters, along with thicker winter

*Original author Helen D. Nienhueser instills the fun of the outdoors in her sons at Rendezvous Peak (Trip 34), circa 1970. Contemporary Leave No Trace principles discourage harming delicate tundra.* (Photo by Nancy Simmerman)

socks, help keep feet warm. Go for insulated winter boots for greater warmth.

Get a set of metal spikes that stretch over shoes with rubber heel and toe fittings. These are not as robust (or expensive) as mountaineers' crampons but are grippy enough for anything but literal ice climbing and much more effective than the tiny metal studs made for slippery pavement. People hike many of the popular trails through the winter and keep the snow packed down. Hiking is cheaper than winter biking, skiing, or skating and should be given its seasonal due.

## HIKING WITH CHILDREN

Experienced hikers can take children along on almost all the trips in this book, but some hikes are too long or difficult for most kids. Try out the easier hikes with your children first. Parents can carry babies almost anywhere in a pack. From three years old and up, children are tougher physically than mentally. Little guys can manage a few miles a day with play breaks and an occasional piggyback ride (for variation, not because of true exhaustion). If they're accustomed to long walks or hiking, children five and older can easily cover 4 to 5 miles a day and often more.

Most important is that a trip has variety—a stream or lake to play in, rocks to climb on. Canoe trips combine short hikes on the portages with time on the water, and kids love them. Contrary to popular opinion, many children find climbing uphill more interesting than flat trails, but too much of anything will do in a youngster. To keep things interesting, pick up a "magic stick"—you carry one end; they take the other. Trade off leads. Use it for follow-the-leader around a tree. Give a boost when needed. Or keep the pace moving with leapfrog hide-and-seek, where kids go a bit ahead and "disappear" while hapless parents "search" for them until they pop out behind and charge ahead to hide again. Always carry favorite nibble foods. Join forces with another family to ensure your child has a playmate.

Parents should set their sights low and worry less about reaching destinations than they normally would, gradually teaching young ones that a steady pace pays off with the reward of hanging out at a lake or on a summit. See Trips at a Glance for suggested trips for kids. And ignore the protests at home when you suggest a hike; kids love it once they're out.

## ESSENTIAL GEAR

Although the outdoor industry pushes enough gear to fill your pack and empty your wallet many times over, the beauty of hiking is how little you really need. That said, it is important to recognize that, just a short distance from the road, you are effectively in the wilderness. You must be self-sufficient, with proper clothing, food, camping equipment, and navigation aids. *Mountaineering: The Freedom of the Hills*, the classic backcountry how-to book, lists the Ten Essentials (developed by The Mountaineers), life-saving gear and supplies that outdoor adventurers should carry on every trip, whether they plan to be out for days or only a few hours.

1. **Navigation.** Traditionally, navigation essentials are a map and compass, the minimum for navigation if you become disoriented or end up off route or in case fog rolls in. This category can include an altimeter, a GPS device or phone app, along with extra batteries, a battery pack, or a solar charger.
2. **Headlamp and extra batteries.** For three to four weeks in midsummer Alaska when darkness never falls, one headlamp per party can be sufficient. Otherwise, bring one headlamp per person. Always bring extra batteries.
3. **Sun protection.** Don't underestimate the Alaska summer sun, particularly on the clearest days of summer when the sun is up during all waking hours and can be inescapable above tree line. Likewise, beware of sun-reflecting snow in winter, particularly in March and April. Sun protection can include sunscreen with SPF 15 or higher, sunglasses, and clothing to protect the skin.
4. **First aid.** Low-risk trips may reasonably be undertaken with a small kit focusing on foot protection, small bandages, insect repellent, and required medications. Long excursions and those with higher risks demand preparation for more serious injury. A first-aid kit can be shared among a group.
5. **Knife and repair items.** Repair items can be one set per group.
6. **Fire.** The ability to start a fire in wet weather can mean the difference between living and dying if you get caught out unexpectedly. Carry a small kit of waterproof matches, a lighter, and compressed wax starter material. A camp stove and fuel may be appropriate.
7. **Shelter.** Carry a bivouac sack, a reflective waterproof blanket, or a small tarp at minimum, or a tent.
8. **Extra food.** This is food you expect to return home with if all goes according to plan—not the lunch and energy bars you expect to eat.
9. **Extra water.** This is more water than you expect to need, or a water purifying method.
10. **Extra clothes.** Imagine the worst-case scenario, such as needing to stay out overnight with a broken bone, and bring sufficient clothing to survive, preferably comfortably.

In Alaska, add **bear protection** to your essentials. For every single summer trip in this book, we recommend that hikers carry bear spray and keep it readily at hand, ideally one canister for each person over about fourteen years old. See Bears and Other Wildlife later in this section for more.

## Clothing

Don't be hoodwinked into thinking you need high-tech clothes to go for a walk outdoors. Knowing the limitations of your clothes and exercising good judgment are more important than owning expensive threads. Invest most in durable raingear. Waterproof, breathable fabrics are expensive and generally better for winter than for summer rainstorms but have become the gold standard for hiking. Fully waterproof raingear, especially lightweight versions made by companies that specialize in waterproof wear for commercial fishing, works and is cheaper but accumulates more sweat without the breathability factor.

Even in midsummer in the mountains, take gloves, a warm hat, coats or sweaters, and raingear. In Alaska's cool and sometimes rainy climate, synthetics are better than cotton for backcountry hiking because they dry quickly and don't absorb water into the fibers. Cotton clothes (most hoodies, T-shirts, and jeans) will not keep you warm if they are wet.

Some clothing associated with winter is necessary for fall and spring travel, especially up high: mittens with windproof shells, an extra pair of wool socks, synthetic or wool long underwear, wind pants, and a buff. Gaiters, worn over boots, keep the snow out and help keep feet warm and dry. Gaiters are useful even in summer, not only for crossing lingering snowfields but for keeping tundra crumbs and grit out of boots as well.

Midwinter trips require a thick parka and insulated pants, primarily for sitting in the cold for a long time, for instance, while waiting for food to cook, or especially in case of injury. Many loose-fitting layers of clothing allow you to fine-tune your body temperature for different levels of activity and changing weather conditions.

## Footwear

Some people swear by traditional leather hiking boots, others by trail running shoes. The goal is protection—you need healthy feet to get you home again. Avoid blisters by making sure shoes are comfortable and by carrying tape or thin, adhesive padding made for feet (available at pharmacies); use it immediately at signs of hot spots (friction points that will quickly blister). If you have weak ankles, make sure you have boots with solid ankle support. Many of these trips take you to country where you'll want to leave the trail and explore. For this, ensure that boots have a decent edge and a solid, non-flared heel that you can plunge into hard snow or rough scree (gravel). Rocky terrain may call for a boot with a beefy toe box for additional protection.

For winter, hiking or snowshoeing boots with a rubber foot, a nylon or leather upper, and thick liners are usually fine. If you will be using snowshoes with bulky boots, make sure they will move freely in the toe opening. See Winter Modes earlier for information on skis and skates.

## Mode-Specific Essential Gear

Depending on the mode of travel, additional gear is necessary for a smooth trip. Bicyclists (fat-tire and mountain) will need to bring a basic bike multitool, chain breaker, spare chain link, pump, patch kit, and tube to get themselves out of the backcountry in case of a breakdown. Additional maintenance items are recommended for beach riding in Trip 3. Canoeists and kayakers will need (in addition to a boat) paddles, life jackets, and a pump, scoop, or sponge for bailing water. When traveling in snowy mountains, additional safety gear is necessary; see Avalanches under Backcountry Safety later in this section.

For overnight trips, a tent, a sleeping pad, a sleeping bag, a lightweight cookstove, cooking utensils, and a bear-proof food storage system are standard (though not strictly necessary if the essentials of food and shelter are covered in more minimalist ways). Human waste should be buried in a cathole 6 to 8 inches deep and at least 200 feet (100 big steps) from water, trails, and campsites; consider carrying a lightweight trowel to dig catholes, and bring a trash bag to pack out used toilet paper.

## PERMITS, FEES, AND REGULATIONS

In Alaska, there are few restrictions on entering public lands or trails, although sometimes we wonder whether there should be more! Likewise, managers generally require no fees for use of the land, but there are small fees for parking at frequented trailheads, particularly Alaska State Parks and Matanuska-Susitna Borough facilities. Some trailheads accept credit and debit cards; some require placing cash or check in an envelope and depositing it into an "iron ranger" drop box. Annual state park and borough parking passes are available online and at outdoor retailers and are more convenient than paying each time you arrive at a trailhead. There are also annual passes for other places, such as the Eagle River Nature Center and Arctic Valley in Anchorage. State and federal land managers typically post important outdoor regulations at popular trailheads.

Some trails pass through Alaska Native corporation lands on easements. These are typically large tracts of land owned by corporations established by the Alaska Native Claims Settlement Act. Although often undeveloped and appearing the same as public land, these areas are private property. Sometimes, the

*Wild Alaska blueberries*

Native corporations allow use of the land by permit, for a fee. However, where there is a public easement across the land, a permit is not necessary to pass through. Easements are narrow, allowing passage on a trail but not enough room for camping. In these areas, either secure a permit or stay on the trail.

## BACKCOUNTRY SAFETY

To stay safe in the backcountry, the key is to think about consequences. Consider a narrow rocky ridge with a long, scary drop. Does it just look scary, when in reality a fall would be stopped quickly in relatively "soft" scree? Or does the slope consist of steep, crusty snow where a fall would mean sliding out of control and off a cliff? It pays to be much more careful in the second instance. If the risk is going without water versus drinking from a stream, the calculation includes risk of ingesting *Giardia*—a parasite that could make you quite ill, require strong drugs, and involve a long recovery. If the water is running off a snowfield high in the mountains and you are seriously dehydrated, out of water, and far from the trailhead, then perhaps it is worth it for you to drink the water without treating it if you do not have the supplies to do so.

The standard for venturing into the mountains is to file a trip plan with a trustworthy person, specifying your intended route, destination(s), and expected return time, with the agreement that the trustworthy person will look for you or alert authorities if you don't return after some specified time. This, too, involves a calculated risk. Clearly, a lot of people head out without alerting anybody or only loosely tossing out "I'm headed up McHugh Valley. See you at the barbecue tonight." If you are headed out alone, and if the trip is longer or riskier (isolated summit climb versus crowded valley stroll), craft a formal plan, and make sure the people you tell know you are counting on them as backup.

Knowing first-aid skills is valuable in the outdoors, where you may be the only source of aid to others. The Resources section lists places that offer wilderness first responder and similar courses. The best approach is to not take undue risks in the first place.

### Satellite Tech

Backcountry enthusiasts can invest in small, lightweight personal locator beacons (PLBs) or satellite messenger devices made for adventuring. PLBs are the most basic way to send an SOS via satellite. Satellite messengers provide more options, including the ability to send nonemergency texts or retract an SOS call. Some can link to a smartphone for further options. Counting on a smartphone alone to have a signal and be adequately charged for an emergency is a poor idea. Costs vary, and satellite messenger services generally require a monthly subscription. Satellite phones are another option. There are plenty of stories of people using these types of devices to get prompt attention.

### Drinking Water

Drinking from lakes and streams could be dangerous. The most serious threat in Alaska's backcountry is the microorganism *Giardia lamblia*, which causes giardiasis ("beaver fever"). Another threat is *Cryptosporidium*, or Crypto. Both are present in the feces of many mammals, including humans. *Giardia* and Crypto survive best in cold water and may be found in any aboveground water body. Both giardiasis and cryptosporidiosis cause diarrhea and cramps, and both are potentially dangerous diseases for some people.

Boiling your water is the most effective treatment. The Centers for Disease Control and Prevention

## BEAR NECESSITIES

These basic tips will help you react appropriately should you see a bear.

**Before heading out:** Mentally rehearse scenarios in which you may encounter a bear and how you should react.

**If you see a bear:** Stop and assess the situation. If the bear has not seen you, retreat quietly, detour widely, or wait for it to leave.

**If you see a bear that is aware of you:** Stop and assess its behavior. Speak calmly, raise your arms to make yourself look large, and gather your group. Unholster your bear spray and retreat slowly.

**If the bear approaches:** Stand your ground, and increase your response. If the bear comes within a few feet or charges, see the next step.

**If a bear suddenly charges:** Stand your ground, make loud noises, and spray its face with bear spray. If the bear makes contact, play dead until it leaves.

advises that to kill *Giardia* and Crypto cysts, as well as bacteria and viruses, drinking water should be boiled for one minute, and three minutes at elevations of 6500 feet or above. To remove *Giardia* and Crypto with a pump-action or gravity-operated backpacking filter, find one with an absolute pore size of 1 micron or less. To filter bacteria, look for a pore size of 0.3 micron or smaller. Normal filters do not screen viruses, but "ultrafilters" do. (Treating backcountry water for viruses is generally not an issue in North America.) More traditionally, water treatment methods, including ones that kill or remove viruses, have depended on chemicals like iodine or chlorine. Ultraviolet light wands also can be effective in clear water. Although boiling water requires a fair amount of fuel, other systems that treat all the bacteria and microorganisms that cause waterborne illnesses are generally more expensive.

Not all handheld backpacking filters are equally effective; read instructions carefully and thoroughly. Chemical methods of disinfecting water do not work on Crypto and are less effective on *Giardia* than boiling or filtering, although they are effective against bacteria. In general, for most day hikes, it is best to take water from home; for overnight trips, purchase a lightweight filter rated for *Giardia* and Crypto. Be sure to understand and follow all instructions, because the system is effective only if you use it correctly.

### Bears and Other Wildlife

Seeing bears, moose, and other species is often thrilling. They *can* be dangerous, but paying attention to animal behavior and your own behavior can make all the difference for a safe encounter.

Books and training videos devoted to bear encounters provide detail to boost your confidence. "Staying Safe in Bear Country" is a thirty-minute YouTube video endorsed by international bear biologists (see Further Reading). Here, we provide the basics of how to avoid and react to encounters with moose, goshawks, and bears.

#### Moose

Often seeming to ignore hikers or skiers, moose appear large, passive, and slow, but they can be fast and lethal, charging and kicking or stomping with sharp hooves and strong legs. When you see a moose calf, expect a protective cow nearby. Avoid stopping near or approaching a moose to take photos. Allow time for a moose to leave, or detour well around it. Clapping and talking loudly may convince a lackadaisical moose to move off a trail. Should you round a bend and encounter a moose at close range, backtrack quickly. If a moose chases you, run behind a tree.

### Goshawks

Goshawks are medium-sized birds of prey, but they have an outsized nest-protection streak. People have had their heads bloodied during the birds' relentless, dogged dive-bombing. Take them seriously. Hold a stick above your head and stoically endure their screeching; the stick should give the bird something other than your head to aim for. Leave the area to stop the attack.

### Bears

Black and brown (grizzly) bears are common in Southcentral Alaska. Learn what to do to avoid an encounter and how to react should you cross paths with a bear. Although black and brown bears have some differences that go beyond fur color, both species can pose risks to humans. The steps below apply to an encounter with either type of bear, except as noted.

Bears will usually avoid an encounter if they know people are approaching, and they are given time, space, and an avenue of escape. Let them know you are coming by traveling with others, talking, and occasionally clapping or saying "Hey-ho!" loudly. Be aware of bear sign (scat, diggings, tracks) and

*Brown bear (grizzly) sow and cubs. Use great caution if you see a bear, especially one with cubs or near a carcass. (Photo by Gayle Nienhueser)*

*A bear canister is the most secure way to store food in the backcountry, particularly in treeless areas where it is not possible to hang food.*

conditions that may mask a bear's knowledge of your presence, such as tall brush, noise from wind or running water, or unfavorable wind direction. In these instances, be more cautious and make more noise, or revise the route plan.

Camp in areas that are as open as possible. Use plastic containers designed to be bear-proof to store food and all scented items, including trash and cosmetics. Keep a clean camp. Bear biologists suggest storing bear canisters and cooking at least 100 yards downwind of your tents.

Carry and know how to use bear spray—a deterrent made of red pepper proven to be effective when used properly. Many Alaskans carry firearms, which work well for those with the proper gun, training, and experience. The Alaska Department of Fish and Game suggests a .300 Magnum rifle or shotgun with rifled slugs; handguns may not be effective. Bear spray is cheaper, proven effective in deterring a bear, and is neither lethal to the bear nor to other humans, although it can severely irritate human eyes, skin, and breathing.

If you see a bear, stop and assess the situation and the bear's behavior. If there is no indication the bear is aware of you, retreat quietly, detour around the bear (make noise if it cannot see you), or wait quietly for it to leave. If a bear is feeding on a carcass or has cubs, be extraordinarily cautious.

If a bear is aware of you, let it know you are human by talking calmly to it. Wave your arms slowly, standing side by side with your companions. Unholster your bear spray and prepare to discharge it. Pick up small children if possible. Slowly back away.

If a bear approaches, stop retreating and increase your response. If you are on a trail, the bear may simply want to pass. Try slowly stepping well off the trail to let it go by. If the bear directly approaches to closer than 20 feet, it is appropriate to discharge bear spray in the path of the bear or at its face (a canister dispenses a stream of pepper spray to at least 20 feet).

If you have been watching a bear and it suddenly charges, or if you first become aware of a bear as it charges out of the bushes, do not run. Stand your ground, be very loud, and deploy bear spray. Spray at close range so that the bear will pass through the cloud, or aim the pepper spray at its face. Charging bears sometimes come very close but veer off. If the bear does make contact, play dead by lying facedown on the ground. If you no longer represent a threat, the bear may leave. Keep your pack on, clasp your hands behind your neck, and keep your legs spread for stability. Stay still and quiet on the ground. After you last hear or see the bear, don't move or make noise for several more minutes to wait for the bear to leave the area. Bears rarely charge humans, and they are even less likely to make contact.

The only exception to playing dead is if a black bear (almost never a brown bear) is predatory. If it continues to attack despite you playing dead, the Alaska Department of Fish and Game recommends you fight back vigorously. Aim for the sensitive nose.

The authors believe that every adult in a group should carry bear spray, and should unholster it and carry it in hand when risk is highest—some combination of low visibility, wind or water noise, plentiful bear sign, and small party size. Carry bear spray in hand when you are alone for a moment, such as when you leave your group to pee behind a tree.

Although thinking about worst-case scenarios can cause stress, it is best to rehearse scenes in your head at home and with hiking companions before venturing out.

For more information, look up "Know Your . . . Bear Facts: The Essentials for Traveling in Bear Country," a leaflet prepared by the Alaska Department of Fish and Game and multiple collaborating agencies (see Further Reading). It is available online and at the Alaska Public Lands Information Center in Anchorage (see the Resources section).

## Plants to Avoid

Although Alaska is free of poison ivy and poison oak, there are a few plants most people will want to avoid, including stinging nettle, devil's club, poison water hemlock, baneberry, poisonous mushrooms, and cow parsnip (pushki). The general rule is: do not eat mushrooms, berries, or other parts of any plant that you cannot positively identify as edible. Musky-smelling cow parsnip is found below the alpine zone everywhere in Southcentral Alaska and is usually harmless, but its sap can make the skin hypersensitive to sun on bright days, and the resulting sunburn can lead to massive, ugly blisters, a particular risk for hikers or mountain bikers crashing through tall plants. Avoid these risks by wearing long sleeves and pants or by washing at a stream soon after you leave the parsnip zone. The Cooperative Extension Service publishes and sells an inexpensive, useful booklet called *Wild, Edible, and Poisonous Plants of Alaska* (see Further Reading).

## Bugs to Watch Out For

Insects cause a buzz among hikers in summer. Wasps can be a hazard whether in a paper nest hanging from a branch or nested in the ground. Hot, dry summers, especially, lead to wasp incidents. Those known or suspected to be anaphylactically allergic to bee stings should always carry an epinephrine injector in the backcountry for relief in case of stings when far from help.

*Mosquitos and biting flies can make eating unpleasant for the unprepared. Here, mesh bug gloves become bug socks at the campground.*

*Even small streams with water levels below mid-calf can be challenging to ford. Use walking sticks and buddy up to improve stability. This crossing of the West Fork of Strelna Creek is en route to Dixie Pass, Trip 51.*

Outbreaks of invasive, fuzzy, rusty tussock moth caterpillars not only strip bushes of their leaves but also result in irritating skin reactions among hikers passing through them. Avoid contact with them in areas where they are prevalent.

Although generally less of a problem in Southcentral Alaska compared to Interior Alaska, mosquitoes are annoying. Currently mosquitoes do not transmit disease in the state, but the warming subarctic could change that. Peak mosquito season in Southcentral Alaska is the end of June and the first part of July. Mosquitoes can be thick in marshy lowlands but are rarely a problem on breezy alpine ridges.

Most Alaskans carry insect repellent during summer, but some repellents should be used cautiously. The US Environmental Protection Agency (EPA) has a registration process for repellents, and the Centers for Disease Control and Prevention recommends using products bearing an EPA registration number. According to *Consumer Reports* testers, the most effective products were those that contained 15 to 30 percent deet, 20 percent picaridin, or 30 percent oil of lemon eucalyptus (OLE). The same article indicated that products made with natural plant oils, including lemongrass oil, cedar oil, and citronella, did not perform well in tests. However, these naturally occurring ingredients are acknowledged to have lower health risks.

Deet is the most well-known active chemical ingredient proven effective against mosquitoes, but it is absorbed by the blood and can have side effects, including skin irritation and (rarely) neurological problems such as confusion and irritability. If you use deet, experts advise using repellents with low concentrations. *Consumer Reports* indicates that formulas with 15 to 30 percent deet are just as effective as ones with 100 percent. Apply deet-based repellents sparingly and only on exposed skin, as trapping the repellent under clothing can increase the possibility of side effects. Deet should not be sprayed on the face, inhaled, or ingested. Avoid putting deet-based repellents on the fingers and hands of small children or letting them apply their own, so they don't lick or swallow any.

Alternatives to using deet repellents on skin include spraying clothing only, especially cuffs, collars, and waistbands, and wearing long sleeves, long pants, head nets, and even gloves. Deet is safe on cotton, wool, and nylon but may damage spandex, rayon, and acetate fabrics. Clothing treated with many deet-based repellents also becomes more flammable.

To avoid mosquitoes and their repellent altogether, stick to the ridges in peak mosquito season!

## Stream Crossings

A few hikes and bike rides described in this book include potentially hazardous stream crossings. When confronted with such a crossing, take the following precautions:

**Cross at the widest part of the stream** where the water will be the shallowest and least swift.

**Wear shoes** to ensure good footing and protect your feet from rocks. Many people are fine with hiking in soggy shoes and socks, but removing just the socks to keep them dry until reaching the other side can reduce discomfort. Some people carry old running shoes for crossings.

**Undo the waist strap of your pack** for ease in getting it off should you fall. Put your phone, GPS, and camera inside the pack in a waterproof sack. Be aware that a camera strap around your shoulders may make it impossible to remove your pack quickly.

**Use a stick, trekking pole, or ice axe** to create a stable tripod with your legs, maintaining two points of contact at all times as you move. If you are traveling with companions, **link arms for stability** in groups of two to four, holding a stick horizontally in front at waist level. Alternatively, face upstream in a line, each holding onto the pack of the person ahead, and sidestep. In either case, line up so that only one person feels the full force of the river and the others support that person. When crossing with others, one person should move at a time.

**Avoid high-water periods.** If a trip will take you across glacial streams, plan the trip in early summer before the peak melt-off period on the glacier, or cross in early morning, when water levels are likely to be lower.

**Consider adding rocks to your pack** for weight, especially if you are small, to "hold you down" and provide more secure footing, so long as you can still heft the weight confidently.

**Expect to be wet and cold, and take the crossing slowly.** You are more likely to lose your balance if you are hurrying, especially in murky glacial waters where the bottom is invisible.

For mountain bikers, when water is too deep, swift, or murky to ride across, it often works to push the bike, using it for support. Be cautious in high water, though, because the force of water on wheels, frame, and any bike bags can knock the bike and person over. The most stable position is one hand on the seat and the other on the handlebars. Remember that tires, especially fat tires, are buoyant, which can keep the bike from anchoring to the streambed. Depending on circumstances, it may work best to walk while carrying the bike or to have

*Seeing a red fox is rare, but such wildlife sightings are possible on virtually every trip in Southcentral Alaska.* (Photo by Dave Wolfe)

two people push a bike across together and then go back for the other bike.

Hikers can cross large, braided streams more easily if they take advantage of natural flow patterns. Scout the river and find an area with many channels. Cross from the upstream end of one gravel island to the upstream end of the next, where the water is shallower and slower due to gravel deposition. The downstream end of a gravel island where channels converge may hide a deep, turbulent hole or soft sand. Avoid crossing toward a vertically cut bank; the water is deepest and swiftest along such banks.

Crossing an icy river in thigh-deep water quickly saps body heat on the best of days. If it is rainy or windy, or if you are fatigued, the crossing could bring on hypothermia (see Hypothermia and Frostbite). Before crossing any stream where there is danger of falling, mentally plan to avoid hypothermia. Are warm, dry clothes and sleeping bags packed in truly waterproof bags? Is there a place on each bank to set up a hasty camp should sleeping bags and hot drinks be needed? A little forethought can go a long way in making a crossing safe.

## Traveling on Ice

Ice skaters and walkers do fall through lake and stream ice from time to time. In Southcentral Alaska, once lake ice forms, it usually can be counted on, but warm storms can affect the integrity of ice. Even in a long, stable cold period, it is possible to encounter thin spots in the ice, for example, where warm spring water is upwelling. Skaters, walkers, or fat-tire bikers should venture only onto good ice, not jumbled ice or white frozen slush, and only with buddies. Take ice picks on a cord, usually designed to wear around your neck for easy access, to aid in self-rescue should the ice break. The best ice to crawl out on may be behind you, where you came from. Carry rope to aid a partner, and bring firestarter and extra dry clothes in a waterproof bag.

The US Army Corps of Engineers indicates that 2 inches of good, clear ice (more if it is whitish frozen slush) is the minimum sufficient thickness for one person on foot or skates; since it is best to travel as a party of two or more, the ice should be thicker. Most sources indicate 3 to 4 inches as the minimum for people to be on lake ice. Often, it is possible to discern ice depth from cracks in clear ice. Testing ice thickness with a drill at several locations is best.

Overflow—water or saturated snow on top of otherwise solid ice—can occur on streams, lakes, and swamps. If there is snow, the surface may look perfect, but it can insulate the wet layer beneath. Venturing into it can result in wet snow freezing to cold skis and snowshoes, and it can be deep enough to result in wet feet (see Hypothermia and Frostbite). Carry a ski scraper if there is risk of such conditions. Test lake and stream surfaces for water with a ski pole.

## Hypothermia and Frostbite

Cold weather is never far away in Alaska, even in midsummer. Excessive loss of body core heat can result in hypothermia, in which the metabolic and physiological processes of the body slow to dangerous levels. Death can result if body heat continues to ebb. Prevention is necessary, because you may not be able to treat a victim of severe hypothermia successfully in the field. Hikers, bikers, boaters, and skiers should travel with extra warm clothing and high-calorie snacks. They should monitor their bodies for exhaustion and dehydration (factors contributing to hypothermia) as well as temperature, and they should keep an eye on the weather. Never overextend a trip to the point that the body's fuel stores are used up.

Cool weather, rain or perspiration, wind, lack of food, fatigue, or poor conditioning can impose a stress on the cardiovascular system. Whenever the rate of cooling exceeds the body's energy supply and ability to produce heat, hypothermia begins. Falling into cold water or wearing a sweaty shirt in windy conditions at 50°F, as just two examples, can easily bring on hypothermia.

Watch for the symptoms of hypothermia: uncontrollable, continued fits of shivering; vague, slow, slurred speech; memory lapses; incoherence; fumbling hands; frequent stumbling; drowsiness; and apparent exhaustion.

The victim often refuses to admit anything is wrong, so companions must insist that treatment begin immediately. To avoid further heat loss, help the victim change into dry clothing and warm layers. Find shelter from the wind. Normal body temperature can be restored in mild cases by exercising, drinking warm liquids, and eating high-calorie foods.

When the body temperature drops below 90°F, symptoms of severe hypothermia appear. This is a medical emergency overcome only by rewarming the body core with external sources of heat, because victims no longer can generate their own heat. Shivering stops; the victim becomes unable to walk alone and shows poor judgment, leaving a parka unzipped or forgetting hat and mittens. Eventually, the victim may lose consciousness.

If help is far away, you must attempt to treat severe hypothermia in the field. Place the victim in a sleeping bag that has been warmed up by somebody else. Place bottles of warm water along the victim's body core in the warm bag. Having someone warm zip up inside the bag with the victim can help immensely; two people warming the victim would be even better. It may be awkward, but other human bodies are often the most readily available source of heat, and skin-to-skin contact speeds the transfer of heat. Simply placing a victim in a sleeping bag will not warm the body core, because the victim's body will be unable to warm the bag.

Do not rewarm the extremities of a severely hypothermic person before the internal organs are warmed. If circulation of blood in the extremities is stimulated through massage or application of heat, that blood (which is still colder than blood in the body core) can cause ventricular fibrillation, an abnormal heart rhythm that can lead quickly to death. Moving or jarring a severely hypothermic person can also trigger ventricular fibrillation, so treat the victim carefully, but don't let these cautions lead to inaction. Get medical help even if recovery seems complete; in severe cases, pneumonia or heart problems can occur later. A victim of severe hypothermia may not have a detectable heartbeat yet may still be alive. Always rewarm hypothermia victims before assuming they have died.

At temperatures below freezing, particularly on windy days, be alert for frostbite, or freezing of body tissues. Fingers, toes, face, and ears are normally the first body parts to show the characteristic white patches that indicate frostbite is beginning. Windchill speeds freezing, as does direct contact with metal. Be careful with camp stove fuel because the very cold and highly volatile gas can freeze flesh instantly. When dexterity is important—for handling cameras, ski bindings, tent poles, and the like—wear thin gloves.

Backcountry partners should make a habit of checking each other's faces and ears. Monitor changing sensation in your hands and feet. If you or your companions lose feeling in your extremities, especially after a period of pain from the cold, check for frostbite. A severely frostbitten extremity may freeze hard to the touch like meat in a freezer, but permanent damage results from more subtle frostbite as well.

Frostnip, the first stage of frostbite, in which the surface of the skin shows waxy patches but the underlying tissue still feels normally soft, should be treated immediately. Hold a warm hand over a frost-nipped nose, ear, or cheek to return the flesh to a healthy color. For fingers and toes, remove tight mittens or boots. Warm nipped fingers in your armpits, between your legs, or on your stomach. Nipped toes may be warmed on a brave companion's stomach. Never rub frost-nipped or frostbitten tissues.

Treatment for frostbite is more complicated than for frostnip. To avoid permanent damage to tissues or joints, study prevention and first aid for frostbite before making trips at low temperatures.

A person with frostbite may also be hypothermic; treat hypothermia first. Do not rewarm a severely frostbitten appendage in the field if there is a chance of it refreezing or if you must walk on it to self-rescue. If it is not possible to evacuate the patient to a hospital within a few hours, frozen fingers or toes may be thawed in water at 104°F to 110°F (a range that feels very warm but not too hot to an uninjured hand) until color, pain, and pliability return. Leave any blisters intact and seek medical help as soon as possible.

Before making a trip to a remote area, read about hypothermia and frostbite in *Medicine for Mountaineering and Other Wilderness Activities*, edited by Dr. James

A. Wilkerson (see Further Reading), or a similar guide to wilderness medicine.

## Avalanches

If you travel through snow-covered mountains, especially in the winter, it is crucial for you to learn about avalanche terrain and conditions. Snowslides kill people every year in Southcentral Alaska, but such accidents are usually avoidable with proper knowledge. Even experienced hikers and skiers are at risk. The mapmaker for the original 1972 edition of this book, Hans Van der Laan, died in an avalanche near Eklutna Glacier (see Trip 37) before the book was published.

### *Avalanche Training*

One of the most dangerous times to travel in avalanche country is during the "ignorance is bliss" period: when you haven't studied avalanche awareness, you don't yet know what to look for, and that dearth of knowledge could kill you. Get smarter: take an avalanche course through the Alaska Avalanche School or a similar course provider (see the Resources section). Learning about avalanche conditions feels like advanced playing in the snow, so don't let the term "course" deter you.

Level 1 avalanche courses for recreationalists (colloquially called "Avy 1") are typically three days, with a combination of classroom and field instruction; a daylong companion course on avalanche rescue fills out the foundation of formal avalanche education. Upper-level courses are available, with separate "rec" and "pro" tracks for recreationalists versus up-and-coming professionals. Getting your Avy 1 is highly recommended for anyone who wants to recreate in snowy mountains. Scholarships for avalanche courses are available through avalanche centers, often in honor of victims. A wealth of excellent books and online sources can contribute to self-education (see Avalanche Resources below). Additionally, seek out mentors willing to share their experience in the field.

*Trees outline an avalanche path, with the "starting zone" in the steep bowl at the mountaintop, the "track" down the gully, and the "runout zone" at the bottom. Avalanches in this path are frequent and powerful enough to prevent trees from growing.*

### *Avalanche Gear*

Three essential items of gear make up the minimum supplies needed for rescuing a companion buried in an avalanche. Carry them, keeping them readily accessible, wherever avalanches are possible:

- **beacon:** a battery-operated radio transceiver for locating buried companions and being located yourself

- **probe:** a long, thin, collapsible metal pole for probing snow to find buried companions' exact locations and burial depths
- **shovel:** a strong, collapsible, lightweight snow shovel for digging out a companion

Invest in these items, learn to use them, and check them off your mental checklist when pulling out of the driveway. This is a reciprocal investment—you carry these items to rescue your friends, and in return, they carry the gear to rescue you. Bring avy gear every time. Turn your beacon "on at the car, off at the bar"—which is to say, turn it on before entering avalanche terrain and off after leaving.

In addition to these three essentials for rescue, other items can increase your chances of avoiding and surviving an avalanche. Avy 1 courses teach about the tools necessary to analyze the snowpack and terrain. Additional safety items such as an airbag backpack and avalanche-specific breathing tube can increase likelihood of survival in the event of an avalanche.

A partner is an essential part of the gear package: not just any partner, but someone you trust to be knowledgeable and well equipped, because that partner is your best chance of rescue if you end up buried. Consider taking an avalanche course with an adventure partner you already know, or sign up for the course alone and make a point of meeting potential partners. To lengthen the buddy list, some people reach out to social media groups of winter backcountry enthusiasts, stating their skill level and recreational interests to find partners with similar objectives. Intentionally vet new acquaintances to ensure you are on the same safety page well before venturing into avalanche terrain with them.

### *Risk Management*

Though the right training and gear can save a buried avalanche victim, managing risky situations is the best way to prevent a burial in the first place. Current training emphasizes the "human factor": the imperfect decision-making process of outdoor enthusiasts. Most fatal avalanches are triggered by people. Not only must backcountry travelers be constantly alert for clues about avalanche danger but they must also pay attention to their thought processes to ensure that route decisions are based on hard evidence and not on mental traps, such as a desire to ski an untracked slope or reach a summit, or on peer pressure, particularly in young-adult groups and mixed-gender groups that are known to expose themselves to higher risk. Instead, travel partners should evaluate their surroundings and communicate clearly to make decisions based on three interdependent variables: the snowpack, the terrain, and the weather.

**Snowpack.** The snowpack is an accumulation of layers of snow from different storms, ice from thaws, and granular crystals that develop within the layers of snow and ice. Most of the layer combinations are no problem, but when there is a more cohesive slab layer above a softer, weak layer, avalanches can happen. The snowpack adapts to changes slowly. When weight is added rapidly and becomes too much for a weak layer, snow slides. Humans trigger avalanches when their body weight is the proverbial straw that breaks the camel's back.

**Five "red flags" indicate an unstable snowpack.** If you observe any of these red flags while you are out in avalanche terrain, proceed home with caution—or better yet, don't venture out if any of these signs are present:

1. Recent avalanches in the area
2. Ominous "whumpfing" noises or shooting cracks as weak layers collapse
3. Significant new snow or rain that loads the snowpack

4. Strong winds blowing and drifting snow
5. A rapid rise in temperature

Level 1, or "Avy 1," courses teach standard tests for assessing the snowpack beyond these red flags.

**Terrain.** Avalanche terrain is anywhere an avalanche can occur, including its starting zone, track, and runout zone. Most human-triggered avalanches occur on slopes between 30 and 45 degrees, the angles on which most skiers love to carve their turns. Lower- and higher-angle slopes can slide in the right conditions. Connected slopes may be dangerous too; for example, a skier on flat terrain can trigger a snowpack failure that brings down snow from a slope above. People often overlook short, steep spots in otherwise gentle terrain, but many avalanche accidents are on slopes less than 300 feet high. Human-triggered avalanches have caught more than ninety people, many of them hikers, on a short foothill to Flattop Mountain (see Trip 31). Additionally, terrain traps such as gullies or streams can funnel an avalanche, burying a victim at an unrescuable depth, and trees or cliffs downhill can cause unsurvivable physical trauma as the victim is swept down with the snow. All of these factors must be considered when planning the safest route.

**Weather.** When wind moves snow, it adds weight on the leeward slope where the snow is deposited and can cause instability in minutes. New snow and rain also quickly add weight to the snowpack. Warming trends can weaken the snowpack. While long periods of cold weather are usually stabilizing, they may create problematic layers in the snowpack that can persist for a long time. Slope orientation, or aspect, is critically important: if natural avalanches are apparent on slopes facing a certain direction—say, north—or if wind is obviously depositing snow on the north-facing slopes in this scenario, beware of any similar north-facing slope on which you want to travel. The slope's aspect to the sun, too, dramatically affects the layers in the snowpack, especially in the springtime as the snow warms.

### *Avalanche Resources*

Avalanche information centers are invaluable, offering daily avalanche forecasts for popular areas in season, crowdsourced observations, and community education. In the morning while your pre-ski coffee percolates, check the avalanche forecast online before committing to plans for the day. For the areas covered in this book, the local information centers are Chugach National Forest Avalanche Information Center, Hatcher Pass Avalanche Center, Valdez Avalanche Center, and the statewide Alaska Avalanche Information Center. See the Resources section.

The information presented here is not enough to keep you safe in avalanche country; learn more from websites, workshops, and books. *Snow Sense: A Guide to Evaluating Snow Avalanche Hazard* by Jill Fredston and Doug Fesler, published in Alaska and used internationally, is a helpful booklet. *Avalanche Essentials: A Step-by-Step System for Safety and Survival* by Bruce Tremper (see Further Reading) is a common textbook for avalanche courses.

Lastly, do not let the fear of avalanches deter you. Winter is a time when rivers, brushlands, and swamps cease to be barriers and become highways to exciting new country inaccessible in summer. Just learn about how to travel through snow and manage risk beforehand to ensure a safe trip.

## ETHICS AND TRAIL ETIQUETTE

We hike to find wilderness, but in hiking we leave tracks that diminish wilderness. Minimizing your impact means more than carrying out litter. It is a state of constant awareness. The phrase "leave only

*Minimize your impact by using a camp stove for cooking, as seen here at Berry Pass (Trip 23), instead of building a fire.* (Photo by Gretchen Nelson)

footprints, take only pictures" rings in our memories, but in fragile areas, even leaving "only footprints" has caused erosion. It is up to each of us to realize that when tiny tundra roots rip underfoot, we must look for a better place for our next footstep. And we must pay attention to more than just damage to ground cover and water quality. Minimizing impact means being continuously aware that our presence, sounds, brightly colored gear, and even the way we smell affect wildlife and other people.

## Leave No Trace

Minimizing impact can be summed up in a three-word directive that's easy to remember: Leave No Trace (LNT). This is not only common sense but is also the name of an education program developed by the National Outdoor Leadership School in cooperation with federal land managers nationwide. The ethic? Make it hard for others to know you are or were there, and Leave No Trace of your visit. There are LNT training books, master courses, and booklets for different environments, but here are seven core principles.

1. **Plan ahead, and prepare.** Know what you are getting into, and take the Ten Essentials (see Essential Gear above). Be sure your body, pack, bike, and other gear are adequately tuned. Plan a small group.
2. **Travel and camp on durable surfaces.** The most durable surfaces are trails, rock, gravel bars, and snow. In vegetated areas, use a trail when there is one, and if there is no

trail, spread out so as not to create one. Use existing campsites, or if there are none, camp 100 big steps from water and trails, on the most durable surfaces available. Spend only a night, maybe two, at any one site. Place cooking and sleeping areas 100 big steps apart or more (see Bears and Other Wildlife above).

3. **Dispose of waste properly.** If you pack it in, pack it out—but don't pack much in to begin with. Carry out poop in a bag designed for that purpose (a "wag" bag), or bury it 100 big steps from water. Carry toilet paper and tampons out in a trash bag. Further protect water by washing yourself and dishes away from lakes and streams, not in them.
4. **Leave what you find.** Good campsites are found, not made. Avoid digging dirt, cutting trees, picking flowers, or removing historical artifacts.
5. **Minimize campfire impacts.** Take a camp stove to reduce forest fire risk and the visual "traces" of fire: broken and sawed limbs and sterile black holes in the ground. It is best to build fires only at formal campgrounds. Ensure there are no fire bans in effect. Put out any campfire completely before leaving it.
6. **Respect wildlife.** Stay well away from birds and other animals, and keep human food for people (see Bears and Other Wildlife). Keep dogs home or under true control so they don't stress or kill wildlife (even squirrels).
7. **Be considerate of others.** Keep your fun clean and quiet, remembering that other hikers and nearby landowners may be out there with you. Respect Alaska Natives and others who subsist off the land. (See etiquette considerations in "Trailheadiquette" and On-Trail Etiquette.)

The Leave No Trace organization (LNT.org) has resources, including an Alaska Wildlands booklet, available from its online store. The organization emphasizes principles and practices that grow out of appreciation of the natural world, rather than strict rules. To that end, LNT also has encouraged outdoor enthusiasts to think carefully before posting to social media about specific outdoor locations. Posting photos, GPS data, and maps to social media (and trail or training apps) can be part of a trend that attracts high numbers of people to fragile places. Sometimes, not posting, or referring to a broader region instead of a specific destination, can keep a place from becoming overrun. The organization also suggests that people can model LNT practices and spread outdoor ethics messages in the posts they choose to share. Respect for and appreciation of Alaska's land come from experience on the trail. So go, always striving to "leave no trace."

## "Trailheadiquette"

Trailheads come in all shapes and sizes, from formal government parking lots to tiny pullouts along narrow access tracks. To make space for everyone, trailhead etiquette is key. Particularly at crowded trailheads, leave the smallest reasonable gap between cars so there is space for others to park. Where a trailhead is near homes, be respectful to keep trail users in the good graces of homeowners. If the formal trailhead is full, and if there are not No Parking signs on the adjacent road, it usually is legal to park off the driving lane (i.e., on the shoulder), but be conscious of the view from homes and yards, the tearing around of your dog or kids, and loud voices, music, or car horns. Don't block sight lines for residents pulling out of their driveways. Remember, you may use a trail only once a year or once in a lifetime, but adjacent homeowners deal with people anxious to hit the trail every day. Trail users should strive to be good stewards of the neighborhood in the same way they work at being good stewards of the backcountry. Multiple trails in Southcentral Alaska have been shut down, not allowed to open, or otherwise contested over neighborhood issues.

Pay the trailhead parking fee when requested; it usually supports a struggling nonprofit or strapped park agency (see Permits, Fees, and Regulations earlier in this section).

Most parking areas are safe, but car break-ins do occur. Before leaving home, remove from your car items of value or items that imply value (such as a purse, bag, or pack, even if nothing important is in it). If you need to leave spare gear or other items in the car, make every effort to lock them away out of sight in the trunk, glove box, or cartop carrier. Even then, never leave cash, credit cards, personal identifying information, or phones that might reward persistent thieves.

*Alpine cinquefoil adds a splash of color near Arctic Valley, Trip 34.* (Photo by Gretchen Nelson)

## A NOTE ABOUT SAFETY

Safety is an important concern in all outdoor activities. No guidebook can alert you to every hazard or anticipate the limitations of every reader. Therefore, the descriptions of roads, trails, routes, and natural features in this book are not representations that a particular place or excursion will be safe for your party. When you follow any of the routes described in this book, you assume responsibility for your own safety. Under normal conditions, such excursions require the usual attention to traffic, road and trail conditions, weather, terrain, the capabilities of your party, and other factors. Because many of the lands in this book are subject to development and/or change of ownership, conditions may have changed since this book was written that make your use of some of these routes unwise. Always check for current conditions, obey posted private property signs, and avoid confrontations with property owners or managers. Keeping informed on current conditions and exercising common sense are the keys to a safe, enjoyable outing.

*—Mountaineers Books*

### On-Trail Etiquette

Walking is the most basic—and slowest—form of locomotion. Cyclists and trail runners will overtake walkers. Walkers usually don't mind stepping aside for other users to pass, but on busy days with multiple user types sharing the same narrow corridor, walkers end up being the ones to step off the trail into the nettles over and over again. Cyclists and runners should instead be first to stop when approaching hikers head-on—to the point of insisting, whenever possible, that walkers come on by. This builds good credit for later overtaking hikers from behind. When overtaking slower people, slow down and pleasantly alert them ("on your left!") as far ahead as possible to avoid startling them. Be prepared to stop if the slower traffic needs to move a bit farther to find a place to get off the trail.

There are trails with downhills that are great fun for cyclists and runners, but if you can't see far ahead because of a winding route or tall grass, avoid really letting go: besides a group of hikers who may be chatting away and unable to hear well, you may speed around a bend to surprise a moose or bear. Use caution, and let people and animals know you are coming.

It is common trail etiquette in the mountain biking world for downhill traffic to yield to uphill traffic. This is a good rule of thumb for all trail users, including hikers.

The primary reason trail builders put in switchbacks is not to make it easier for citified people to climb the hill; it is to prevent trail erosion. Respect the efforts of the trail builders—don't shortcut switchbacks. In the age of limited state and federal outdoor recreation budgets, it is best that everybody participate in minimizing impact.

Letting wildlife know of your presence by talking and by occasionally clapping or saying "hey ho!" is much more acceptable in the backcountry than playing music over speakers. Endeavor to enjoy the quiet and natural sounds, and avoid disturbing the audible part of nature for others as much as possible.

# How to Use This Book

**This book is organized geographically (see the overview map). The trips are all accessible by** road, as opposed to access by small airplane; we make minor exceptions for the use of water taxis. We present trips following the Southcentral Alaska highway system. Book sections correspond with major geographic and government boundaries, starting with the Kenai Peninsula Borough and proceeding through the Municipality of Anchorage, Matanuska-Susitna Borough, and the Copper River watershed.

## TRIP DATA AND DIFFICULTY

Key data for each trip appear before the detailed description of the route itself. Each trip begins with at-a-glance summary information, including trip distance, time, elevation gain, high point, season, surface, and grade. There is no commonly accepted rating system for trail difficulty, but there have been attempts to create one. In addition to distance and elevation gain, these systems usually factor in the route's surface (obstacles or hazards) and its grade, either steepness or length of grade or both. To determine trail difficulty, consider the distance, elevation gain, surface, and grade.

The following rundown explains how we evaluated trails and the characteristics we considered most important to share up-front about each trip.

**Distance:** This category provides the total distance (in miles) of the primary route we describe and type of route (roundtrip, loop, or point to point).

**Time:** Trip time is provided as half day, full day, and extended day. If a trip will take more than one day, we list the number of days. Time guidelines assume people stop occasionally for a breather, snack, photo, layer break, or bathroom break. While different people clearly operate at different paces, probably the biggest difference in time on the trail will be the amount of time they spend stopped. Some people are "go, go!" types who don't like stopping except maybe at the summit, others are "stop and smell the wild roses" types who enjoy investigating nature's details, and some love the long conversations that come up when someone needs a "quick" stop to grab an energy bar. We tend to land somewhere in the middle. With luck, readers will be able to gauge their pace against our guidelines. We considered the trail difficulty in presenting trip time. Finally, we give some consideration to the remoteness of a trip from population centers. If a day hike requires a long drive for most hikers, it may tip from half day to full day.

A half day is up to three to four hours. A full day is anything likely to go beyond about four hours on the trail, but not longer than seven to eight hours. Extended day is anything in excess of seven to eight hours on the trail but with the assumption that the excursion is still a day trip, in which the hiker likely is

OPPOSITE: *The mouth of Tonsina Creek with Resurrection Bay beyond, en route to Caines Head, Trip 8, in June* (Photo by Shawn Horning)

not carrying a sleeping bag, tent, or stove. Summers in Southcentral Alaska mean extended midsummer daylight, and hiking without a headlamp is possible around the clock roughly from the end of May through mid-July. For this book, we do not assume any day trip would eclipse a normal night's sleep.

**Elevation gain:** The approximate cumulative elevation gain is noted in this category. Sometimes, this is just the difference between the starting elevation and the high point, but some trips go through dips on the way up and therefore have stretches of uphill during the return. In these cases, the number given adds up the smaller and larger climbs. It is estimated from topographic maps and GPS data.

**High point:** Here you'll find the highest elevation attained on the primary route. It is not necessarily the elevation of the end point.

**Season:** We report our estimate of the best season for the trip. For summer outings, this typically means when the trip is most likely to be reasonably (but not entirely) snow-free.

**Surface:** To describe the route surface in terms of ease and obstacles, we selected up to three descriptors—the most applicable—from the following: boardwalk, boulders (hiker must step or climb from one boulder to another), bog, bushes (low), brush (high), hardpack (normal, hardened trail, typically built by a trail crew, or a portion of a trail on an old mining or service road), handholds (scrambling), mud (shoes may get messy, and walking will be more difficult), rocks, roots, sand and/or gravel, snow, tundra, and water. A surface described as "water" typically means you cannot avoid getting your feet wet because of stream fords, swamps, or substantial and persistent puddles.

**Grade:** We selected the best description from a limited number of options to describe grade: low angle, rolling, moderate, steep, and sustained steep. A combination, such as moderate with steep segments, means there is at least one long steep segment mixed with other terrain—in this case moderate terrain.

**Indigenous land:** For each trip, we briefly acknowledge the Alaska Native people on whose traditional land the trip occurs. See Indigenous Land Acknowledgment in the Preface and Alaska Native Entities in the Resources section.

**Managing agency:** This line identifies the formal land manager, usually a local, state, or federal government agency but occasionally a private entity or Alaska Native corporation. See the Resources section for contact information.

**Map and trailhead information:** In the trip data, we include a line with information about maps for the trip (see more in Maps below). Sometimes further map information appears in the text. We then provide an online map search term that will allow you to zoom into the trip area on mapping websites like CalTopo. We also provide GPS coordinates for the trailhead (in decimal degrees based on the WGS84 datum), or multiple sets of trailhead coordinates for point-to-point trips and situations where alternate trailheads occur. In cases with more than one trailhead, the coordinates are titled to match trailhead names.

## DRIVING DIRECTIONS

Often, getting to the trailhead is an interesting excursion in itself. Outside of the larger communities, Alaska's highway system is mostly two-lane paved roads that pass through wonderful scenery. A few of the access roads are not maintained or marked. Each trip description gives specific turn-by-turn directions. Highways and primary side roads have mileposts. We used car odometers to measure from mileposts, or from an intersection or bridge on side roads. Because odometer readings vary with the car, tire size, and reference points, our distances may vary slightly from yours, but by using the distances we provide, you will be close to the trailhead and should find it with ease. Our driving directions often provide an online search term at the beginning of the paragraph. We used Google Maps to test search terms, and where a term succeeded in generating turn-by-turn driving directions to the desired destination, we listed it. Note, however, that many trailheads are outside the reach of cell signals, and just when you need the driving directions most, your phone may say "No Service." Either download the directions for use offline or follow our written directions.

Alaska's highways are known by their names, not numbers. It may be helpful to understand the milepost system for each. Mile 0 for the Glenn Highway (Alaska Route 1) and George Parks Highway (Route 3, known simply as the Parks Highway) are in Anchorage. Richardson Highway (Route 4) mileposts begin in Valdez. Seward Highway (Routes 1 and 9) and Sterling Highway (Route 1) mileposts start in Seward. Edgerton Highway (Route 10) mileposts begin at the Richardson Highway. Straightening highways over time has created inconsistencies in the milepost system. Our figures are generally derived from the nearest standing milepost.

Driving directions are from what we believe to be readily recognizable locations—a major intersection or a mileage point along a major highway. If a starting intersection is not familiar, an online search should help you pinpoint it.

When a road does not receive public maintenance, its condition may vary from year to year, with no guarantee it will be drivable. We note which roads may present problems. If you have doubts about whether your car can make it, don't proceed beyond where you are willing to back up. Getting a tow truck may take hours and be very expensive. Furthermore, driving on a soft, muddy road tears it up, which is unfair to residents who may maintain it themselves.

## TRIP DESCRIPTION

Following the trip data and driving directions are the narrative sections describing the trip and associated options. Each trip includes an overview that sets the scene for the route, sometimes describing the scenery you can expect and sometimes sharing historical context. After that, the featured trip and associated options are described in detail in a couple sections:

**On the Route:** This section provides the more detailed information that may be desired while underway, such as turn-by-turn directions and points of interest.

**Options:** Most trips include some combination of options for shortening or extending your trip, as well as seasonal opportunities where applicable. Because several of the trips are point-to-point traverses, look to Shorter Options for out-and-back excursions that do not require a car shuttle. Forty of the fifty-five trips identify shorter options, and many of these indicate several shorter excursions.

## MAPS

Topographic maps are the standard for determining routes and tracking progress in the backcountry. They are key to determining difficulty by showing distance, elevation, and grade visually, often with hints about stream crossings, boulder fields, permanent snow and ice, and vegetation. Being able to interpret topographic maps is a great skill and confidence booster.

The maps in this book present a snippet of full topographic maps. Our maps compile tracks recorded in the field, traced from aerial photos, or drawn by us based on personal experience, along with other important features, and place these elements on a topographic base created by the US Geological Survey (USGS). We used CalTopo, a free online resource, to help create the maps. Although the maps in the book may work for the simplest trips, the scale and lack of context make them insufficient for complex trips, which demand bigger and better maps. Whether hikers use an electronic device, print physical maps from websites, or purchase printed map sheets from USGS by mail or from an outdoor store, an accurate map is indispensable.

Many of the trips in this book do not follow typical, hardened trails built by a skilled trail crew. Our maps differentiate between defined trails, intermittent or informal trails that may have been created by moose or hikers repeatedly using the same path, and cross-country routes on tundra, gravel bars, rock, or snow and with little or no visible evidence on the ground. Refer to the map legend to learn how these trails are differentiated. In many areas, trails are still forming. After fifty years of revising this book, it is clear that trails develop and push farther into the mountains as time goes by. Places noted with dotted lines as routes without trails today may, in the near future, become social trails or undergo formal construction to enhance sustainability and minimize erosion.

Each trip lists an online map search term so that the reader may easily look up the area on mapping websites. We tested these search terms with CalTopo. The trip data also list the USGS map for the area. The online USGS map store (see the Resources section) allows free PDF downloads of maps, and you may order paper maps by mail for a price. The most popular USGS maps tend to be sold at outdoor

*While smartphones and GPS devices make it easy to track your route and pinpoint your location, there are advantages to paper maps that do not depend on batteries and are not limited to a small screen.*

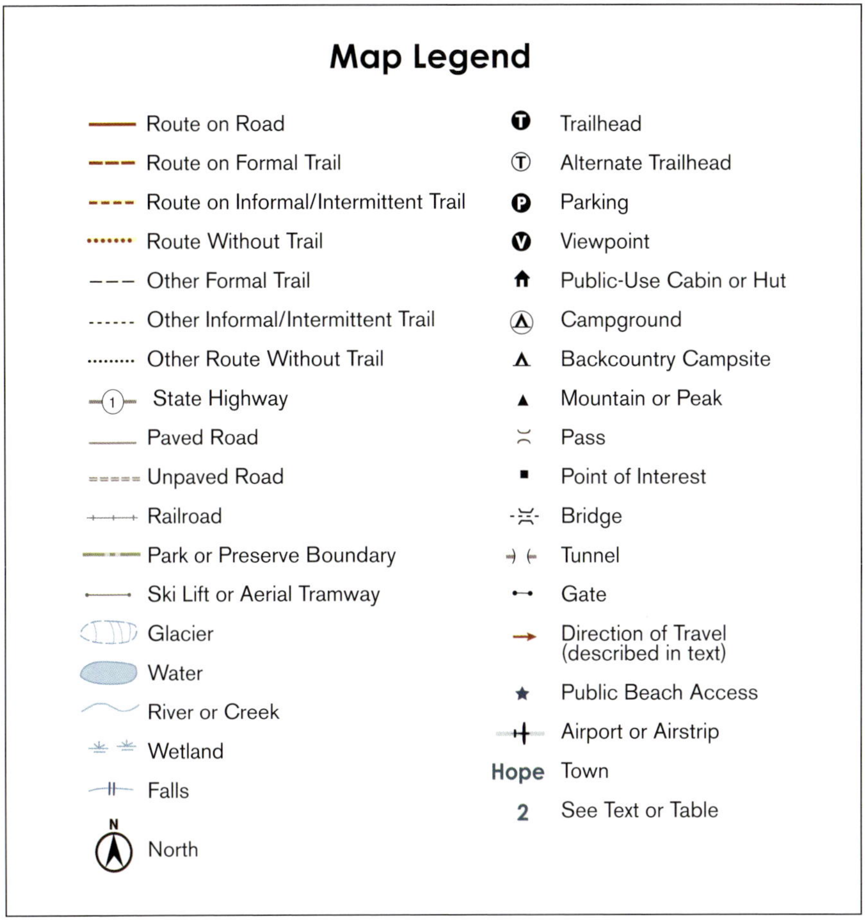


retailers. There are several other map products that may be useful:

**Imus Geographics: "Chugach State Park."** This good-quality, hard-copy map is considered the official map of Chugach State Park. The only downside is that its scale does not offer as much detail as USGS map sheets.

**National Geographic Trails Illustrated Maps.** This nationwide series covers most of the areas addressed in this book. It is not clear how often they are updated, but they are almost always more up to date than USGS maps.

**OuterSpatial.** This app and website (outerspatial.com) features maps of trails and outdoor facilities. For Alaska, it covers primarily Southcentral Alaska. The trails are curated by the trail managers themselves and are not crowdsourced like some online mappers, so there is reasonable assurance that trails shown are legitimate and don't involve trespassing. Included are trails of the State of Alaska (non-park and state parks) and the Matanuska-Susitna Borough.

The OuterSpatial app displays a phone's location by GPS on a map of trails, and this function works even without cell service, although the maps will not update without service. Popular trails appear to be reasonably accurate. Outlying trails may have been taken from generalized maps or old state records and may be less accurate but do indicate where public access is available. The app provides driving directions.

USGS publishes Southcentral Alaska maps at 1:63,360 scale (1 inch on the map equals 63,360 inches, or 1 mile, on the ground). These maps have titles like "Anchorage A-7" and "Seward D-8." USGS also publishes more recent 1:25,000-scale maps that divide the 1:63,360 maps into four sections (labeled northwest, northeast, southwest, and southeast) and enlarge them. The 1:25,000 maps show more up-to-date features, and the scale offers greater detail. But these maps can be cumbersome: the sheet sizes are larger, it often takes more sheets to cover one trip, they are in metric, and often only maps of the most-settled areas are widely available. When this book indicates "Anchorage A-7 NW," you may acquire "Anchorage A-7" at 1:63,360 or "Anchorage A-7 NW" at 1:25,000.

Elevations for the same point on different maps may not match exactly. This is, in part, because advances in technology have allowed the USGS to refine its elevations on newer maps, which are published in meters. The Imus Geographics "Chugach State Park" map converts these to US standard (nonmetric) units. We list elevations in feet.

Note that true north differs substantially in Alaska from magnetic north, to which a compass needle points. Learn how to correct for the difference if using a compass.

Contact information for the USGS and outdoor shops that carry maps is listed in the Resources section, along with select mapping websites.

OPPOSITE: *A late evening July sunset from Ninilchik View Campground over Redoubt Volcano along the Cook Inlet Beach Bike route, Trip 3*

# Kenai

THE KENAI REGION INCLUDES THE KENAI PENINSULA BOROUGH AND WHITTIER, A RICH mountain and coastal area. The western Kenai Peninsula includes extensive flats of forest, lakes, and marshes. Adjacent to these western flats facing Cook Inlet, the coast is a true beach, suitable for walking and biking for dozens of miles. These are Dena'ina Athabascan lands. The peninsula's other coasts are dramatic and rocky—land of the seagoing Sugpiaq (Alutiiq) people—but some are walkable.

The position of the peninsula adjacent to the Gulf of Alaska means the peaks have gathered moisture in the form of snow and ice, including extensive icefields that spill over as valley glaciers in many directions. The iconic blue-green waters of Kenai Lake and the Kenai River are one result of that glaciation. The peninsula marks the northwestern limits of coastal rainforests, and the thick green hemlock-spruce cover is completely different from less-coastal forests in other parts of Southcentral Alaska. The northeastern peninsula abuts the fjords of Prince William Sound, with its glaciated ridges and deep-blue waterways. The Kenai National Wildlife Refuge and Chugach National Forest are the oldest formal conservation lands in Southcentral Alaska, and their trails are well established.

# 1 TUTKA BACKDOOR TRAIL

**DISTANCE:** 22.6 miles roundtrip (extensions to 40 miles or more)
**TIME:** 2–4 days
**ELEVATION GAIN:** 5000 feet
**HIGH POINT:** 2300 feet
**SEASON:** July–September
**SURFACE:** Hardpack, tundra, rocks
**GRADE:** Moderate with steep segments
**INDIGENOUS LAND:** Dena'ina Athabascan and Chugach Sugpiaq (Alutiiq)
**MANAGING AGENCIES:** Kachemak Bay State Park and Kachemak Bay State Wilderness Park
**MAPS:** USGS Seldovia B-3, B-4; Ground Truth Alaska "Tutka Backdoor"
**ONLINE MAP SEARCH:** "tutka backdoor trail"
**TRAILHEAD GPS:** 59.415623°N, 151.308866°W

**The recently developed Tutka Backdoor Trail traverses Kachemak Bay State Wilderness Park,** inviting unprecedented access to the mountainous outer fringes of the Kenai Peninsula. Follow Backdoor Creek from its mouth at the head of Tutka Bay through big, friendly forests, up tundra knobs, along bright, mossy gravel bars, and above crystalline falls to the creek's origin at Tutka Pass. Few routes feature such magical country and such impressive trail building, thanks to the efforts of a visionary volunteer trail crew headed by nonprofit Ground Truth Alaska, based in Seldovia. This trip plan, from upper Tutka Bay to the pass and back, is ideal for three days and easily executed with the help of a water taxi from Homer or Seldovia. Determined expert hikers may pound it out in a weekend. Those wishing to stay longer can easily fill a week or more (see Extending Your Trip).

## DRIVING DIRECTIONS

Search online for "homer spit ak," then follow these directions. Hikers not living on Kachemak Bay will likely access this trip via water taxi from Homer. Follow the Sterling Highway nearly to its terminus on the Homer Spit, a narrow, 4-mile peninsula that juts into Kachemak Bay. The small boat harbor and signs advertising water taxis are near the end of the spit (see the Resources section).

Ask about current rates (not cheap) for drop-off and pickup at the upper Tutka Bay trailhead, which requires a tide higher than four feet for boat access at low tide. Allow an hour for the water taxi trip one way, assuming some stops for other passengers. An invaluable, regularly updated hard-copy map for this route is available from Ground Truth Alaska; order ahead online or ask if the water taxi office has the map.

Access by land or water from Seldovia is also possible. The connecting Tutka–Jakolof Trail starts from Jakolof Bay Road, about 13 road miles east of Seldovia (see Extending Your Trip below).

## ON THE ROUTE

The trail begins at a water taxi landing in upper Tutka Bay, a small rocky point on the south side of Tutka Bay marked with an orange triangle. Clamber up off the rocks at an evident, worn path and find yourself immersed in a mossy Sitka spruce forest. The initial wooded portion of this trail is newly built and easy to follow but may become overgrown. Look for neon flagging if in doubt. After following the trail 0.6 mile, reach an unsigned junction. The left fork descends rock steps to the tidal flats, leading shortly to an established campsite with a fire ring and an old outhouse. To continue, take the right fork.

Another junction, this one signed, appears shortly. The right fork leads to the Sentinel Ridge Trail (see Extending Your Trip for details). Take the left fork signed for Taylor Bay, and shortly after, cross a small creek. Stream crossings and substantial river fords pepper this trip; do not shy away from wet feet. On the far side of the creek is yet another unmarked junction, the left fork leading back to the campsite on the flats; take the right fork uphill. Another signed spur trail about three-quarters of a mile farther leads to the tidal flats where there is a lightly used older trailhead, accessible when the tide is very high. Keep right.

Now roughly 2 miles from the trailhead, come to a rocky streambed, likely dry. Beyond, the big, friendly forest transitions to a spooky forest. The trail meets and begins paralleling the blue-green waters of Backdoor Creek, then turns onto a gravel bar on the riverbank; follow cairns and flags here. This spot is good for a snack break or even camping, but avoid lingering in late summer when bears may frequent the area to fish for salmon. About a quarter mile past the gravel bar is another stream ford, a tributary of Backdoor Creek. From here, the trail begins a switchbacking ascent, hugging the edge of a gorge where Backdoor Creek careens through below and climbing the face of Lunch Mountain.

While pushing up the hill, look for high-bush blueberries at first and salmonberries with increasing altitude. The path swings left around the back side of Lunch Mountain before reaching the 1227-foot

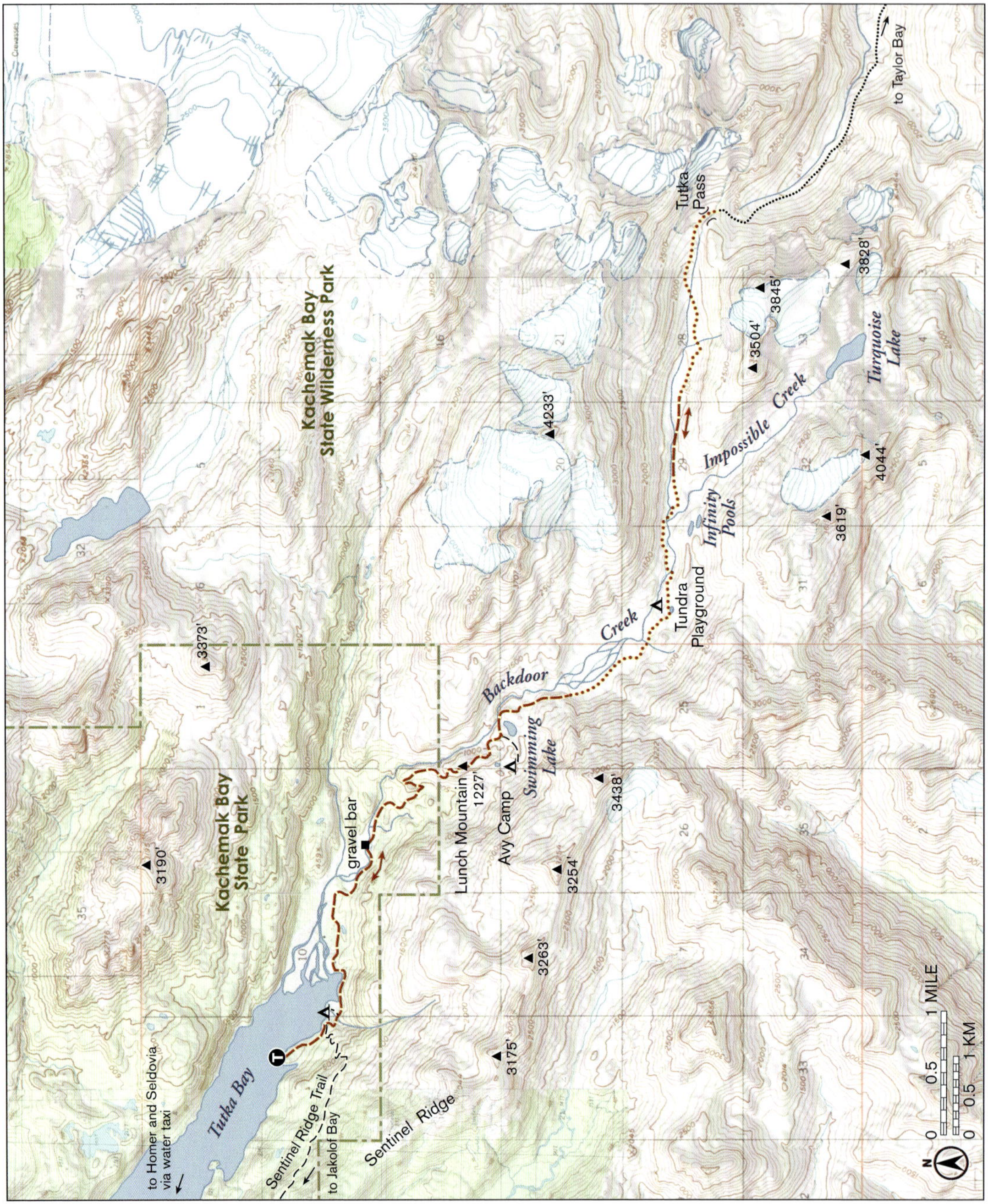
Kachemak Bay State Wilderness Park
Kachemak Bay State Park
Tutka Bay
to Homer and Seldovia via water taxi
Sentinel Ridge Trail
to Jakolof Bay
Sentinel Ridge
gravel bar
Lunch Mountain 1227'
Avy Camp
Swimming Lake
Backdoor
Creek
Tundra Playground
Infinity Pools
Impossible Creek
Turquoise Lake
Tutka Pass
to Taylor Bay
3190'
3373'
3175'
3263'
3254'
3438'
4233'
3619'
4044'
3504'
3845'
3828'
0 0.5 1 MILE
0 0.5 1 KM
N

"summit," 4.5 miles from the trailhead. This is not a real mountain but a rock outcrop, though it features views in all directions. It is aptly named, however, because it makes a nice midday turnaround point for a day hike, popular among maritime Kachemak Bay residents for whom a boat trip to the trailhead is easy. Lunch Mountain is also a geographic hinge point: look back (northwest) to coastal forests and a long view, weather permitting, of Tutka Bay framing Mount Iliamna, a volcano that rises high and white on the far side of Cook Inlet; look ahead (southeast) to an increasingly alpine landscape hemmed in by mountainsides.

Continuing on the trail from Lunch Mountain, a signed junction at less than a mile indicates a campsite on a spur trail 0.4 mile to the right. This place, known as Avy Camp (5.5 miles from the trailhead to camp), is not an established campsite but does offer a large, level place that can accommodate multiple tents, with nearby rivulets as water sources. If you are hiking farther, pass the spur trail to skirt left around Swimming Lake. The trail rolls along with minimal elevation gain and shortly enters a cliffy section, where serious trail work allows hikers to traverse the wooded hillside above Backdoor Creek for 0.4 mile. Mid-traverse, an opening in the trees to the left allows access to the parallel creekside gravel bars. At 6.1 miles from the trailhead, the main trail drops onto the gravel bar as the creek spreads out into a wide, braided section. Alluring bright-green moss blankets the gravel footing, complemented by dwarf fireweed in season, as a Dr. Seuss–like mountain peak punctuates the distant view. Follow a faint trail for 0.7 mile toward the far end of this valley, looking for intermittent cairns to guide the way.

At 6.8 miles, leave the gravel bar as the trail crosses a small stream and enters the knobby alpine landscape of Tundra Playground, where trickling water sources and good, informal camping opportunities abound. The route can be confusing here, as no worn trail is evident, but cairns guide the winding way through rock and tundra bumps. (Avid cross-country explorers can find a prized camp spot at the Infinity Pools a little more than a mile from here, up valley on the south side of Backdoor Creek, but no trail currently leads there.) If you are continuing to Tutka Pass, pick your way from cairn to cairn and flag to flag, encountering another minor side stream ford, until you reach the first major ford of Backdoor Creek, 7.8 miles from the trailhead.

This is one of two serious, potentially hazardous river fords on the route to the pass; see Stream Crossings in the Introduction for safety tips. Hikers should be prepared to turn back at this point or camp and wait if the creek is prohibitively swollen by heavy rains or snowmelt. The water spreads wide here, however, providing a relatively shallow section. Angle downstream as you cross to the north side of the creek, reaching the far bank at an obvious cairn-marked trail. After less than half a mile paralleling Backdoor Creek on the north side, come to its confluence with Impossible Creek, which flows in from the south. Take a moment to marvel at the deep river pools here: the clear, azure-tinted waters of Backdoor colliding with a milky, glacial blue from Impossible. Ford Backdoor Creek again immediately upstream of the confluence, avoiding the need to cross Impossible Creek. From here, a cross-country side trip upstream along Impossible Creek to Turquoise Lake is possible, but unmarked.

Continuing along Backdoor Creek to Tutka Pass, cairns become increasingly hard to pick out as the landscape becomes rockier. At a pinch point in the valley 0.7 mile from the second ford, follow a stretch of obvious trail cut into the cliff edge, as crystalline waters dance through pools and falls in the gorge

*Approaching Tutka Pass*

50 feet below. The valley widens out beyond, a field of talus that makes for slower going. Follow cairns and a trail tread where visible, but hikers may have to pick their own way in some sections here, always searching for another marker. You will most likely have to cross snow well into July.

About 9.5 miles from the trailhead, cross a notable stream tumbling steeply down from a hanging glacier on the right. Be wary of lingering snow bridges. Not long after, the route turns slightly left, returning to Backdoor Creek. Fording the now smaller creek is unlikely to be a problem; cross to the north side again at a large, light-colored boulder. Search for cairns on the far side, swinging slightly uphill at the base of green tundra vegetation. Continue heading east and traverse above the creek toward the pass on a logical line, spotting a few cairns along the way. Be prepared for whipping winds.

At the pass is a wide, flat gravelly area (a snowfield in early season); a glacier occupied this spot within the last half century but has since retreated to peer down from the mountaintop above to the left. On the far side of this gravel field is a crest, 11.3 miles from the trailhead and at 2300 feet elevation, on which to stand at the high point of the route. Gaze into the deep valley beyond, which leads down to the Taylor River and ultimately Taylor Bay. The return route from the pass to the upper Tutka Bay trailhead is the same.

Many backpackers on Kachemak Bay trails will need to plan their hiking days around a culminating water taxi pickup. Some say "Katch-a-boat Bay" would be a more appropriate name. Schedule extra time to hike to your pickup point, and do not plan a trip that exceeds your party's capabilities. Rushing to meet the boat will surely reduce enjoyment and can increase your chance of injury. If you miss your scheduled time, know that various water taxis frequent the pickup points in Tutka Bay and can contact each other via radio.

## SHORTER OPTION

Lunch Mountain is a 9-mile roundtrip quasi-summit with sweeping views of Tutka Bay and Mount Iliamna. It makes for a solid day hike.

## EXTENDING YOUR TRIP

Intrepid backpackers can descend the far side of Tutka Pass to complete the epic trek between Tutka Bay and Taylor Bay on the outer coast, to be met by floatplane (20.6 miles one way). Or, with some gumption, hike Tutka Bay to Taylor Bay roundtrip (41.2 miles). Be prepared for significantly more cumulative elevation change on the Taylor side (roughly 9300 feet roundtrip from the pass and back), along with more routefinding, bigger river crossings, and steep snow in early season. Study the Ground Truth Alaska map. Hiking one way requires a chartered floatplane; the safest bet is to book a drop-off at Taylor Bay and hike in reverse back to Tutka Bay, as any flight delay due to stormy weather on the outer coast would then affect your trip start rather than leaving you stranded.

To extend the trip along Tutka Bay, head uphill at the signed fork 0.6 mile from the upper Tutka Bay trailhead onto the Sentinel Ridge Trail. This trail gains about 2800 feet and offers views of Tutka Bay islands and Grace Ridge (another popular Kachemak Bay hike); camping is possible in the tundra zone near the apex of Sentinel Ridge, about 3 miles from the fork. From there, the Sentinel Ridge Trail drops into a parallel valley and connects to the Tutka Lake Trail. Hikers can reach Sea Star Cove from a junction at the northwest edge of Tutka Lake (7.6 miles from the fork), taking a right turn uphill to reach a well-kept public-use cabin in 1.1 miles (8.7 miles from the fork near the upper Tutka Bay trailhead). Make reservations through the Alaska State Parks website (see the Resources section). Water taxis can pick up or drop off hiking parties at Sea Star Cove.

To reach Seldovia by land, keep left at the trail junction at Tutka Lake, following signs for Tutka Bay Lagoon. The route skirts the shore of the lagoon; passability is tide dependent. The Tutka–Jakolof Trail leads west from the lagoon, departing Kachemak Bay State Park and entering private Seldovia Native Association Inc. (SNAI) lands; you must secure a personal-use permit through the SNAI website before your trip (see the Resources section). The trail ends at Jakolof Bay Road, about 13 road miles from Seldovia. The distance from the junction at Tutka Lake to Jakolof Bay Road is 3.2 miles. Check Ground Truth Alaska's website for more details, including a planned hiking trail from this point into Seldovia.

# 2 ALPINE RIDGE TRAIL AND GREWINGK GLACIER

**DISTANCE:** 9 miles point to point
**TIME:** Full day to 2 days
**ELEVATION GAIN:** 2600 feet
**HIGH POINT:** 2100 feet
**SEASON:** June–October
**SURFACE:** Tundra, hardpack, handholds (scrambling)
**GRADE:** Low angle with steep segments
**INDIGENOUS LAND:** Dena'ina Athabascan and Chugach Sugpiaq (Alutiiq)
**MANAGING AGENCY:** Kachemak Bay State Park
**MAPS:** USGS Seldovia C-4 NE, C-4 SE, C-3 NW, C-3 SW
**ONLINE MAP SEARCH:** "glacier spit ak"
**TRAILHEAD GPS:** Glacier Spit trailhead 59.622366°N, 151.196299°W
Saddle trailhead 59.601370°N, 151.164164°W

**Kachemak Bay State Park offers hikes for everyone—from families with infants to experienced** backpackers—and even the easiest comes complete with a glacial lake, icebergs, towering peaks, and a spectacular coast. One of the more strenuous options is a hike up a high ridge rewarded by views overlooking the iceberg-dotted lake at the foot of Grewingk Glacier and Kachemak Bay beyond. (See Shorter Options for a lowland stroll to the same Grewingk Glacier Lake.) The Alpine Ridge Trail provides access through forest and brush to spectacular alpine country. Camping is possible at this route's destination, where rolling tundra knobs are interspersed with tiny ponds. Extended exploration along the broad ridge crest allows views across the mile-wide glacier and the much larger icefield that feeds it.

This point-to-point route offers variety and possible spur trails along the way, but hiking out and back from either trailhead is also possible. The quickest access to Alpine Ridge is from the Saddle trailhead, a 5.7-mile round-trip.

## DRIVING DIRECTIONS

Search online for "homer spit ak," then follow these directions. Hikers not living on Kachemak Bay will likely access this trip via water taxi from Homer. Follow the Sterling Highway nearly to its terminus on the Homer Spit, a narrow, 4-mile peninsula that juts into Kachemak Bay. The small boat harbor and signs advertising water taxis are near the end of the spit (see the Resources section). Ask about current rates (not cheap) for drop-off at the Glacier Spit trailhead and pickup at the Saddle trailhead. Allow forty-five minutes for the water taxi trip each way.

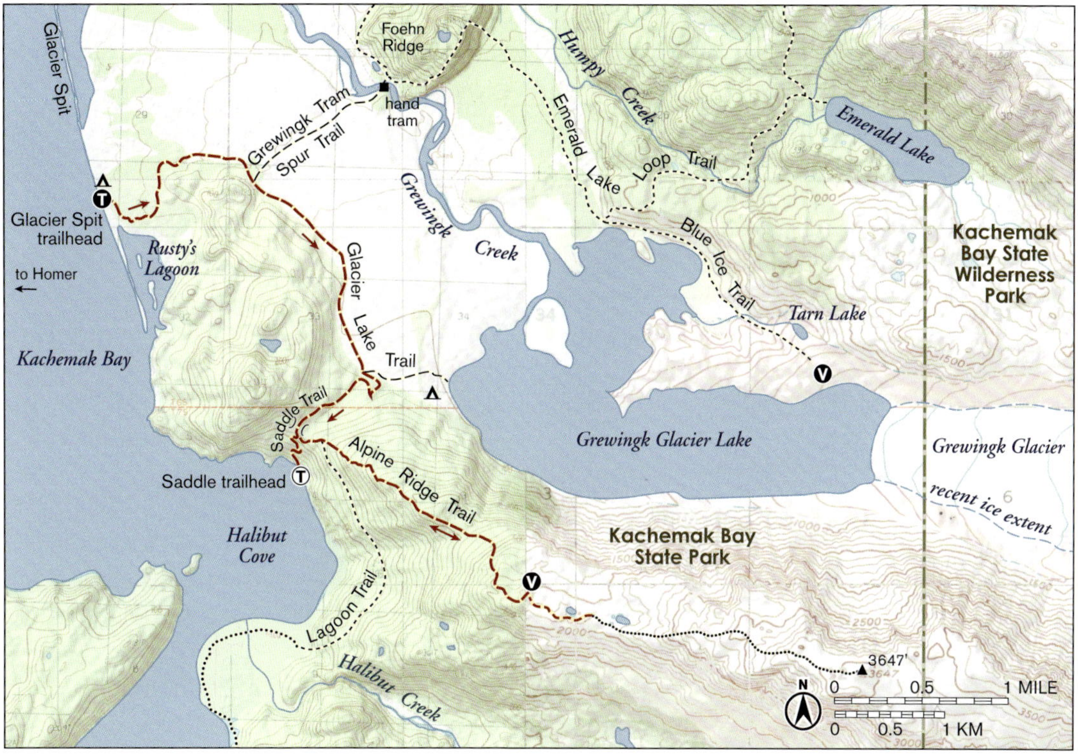


## ON THE ROUTE

Start with a water taxi drop-off at the Glacier Spit trailhead. The trail begins between the long Glacier Spit and a shorter spit enclosing Rusty's Lagoon. The beachfront trailhead is designated by an orange marker, a helpful beacon if the water taxi needs to land down the shoreline due to the tide. Just behind the beach, the trail passes a food storage locker, a trail register, and an aging outhouse. There is flat ground to nestle tents in the beachside grasses here, but pack in fresh water if staying.

This main trail in the Grewingk area, called the Glacier Lake Trail, initially wanders through cottonwood and spruce forest, then emerges on a glacial outwash plain covered with low vegetation, which makes for easy going on nearly flat terrain. At 1.4 miles, a left fork off the route leads to a hand tram across Grewingk Creek on the Grewingk Tram Spur Trail. Stay on the Glacier Lake Trail (right fork). At mile 2.7 the Glacier Lake Trail intersects the Saddle Trail. Grewingk Glacier Lake is worth a side excursion, time permitting, a 1-mile round-trip from this junction; see Shorter Options. For Alpine Ridge, take the right fork to start up the Saddle Trail.

The Saddle Trail leaves the glacial plain, climbing 300 feet in 0.9 mile to a junction near the topographic saddle, 3.6 miles from the Glacier Spit trailhead. Look for a sign pointing the way left toward the Alpine Ridge Trail. This trail takes off steeply and is less maintained than the Saddle Trail; expect grassy overgrowth. After 0.2 mile, reach another signed junction, and take the left fork toward the ridge. The large Sitka spruce (many killed by spruce bark beetles) and the thick green understory in this area create a different forest than is found along most trails in Southcentral Alaska. Depending on the latest trail maintenance, hikers may find a few of these big trees across the trail. By midsummer, the lower parts of the Alpine Ridge Trail may be badly overgrown, and after rainy weather, the grass and bushes may be wet. The trail has few flat spots, and because the forest is thick, the climb features few vistas. Nonetheless, keep an eye out between the trees for peeks at Halibut Cove to the right or Grewingk Glacier and its berg-studded lake to the left. From the junction with the Saddle Trail, the Alpine Ridge Trail gains 1870 feet in 2 miles, climbing so steeply in some segments that ropes are in place as handholds to supplement eroding footing.

*Meeting a water taxi in Halibut Cove after a day on the Alpine Ridge Trail*

Finally, the trail enters the alpine zone where the ridge levels off, 5.6 miles from the Glacier Spit trailhead. A viewpoint just off the trail to the left affords an expansive look at the white ice of Grewingk Glacier, now below, and the surrounding peaks. A series of knobs and pocket-sized valleys lies ahead, rolling on for nearly a mile on the broad ridge crest. The viewpoint is a fine destination, but venturing into the rolling terrain to rest, stretched out on a tundra cushion by an alpine pond, is recommended. Camping is possible here, although water may be scarce after the last snow patches melt in mid- to late June. Water from small ponds should be purified before drinking.

On the descent, follow the Alpine Ridge Trail back down to its junction with the Saddle Trail. Turn left to reach the Saddle trailhead. This last leg is a switchbacking 0.4 mile that quickly loses 350 feet through thickening forest, ending at sea level on a wooden platform above a rocky beach. Await your water taxi here.

Many hikers on Kachemak Bay trails will need to plan their hiking days around a culminating water taxi pickup. Schedule extra time to hike to your pickup point, and do not plan a trip that is longer than your party's capabilities. Rushing to meet the boat will surely reduce enjoyment and can increase the chance of injury. If you miss your scheduled time, know that various water taxis frequent the trailheads around Grewingk Glacier and can contact each other via radio.

*Alpine Ridge offers views deep into Kachemak Bay State Wilderness Park and back over the ocean.*

## SHORTER OPTIONS

The easy 6.4-mile roundtrip trail to Grewingk Glacier Lake begins at the Glacier Spit trailhead, proceeding as described above. At the intersection of the Glacier Lake Trail and the Saddle Trail, take the left fork, reaching the lake in about half a mile. This last part of the route is marked with cairns, but these rock piles may be difficult to pick out against the background of glacial cobbles. The lake's broad beach invites picnicking, camping, or just sitting and watching the light and clouds play on the mountains and the big glacier across the lake. If you camp near the lake, pick a site away from the water to avoid blocking other hikers' access to the beach, as well as for safety: landslides falling into the water could generate large waves.

Drinking water is an issue here. The lake is glacial; the silty water is drinkable (with treatment) but will quickly clog a filter. Let it settle as much as possible and skim off the clearer water for boiling before consumption. A better bet is to melt icebergs. Take an ice axe or other chipping tool to break ice into pot-sized chunks, and be prepared to take a step into the frigid water to reach a grounded berg.

For alternate access to Grewingk Glacier Lake, use the Saddle trailhead, a shorter but steeper 3.7-mile round-trip. Make it a point-to-point trip, from the Glacier Spit trailhead to the Saddle trailhead with a side trip to the lake, for a total of 5 miles.

For another shorter option, consider the Grewingk Tram Spur Trail. A hand tram is a curiosity in wilderness settings and makes a fun destination in itself, at 4.8 miles roundtrip from the Glacier Spit trailhead. At the intersection 1.4 miles in, take the Grewingk Tram Spur Trail northeast out of the woods and across an inviting dryas-covered bench. The trail passes through a forest of young spruce and cottonwood to the tram across Grewingk Creek, 1 mile from the intersection. The tram requires significant upper-body strength to operate but is manageable for two people, with one in the cable car and one on the platform, both pulling. Take gloves. Hanging, suspended on a thin cable, above glacial waters roaring below is a thrill.

There are possible campsites just north of the tram. For water, follow the Emerald Lake Loop Trail west from the tram a few hundred yards to a small, clear-water lake. Near the far end of this lake is a dryas-covered bench that offers good camping. Camp as far off the trail as possible. Bears frequent the Grewingk Creek area, especially when the salmon are running, so take appropriate precautions (see Bears and Other Wildlife in the Introduction).

### EXTENDING YOUR TRIP

The most obvious extension lies before you as you hit the viewpoint on Alpine Ridge—keep hiking up! The ridge itself continues east for miles, paralleling Grewingk Glacier. The trail gradually disappears on the rolling bench at 2100 feet elevation, but routefinding up roughly 1500 feet to point 3647, another 3 miles roundtrip, will provide a good workout. The views increase with elevation. Achieving yet farther points on the ridge is enticing for the most adventurous but becomes trickier with a narrowing ridgeline and the time constraints of water taxis. If you want a long ridge day, consider hiking out and back from the Saddle trailhead to reduce lowland time.

The Lagoon Trail that intersects the Alpine Ridge Trail is a connector to more Kachemak Bay State Park trails to the south but sees scant use and maintenance. Hike only with caution and research. Similarly, the extensive trail system north of the Grewingk hand tram is not as well used and may be overgrown or blocked by deadfall, although the Blue Ice Trail offers a stellar view of the glacier. Check the Alaska State Parks website for information on trail conditions (see the Resources section).

# 3 COOK INLET BEACH BIKE

**DISTANCE:** 90 miles point to point
**TIME:** 3–5 days
**ELEVATION GAIN:** Less than 500 feet
**HIGH POINT:** 290 feet
**SEASON:** Late May–September
**SURFACE:** Sand and/or gravel, water, hardpack
**GRADE:** Low angle
**INDIGENOUS LAND:** Dena'ina Athabascan
**MANAGING AGENCY:** Alaska Division of Parks and Outdoor Recreation; Alaska Division of Mining, Land, and Water

**MAPS:** USGS Seldovia C-4, C-5, D-5; Kenai A-5, A-4, B-4, C-4
**ONLINE MAP SEARCH:** "kenai peninsula ak"
**TRAILHEAD GPS:** Port of Homer 59.605016°N, 151.430671°W
City of Kenai Dock 60.543930°N, 151.220042°W

**Cruise the western edge of the Kenai Peninsula on a fat-tire bike: beachy gravel under tread, three** shining white volcanoes across the ocean waters lapping at your left, a steep bluff defining the beach to your right, sunshine on your shoulders, and a breeze in your hair. This trip offers a glimpse into the seaside world that goes on below the Cook Inlet bluff, hidden from the parallel Sterling Highway. On the beach, abundant salmon fisheries are on full display in the height of summer. Sea otters, eagles, and even sea lions make their appearance beachside, feasting on fish scraps or snagging a sunbath. Bluff-perched and stilt-legged specimens of coastal architecture, ranging from grand to ramshackle, peer out to the inlet. For a smaller sample of this coastal flavor, try a simple beach walk from Homer (see Shorter Options).

These 90 miles of unique beach experience are made possible by a unique ride: the fat bike is an Alaska-grown innovation, its wide tires developed to float across snowy landscapes and proven in early testing on the Iditarod Trail in the 1980s. The wide tread works wonderfully on the sand and gravel of Cook Inlet's shore too. With surfaces ranging from borderline bouldery on the Homer end to serious sand near the Kasilof and Kenai Rivers, and with river crossings to navigate in between, this trip presents a delightful romp for experienced fat-tire bicyclists and a rewarding challenge, at a slower pace, for the beginning to intermediate crowd.

## DRIVING DIRECTIONS

This description assumes a two-car shuttle, with "trailheads" at multiday parking lots, one at each end. Both cars would ideally be capable of carrying all the bikes. A less cumbersome option for bigger groups: take advantage of shuttle services offered by Cycle Logical bike shop in Homer, which has the rig to pick up a crew and their bikes in Kenai for a fee; book well in advance (see the Resources section for website). Yet another variant is to ride with a sag wagon: a vehicle that follows along on the Sterling Highway, carrying gear and meeting up with the group at camp each night. Advantages include no-holds-barred car camping and no shuttle logistics, but someone has to drive instead of bike. In these alternative scenarios, coordinate with a hired shuttle or sag wagoneer for start and end points.

**Port of Homer parking (south trailhead).** Search online for "homer spit road ak," then follow these directions. Follow the Sterling Highway nearly to its terminus on the Homer Spit, a narrow, 4-mile peninsula that juts into Kachemak Bay. The small boat harbor and associated parking are near the end of the spit. Look for the intersection with Freight Dock Road; immediately thereafter, a large gravel lot on the left boasts seven-day free parking. Additional lots on the northeast side of the harbor offer the same, along with parking for trailers.

**City of Kenai Dock parking (north trailhead).** Search online for "city of kenai boat launch ak," or follow these directions. Take the Sterling Highway to

Kenai
City of Kenai Dock
SEE KENAI DETAIL
South Kenai Beach access
Sterling
to Anchorage
Sterling Hwy
Kenai River
Watsjold Lane
Soldotna
Buchanan Rd
Kalgin Island
Kasilof River Special Use Area
SEE KASILOF DETAIL
Kasilof
Kasilof River
Cook Inlet
Clam Gulch State Recreation Area
Tustumena Lake
Crooked Creek
Ninilchik River
SEE NINILCHIK DETAIL
Ninilchik River, north side
Ninilchik River Campground
Ninilchik Beach Day Use Area
Deep Creek State Recreation Area
Ninilchik
Deep Creek
South Fork
Happy Valley
Stariski Creek
Stariski State Recreation Site
Whiskey Gulch
SEE ANCHOR POINT DETAIL
North Fork
Anchor River State Recreation Area
Anchor Point
Anchor River
Diamond Creek
Kachemak Bay
Diamond Gulch
Homer
Bishop's Beach
Mariner Park
Port of Homer
SEE HOMER DETAIL
0 5 10 MILES
0 5 10 KM

## PUBLIC BEACH ACCESS POINTS BETWEEN HOMER AND KENAI

| BEACH ACCESS NAME | GPS | MILEPOST | ACCESS ROAD (ALTERNATE NAME) | CAMPING |
|---|---|---|---|---|
| 1. Mariner Park, Homer | 59.632249°N, 151.497137°W | SH 175.2 | N/A | ✓ |
| 2. Bishop's Beach, Homer | 59.637732°N, 151.540475°W | SH 173.1 | Main Street to E. Bunnell Avenue to Beluga Place | |
| 3. Diamond Gulch | 59.670496°N, 151.705763°W | SH 167 | Unmarked, opposite Diamond Ridge Road | |
| 4. Anchor River State Recreation Area | 59.773070°N, 151.867889°W | SH 157.1 | Old Sterling Highway to Anchor Point Road | ✓ |
| 5. Whiskey Gulch | 59.833049°N, 151.821261°W | SH 152.6 | Whiskey Gulch Road (Whiskey Gulch Spur Road) | ✓ |
| 6. Deep Creek State Recreation Area | 60.028554°N, 151.704408°W | SH 137.3 | Wayside Road (Deep Creek Way) | ✓ |
| 7. Ninilchik Beach Day Use Area | 60.049071°N, 151.672016°W | SH 135.1 | Mission Avenue (Beach Access Road) to Valley Avenue | |
| 8. Ninilchik River, north side | 60.054994°N, 151.664986°W | SH 135.1 | Mission Avenue (Beach Access Road) | |
| 9. Clam Gulch State Recreation Area | 60.239449°N, 151.401024°W | SH 117.5 | Clam Gulch Road to Per Osmar's Way | ✓ |
| 10. Kasilof River Special Use Area, south side | 60.382653°N, 151.321680°W | CL 9.7 | Cohoe Beach Road (Cohoe Loop Road) | |
| 11. Kasilof River Special Use Area, north side | 60.389802°N, 151.296770°W | KBR 4.8 | Kasilof Beach Road (Kasilof Beach Stub) | |
| 12. Buchanan Road | 60.423337°N, 151.289892°W | KBR 7.4 | Buchanan Road | |
| 13. Watsjold Lane | 60.481413°N, 151.280550°W | KBR 11.5 | Watsjold Lane | |
| 14. South Kenai Beach access | 60.527405°N, 151.273056°W | KBR 13.8 | Cannery Road to Dunes Road | |

**Notes:** For milepost column, SH = Sterling Highway; CL = Cohoe Loop; KBR = Kalifornsky Beach Road.

Soldotna, turning west onto Kalifornsky Beach Road just south of the Kenai River bridge. Drive 6 miles, then turn right onto Bridge Access Road. Drive north on Bridge Access Road for 1.7 miles, then take a left on Boat Launch Road where a sign announces the City of Kenai public dock. Here, plentiful overnight parking in a gravel lot is free for noncommercial use, except between July 10 and 31, when the Kenai personal-use fishery raises demand and a daily fee.

**Intermediate beach access points.** The accompanying table helps with planning shorter options, meeting up with a sag wagon, and arranging beachside camping (additional, inland camping options are available; see maps and On the Route). The place names listed under "Beach Access Name" double as online search terms. GPS coordinates are where the public access meets the beach. The access road names are marked on street signs; alternate names in parentheses are for the same road, when it is called something different by digital mapping sources.

### ON THE ROUTE

By necessity, the following description is heavy on directions at obstacles along the route. Rest

*Cyclists and walkers share the beach near Homer.*

assured, between each complex section (see detail maps) is a long stretch of beach perfect for untroubled pedaling.

You can ride this route in either direction, but Homer to Kenai is featured so that summer's prevailing winds (and sun) will be at your back. If you don't have a fat bike in your garage, rent one and the related gear through Cycle Logical in Homer, Beemuns in Soldotna, or various locations in Anchorage. Cycle Logical offers beach tours as well (see the Resources section). Plan riding days to suit your pace, as overnight options dot the route. The many state campgrounds along the way are a good bet, with views and ambiances well worth the fee. Stringing together inns and vacation rentals is a feasible, cushier option.

Riding the beach comes with water-related risks: track the tides with a printed table or app, as finding yourself trapped against the bluff by the encroaching sea is a possibility. Particularly between Homer and Anchor Point, a tide higher than 18 feet will get you wet. The danger of getting stuck on the remainder of the route is lower, but choice of riding line is poor when the beach is narrow in the hours around high tide. It is safest to stop and wait out the tide at a place above the high-water line, taking the opportunity for a snooze or a snack—this pace is part of the joy of the trip.

River crossings, too, present risks. The route necessarily detours around the mighty Kasilof and Kenai Rivers. Three other notable waterways, the Anchor River, Deep Creek, and Ninilchik River, are crossable at low tide but will be daunting enough for most that roadway detours are provided as the primary route, easing scheduling too. Smaller drainages are frequent, ranging from splashy crossing puzzles to hardly noticeable, so expect wet feet, and see Stream Crossings in the Introduction.

Optionally, the most gear-equipped bikers could bring packrafts and the skills to cross rivers and keep off the roads.

A freshwater source at each camp is necessary on this route, not just for hydration but also for nightly bike maintenance against the salt and grit of beach riding. The crew at Cycle Logical, experts in keeping their rental fleet rolling, recommends the following maintenance regimen at each camp. In addition to the typical bike toolkit (see Mode-Specific Essential Gear in the Introduction), beach riders should also pack a rag, a brush, and lube. Remove the wheels, brush sand off the bike, and rinse everything thoroughly with fresh water. Let it dry off, reinstall the wheels, clean the chain with a rag, brush off the cassette, lubricate the chain, and then clean the chain again with your rag. Depending on the bike, an Allen wrench may be all that is needed to pull out and clean the crank as well.

## Homer to Anchor Point

For this 21.2-mile section in particular, plan to be off the beach for two hours on either side of high tide. Depart from the Port of Homer parking lot to head northwest on the Homer Spit Trail, a paved, separated path that runs along Homer Spit Road. Pass Mariner Park on the left in 2.8 miles, which offers camping and marks the start of a low-tide shortcut along the beach, passing below the Ocean Drive Loop seawall to reach Bishop's Beach. To continue through town, pedal uphill at the base of the spit, following the sinuous Sterling Highway route (street names change along the way; just follow the clear main road). At the intersection with Poopdeck Street, just before the Alaska Islands and Ocean Visitor Center, take a path left around the visitor center parking lot and downhill on a portion of the Beluga Slough Trail to meet the north end of Beluga Place, taking that road straight (south) to

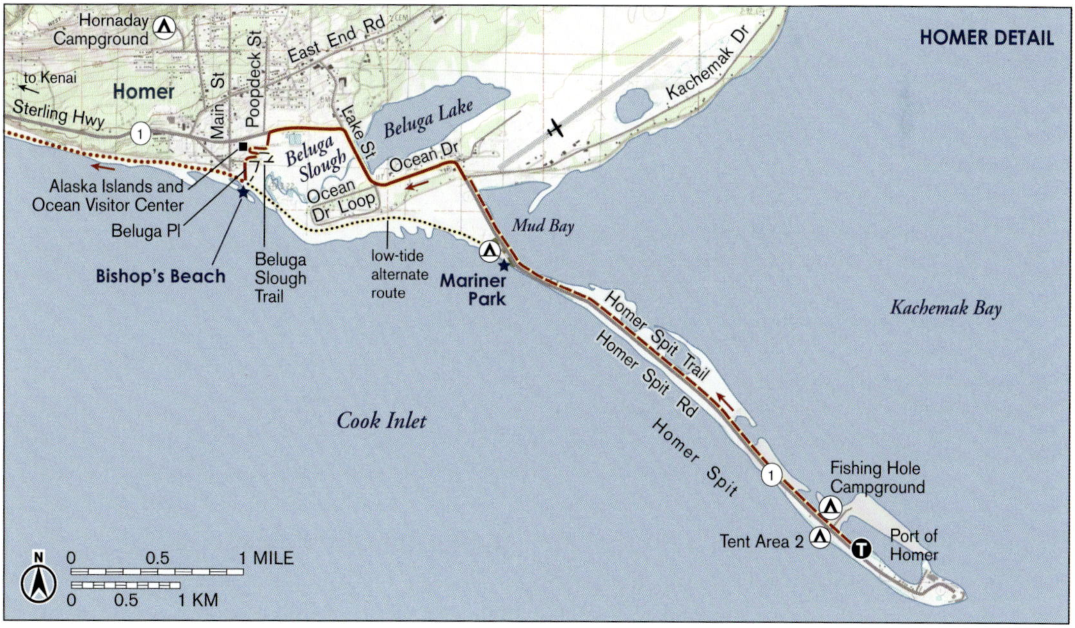

Bishop's Beach. Bikes are not allowed on the boardwalks along Beluga Slough. Bishop's Beach marks 5.3 miles from the trailhead through town, or about 4.7 miles on the low-tide beach route.

The Homer end of the beach ride is the most technical, with stretches of rounded rocks that require either mountain bike skill or some bike pushing (though timing your passage carefully at low tide can make for easy cruising on exposed sands). Reducing tire pressure may be useful over rocky tread. Enjoy the challenge for 6.4 miles from Bishop's Beach before reaching Diamond Gulch, where a popular beach access trail and Diamond Creek meet the shore at a grassy gap in the bluff. The 0.6-mile Diamond Gulch trail is an opportunity to connect to the highway if needed; it traverses the side of a green gully where alders line the way to the top of the bluff. The trail is well traveled but badly eroded, not maintained, and muddy in wet weather; use caution, and expect a difficult time if hauling loaded bikes. A small parking lot at the Diamond Gulch trailhead is accessible by a 1-mile four-wheel-drive road from Sterling Highway milepost 167. Pullouts closer to the highway provide parking for less capable vehicles.

Continue on the beach another 9.5 miles from Diamond Gulch to Anchor Point. Your bearing points across Cook Inlet toward Mount Iliamna, with its neighbor volcano, Redoubt, coming into view as the beach curves north. The surface gradually becomes tamer, giving more chances to look up at the scenery. Reach Anchor River State Recreation Area at a large gravel parking lot on the beach. Here, a tractor-assisted boat launch operates throughout the summer, helping boaters get out on the water for fishing. At the south end of the parking area, Anchor Point Road heads east past five state campgrounds toward the highway and small-town amenities. This

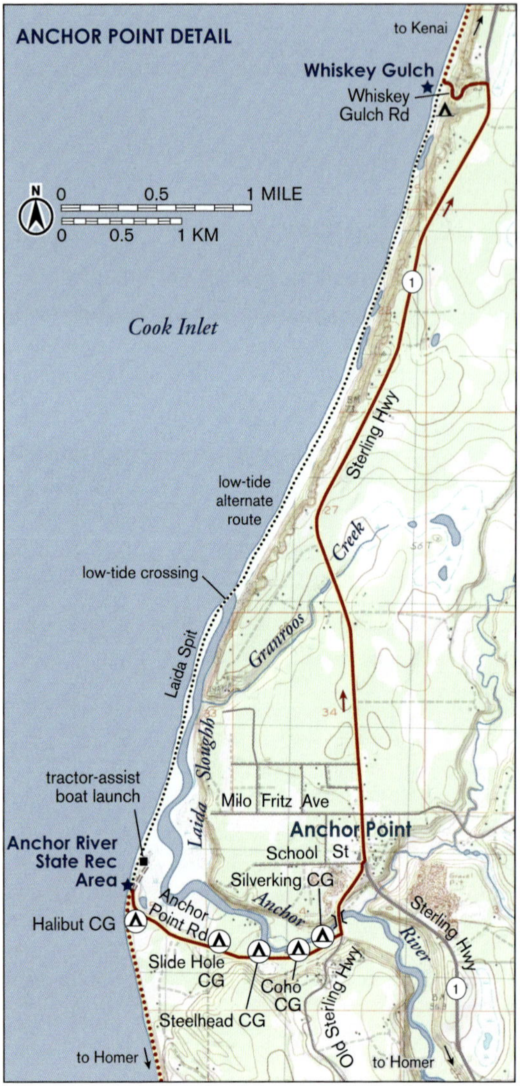


is the westernmost point on North America's continuous road system.

## Anchor Point to Ninilchik

In this 23.1-mile section, detouring around the mouth of the Anchor River on the road is the safest

plan, as outlined below, but it won't hurt to pedal 1.5 miles north along Laida Spit to check out the mouth of the river. If you attempt to cross Laida Slough (Anchor River's estuary), do so only at low tide and use caution. To detour instead, take Anchor Point Road east off the beach for 1.2 miles to its end, then turn left onto the Old Sterling Highway just before it crosses the Anchor River Bridge, and continue 0.4 mile to intersect the Sterling Highway at School Street. Cross the two-lane highway cautiously and pedal north. Several eateries and convenience stores greet the hungry bicyclist here. Ride on the highway shoulder for 4.2 miles to Whiskey Gulch Road at milepost 152.6. Turn left to descend steeply on the 0.3-mile dirt road to the beach. (There is a pleasant, bluff-perched campground off the highway 0.6 mile north at Stariski State Recreation Site, but it lacks beach access.)

Undeveloped beach camping is allowed at Whiskey Gulch, free and limited to fourteen days. Good spots beckon among the beachside trees, but expect neighbors, as the place becomes an elaborate camp city in the summer. Portable toilets are marginal, if any, and plan to haul in potable water. From here, take the beach north again toward Ninilchik. Three volcanoes now rise up across the inlet on clear days: Iliamna, Redoubt, and Spurr (think "IRS"). Come to Stariski Creek in 4.2 miles, one of the more substantial necessary crossings. Wade across if in doubt. Reach Happy Valley 7.8 miles from Whiskey Gulch, where a charming waterfall tumbles to the shoreline. There is no public access to the highway here, but the falls make an excellent lunch spot. Deep Creek is 6.8 miles ahead, with a smattering of state camping options from there to Ninilchik. The first is a beachside Deep Creek State Recreation Area campground, a well-appointed but somewhat exposed gravel lot. At the north end of the campground is Cape Ninilchik (not yet Ninilchik Village; see Ninilchik detail map), the spot to scope out the Deep Creek crossing.

To opt for the highway detour around Deep Creek, turn east at the south end of the campground onto Wayside Road. Go 0.3 mile on a shallow slope to the Sterling Highway. Cross the highway carefully, and turn north. Ninilchik Village lies 2.2 miles ahead. After 0.5 mile, a turnoff to the right leads to Deep Creek South Scenic Overlook with close-quarters camping popular among anglers. Deep Creek North Scenic Overlook just beyond the Deep Creek bridge offers the same. Continue on the highway through the commercial drag of Ninilchik, passing eateries and the Kenai Peninsula Fairgrounds. After 1.8 miles on the highway, an oblique left turn leads to Ninilchik View Campground, which has a lush setting, secluded campsites, and a set of stairs to the beach. Continue on the highway 0.4 mile to Mission Avenue at milepost 135.1, which leads to Ninilchik Village and back to the beach. To detour for yet more camping, continue 0.5 mile on the highway to Ninilchik River Campground, where sites sit tucked into a spruce-and-birch forest. Ninilchik River Scenic Overlook, 0.2 mile north from Mission Avenue, is another close-quarters riverside option.

## Ninilchik to Clam Gulch

To start this next section of 17.1 miles, turn north onto Mission Avenue, which forks just 0.2 mile from the highway. Take the right fork across the Ninilchik River bridge. If you braved the Deep Creek crossing and approach the Ninilchik River from the beach, it is best to concede a 0.5-mile detour to avoid the active harbor at the Ninilchik River's mouth. Continue through Ninilchik Village, originally settled by the Dena'ina people, home of the Ninilchik Village Tribe and the oldest community on the Kenai Peninsula. The Dena'ina name for this place is Niqnalchint, meaning "a place where a lodge is built" (see Ninilchik Village Tribe in the Resources section for more). Subsequent Russian influence is evidenced by the Russified village name and the Orthodox church; its cross-topped, onion-shaped spires stand visible high on the hill to the north, worth a switchbacking detour up the bluff. Both the village and church are recognized in the National Register of Historic Places.

Mission Avenue ends 0.2 mile from the bridge after passing quaint historic structures, some now housing art galleries and gift shops. At the road's terminus, follow an informal track to the right along the Ninilchik River, passing the Ninilchik Small Boat Harbor on your left. With luck, the harbor will be packed with drift gillnetters, small commercial salmon fishing boats moored one to the next, their fine nets coiled on drums (big spools) on their decks. Look for deckhands returning from town with groceries and supplies, hopping from boat to boat to reach their own. After 0.4 mile along the harbor, it's back to the beach.

Keep the ocean on your left, bluff on your right for 15.8 miles to Clam Gulch, the longest uninterrupted stretch of the route. The surface becomes ideal for carefree cruising; those with some drive can hit 8 to 10 miles per hour in sections. The upper Cook Inlet commercial set gillnet salmon fishery extends north from Ninilchik, a beach-based operation with nets staked close to shore extending to buoys anchored far out in the water. Bikers will pass fish camps, four-wheelers, tractors, skiffs, totes, and nets. Respect private equipment by steering clear, but no need to circumnavigate every line lying flat on the beach. (Do be alert for the occasional line suspended above the beach.) Digging for razor clams, too, is a historic pastime along this stretch but has been prohibited in recent years due to declining clam populations.

Two monolithic boulders off the shore are a sign to look for the turnup at Clam Gulch. The dirt road up the bluff is marked "Per Osmar's Way" on a street sign at the beach, though it is called Clam Gulch Road where it meets the Sterling Highway. This climb is the most strenuous of the route—250 feet elevation gain in 0.7 mile. Clam Gulch State Recreation Area has a pleasant campground partway up the access road—the only formal camping option in this area.

## Clam Gulch to Kasilof North

This 13.8-mile segment covers the longest road detour of the route, around the Kasilof River. The Sterling Highway cuts inland from Clam Gulch, so crossing the Kasilof at the highway's bridge takes the route far from the shore and cuts out about 11 miles of beach. For those with time in their schedule and a dedicated spirit, continuing on the beach from Clam Gulch north to the south bank of the Kasilof, then backtracking south on N. Cohoe Loop to the Sterling Highway, is a grand plan. The pavement miles are nearly equivalent in either scenario.

To shortcut, turn onto the Sterling Highway northbound from Clam Gulch Road. Ride defensively on the shoulder, as bikes are relatively unexpected by motorists here. Meet N. Cohoe Loop (the end of the alternate longer route) after 6.1 miles. A popular sport fishing campground at Crooked Creek State Recreation Site is 2.2 miles away up N. Cohoe Loop, and more secluded campsites at Johnson Lake State Recreation Area are accessed from the highway

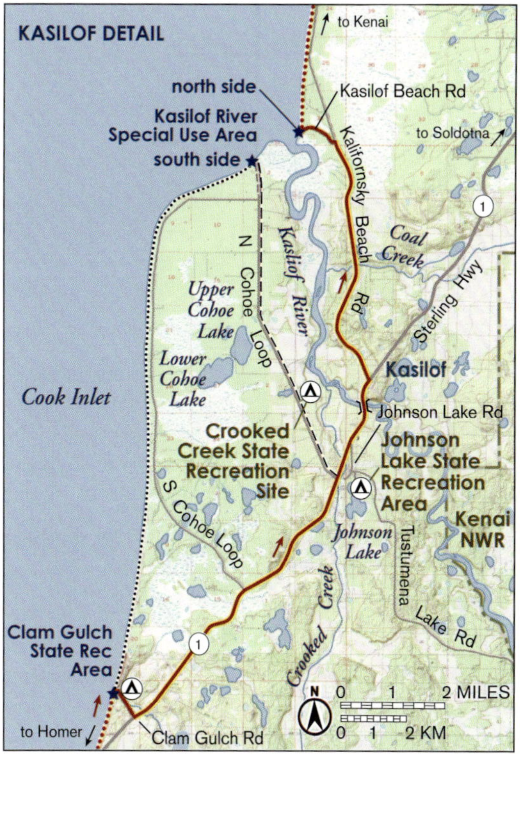


at Johnson Lake Road, 0.7 mile north. At 8.1 miles from Clam Gulch, after crossing the Kasilof River bridge, take a left onto Kalifornsky Beach Road. Head north 4.8 miles, then turn left onto Kasilof Beach Road, which reaches the north unit of the Kasilof River Special Use Area in 0.9 mile. In July, Alaska residents flock to the mouth of the Kasilof (and the Kenai) for the personal-use dipnet salmon fishery, a festive atmosphere that may find bikers momentarily dodging aluminum nets, flopping fish, and running children. Escape the melee for the solitude of a continued beach ride north.

## Kasilof North to Kenai

This 15.3-mile stretch begins along Kalifornsky Beach, which runs directly north for 9.6 miles, featuring mostly soft-sand beaches; aim for harder, wet sand near the water. Kalifornsky Beach Road parallels closely, lined with private lots that span between it and the beach. Two short public access roads squeeze between properties. The first, at 2.3 miles from the north Kasilof River Special Use Area, is Buchanan Road, which turns up from the beach immediately past a quaint cottage on stilts with a distinctive, curved metal roof. The access road weaves between private homes to reach Kalifornsky Beach Road in 0.2 mile. The second public access is at Watsjold Lane, which occurs 6.4 miles into Kalifornsky Beach and is unmarked at both ends, though it is less than 500 feet long. For both of these access points, there is no turnaround and no public parking; motor vehicles should stay on Kalifornsky Beach Road.

The bluff drops gradually along the ride north, bringing residences closer to beach level and increasing the prevalence of private drives accessing the beach. Keep in mind that, with the exception of access roads noted here, land above the high-water

mark is private; act respectfully. Many property owners on Kalifornsky Beach have erected minor seawalls to protect their lawns from erosion, which can create pinch points and unfavorably cobbled surfaces for riders traveling near high tide; plan accordingly. Savor the last 3.2 miles with the beach, now a familiar friend, from Watsjold Lane to the South Kenai Beach access point at Dunes Road.

The bluff gives way to grassy flats at the mouth of the Kenai. Turn up through the grasses at Dunes Road, a public access with three or four parking spaces just up from the beach. Do not park in neighboring private lots. Follow Dunes Road 0.2 mile to its terminus, turn right (south) to travel 1 mile on Cannery Road, then turn left onto Kalifornsky Beach Road. Ride east 2.4 miles on the paved shoulder, then turn left (north) onto Bridge Access Road. Enjoy a triumphant pedal across the Kenai River at the scenic Warren Ames Memorial Bridge, keeping an eye out for wildlife in the surrounding marshes: sandhill cranes in May, caribou in summer, moose browsing in mornings and evenings, along with many shorebirds and maybe even a coyote. After 1.7 miles on Bridge Access Road, reach a sign indicating the left turn to the City of Kenai public dock. The final 0.4 mile of the trip leads downhill to your waiting car. Refreshment and rest may be first on your mind, but remember to wash off your bike as soon as possible!

## SHORTER OPTIONS

For those less wheel-inclined, enjoy a walk west from Bishop's Beach in Homer, returning to suit your schedule, or venture the 7 miles between Bishop's Beach and Diamond Gulch for a one-way trip (shuttle required). On the beach at low tide, look for sea stars, many kinds of clamshells, mussels, whelk (neptune) shells, rocks covered with barnacles, sea urchins, snails, crabs, small shorebirds, gulls, scoters, loons, harlequin ducks, and kittiwakes. Coal and sometimes fossils can be found below the cliffs that border the beach. Bald eagles often soar along the eroding bluffs, and driftwood logs thrown up by storm waves provide ready benches and tables for picnics. Walkers of all ages will enjoy a stroll in the brisk salt air. If you plan to hike between the two access points, the view is better starting at the Diamond Gulch end because you walk toward the Kenai Mountains. In deciding which way to walk, pay attention to the wind; walking with the wind to your back is recommended because of blowing sand. See details on the Diamond Gulch trail under Homer to Anchor Point, previously.

Bishop's Beach is also a trailhead for the wheelchair-accessible Beluga Slough Trail, a 1.2-mile out-and-back route that is mostly boardwalk and gives access to good bird-watching, particularly for shorebirds such as spotted and western sandpipers. As you face Kachemak Bay, the trail goes left and skirts Beluga Slough. The trail is best when the tide is in and there is water in the slough. The walk takes about ten minutes one way and comes out at the Alaska Islands and Ocean Visitor Center (parking and second trailhead). Bikes and pets are not allowed on the boardwalk.

Homer to Clam Gulch is a shorter, 61.4-mile fat-bike route that gives plenty of beach riding flavor but stops before the highway detour around the Kasilof River. Plan for three days, though the speedy could do it in two.

Anchor Point to Kenai is a 69.3-mile option that avoids the trickiest riding and timing of the tides at the rocky beaches on the Homer end.

### EXTENDING YOUR TRIP

Beach riders have been known to extend this trip at both ends. Cycle Logical leads tours from Kachemak Selo to Homer, 16 beach miles from the east end of East End Road to Mud Bay by the Homer Spit, accessed from Kachemak Drive. On the Kenai end, Nikiski or Captain Cook State Recreation Area are possible destinations. The truly adventurous might make it along the wild north shore of the Kenai Peninsula to Point Possession, or even to the Chickaloon River across Turnagain Arm from Anchorage with the help of a bush plane, like the pioneers of the Kenai Peninsula beach fat-bike ride, the Homer-based owners of Free Spirit Wear Bike Jerseys (check out their gear and adventure blog at freespiritwear.com).

### SEASONAL OPTIONS

Beach riding is ultimately a year-round sport. Snow may cover some sections of beach, but luckily you are on a fat bike. With the willingness to carry more insulating layers and brave biting cold, winter riders get an entirely new take on the beauty of the beach. As always, consult the weather forecast and tide tables ahead of time. Walking in winter from Bishop's Beach at low tide is lovely, too, though the slippery Diamond Gulch trail is not recommended.

## 4 SWAN LAKE CANOE SYSTEM

**DISTANCE:** 13–60 miles point to point
**TIME:** 2 days to 1 week
**ELEVATION GAIN:** Less than 500 feet
**HIGH POINT:** 280 feet
**SEASON:** Late May–early October
**SURFACE:** Water, roots, mud
**GRADE:** Low angle
**INDIGENOUS LAND:** Kahtnuht'ana (Kenaitze) Dena'ina Athabascan
**MANAGING AGENCY:** Kenai National Wildlife Refuge
**MAP:** USGS Kenai C-2
**ONLINE MAP SEARCH:** "gavia lake ak"

**TRAILHEAD GPS:** East entrance 60.722969°N, 150.698027°W
west entrance 60.729730°N, 150.549675°W

**A long chain of lakes, streams, and rivers in the wooded northwestern Kenai Peninsula, the Swan** Lake canoe system offers outstanding paddling. Take a day or a week—many route variations are possible. More time means more fun exploring and fishing. Portages between lakes are marked trails; most are short at 0.2 to 0.4 mile, with the longest around 0.7 mile. The lakes come in a variety of sizes and shapes, the smaller ones usually protected from wind and rough water, the larger ones offering bays for exploring and views of the Kenai Mountains. A rich variety of waterbirds inhabits the area, including many species of ducks and shorebirds, loons, snipes, and of course, swans. Anglers will find rainbow trout, Dolly Varden, arctic char, and landlocked salmon. Watch for moose, beavers, muskrats, river otters, and bears.

Print a detailed map from the Kenai National Wildlife Refuge website, or pick up a brochure at the trailhead or the refuge visitor center in Soldotna (see the Resources section). Businesses in Anchorage, Soldotna, and Sterling rent canoes (see the Resources section). Guided trips are available. The Swan Lake canoe system is part of the National Recreation Trails system and is in the Dave Spencer Unit of the Kenai Wilderness. Wheeled or motorized vehicles, including powerboats, snowmachines, aircraft, off-road vehicles, mountain bikes, and wheeled canoe carriers, are prohibited in the wilderness. Groups are limited to a maximum of fifteen people.

## DRIVING DIRECTIONS

Search online for "swan lake road ak," then follow these directions. Two cars are necessary for shuttling, unless planning an out-and-back route. Access the trailheads for all routes from mile 83.2 of the Sterling Highway, 1.4 miles west of the Moose River bridge (on the western edge of Sterling). Turn north onto Swanson River Road here; expect no gas stations beyond the turn. Drive past free campgrounds at Dolly Varden and Rainbow Lakes (14.4 and 15.8 miles from the turnoff, respectively) with drinking water, picnic tables, and outhouses.

At 17.5 miles from the Sterling Highway, turn right (east) onto Swan Lake Road. The Swan Lake canoe system lies south of the road. The system has two entrances, the west entrance at Canoe Lake (mile 4 of Swan Lake Road) and the east entrance at Portage Lakes (mile 9.8). Both east and west trailheads feature free parking and an outhouse. The takeout that concludes the Moose River route is at the Izaak Walton State Recreation Site boat ramp adjacent to the Sterling Highway bridge, accessed at mile 81.

## ON THE ROUTE

The Swan Lake canoe system contains several possible lake-to-lake routes and a mild Moose River float route. There are many ways to link the lakes. Paddling from one entrance to the other via the shortest route, which is 13 miles, makes a good two- to three-day trip; strong paddlers can expect to reach Gavia Lake late the first day from either entrance (it is slightly closer to the west entrance), but many will be happier to take it more slowly. Alternatively, cast a wider route of roughly 15.5 miles entrance to entrance via Loon Lake for larger lakes and less-used portages. Spur routes to outlying lakes (Moosehorn

*Family fun on a water portage between two lakes* (Photo by Denny Wells Photography)

or Camp Island Lake) ensure long-term solitude for those looking to explore the wilderness for a week or more. When planning with skill and weather in mind, consider that winds can create whitecaps and difficult-to-dangerous canoeing on Swan Lake and other larger lakes. Look for a loon on every lake—they are almost guaranteed.

Each portage or connecting channel is marked with a small, unobtrusive brown sign bearing a white canoeist symbol; these are difficult to see from a distance. A map from the refuge showing the canoe system routes is a must for finding the general location of each portage. Most lakes in the Swan Lake system have primitive, cleared campsites, often near portage entrances; they are many and informal (not marked). Combing lakeshores for campsites on the mossy forest floor may also yield results with patience. Use of islands is discouraged because of impact to wildlife; if you must, use only existing campsites. A camp stove is generally best in this popular area. If you do build fires, do so only in existing firepits, not on moss or peat. Do not enlarge firepits, and be sure to pour a lot of water on the fire and surrounding earth when you are finished. Campfires may be restricted in dry years. Only dead and down trees may be cut.

From either entrance, the canoeist can reach the Moose River and float it to the Sterling Highway bridge (near the beginning of Swanson River Road). The river's tame gradient of 4 feet per mile makes for easygoing flat water, though intermediate paddling skills are necessary to navigate tight turns.

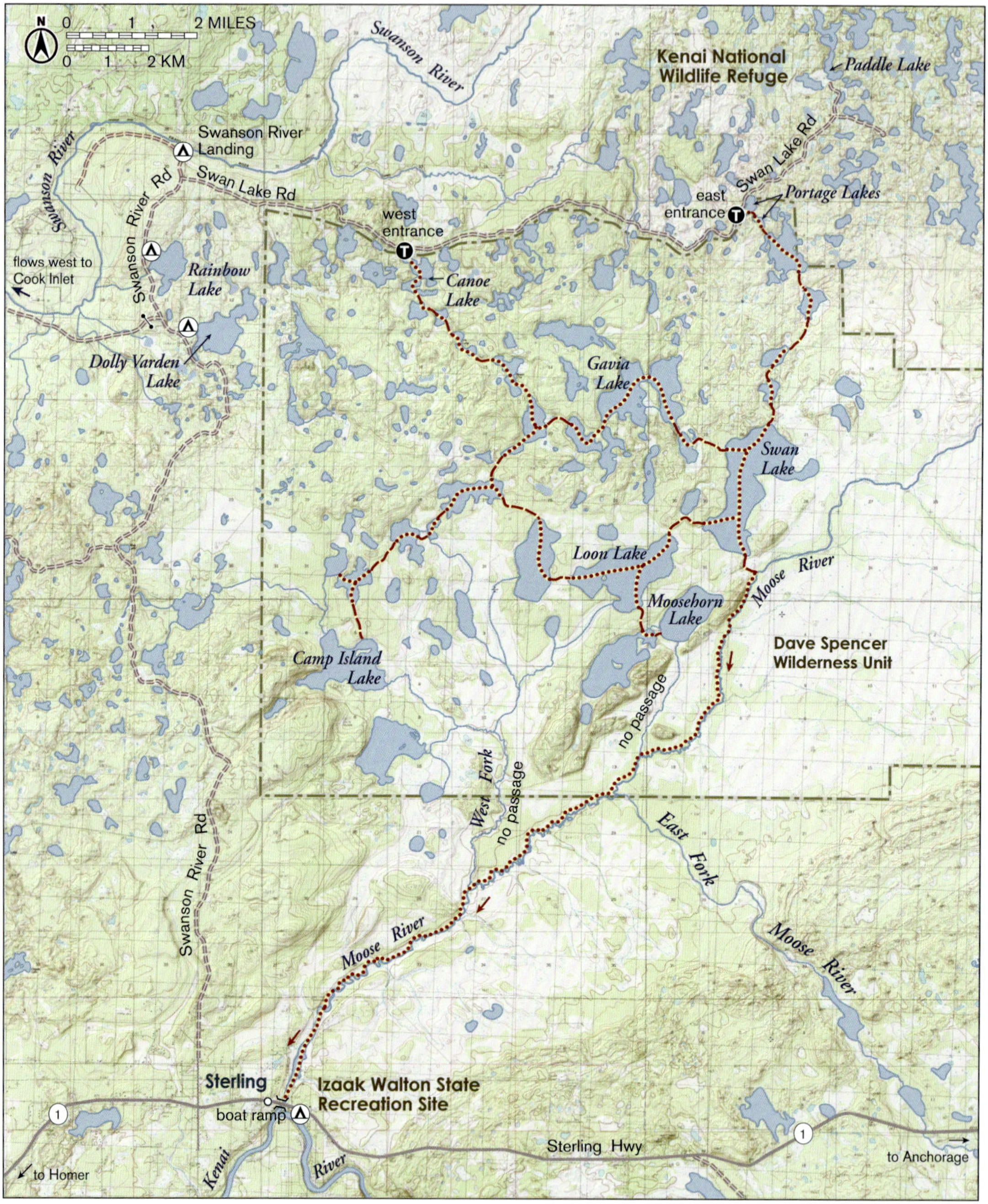

0 1 2 MILES
0 1 2 KM
Swanson River
Kenai National Wildlife Refuge
Paddle Lake
Swanson River Landing
Swan Lake Rd
Swanson River Rd
Portage Lakes
east entrance
west entrance
Canoe Lake
Rainbow Lake
flows west to Cook Inlet
Dolly Varden Lake
Gavia Lake
Swan Lake
Loon Lake
Moose River
Moosehorn Lake
Camp Island Lake
Dave Spencer Wilderness Unit
no passage
West Fork
East Fork
Moose River
Sterling
Izaak Walton State Recreation Site
boat ramp
1
Sterling Hwy
to Anchorage
to Homer
Kenai
River

Most people can do this float in three days; strong, seasoned canoeists may complete it in two long, hard days, but more time is recommended. From the east entrance (Portage Lakes), expect to reach Swan Lake to camp on the first night. Plan to take at least six to eight hours to paddle the river from Swan Lake to the Sterling Highway over two days, camping the second night along the river. Riverside camp spots are reasonable below the confluence with the East Fork of the Moose River but are poor above this. Fishing on the Moose River north of the Sterling Highway is closed year-round for salmon and in early season for all fish; check regulations. The Moose River takeout at Izaak Walton State Recreation Site offers a popular campground and day-use parking for a fee.

Your canoe and gear can make or break the fun of this trip. Test your ability to carry fully packed bags and the canoe in the comfort of your own neighborhood. Consider: Will you make one trip or two per portage? Will two people carry the canoe, or will one person balance it like Atlas while another doubles down on gear? Will you pack in dry bags or backpacks? Will you hand-carry the paddles or lash them to the canoe? Many systems are workable, but do test for comfort. Wear rubber boots because lakeshores are often wet and boggy. Carry ample insect spray and impenetrable layers against the certain bugginess of mid-season.

## EXTENDING YOUR TRIP

Yet another option in this system is to float the Swanson River. From the junction with Swan Lake Road, Swanson River Road continues north 0.4 mile to Swanson River Landing, a parking area with a small, free campground nearby. This is the access point for a twelve-hour float (allow two days) downstream to Captain Cook State Recreation Area where the Swanson River empties into Cook Inlet. Highway access to the canoe takeout is from the city of Kenai. Drive to mile 38.5 of N. Kenai Road (Kenai Spur Highway) and follow a side road 0.5 mile south to the canoe landing.

The Swanson River is part of a larger, 80-mile canoe system starting at Paddle Lake, accessed from the end of Swan Lake Road. This full route is more difficult, and the upper river can be nearly impassable if water levels are low. Contact the Kenai National Wildlife Refuge (see the Resources section) for a water-level report and maps.

## SEASONAL OPTIONS

In early winter the lakes can offer long-distance lake-to-lake ice skating using Nordic skates (see Modes of Travel in the Introduction), and after the snowpack is in place, the potential for ski touring is endless.

*A calm day on Canoe Lake* (Photo by Denny Wells Photography)

# 5 SKYLINE TRAVERSE

**DISTANCE:** 12.4 miles point to point
**TIME:** Extended day
**ELEVATION GAIN:** 5300 feet
**HIGH POINT:** 3520 feet
**SEASON:** June–September
**SURFACE:** Hardpack, tundra, roots
**GRADE:** Rolling with steep segments
**INDIGENOUS LAND:** Kahtnuht'ana (Kenaitze) Dena'ina Athabascan
**MANAGING AGENCY:** Kenai National Wildlife Refuge
**MAPS:** USGS Kenai C-1 SE, B-1 NE
**ONLINE MAP SEARCH:** "mystery hills alaska"
**TRAILHEAD GPS:** Skyline 60.518184°N, 150.187925°W
Fuller Lakes 60.485055°N, 150.075661°W

**A point-to-point route for energetic hikers connects the Skyline Trail and the Fuller Lakes Trail,** farther east, via the Mystery Hills. This meandering ridge is the last of the Kenai Mountains for

*A sheep skeleton on the Mystery Hills ridge, near the western end looking east along the route*

drivers heading west, and the first for those heading east from the flats of the western Kenai Peninsula. The typical day hiker may prefer to hike out and back for ridgetop views on the steep Skyline Trail or, from the other trailhead, up to Fuller Lake, a tree line jewel surrounded by scattered hemlock, spruce, willow scrub, and grassy meadows. Lower Fuller Lake, smaller and nestled just below tree line, is a good out-and-back destination for families at just 2 miles from the Fuller Lakes trailhead. After a 2019 wildfire affected the area, the landscape is renewing with bright new plants complementing black earth.

The route described here is within the Kenai National Wildlife Refuge's Mystery Creek wilderness unit. Off-road vehicles (including mountain bikes) and snowmachines are prohibited.

## DRIVING DIRECTIONS

The traverse requires a two-car shuttle.

**Skyline trailhead (west).** Search online for "skyline trail ak," or follow these directions. The Skyline trailhead is at mile 61.3 of the Sterling Highway; park on the south side of the highway at a paved parking lot (elevation 500 feet). The trail begins by relaying hikers to the north side of the highway through a pedestrian underpass.

**Fuller Lakes trailhead (east).** Drive to mile 57.4 of the Sterling Highway, and park in an easy-to-miss gravel pullout on the north side of the highway, marked with a small trailhead sign (elevation 300 feet). The trail begins up a set of steps from the parking lot, though planned Sterling Highway reconstruction in this area may reconfigure the trailhead.

## ON THE ROUTE

Hiking the Mystery Hills ridgetop is mostly easy, but the rolling crests go on and on over at least six summits without water, and it is easy to underestimate the effort this hike requires. A couple of the ascents of these summits are long and steep. A one-day traverse is best done in mid-June or July when there is plenty of light. People have been caught by darkness on this route. Camping locations are nearly nonexistent, and early summer snowbanks provide the only water. A small, intermittent path is worn in over much of the route, but not all of it, and there are no route markers. Hiking in either direction is possible, though the Skyline-to-Fuller direction is recommended here due to a short section of possible bushwhack routefinding where the ridge ends on the Fuller Lakes end, easiest to scout from a high vantage point. For those adequately prepared for a long day, the ridge presents fine views, and its variety is rewarding.

The Skyline Trail itself is relatively short, about 2.25 miles from the highway to point 3295 on the ridge, with 2800 feet of elevation gain in this section. The trail is maintained but climbs very steeply and can be slippery. Help prevent erosion by sticking to the trail. About 1.5 miles in, the terrain levels out at a minor pass, framing the first view north across the Kenai flats to Cook Inlet and even, on a clear day, as far as Denali. Those in search of camping and water may be rewarded by scouting north from the pass down the wide drainage a short ways, but even then the options are marginal. To continue, hike on a clear trail from the pass, following a left fork steeply up through brush (the right fork dead-ends immediately). Climb an increasingly rocky surface, cutting below the first of the Mystery Hills (Point 3250, above to the left), before hitting another small saddle, then gaining the ridge at point 3295. This peak is not particularly prominent but is often marked by a

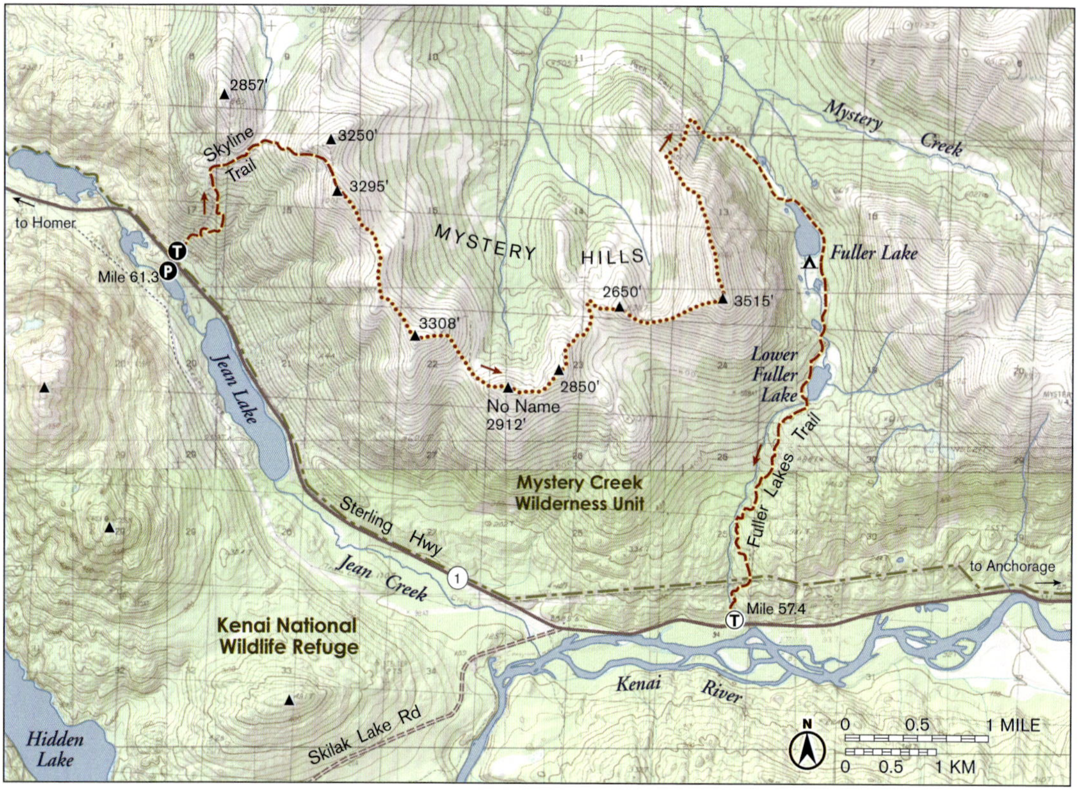


rock pile or other makeshift indicator. If this is your turnaround point, celebrate here, gratified by views of Jean Lake down by the trailhead and vast Skilak Lake beyond.

Continuing ridge hikers will find little to no trail beyond this point, but the natural ridge crest is easy to follow, with a mix of tundra and rocky outcroppings for footing. Walk pleasantly for over a mile, enjoying the panoramic vantage. At 3.5 miles from the trailhead, just past a high point of 3308 feet, the ridge takes a steep plunge, losing 800 feet of elevation before climbing again. Choose a descent line that swings left to avoid the steepest slope, and beware of thick, slippery mud left behind in the wildfire's wake until vegetation becomes reestablished. From the col, a faint trail may be evident on the opposing slope ascending to the next high point, No Name, at 2912 feet. The ridge elevation is more variable in the next section, rolling over several peaks within the next 2 miles, but following the ridgetop is still straightforward. The uphills look daunting but mostly aren't bad. Throughout, look for Dall sheep, ptarmigan, and bears grazing in the high tundra. The roller coaster ends with a climb to the ridge's apex at point 3515, located 6.3 miles from the Skyline trailhead.

From here, the long toe of the ridge tapers gradually to the north, descending toward the lush expanse of the Mystery Creek valley. Follow the ridge crest for another mile or so of easy walking, with a worn footpath giving reassurance now and again. Hike nearly to the end of the ridge, past all rock outcrops and brush that might thwart descent to the east. Just before a last gentle rise in the ridge, look below to the right for a bare, gravelly hump, where a rock cairn may be visible marking the route. A smaller cairn at the ridge and, possibly, a very small but helpful metal tag staked into the ground indicate the spot to turn and head downslope. Descend steeply, losing 660 feet, to the aforementioned bare hump and cairn.

Between this point and Fuller Lake is the trickiest part of the route—the area that burned a few years ago. It appears the route had been flagged and partly worn in on the ground, but the fire melted many of the flags and burned over the trail. The route will likely reform as hikers pass this way, but it may not be possible to follow a continuous thread of trail. If the route is not evident, pick your way southeast across the hillside through stands of trees and thickets of brush, descending gradually and picking up the trail as it appears intermittently. The trail becomes more solid as it approaches the valley bottom, well before reaching Fuller Lake. Cross the outlet at the north end of the lake, 8.5 miles from the Skyline trailhead, then turn right to follow the patchy trail that hugs the east shore.

By the south end of Fuller Lake, 0.5 mile farther, where the fire left no effect, the trail is well established. A small offshoot leads to a flat lakeside camping spot, for those who may have hiked up from the east trailhead. Continuing past Fuller Lake, follow the trail on a gentle descent to reach Lower Fuller Lake within another mile, passing small ponds along the way. Be careful on small bridges that may be ill-maintained. The shores of Lower Fuller Lake are much brushier than those of its counterpart, offering little to no camping. Cross the lower lake's outlet on a bridge, and begin a steeper but moderate descent of 2 miles through forest and meadows to the Fuller Lakes trailhead. Exposed roots and occasional fallen trees may cross the trail along the way, but look up frequently for glimpses of Skilak Lake and the mountains to the south. The trail ends with a set of steps to the parking pullout, 3.2 miles from Fuller Lake and 12.4 miles from the Skyline trailhead.

### SHORTER OPTIONS

For a steep out-and-back half-day trip with rewarding views, hike to point 3295 from the Skyline trailhead (4.5 miles, 2800 feet elevation gain). For a more gradual option, try an out-and-back trip from the Fuller Lakes trailhead to Lower Fuller Lake (4 miles, 1300 feet elevation gain) or Fuller Lake (6.4 miles, 1500 feet elevation gain).

# 6 RESURRECTION PASS TRAIL SYSTEM

**DISTANCE:** 38.4 miles point to point
**TIME:** Hiking 3–5 days, biking 1–2 days
**ELEVATION GAIN:** 2400 feet
**HIGH POINT:** 2600 feet
**SEASON:** June–September

**SURFACE:** Hardpack (mud and snow possible)
**GRADE:** Rolling with steep segments
**INDIGENOUS LAND:** Kahtnuht'ana (Kenaitze) Dena'ina Athabascan
**MANAGING AGENCY:** Chugach National Forest
**MAPS:** USGS Seward B-8, C-7, C-8, D-8
**ONLINE MAP SEARCH:** "juneau lake ak"
**TRAILHEAD GPS:** Hope (north) 60.869885°N, 149.630239°W
Sterling Highway (south) 60.484584°N, 149.953340°W

**The Resurrection Pass Trail offers miles of relatively mellow hiking through rolling alpine and sub-**alpine meadows, backed by a mix of comfortable mountains and forest. Except at the lowest elevations, the trail abounds in views. Hikers looking for a long trip, a good trail, mountain scenery, well-spaced cabins, and lake fishing will find all that and more along the Resurrection Pass Trail. The most popular route, 38.4 miles between the Hope trailhead and the Sterling Highway near Cooper Landing, normally takes three days for strong hikers in good condition. Some may enjoy it over five days or more. It is one of few singletrack trails that make a two-day or even three-day bikepacking trip, but the trail is very popular, and cyclists should take care to spread goodwill and avoid surprising hikers.

The southern trailhead area, near the salmon-rich confluence of the Kenai and Russian Rivers, is a site of extensive Dena'ina activity and still is important to the Kenaitze people. It seems likely ancestors of today's Kenaitze were the first to cross Resurrection Pass. Prospectors staked the first gold claims on Resurrection Creek in 1893. Three years later, and a year before the Klondike Gold Rush, thousands of gold seekers poured into this country. Over the next few years, the route over Resurrection Pass provided one method of connecting Seward and Hope and an avenue for prospecting upper Resurrection Creek and its tributaries. Today, the trail is an entirely different kind of gold mine—a designated National Recreation Trail that provides thousands of people access to the mountain high country. Several access options create a variety of possible trips, and the route can be linked to the Russian Lakes Trail (Trip 7) and the Resurrection River trail system for a more adventurous trek of 60 to 70 miles.

## DRIVING DIRECTIONS

The point-to-point traverse of the Resurrection Pass Trail requires a car shuttle between the Hope area and the Cooper Landing area. Out-and-back trips are good from each end and avoid the shuttle.

**Hope trailhead (north).** Drive to mile 56.3 of the Seward Highway. Turn north onto Hope Highway, drive to mile 16.1, and then turn left onto the gravel Resurrection Creek Road (marked; sign indicates the Resurrection Pass Trail). Drive 3.9 miles more to the trailhead (elevation 400 feet). The trail begins by crossing Resurrection Creek on a bridge.

**Sterling Highway trailhead (south).** The trail (marked) begins in a parking lot up a short driveway off the Sterling Highway at mile 53.1, just west of the Kenai River near Schooner Bend. Note,

*Heading south toward Cooper Landing on rolling terrain near Resurrection Pass*

however, that a multiyear highway reroute project began in 2020; Sterling Highway mileposts in the Cooper Landing area may change as the highway is rerouted around the community. While the existing Sterling Highway trailhead is expected to remain, most long-distance use of this trail is likely to begin or end at a planned new trailhead. The new trailhead is expected to be just west of a long bridge over Juneau Creek. See map.

## ON THE ROUTE

The accompanying table lists points of interest along the main route, keyed to the map. The trail from Hope follows the wooded Resurrection Creek valley and quickly narrows to a well-maintained Forest Service path that occasionally climbs in and out of side drainages. The overall gradient is low, so the trail remains in forested country for more than 15 miles, but frequent bluff edges and openings provide a changing sequence of views. Above tree line, the trail is a narrow ribbon buried deep in wildflowers. Watch for moose, Dall sheep, marmots, and grizzly (brown) bears. Resurrection Pass itself (4 on the map) is covered in low alpine tundra. At and just south of the pass are junctions with side routes to the Seward Highway—the Summit Creek and Devils Creek Trails, the first less used, the second a popular cross-connection. The main trail descends gradually through upper Juneau Creek, then passes through a steep segment from elevation 2200 feet to 1600

N
0 1 2 MILES
0 1 2 KM
Resurrection Creek Rd
to Hope
to Hope
Resurrection Pass Trail
Palmer Creek
Hope Hwy
Chugach National Forest
Caribou Creek
to Anchorage
Resurrection Creek
Fox Creek
Kenai National Wildlife Refuge
KENAI MOUNTAINS
East Creek
Seward Hwy
Canyon Creek
Lower Summit Lake
Chickaloon River
Resurrection Pass
Summit Creek Trail
Upper Summit Lake
Swan Lake
Devils Pass
Thurmond Creek
Juneau Creek
Devils Creek Trail
Juneau Lake
Chugach National Forest
Quartz Creek
Trout Lake
five campsites
proposed reroute of Sterling Hwy
Seward Hwy
Slaughter Ridge Rd
Sterling Hwy
Upper Trail Lake
Round Mountain
Juneau
Cooper Landing
to Soldotna and Homer
Bean Creek Trail
1 Points of interest align with trip table
to Seward
Kenai
River
Kenai Lake

## POINTS OF INTEREST ALONG RESURRECTION PASS TRAIL

| NUMBER ON MAP | POINT OF INTEREST | MILEAGE FROM NORTH | MILES TO NEXT | MILEAGE FROM SOUTH | MILES TO NEXT |
|---|---|---|---|---|---|
| | **Hope trailhead (north end)** | 0 | 7.2 | 38.4 | 0 |
| 1 | **Caribou Creek Cabin** | 7.2 | 4.5 | 31.2 | 7.2 |
| 2 | **Fox Creek Cabin** | 11.7 | 2.9 | 26.7 | 4.5 |
| 3 | **East Creek Cabin** | 14.6 | 4.9 | 23.8 | 2.9 |
| 4 | **Resurrection Pass and Summit Creek Trail junction** | 19.5 | 2.2 | 18.9 | 4.9 |
| 5 | **Devils Pass Cabin and Devils Creek Trail junction** | 21.7 | 3.8 | 16.7 | 2.2 |
| 6 | **Swan Lake Cabin upper junction (0.6-mile spur)** | 25.5 | 0.5 | 12.9 | 3.8 |
| 7 | **Swan Lake Cabin lower junction (0.4-mile spur)** | 26.0 | 3.0 | 12.4 | 0.5 |
| 8 | **Juneau Lake Cabin** | 29.0 | 0.4 | 9.4 | 3 |
| 9 | **Romig Cabin on Juneau Lake** | 29.4 | 1.8 | 9.0 | 0.4 |
| 10 | **Trout Lake Cabin junction (0.5-mile spur)** | 31.2 | 2.7 | 7.2 | 1.8 |
| 11 | **Bean Creek Trail junction** | 33.9 | 0.5 | 4.5 | 2.7 |
| 12 | **Juneau Creek Falls** | 34.4 | 0.3 | 4 | 0.5 |
| 13 | **Proposed new Sterling Highway trailhead parking** | 34.7 | 3.7 | 3.7 | 0.3 |
| | **Sterling Highway trailhead (south end)** | 38.4 | 0 | 0 | 3.7 |

**Note**: Swan Lake Cabin (6, 7) is accessible by trail. West Swan Lake Cabin is accessible by float plane or over lake ice. The new trailhead near Juneau Creek Falls (12 and 13) had not been constructed when this book went to press. Its construction is expected to result in new connector trails and a new overlook of the falls.

feet—bikers going either direction will be walking some of this, and hikers will feel the grade change. The trail in the lower segment of the Juneau Creek valley winds through forests and meadows, along the shores of Juneau Lake, and past Juneau Creek Falls to the Sterling Highway (elevation 400 feet). The Department of Transportation is substantially rerouting the Sterling Highway. It will bridge over the trail near Juneau Creek Falls and will include a new trailhead nearby (elevation 1100 feet).

There are eight cabins on the trail spaced for a five-day hike, but it is not possible to reserve sequential cabins with a single reservation, and many people reserve only one. If you wish to stay in these cabins on successive dates in summer, you will need to reserve your dates on successive days the previous winter. Reservations can be made up to six months ahead of time at recreation.gov. The lake cabins have boats for cabin renters, and there are several species of fish in the lakes, including Dolly Varden, rainbow trout, lake trout, and sockeye salmon. The Forest Service has created many designated campsites. Each generally has a good water source and a bear-proof food locker, and often an open-air pit toilet (the "out" without the "house"). Designated campsites are first come, first served. Over most of the trail, and particularly at the higher elevations, it is possible to find other campsites. Use of the area within 300 feet of cabins is limited to those with reservations.

The trails in this system are closed to horses April 1 through June 30 because of soft spring trail conditions. Mountain bikers should observe the horse prohibition to help prevent mudholes and erosion.

## OPTIONS

Three other trails connect with the main route to make an intriguing trail system: the Devils Creek Trail and the Summit Creek Trail to the Seward Highway and the Bean Creek Trail to Slaughter Ridge Road near the Sterling Highway. A hike from the Hope trailhead to either of the Seward Highway trailheads is about 31 miles. From either of the Seward Highway trailheads to the original Sterling Highway trailhead is about 27 miles. From one Seward Highway trailhead to the other is about 20 miles. The Bean Creek Trail is an alternate southern access that reduces the overall distance by up to 2.5 miles, depending on where you park, and may be the best winter access route, because the first few miles at the southern end of the standard route can be sloped and icy.

*Hiking Summit Creek Trail in fall*

**Driving directions for Bean Creek Trail.** Drive to mile 48.6 of the Sterling Highway and, just east of the Kenai River, take Bean Creek Road north. Drive 0.9 mile, and turn right on Slaughter Ridge Road, which may not be marked. Follow this road 0.6 mile to a wide turnaround area. In dry conditions most cars can proceed straight ahead on an old logging road another 0.9 mile to the base of a large hill. To go another 0.3 mile beyond the hill, or to go at all in wet conditions, four-wheel drive may be desirable. A gravelly area 1.2 miles from the end of the main road is good for parking (elevation approximately 750 feet). Winter parking is generally at the turnaround at the end of the main road (elevation approximately 600 feet).

**Driving directions for Devils Creek Trail.** The Devils Creek Trail begins at mile 39.5 of the Seward Highway. The trailhead is marked.

**Driving directions for Summit Creek Trail.** Turn west off the Seward Highway at mile 43.9, just south of Upper Summit Lake. Hidden behind trees is a parking area and a trailhead bulletin board (elevation 1350 feet). There is no sign on the highway.

**Trail details:** The Devils Creek Trail climbs from its trailhead (elevation 1000 feet) to 2400-foot Devils Pass. It joins the Resurrection Pass Trail at about the same elevation. The trail has a steady, moderate grade. Near the beginning and near the pass, the trail can be muddy. The Summit Creek Trail, similarly, climbs steadily, traversing the slope north of Summit Creek. The route crosses two passes (elevations 3450 and 3350 feet) and descends, heading north to Resurrection Pass proper to avoid wet areas. Finding the Summit Creek Trail from the Resurrection Pass Trail can be difficult.

The Bean Creek Trail begins by following the old logging road. About 0.2 mile beyond the upper parking area, there is a fork. Go left, descending briefly, and cross Bean Creek on a bridge. There may be orange, diamond-shaped markers. The trail in this area may be rerouted during highway reconstruction. Beyond the creek, the route bends to the right and winds its way about 2 miles gradually uphill to the Resurrection Pass Trail.

The trail from Hope to the Bean Creek trailhead makes a fine ski or snowshoe tour in winter, but prepare for featureless whiteout conditions and cold winds above tree line. The Devils Pass Cabin has an oil heater, but users must haul their own diesel or stove oil. The Devils Creek and Summit Creek Trails are not recommended for winter use due to avalanche hazard.

The Resurrection Pass Trail and upper Devils Creek Trail are open to snowmachines in alternating years. Snowmachine season generally runs December 1 through April 30. When the December 1 opening date falls in an odd-numbered year (2023, 2025, etc.) snowmachines are allowed.

# 7 RUSSIAN LAKES TRAIL

**DISTANCE:** 21.5 miles point to point
**TIME:** Hiking 2 days, biking full day
**ELEVATION GAIN:** 1600 feet southbound, 2000 feet northbound
**HIGH POINT:** 1350 feet
**SEASON:** June–October
**SURFACE:** Hardpack, roots
**GRADE:** Rolling
**INDIGENOUS LAND:** Kahtnuht'ana (Kenaitze) Dena'ina Athabascan
**MANAGING AGENCY:** Chugach National Forest
**MAPS:** USGS Seward B-8; Kenai B-1
**ONLINE MAP SEARCH:** "upper russian lake ak"
**TRAILHEAD GPS:** Cooper Lake 60.377001°N, 149.710052°W
Russian River Campground 60.4778175°N, 149.962811°W

**The trail that links Upper and Lower Russian Lakes traverses broad valleys and a flat pass. It is** good for anything from an afternoon jaunt to a relatively gentle backpacking trip of two or more days. On a mountain bike, the trail provides challenges but requires no overly long climbs. In fact, the route from Cooper Lake to Russian River Campground is downhill overall, even though the route has plenty of little climbs along the way. The trail offers big forests breaking to alpine meadows, clear cascading streams, fine lakes, brilliant wildflowers and berries in season, moose, and bears. Glaciated mountains pop out at openings in the trees. This trail may be linked to the Resurrection Pass Trail headed north across the Sterling Highway for a trip of about 60 miles and, for the truly hardy adventurer, may be linked south to the primitive Resurrection River Trail (see Extending Your Trip).

The Russian River is known for its run of red salmon, but fishing for salmon is allowed only in the lowest portion of the river, below Russian River Falls. Fishing for rainbow trout can be excellent in the lakes and upstream. Check regulations before casting.

Regarding the two USGS maps listed: Seward B-8 shows the entire route except for one bend of the Russian River, and Kenai B-1 shows the bend and context for mountains visible across the river.

## DRIVING DIRECTIONS

This trip requires a car shuttle (about 16 miles). There are also out-and-back options from each end. Note that Sterling Highway mileposts in the Cooper Landing area may change because the state is rerouting the highway. Trailhead access will be on the old highway, which may have different mileage markers following construction.

**Cooper Lake trailhead.** Search online for "rainbow lake trail, ak" which will take you to a nearby trailhead, and proceed 0.5 mile farther along the road, or follow these directions. From mile 47.9 of the Sterling Highway, just west of a bridge over the Kenai River in Cooper Landing, turn southeast on Snug Harbor Road, and follow it 11.5 miles to a small parking area marked by a sign for the Russian Lakes Trail. Don't be confused by the Rainbow Lake Trail at mile 11, which is a separate, short (and pleasant) trail with a more prominent trailhead; go another half mile to a small and nondescript parking area for the more adventurous Russian Lakes Trail.

**Russian River Campground trailhead.** Search online for "russian river campground ak," then follow the directions below. From mile 52.6 of the Sterling Highway, turn south onto a paved side road marked with a sign for Russian River Campground and the Russian Lakes Trail (do not confuse it with the Kenai National Wildlife Refuge's Kenai–Russian River Campground at mile 55). Follow the side road to a stop sign and gatehouse. During salmon runs from mid-June through mid-August, the area is crowded with anglers, and the Forest Service charges fees for parking, camping, and fishing. Beyond the gatehouse, go left, and follow the road 0.8 mile to the Russian Lakes trailhead (marked).

## ON THE ROUTE

This trail works well in either direction. This description is from the Cooper Lake end (elevation 1300 feet) to Russian River Campground (elevation 500 feet), which is downhill overall. The grade is mellow enough that direction of travel is not a critical factor. Note that although Cooper Lake is a major topographic feature near the trailhead, it is not on the route. Drive to see it if desired. Mountain bikers on this route should note the high likelihood of surprising hikers en route; crossing paths with others is more likely near the Russian River end of the trail. Spread goodwill by being the first to stop and let walkers pass whenever possible.

The trail begins to the right (west) of the parking area and rolls through small dips and rises and in and out of forest and meadow for about 6 miles. Vegetation nicely frames the mountain views. An unmarked fork at mile 1.6 is a split between old and new trails; go right; the trails merge again. The first in a series of Forest Service backcountry campsites, each with a bear-proof food container and some with open-air pit toilets, appears near mile 3 and a second near mile 4.7. Another trail fork occurs at about mile 5.5 in a meadow. The left fork is the Resurrection River Trail (marked; see Extending Your Trip). Take the right fork.

*Resting on the porch of Upper Russian Lake Cabin*

Near the trail's midpoint is Upper Russian Lake, a large lake set below a mountain backdrop. The far side of the lake is designated federal wilderness in Kenai National Wildlife Refuge. This is a logical place to camp, both for the visual amenities and location that provides for close-to-equal days. Upper Russian Lake Cabin (a reservable log cabin) and two campsites are situated near the north end of the lake, at around mile 9.7. Aspen Flats Cabin lies another 3 miles down the trail on a spur toward the river.

Parts of the trail beyond Upper Russian Lake closely follow the Russian River. Look for salmon in these waters after midsummer, and be sure to alert four-legged wildlife of your presence in this area (see Bears and Other Wildlife in the Introduction). The trail also climbs up bluffs well above the river, providing views from a higher vantage over the valley.

Approaching Lower Russian Lake, the trail transits a steep hillside that in some places avalanches in winter. These areas have few trees and, by midsummer, are tall with grass. The open landscape provides grand views of the lake from this hillside.

Near mile 19 (2.5 miles from the Russian River Campground trailhead), the narrow trail merges with a broad trail that continues to the trail's end. This portion is built to backcountry wheelchair standards, with relatively low grades and a wide surface. Doubling back to the left at this intersection leads to

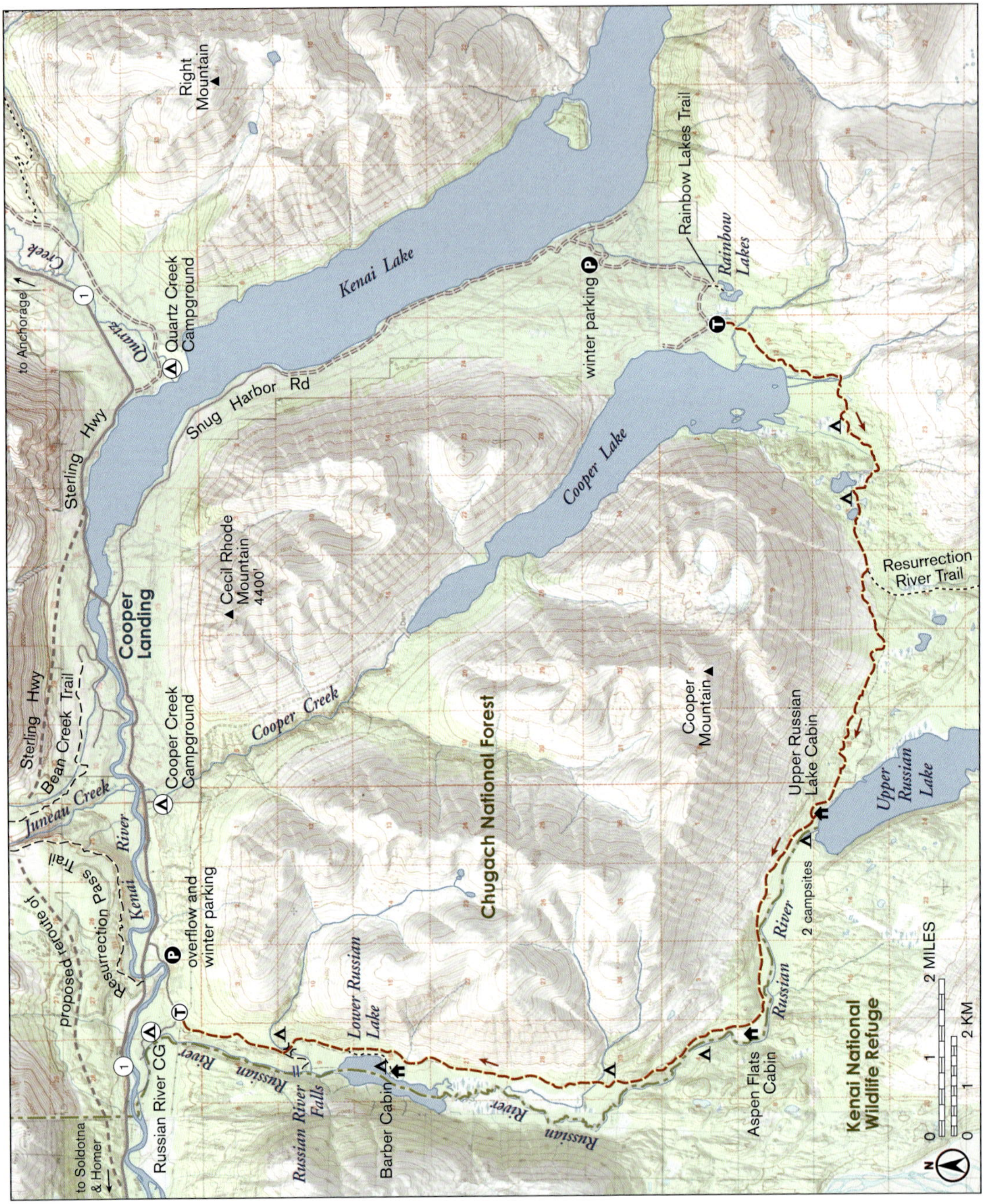
to Anchorage
Right Mountain
Quartz Creek
Quartz Creek Campground
Kenai Lake
Rainbow Lakes Trail
Rainbow Lakes
winter parking
Sterling Hwy
Snug Harbor Rd
Cooper Lake
Cecil Rhode Mountain 4400'
Cooper Landing
Resurrection River Trail
Sterling Hwy
Bean Creek Trail
Juneau Creek
Cooper Creek Campground
Cooper Creek
Chugach National Forest
Cooper Mountain
Upper Russian Lake Cabin
Upper Russian Lake
Kenai River
proposed reroute of Resurrection Pass Trail
overflow and winter parking
2 campsites
Russian River
Lower Russian Lake
Russian River CG
Russian River Falls
Barber Cabin
Aspen Flats Cabin
Kenai National Wildlife Refuge
to Soldotna & Homer
2 MILES
2 KM
N

Lower Russian Lake and Barber Cabin (reservable) and to a campsite. The spur to the cabin is nearly 0.9 mile, but the trail hits the lakeshore within 0.3 mile. After the merge point, the trail has a more open feel. About 1.5 miles from the Russian River Campground trailhead, just beyond a bridge, a trail takes off to the left. This is a short spur to Russian River Falls and a viewing deck.

Check with the Forest Service before setting out, especially on spring trips, to be sure trees blown down across the trail during winter have been cleared. Make cabin reservations through recreation .gov (see the Resources section). Note that lake cabin rentals include the use of a rowboat for exploring these large lakes. Check at time of reservation regarding life jackets.

In winter, the main trail along Lower Russian Lake is not recommended because of avalanche runout zones there. For people heading south from the Russian River Campground trailhead, go to the trail junction that leads to the falls, go left across the bridge, and follow a winter route to the right (left of the creek). It is marked by blue diamonds and leads to the lake. Note that the access road to the summer trailhead is not plowed; park in the parking area near the Sterling Highway (see map).

From the Upper Russian Lake Cabin westward, the trail is closed to motorized use year-round. The other trails are closed to motorized use May 1 through November 30. All are closed to horses April 1 through June 30. Early season bikers should ride only if the trail is dry.

The Cooper Lake area is popular with snowmachines in winter. Snug Harbor Road is plowed to a parking area at mile 9.1. Skiers can use the area, but the road up the hill from mile 9.1 may be well packed in by snowmachines and hummocky or icy.

## SHORTER OPTIONS

The trail from the Russian River Campground trailhead to Lower Russian Lake or Barber Cabin (6 or 7 miles roundtrip) is a nice one-day or overnight trip for families and a pleasant, easy mountain bike trip (550 feet elevation gain roundtrip).

Continuing to Aspen Flats Cabin or a nearby tent site from the Russian River Campground trailhead makes for a round-trip of about 19 miles. Going still farther to Upper Russian Lake is about 24 miles roundtrip—not necessarily shorter, but these are good options if avoiding the car shuttle. Elevation gain for the route to the upper lake is about 1600 feet roundtrip.

From the Cooper Lake trailhead, hiking in to the second campsite, located near a pond, can be a good short overnight trip or a longish day hike—9.4 miles roundtrip.

## EXTENDING YOUR TRIP

Hikers can extend their trips south on the primitive Resurrection River Trail and north across the Sterling Highway on the Resurrection Pass Trail (Trip 6). From the Russian River Campground trailhead to the Resurrection River trailhead near Seward is 32 miles; from the Cooper Lake trailhead, it is 21.5 miles. "Primitive" means the Forest Service does not have bridges at creek crossings and may not send crews in to cut out blowdowns for seven years or more. One season of blowdowns can create several dozen big trees across the route. Brush and flooding may obscure the path. Finding the trail may require bushwhacking, patience, and map-reading skills. Note also that the Kenai Peninsula's largest concentration of grizzlies feeds along this route. Tackling this trail is a true adventure undertaken by relatively few. Contact the Seward Ranger District of Chugach

National Forest (see the Resources section) for current conditions.

The Resurrection Pass Trail, by contrast, is well used and generally well maintained. To link the Russian Lakes Trail to the Resurrection Pass Trail, walk about 0.9 mile along the access road for the Russian River Campground trailhead and 0.6 mile west along the Sterling Highway to the southern end of Trip 6, at mile 53.1. Combining all three trails would make for a 70-mile trek.

# 8 CAINES HEAD

**DISTANCE:** 10 miles roundtrip to North Beach, 14 miles roundtrip to Caines Head
**TIME:** 2 days
**ELEVATION GAIN:** 950 feet
**HIGH POINT:** 650 feet (Caines Head)
**SEASON:** May–September
**SURFACE:** Hardpack, sand and/or gravel, rocks
**GRADE:** Low angle with rolling segments
**INDIGENOUS LAND:** Chugach Sugpiaq (Alutiiq)
**MANAGING AGENCY:** Alaska Division of Parks and Outdoor Recreation
**MAPS:** USGS Seward A-7, Blying Sound D-7
**ONLINE MAP SEARCH:** "lowell point ak"
**TRAILHEAD GPS:** 60.068227°N, 149.442577°W

**Caines Head, with an abandoned World War II army fort and bay views of rounded islands and** jagged, snowcapped peaks, all framed by coastal rainforest, offers a blend of historical curiosity and natural wonder. Find rock outcrops, soaring coastal cliffs, and long beaches with cobbles and slate. Part of the main access trail is not a trail at all but a beach walk, and segments of the beach route appear only at low tide. Look for a variety of seabirds, shorebirds, and songbirds en route, along with bald eagles, black bears, rafts of sea otters, curious seals, and spawning salmon. If the tide is not favorable when you can go, consider launching a sea kayak and exploring this area from the water. Rent kayaks in Seward or at Miller's Landing near the trailhead (see the Resources section). You can extend the trip by following a trail to alpine country, with the possibility of a loop.

The cabins along this route at Tonsina Point, Callisto Canyon, and Derby Cove are among the state's most popular. Visitors can make reservations up to seven months before their summer trip. Learn more and make reservations through alaskastateparks.reserveamerica.com.

## DRIVING DIRECTIONS

Search online for "caines head trailhead ak," or follow these directions. Follow the Seward Highway into Seward (it becomes 3rd Avenue), and proceed until the road ends at an intersection with Railway Avenue. Turn right, and follow Railway Avenue as

*Kayakers and hikers alike commonly visit North Beach.* (Photo by Kjerstin and Joe Thomas)

it parallels the coastline, becomes the gravel Lowell Point Road, and ultimately bends left toward Lowell Point, becoming Border Avenue. Here, 2.1 miles from 3rd Avenue, turn right onto Pinnacle View Road and almost immediately right again at a sign for Lowell Point State Recreation Site. A short driveway leads uphill to the trailhead.

Pinnacle View Road continues south to another, sea-level parking area. Both have outhouses and information. A 500-foot trail connects the two. Pinnacle View Road forms a small loop with Beach Drive (parallel to the coast) and Border Avenue. Kayak rentals and water taxis may be arranged at Miller's Landing at the corner of Border Avenue and Beach Drive. At the southern end of Pinnacle View Road, there is a walk-in boat launch ramp for kayaks. Cliffs prevent walking the beach from here; if on foot, use the trail.

## ON THE ROUTE

From the trailhead, the route joins a private road, which becomes a footpath through coastal rainforest and then descends switchbacks to Tonsina Creek and the Caines Head State Recreation Area. At the first big bridge, look for spawning salmon. Beyond a second bridge lies a small, run-down but serviceable campground in the forest with tables, firepits, a shelter, and an outhouse. Beyond tall grass is a broad beach kids will love. A trek to the campsites (2 miles each way) makes a good overnight trip for children. Tonsina Cabin is a reservable public-use cabin located at the south end of the Tonsina Point beach (marked). Unless staying at the cabin, keep to the beach. The coastal route is from the Tonsina Point beach to Derby Cove, another 2.5 miles.

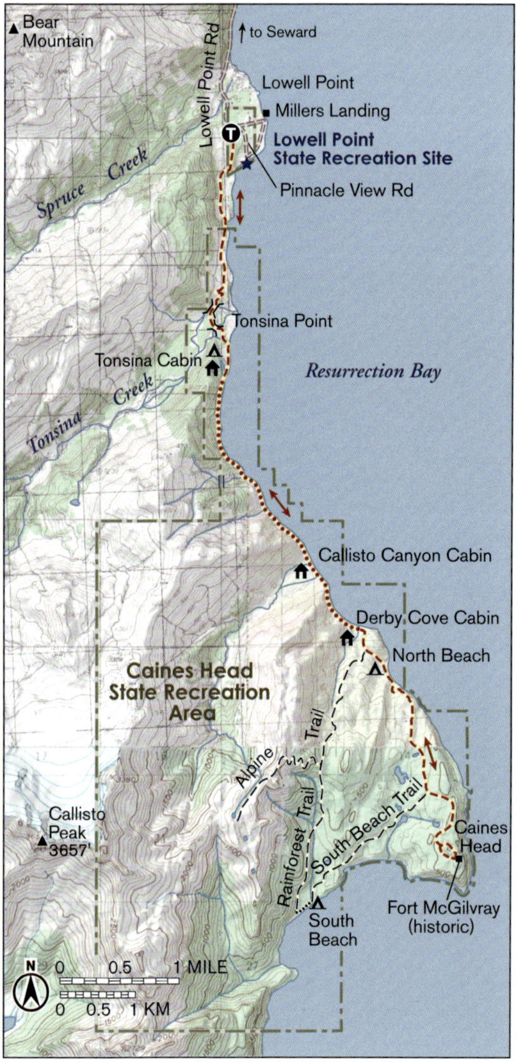


Water covers the route between the Tonsina Point beach and Derby Cove except for a couple of hours before and after low tide. Cliffs plunge right to the water. There is no reasonable way around; a man fell and died making an attempt. Luckily, the ocean pulls back twice a day and, on most days, leaves a continuous thread of walkable beach for those paying attention to their tide tables (search "noaa seward tide table" online, or download a tide app).

This route is recommended during a low tide of less than 3 feet. The tides fluctuate day to day around an average sea level. When weather is stormy and gray, the barometric pressure is lower and the ocean can come up higher on the shoreline because there is effectively less air pushing down on it. Low pressure and the wind-driven waves common in stormy weather mean that hikers are more likely to get wet, so use extra caution if the weather is poor.

A couple of small but difficult rocky headlands are at the heart of this otherwise simple beach walk. People who don't time the tides carefully will find themselves scrambling over these low headlands. The highest is perhaps 15 feet above water and is slippery with seaweed. Some hikers have skidded into the water. Those uncomfortable with scrambling over the slippery headland should plan their trip particularly carefully. Leave plenty of time to get from the trailhead to this area by the lowest part of the tide cycle. It's a bit more than 2 miles; allow an hour or more depending on your pace.

The route passes a short side trail to Callisto Canyon Cabin (3.5 miles from the trailhead). People have reported dry creeks at Callisto Canyon Cabin at some times; more reliable drinking water is within 0.2 mile south of the cabin along the shore, but it is accessible only when the tide is down. Upon reaching the beach in front of Derby Cove Cabin (4.5 miles), you can leave all fretting about the tide behind.

Where the Derby Cove beach pinches out, the trail (marked) climbs into the woods and goes less than 0.5 mile to North Beach. North Beach is the site of a former military dock and the beginning of an old road up to Fort McGilvray. There are picnic pavilions, outhouses, multiple tent platforms, bear-proof food storage lockers, and a ranger cabin at North Beach, and it is the best camping option.

The historic military road (trail) leads 2 miles to the concrete fortress buried in the ground at the top of Caines Head (elevation 650 feet). Two concrete circles, where big guns aimed over the bay to protect the Port of Seward during World War II, flank the fort. The concrete passageways are fun to explore (take a headlamp), and the command room with its slit windows overlooking Resurrection Bay stokes the imagination. The trail to the fort passes old concrete ammunition bunkers. Poke your head in and yodel; the acoustics ring!

*Boardwalk trail near Tonsina Beach (Photo by Shawn Horning)*

## EXTENDING YOUR TRIP

The distance from North Beach to South Beach is about 2.5 miles. Take a fork to the right, marked, midway to the fort. Behind South Beach is a large collection of collapsed buildings that once housed hundreds of soldiers who built and operated the place. There is a tent platform at South Beach, which sees substantially less overnight action than North Beach. If you are traveling by kayak, note that South Beach is exposed to more wind and wave action and is a difficult beach to land on and launch from.

At the crest between Derby Cove and North Beach is a trail junction (marked) for the Alpine Trail. It climbs steadily but never too steeply out of the forest to the tundra zone and peters out at about 1600 feet. The trail snakes in and out of dense forest, open meadow, tall grass, and wrinkles in the topography, providing new views at every turn. The walking is easy below Callisto Peak (elevation 3657 feet) after the trail runs out.

About halfway to the end of the Alpine Trail, near elevation 800 feet and just as the continuing trail begins the first in a series of switchbacks, the Rainforest Trail takes off downhill to the south. Following this fork can make for a grand loop of about 5.5 miles via South Beach back to the junction above Derby Cove. Find this connector from South Beach by walking westward over the beach cobbles, seeking a small trail marker to indicate where to duck into the woods and start up the trail. The Rainforest Trail from the Alpine Trail to South Beach has typically been less defined and less well marked than the other trails. The lower end of the descent provides some glimpses of the collapsed old barracks if you are looking for them, but they are being covered by new growth.

Resurrection Bay is often breezy. Drizzle is common. The snowpack can stay in the shady forest until late May near sea level and well into June on the Alpine Trail. By mid-June portions of the Alpine Trail are lined with head-high grass that holds moisture; take raingear. Some streams dry up, but drinking water should be locatable.

# 9 MOUNT MARATHON

**DISTANCE:** 5.2 miles roundtrip on Hiking Trail, 2.5-mile loop on Runners' Trail
**TIME:** Half day
**ELEVATION GAIN:** 2800 feet
**HIGH POINT:** 3022 feet
**SEASON:** Late May–October
**SURFACE:** Hardpack, sand and/or gravel, rocks, mud when wet
**GRADE:** Moderate with steep segments on Hiking Trail, sustained steep on Runners' Trail
**INDIGENOUS LAND:** Chugach Sugpiaq (Alutiiq)
**MANAGING AGENCIES:** City of Seward and Alaska Division of Mining, Land, and Water
**MAP:** USGS Seward A-7 SW
**ONLINE MAP SEARCH:** "lowell point ak"
**TRAILHEAD GPS:** Hiking Trail 60.108418°N, 149.445559°W
Runners' Trail 60.104053°N, 149.451014°W

**In 1915, a bet in Seward started a race up Mount Marathon that repeats every Fourth of July.** Back then, there was no Seward Highway, no city of Anchorage, and railroad construction was just beginning, but there was a Mount Marathon race. The runners start from the town center near sea level, climb to Race Point (elevation 3022 feet) on the southeast ridge of Marathon Mountain, and return. The women's record is forty-eight minutes, the men's forty-two minutes. Independence Day is the most exciting time to make the climb, whether or not you participate in the race, but these hikes are great anytime during the summer.

The Mount Marathon Hiking Trail and the Runners' Trail climb separately toward Race Point. Each has easier destinations as well. The hikers' trail is steep, the Runners' Trail steeper. Both provide far-reaching views of Resurrection Bay, its mountainous rim, and the far southern horizon over which the next thing to see would be Hawaii. Thankfully, the views give a ready excuse to

*Watching boats on Resurrection Bay from Race Point* (Photo by Marty Welbourn Freeman)

pause. Hikers may choose to go up the hikers' trail and down the Runners' Trail; the lower ends connect via a crossover trail and are also within reasonable walking distance via city streets. The same crossover trail allows people to bypass the cliffiest part at the bottom of the Runners' Trail by using the hikers' trailhead.

## DRIVING DIRECTIONS

Two trailheads and their respective trails lead to the same destination.

**Hiking Trail.** Search online for "mt marathon trailhead ak," or follow these directions. Drive to 1st Avenue and Monroe Street in Seward. The trail starts behind a gate as an extension of Monroe Street. Park on the street, being cognizant of private property.

**Runners' Trail.** Search online for "lowell canyon trailhead ak," or follow these directions. Find Jefferson Street in Seward and drive it west toward the base of Mount Marathon. At 1st Avenue, Jefferson Street becomes Lowell Canyon Road, which soon ends at the Lowell Canyon picnic area and a gate. Park at the picnic area.

## ON THE ROUTE

A segment of the Runners' Trail near the bottom has terrain beyond what this book generally includes as a reasonable hiking route. However, the July Fourth event is so well known that people want to try it—to prepare for the race themselves, for the personal challenge, or just to see what the hoopla is

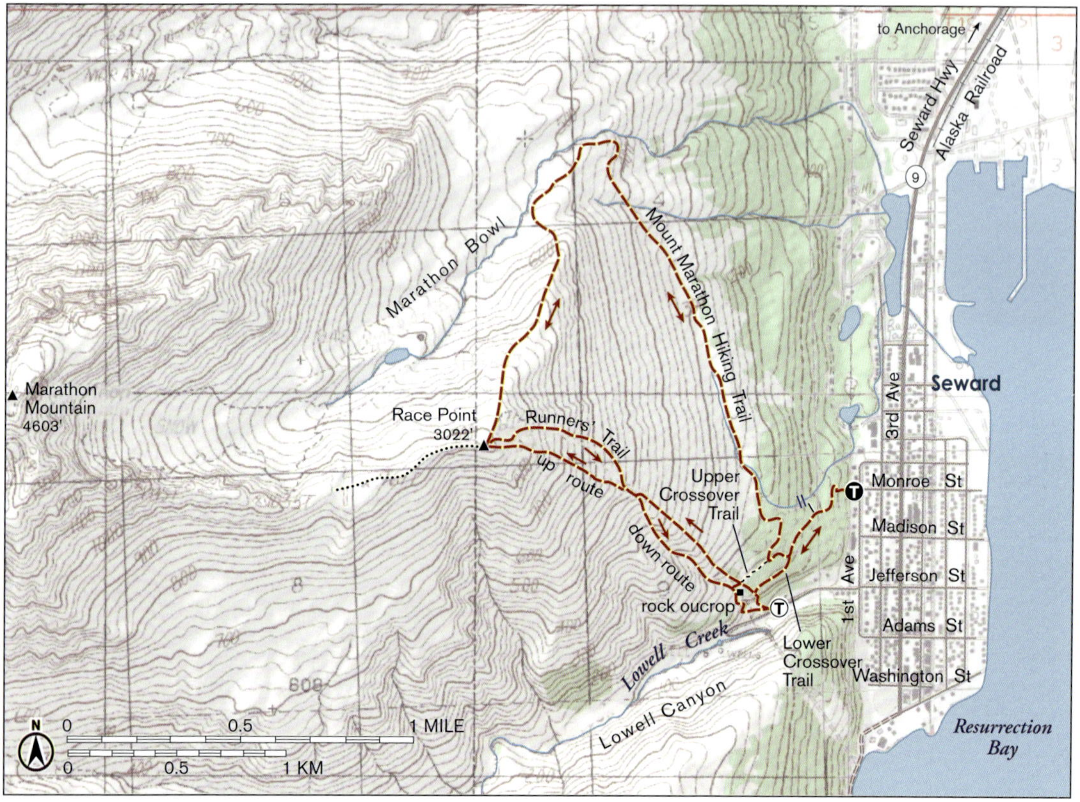


about. Therefore, below is guidance about doing it as safely as possible. That said, the Mount Marathon Hiking Trail is the recommended route to surmount the initial couple hundred vertical feet.

## Mount Marathon Hiking Trail

A yellow gate between houses at 1st Avenue and Monroe Street (elevation 150 feet) blocks vehicle access to an old track up the hillside formerly called the Jeep Trail. The City of Seward has renamed it as the Mount Marathon Hiking Trail. Start going uphill immediately.

Beyond the gate, follow the main route and trail signs around two switchbacks. A spur to the right (marked) leads a short distance to a cascade. A few minutes later, first the Lower Crossover Trail and then an Upper Crossover Trail (both marked) go left to connect with the Runners' Trail. The lower is easiest.

The hikers' trail transitions from the Jeep Trail to the Bench Trail and traverses northward across an angled topographic bench on the lower slopes below Race Point. The mostly gentle grade leads to a ridge that drops to the northeast off Race Point. Round this ridge, and step into Marathon Bowl, a beautiful alpine cirque beneath the true summit of Marathon Mountain. The route hits the bowl about where shrubs transition to tundra. Where the main trail hooks left and up the ridge, a small trail proceeds straight ahead to a creek. Access to flowing water is not likely above this point. Take a break where the views open up. Look for ptarmigan, ground squirrels, marmots, mountain goats, Dall sheep, and wildflowers.

Follow the ridge to Race Point or beyond. The views will lead you on—the city below, Mount Alice across the head of Resurrection Bay, and the islands of the outer bay. Snow can obscure the upper end of this route early in the season.

To climb the true summit of Marathon Mountain (elevation 4603 feet) by any route requires experience and mountaineering gear. That said, a clear if airy trail continues along the ridge beyond Race Point, traversing small knobs, with views of Bear Mountain across Lowell Canyon. While there is a sharp drop, particularly to the south, the route is walkable for at least a quarter mile.

### Runners' Trail

The race begins and ends in downtown Seward, starting at 4th Avenue and Adams Street, ending at 4th Avenue and Washington Street, and using Jefferson Street. This description assumes parking at the Lowell Canyon picnic area, per the driving directions.

The Runners' Trail has separate up and down routes that form a figure eight (see map). It is worth scoping the overall scene at the bottom before choosing your route up. Beyond the gate (elevation 200 feet), walk the service road about 500 feet to see a gravel fan at the base of a gully. Above this fan is a smooth section of rock outcrop that looks impassable. The descent route is in the gully, and many runners come down over the outcrop. The standard ascent route is on the forested cliffs to the right (east), between the gully and the picnic area, and behind two large tanks. The easiest route may be to get on top of an engineered pile of gravel just east of the gully and follow a path on its top into the brush and trees. Abruptly, the route turns upward.

You will see that runners have tried all possible routes up the cliffs. It appears best to err to the right on a sloping traverse trail of sorts, then head more directly up, looking for places with good roots and trees for handholds and avoiding areas of spiky bare rock where a fall would be particularly bad. Be willing to back off and try a different route. To avoid a rescue mission, don't take your dog this way. The cliffy section is short but intense and not for everyone. At the top, the ground is comparatively flat, and the edge is peppered with signs that read "Danger Cliffs." A wide trail heads left and up (the main trail); to the right is the Lower Crossover Trail to the Mount Marathon Hiking Trail.

Back at the bottom, a less traditional but less intimidating route avoids the engineered gravel pile and instead begins beyond the rock outcrop on the far side (west side) of the gravel fan. Pick up a steep switchback trail in the brush (marked, but minimally) that goes up left of the gully. The tread underfoot is a steep compaction of fine silt and organics, at once hard and very slick when wet. If it has been raining, this is a poor route. However, above the rock outcrop, this trail leads directly into the gully with no cliff or rock outcrop to cross. At this point, proceed some 70 feet up the gully, and find a nearly level trail that cuts back to the right and traverses out of the gully to the top of the cliff area described above. It then joins the runners' usual ascent route.

After these initial options, the route is clearer. An upward track follows a line (also very slick when wet) above and to the right of the gully. Emerging from the trees, the ascent route continues directly up and is crossed by the down route, which enters from the right (east) and descends into the gully on the left. Unless you are a runner, sit awhile to enjoy the glacier-streaked mountain view. The trail crossing (elevation 1600 feet) is the turnaround point for the junior race.

The trail to the "summit" of Race Point at 3022 feet becomes less defined on the rocky ridge; just continue toward the skyline. Race Point is the nearly level ridgetop that appears suddenly. The descent route starts down the east face of the mountain. Snow patches commonly remain at the top of the descent route into July. Although runners slide on the snow for a quick descent, this is where some injure themselves. The snow is steep and fast and ends in rock. Better to skirt the snow. Below, descending with long strides in loose gravel (scree) to the crossover point can be fun.

Descending the gully in early summer often involves walking on snow. The gully ends in the rock outcrop. Top runners descend the outcrop. Most hikers will want to exit the gully, either left, to follow the Lower Crossover Trail to the hikers' trail, or right, to use the switchback route described above.

# 10 HARDING ICEFIELD TRAIL

**DISTANCE:** 8.4 miles roundtrip
**TIME:** Full day
**ELEVATION GAIN:** 3150 feet
**HIGH POINT:** 3500 feet
**SEASON:** June–September
**SURFACE:** Hardpack, rocks, snow (early season)
**GRADE:** Moderate
**INDIGENOUS LAND:** Chugach Sugpiaq (Alutiiq) and Dena'ina Athabascan
**MANAGING AGENCY:** Kenai Fjords National Park
**MAP:** USGS Seward A-8 NE
**ONLINE MAP SEARCH:** "exit glacier ak"
**TRAILHEAD GPS:** 60.188307°N, 149.631143°W

**Valley glaciers nestle between high peaks, but icefields bury mountains entirely or leave just** their tops—called nunataks—jutting out of the ice. The Harding Icefield Trail may be the only established trail in the country that leads to an icefield overlook. Getting there is a steady uphill walk, but the trail parallels the frozen blue-white waterfall that is Exit Glacier, providing frequent views. The bright white ice contrasts sharply with the deep green of thick summer foliage and the magenta of fireweed blooms to create a memorable walk even for those who tire before reaching the highest point. Keep an eye out for mountain goats on the rocks above the trail and for black bears in the lower green meadows. Bikes and pets are prohibited on the trail.

*Exit Glacier spills off the Harding Icefield, as seen from the Top of the Cliffs viewpoint.* (Photo by Joseph Brylle M. Casquejo)

## DRIVING DIRECTIONS

Search online for "exit glacier trailhead ak," or follow these directions. Drive to mile 3.7 of the Seward Highway, on the edge of the city of Seward, and turn west on Herman Leirer Road (marked), also known as Exit Glacier Road. Proceed 8.6 miles on this paved road to a parking area a short distance from a National Park Service nature center. The trail starts adjacent to the nature center. This is one of few national parks without an entrance or parking fee.

## ON THE ROUTE

The trail starts (elevation 400 feet) as a paved, wheelchair-accessible path that leads beyond the nature center toward the hunk of ice spilling off the mountainsides. The paved trail ends near an information kiosk, where a nature trail loops back to the nature center as an option. Proceed straight. A short distance farther, 0.4 mile from the start, a sign for the Harding Icefield Trail directs hikers to the right. The less ambitious will enjoy a network of short trails around the toe of the glacier—straight ahead from this sign—including close-up views (stay on trails to avoid falling ice).

On the Harding Icefield Trail, hikers will appreciate the work of the Student Conservation Association. Young people worked for many summers to carve a beautiful trail with relatively easy grades into the steep hillside, and the trail has been continually upgraded over the years. For its rough, sometimes-cliffy terrain, it is one of the best-made trails in the state. The hike starts in forest, with frequent glimpses out to mountains, hanging glaciers, and the big valley that drains to Seward. Exit Glacier proper does not come into view for the better part of an hour, at what the National Park Service calls

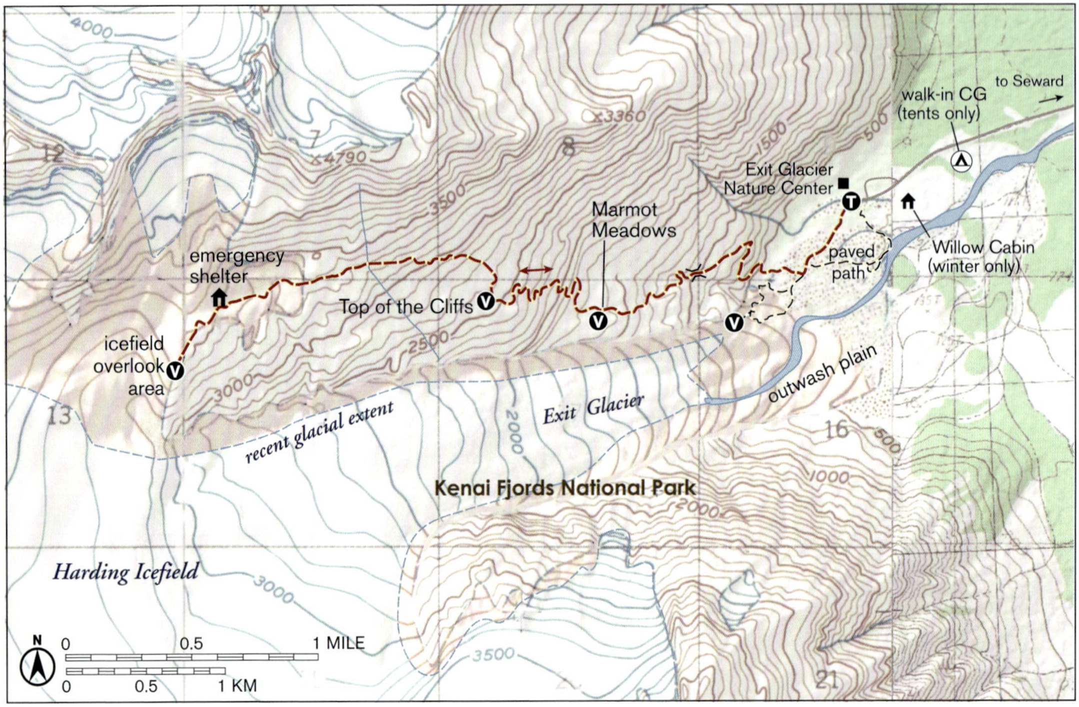


Marmot Meadows (1.4 miles, 1600 feet elevation). Then, views of the glacier steadily improve. The Top of the Cliffs area in another mile (and another 1000 vertical feet) is fully above tree line and provides the first sense of the breadth of a fully ice-draped landscape.

Above tree line and into July, snow covers parts of the trail. Steps in the leftover snow usually guide hikers. The high point is a gray, gravelly knob, relatively recently deglaciated. From here, hikers look out at the rolling sweep of ice stretching into the distance, punctuated with many nunataks. The icefield stretches 25 miles to the southwest, and interconnected ice reaches almost to Kachemak Bay 40 miles away.

Hikers should prepare for cold winds that often blow off the icefield, even on sunny summer days. Bad weather can roll in quickly in this area, and because of this, the Park Service has established an emergency shelter cabin near the icefield. It is on a hill of gravel and rock on the route, but it does not overlook the icefield. It cannot be reserved but may be used by anybody in bad weather. Limited camping is possible in this area. Above tree line, hikers should stay on the main trail and observe any park signs about trail use. Old scars evident on the tundra are a reminder that walkers can impact the land. Those camping should set up only at the top end of the route, 700 feet or more off the trail, on bare rock and gravel or on snow to avoid damaging fragile alpine plants that take decades to regenerate.

While it is possible to hike down for a closer look at the ice edge (up to 0.4 mile, 500 vertical feet), only experienced mountaineers with crevasse rescue training and proper equipment should venture onto the ice. Park rangers lead summer naturalist walks on area trails, including treks to the icefield.

Some other notes: (1) a small, tents-only campground along the access road, 0.5 mile from the parking lot, offers the only free camping in the Seward area, though it typically fills early in the day in July and August; (2) Herman Leirer Road is not maintained for cars from November 1 to May 1 beyond mile 1.3, but the road is often groomed for use by skiers, fat-tire bikers, dog mushers, and snowmachiners, and the Park Service rents its Willow Cabin near the Exit Glacier trailhead for public use in the winter (contact the park; see the Resources section); and (3) the park's information center, which is open in the summer, is at 1212 4th Avenue in Seward, adjacent to the small boat harbor.

## SHORTER OPTIONS

A paved, wheelchair-accessible trail makes a 1-mile loop from the nature center to an Exit Glacier viewpoint. To reach the glacier's toe, see above for directions to a network of side trails that reach the ice in an additional 0.6 mile one way.

*Harding Icefield blankets dozens of miles of high country in the Kenai Mountains.*

# 11 LOST LAKE

**DISTANCE:** 14.8 miles point to point
**TIME:** Extended day to 2 days
**ELEVATION GAIN:** 2230 feet southbound, 2430 feet northbound
**HIGH POINT:** 2221 feet
**SEASON:** July–mid-October
**SURFACE:** Hardpack
**GRADE:** Moderate
**INDIGENOUS LAND:** Dena'ina Athabascan and Chugach Sugpiaq (Alutiiq)
**MANAGING AGENCY:** Chugach National Forest
**MAPS:** USGS Seward A-7 NE, B-7 SE (A-7 NW, B-7 SW for areas west of Lost Lake)
**ONLINE MAP SEARCH:** "lost lake ak"
**TRAILHEAD GPS:** North 60.340694°N, 149.369702°W
south 60.172457°N, 149.411022°W

*Lost Lake has several peninsulas. The tents in the center of the photo violate a Forest Service prohibition on peninsula camping.* (Photo by Anne Raup)

**Climbing through a hemlock-and-spruce forest, the Lost Lake Trail emerges above tree line on** tundra and flower-covered meadows. The area was once heavily glaciated. Now, brilliant blue and green lakes fill every depression, reflecting the snowcapped summits of surrounding mountains. The glacial topography forms Lost Lake, the largest of these lakes, into a picturesque shape with several peninsulas. Stands of weathered, gnarled hemlocks punctuate the alpine portion of trail. From the bald ridges along the lake, views extend to the rounded islands and steep mountainsides that define Resurrection Bay. The area invites camping and exploring. Water is plentiful. A few small fish populate Lost Lake, and marmots abound in the nearby rockslides. The trail is good for family camping when kids are old enough to tackle about 7 miles.

There are two trailheads. The northern trailhead is in Primrose Campground adjacent to Kenai Lake, and the southern trailhead is in a housing subdivision outside Seward. Lost Lake lies halfway between these points. This description runs north to south between the trailheads because the views are best looking south, but traversing either direction works well. Trips out and back from either end provide the same high-country views without the need for a car shuttle. Mountain bikers may prefer riding south to north because the northern end has short, steep, and somewhat technical segments that are easier to descend. The trail is very popular in July and August; expect to encounter multiple parties of hikers, mountain runners, and mountain bikers on weekends (see On-Trail Etiquette in the Introduction).

## DRIVING DIRECTIONS

The traverse requires a car shuttle. Out-and-back options are possible from each end.

**Northern trailhead (Primrose Campground).** Search online for "primrose campground ak," or follow these directions. Turn off the Seward Highway at mile 16.9 on Primrose Spur, which becomes gravel. Drive 1.1 miles to the end of the access road at Kenai Lake, and park in the boat ramp area at the entrance to Primrose Campground. The trailhead is about 800 feet from the parking area, at the end of the campground road, and is marked.

**Southern trailhead.** Search online for "lost lake trail ak," or follow these directions. Drive to mile 5.3 of the Seward Highway, just north of Seward. Turn west on Scott Way, which becomes gravel, and follow the road uphill 0.2 mile to a T intersection. Turn left on Heather Lee Lane. In 0.2 mile, just beyond a bend in the road, turn right on Hayden Berlin Road. Drive another 0.3 mile to the end of the road and the trailhead.

## ON THE ROUTE

Beginning at the Primrose Campground trailhead (elevation 450 feet), the trail climbs 5 miles to tree line. Officially, the Forest Service calls the northern end the Primrose Trail, but most people refer to the whole thing as the Lost Lake Trail. The Primrose Trail grade is gradual, but there are a couple of steeper sections. A trail junction within a half mile of the start is the Meridian Lakes Trail. A short, informal side trail near mile 2 leads to a waterfall view. The trail is in generally good condition, pleasant and woodsy until tree line. Beyond the forest, the trail crosses 2 miles of rolling tundra ridgetops to Lost Lake, which sits below the trail at elevation 1913 feet. Mount Ascension (elevation 5710 feet) above the lake and Paradise Peak across the valley to the east make up just part

Primrose Campground
Kenai Lake
to Anchorage
Primrose Creek
Primrose Spur
Seward Hwy
Long Lake
Porcupine Creek
Meridian Lakes Trail
Snow River
Chugach National Forest
Martin Creek
Primrose Trail
Meridian Lake
Grayling Lake Trail
Lost Creek
Lost Lake
Grayling Lake
Leech Lake
Mount Ascension 5710'
2 sites
Ski Lake
Divide
South Fork Snow River
Lost Lake Trail
Lost Creek
Box Canyon Creek
Seward Hwy
Alaska Railroad
Chugach National Forest
Resurrection Peaks
Dale Clemens Cabin
Bear Lake
winter route
to Exit Glacier
Bear Lake Glacier
Salmon Creek
Herman Leirer Rd
Lost Lake trailhead
Scott Way
Resurrection River
to Seward
0 1 2 MILES
0 1 2 KM

of the "mountains everywhere" scenery surrounding the green-carpeted foreground. In some years, snow persists into July, which could make portions of the route above tree line hard to follow. Be prepared to navigate cross-country or retreat. Particularly in midsummer, flies and mosquitoes can be pesky in subalpine areas without a breeze.

The best places to camp are in Forest Service backcountry sites in the alpine area. Each generally has a bear-proof food storage box, places for tents, access to water, and, except for the northern two, open-air backcountry toilets. Use these campsites to consolidate impact and safely store food. If these campsites are full, walk well off the trail to camp. The Forest Service forbids camping on the peninsulas in the lake to prevent trampling of the fragile vegetation and asks that all camping occur out of sight of Lost Lake and the trail. This protects the experience for all who use this popular area.

The trail skirts Lost Lake to the east, crossing Lost Creek on a bridge at mile 7.5 (there are campsites downstream). The bridge is usually snow-free from mid- to late June into September. Consider exploring while camped near the lake. Climbing to the summit of Mount Ascension, the prominent peak west of Lost Lake, is a goal best left to mountaineers with training, ice axes, and crampons. However, scrambling partway up the steep, lower slopes for a sweeping view is definitely recommended. A side trip, with easy walking over firm tundra, around the southwest edge of the lake and up the valley to the west brings a splendid view of the steep north side of Mount Ascension. Look for mountain goats and bears.

South of the lake, the continuing trail climbs a bit, crossing a broad, glacier-scarred bedrock ridgetop before beginning a gradual descent. On a good day, the views across meadows, bent-low hemlocks, and thickly forested hills below to the islands of Resurrection Bay make this as fine a walk as there is anywhere. Finally, the trail drops into the forest proper for the last 3 to 4 miles to the trailhead (elevation 320 feet).

About 11 miles from Primrose Campground and nearly 4 miles above the southern trailhead, there is a fork to the east. Look for ripe salmonberries in this area in August. The fork (marked) leads downhill 1.5 miles to the Dale Clemens Cabin. The cabin, with views to Resurrection Bay, Seward, and the nearby Resurrection Peaks, can be booked at recreation .gov. In summer, the standard is to backtrack from the cabin to the main trail and descend to the southern trailhead. In winter, the main trail to and from the high country goes past the cabin. The standard (summer) trail is not recommended in winter because of avalanche hazard. South of the cabin, this winter route is not maintained for summer use. If you start at the southern trailhead in summer, don't be confused by the winter trail taking off to the right at about 0.4 mile, after a switchback.

There are active mining claims off the Primrose end of the trail. At least one miner has a permit to use an all-terrain vehicle on this portion of the trail to reach the claim. The trail is otherwise closed to motorized vehicles from May 1 to November 30 and closed to horses from April 1 to June 30.

## EXTENDING YOUR TRIP

It is possible to hike off-trail from Lost Lake westward and then northward into miles of wide, high-country drainages, with overlooks to Kenai and Cooper Lakes. Consult topographic maps, and plan a day trip or stay out a night or two.

Mountain bikers seeking to avoid a car shuttle can make a 30-mile loop that includes 6 highway miles. Park at the Grayling Lake trailhead at Seward Highway mile 13.2. Ride uphill via the trail, then down to the Divide trailhead at highway mile 11.4, then on the highway shoulder toward Seward. Or just start on the highway to avoid the singletrack climb and additional 2 miles. Follow driving directions to the southern trailhead. Follow the Lost Lake Trail nearly to its northern end, and double back to the south on the Meridian Lakes Trail. This forested trail is fun to ride and passes several fishing lakes, two with campsites. A left fork down to the Grayling Lake trailhead (rather than up) should be marked.

### SEASONAL OPTIONS

The winter route of the Lost Lake Trail provides access for snowmachiners and skiers to the open high country. This is a popular winter motorized trail. Lower elevations of the winter trail can be icy, are fairly steep, and can make for poor skiing, although the vicinity of the cabin and above can offer excellent skiing. Skiers should prepare to hike the first part of the trail. "Spring" skiing can last into June at lake elevations for those willing to carry their skis at lower elevations.

# 12 PTARMIGAN AND VAGT LAKES

**DISTANCE:** 10.7 miles point to point
**TIME:** Full day to 2 days
**ELEVATION GAIN:** 2000 feet
**HIGH POINT:** 940 feet
**SEASON:** May–October
**SURFACE:** Hardpack, boardwalk, roots
**GRADE:** Moderate
**INDIGENOUS LAND:** Dena'ina Athabascan
**MANAGING AGENCY:** Chugach National Forest, Alaska Division of Mining, Land, and Water
**MAP:** USGS Seward B-7 NE
**ONLINE MAP SEARCH:** "crown point ak"
**TRAILHEAD GPS:** Ptarmigan Creek (south) 60.405337°N, 149.362768°W
Vagt Lake (north) 60.434952°N, 149.372287°W

**A turquoise beauty, Ptarmigan Lake reflects its surroundings: forested mountain slopes rising to** hanging glaciers. Its much smaller counterpoint, Vagt Lake, is tucked in among spruce and aspen, a secret mirror for towering peaks along Trail Creek valley. Linking the two lakes is a section of the Iditarod National Historic Trail (INHT); see Iditarod Trail and Alaska Long Trail in the Introduction. This trip plan meanders on a point-to-point route from one lake to the other, caring more about enjoying the way than hastening to the destination. See the options below for the many shorter day hikes as well as overnight options in the area. Anglers will find grayling, salmon, Dolly Varden, and rainbow trout in Ptarmigan Creek and grayling in Ptarmigan Lake. Vagt Lake is stocked with rainbow trout and is a popular destination for anglers.

*Taking a dip in cold Ptarmigan Lake on a hot midsummer day*

## DRIVING DIRECTIONS

A car or bike shuttle is required to complete the route as described.

**Ptarmigan Creek trailhead (south).** Search online for "ptarmigan campground ak," or follow these directions. The Ptarmigan Creek Trail leaves from Ptarmigan Creek Campground at mile 23.2 of the Seward Highway. Use the campground driveway, then find the trailhead parking lot (marked) on the right. For those staying in the campground, there is a shortcut to the trail across from site 16 and near the campground host.

**Vagt Lake trailhead (north).** Drive to mile 25.2 of the Seward Highway, just south of a highway bridge across the outlet of Lower Trail Lake, and turn east onto Mine Road. There is some parking near the start of Mine Road, or follow a rough track 0.1 mile north to the shore of Lower Trail Lake and more parking. At the time of publication, the Forest Service was planning to upgrade the trailhead here, so details may change slightly. Follow signs for the Vagt Lake Trail.

## ON THE ROUTE

The route is doable in either direction; this description begins on the south end from Ptarmigan Creek Campground (elevation 450 feet). The Ptarmigan Creek Trail follows tumbling, opalescent waters upstream. After 0.8 mile, the trail meets the INHT, where a sign indicates a left turn for "Falls Creek

Mine Road." Take the right fork for Ptarmigan Lake. Eventually, the trail turns away from the creek to climb through a quiet conifer forest, then descends slightly through tall grass to Ptarmigan Lake (elevation 755 feet, 3.4 miles from the trailhead). This is a good stopping point for a picnic, a swim on a warm day, or overnight camping at designated campsites with a bear-proof food lockers and pit toilets. For more campsites, continue around the north shore of the lake on a grassy, primitive trail. The route once continued beyond Ptarmigan Lake into Paradise Valley, but that trail no longer exists. Although the walking and routefinding are tough, those with an exploring bent might want to bushwhack into this wild country.

After soaking up the view at Ptarmigan Lake, backtrack 2.6 miles to the INHT junction in the forest, this time taking the signed fork toward Falls

Creek Mine Road. The trail climbs gradually, then levels. In about 1 mile, reach the junction with the Falls Creek Mine Trail (formally, it is designated a trail, but it is an old road). Continue straight on the INHT toward Falls Creek. The elevation rolls slightly, and mountain views appear periodically between the conifers. Just before reaching Falls Creek, 1.1 miles past the Falls Creek Mine Trail, a small rivulet marks a forested, workable spot to pitch a tent. At the deep gorge of Falls Creek, cross a high footbridge with a view of roiling waters below. Continue north to another junction with an old road 0.1 mile ahead, the Crown Point Mine Trail. Continue straight through the junction on the INHT, following signs for Vagt Lake. The trail makes a large zigzag around topographical features, gradually losing elevation, before meeting the Vagt Lake Trail 1 mile past the Crown Point Mine Trail and a total of 3.2 miles on the INHT from the Ptarmigan Creek Trail.

A signed, 0.1-mile spur trail leads to the edge of Vagt Lake. Dispersed camping here is possible, though scarce; follow Leave No Trace guidelines to avoid over-impacting the area. The Forest Service plans a continuation of the INHT north of Vagt Lake from here. To complete the route, retrace your steps from the lake, then take the Vagt Lake Trail toward the Seward Highway. The trail parallels a small creek through a mini canyon, crossing it near a vista of Lower Trail Lake. The route concludes with a forested walk along the south edge of Lower Trail Lake to the trailhead, 1.4 miles from Vagt Lake.

The INHT and the Ptarmigan Creek and Vagt Lake Trails are closed to horses from April 1 through June 30 and to motorized vehicles from May 1 through November 30. Mountain bikers may find the INHT entertaining, though the distances are relatively short and bikers should observe the same closure as horses to avoid impacting wet trails. All-terrain vehicles use the old mining roads.

## SHORTER AND SEASONAL OPTIONS

Hiking out and back to Ptarmigan Lake from the Ptarmigan Creek Campground trailhead is a classic Kenai adventure, with timelessly rewarding mountain lake views, at 6.8 miles roundtrip. Vagt Lake, too, is a popular day hike and great for kids, offering a gradual 2.8-mile round-trip with only 400 feet of total elevation gain and the possibility of fishing for trout.

Several shorter point-to-point day hikes are possible along the INHT, using any of the east-west trails (Ptarmigan Creek, Falls Creek Mine, Crown Point Mine, or Vagt Lake Trail) to connect back to the Seward Highway. The Falls Creek Mine Trail begins off Solar Mountain Road (milepost 24.2). Park on the east side of the railroad tracks, respect private property, and hike around a Forest Service gate on a signed track, then proceed 0.7 mile to intersect the INHT. The Crown Point Mine Trail begins at Mine Road (milepost 25.2; the same turn for the Vagt Lake Trail) and leads 1.4 miles uphill to meet the INHT. For those without a shuttle car, it is reasonable to walk

*Shelf fungus in the rainforest along the Iditarod Trail*

back to your starting point along the highway; much of the way, it is possible to walk well off the shoulder.

Avalanche hazard precludes winter use of most of these east-west trails beyond the first mile from the highway. Vagt Lake, however, makes a possible winter destination for hiking, snowshoeing, or cross-country skiing, especially when the lake is frozen and covered with snow. The INHT does not cross avalanche terrain.

### EXTENDING YOUR TRIP

Hiking out and back from the Ptarmigan Creek Campground trailhead to the far end of Ptarmigan Lake makes a 14-mile trip, though the trail along the lake is primitive and likely to be overgrown with tall grass past midsummer. There is a designated campsite at the very end of the lake, 7 miles from the Ptarmigan trailhead, and another midway along the lakeshore, 4.5 miles from the trailhead. Alternatively, try one overnight along Ptarmigan Lake and another at Vagt Lake.

Trail building is underway to extend the INHT north along Vagt Lake to Grant Creek, about 1 mile past first contact with the lakeshore. Further plans are afoot to bridge Grant Creek and continue the INHT north from there, which would create a nearby connection to Grant Lake, another photogenic, aquamarine sibling of Kenai and Ptarmigan Lakes.

If elevation is what you seek, take the Crown Point Mine Trail uphill past its intersection with the INHT. The old track is easy to follow, winding steeply up through myriad switchbacks to the base of a glacial bowl at 3900 feet. Sweeping views that are destination enough begin much lower. Be prepared to share the track with motorized vehicles.

# 13 JOHNSON PASS IDITAROD TRAIL

**DISTANCE:** 23 miles point to point
**TIME:** Hiking 2 days, biking full day
**ELEVATION GAIN:** 2000 feet southbound, 2200 feet northbound
**HIGH POINT:** 1450 feet
**SEASON:** June–September
**SURFACE:** Hardpack, roots
**GRADE:** Moderate
**INDIGENOUS LAND:** Dena'ina Athabascan
**MANAGING AGENCY:** Chugach National Forest
**MAPS:** USGS Seward C-6, C-7
**ONLINE MAP SEARCH:** "johnson pass ak"
**TRAILHEAD GPS:** North 60.724097°N, 149.277799°W
south 60.503562°N, 149.433620°W

**The Johnson Pass Trail is a "shortcut" between points on the Seward Highway and makes for a** fine point-to-point hike or mountain bike ride. It starts just high enough on the northern end that subalpine meadows are a feature from the beginning. The country is a mix of forest and alpine

*Pedaling north along the Johnson Pass Trail with Bench Peak in the background* (Photo by Anne Raup)

terrain, placid lakes, small canyons, and rowdy streams. Vegetation is a combination of hemlock-and-spruce forest, tall-grass meadows, and open muskeg. The route ducks into forest patches and emerges into mountain views. Bench Lake and Johnson Lake, on either side of the mostly indistinguishable pass, are fine high-point and midpoint rewards, reflecting the mountains.

By 1900, miners recorded using a trail over the pass to connect the port at Seward with the newly populous gold-fever towns of Hope and Sunrise. Dog team mail delivery started soon after. In 1907, the Alaska Road Commission constructed a wagon road through the pass, starting at a new railroad line built from Seward that did not yet extend up Turnagain Arm. These days, this popular point-to-point trail, with bridges over the most substantial streams, is designated part of the Iditarod National Historic Trail. The terrain is good but challenging for mountain biking; most will push bikes on a few loose rocky hills. The trail can be muddy, and there is potential for conflict with hikers. There is a narrow window in summer that is optimum for biking: usually two to three weeks in mid- to late June, after the last of the snow at the pass has melted from the trail (and spring mud has dried out) and before the cow parsnip and grass grow so tall they obscure the trail. Summertime hikers will enjoy it anytime but should expect many cyclists during that period, particularly on weekends. Cyclists should take care to stop for walkers whenever possible to spread goodwill (see On-Trail Etiquette in the Introduction).

*Wild skating on Bench Lake early in winter, with access by mountain bike* (Photo by Taylor Horne)

## DRIVING DIRECTIONS

The traverse requires a car shuttle. It is 31 driving miles between trailheads. Out-and-back options are good as well.

**Northern trailhead.** To reach the northern trailhead, search online for "johnson pass trail north," or follow these directions. Drive south of Turnagain Pass to mile 63.7 of the Seward Highway. A 0.4-mile side road, marked Johnson Pass Trail, leads south to a parking area.

**Southern trailhead.** The southern trailhead is at mile 32.7 of the Seward Highway, near Upper Trail Lake and its fish hatchery.

## ON THE ROUTE

Hike or bike the route in either direction. From the northern trailhead (elevation 700 feet), the route winds through open meadows and forest, crossing Center Creek (mile 2.2) and Bench Creek (mile 3.8) on bridges. Beyond the second bridge, the trail enters the Bench Creek valley and follows the creek to Bench Lake. There are a couple of short, steep, rocky stretches before the lake. At the top of a long hill near mile 6 (elevation 1250 feet), an informal footpath leads to an airy overlook of a waterfall. In this area, and through the pass, the grass grows tall and dense, as does cow parsnip (see Plants to Avoid in the Introduction). The wildflowers hold their own. Note that the trail shown on the USGS maps is based on historic alignments that have changed in a few places. The main trail is easy to follow.

The trail follows the eastern shore of Bench Lake. There is a ford required at a stream that flows into the lake. The route climbs imperceptibly to Johnson Pass (mile 10, elevation 1450 feet). South of Johnson Lake, the trail parallels Johnson Creek but is above the creek in the woods. About 9 miles south of the pass and nearly 19 miles from the northern trailhead, after dipping down and climbing up through several creek drainages, the trail emerges on the shore of Upper Trail Lake and roughly parallels the shore to the southern trailhead (elevation 500 feet). While the northern half of the trail is rocky in some places, the southern half has more roots.

to Anchorage
Sixmile Creek
Granite Creek
Seward Hwy
1
Granite Creek Campground
Johnson Pass Trail
Center Creek
Bench Creek
Tincan Peak
Placer River
Spencer Glacier Whistle Stop
Seward Hwy
Canyon Creek
Silvertip Peak
to Seward and Kenai
Manitoba Mountain
Juneau Creek
Spirit Walker Ridge
Lower Summit Lake
Mills Creek
Timberline Creek
Groundhog Creek
Bench Peak
Chugach National Forest
Grandview Whistle Stop
Bench Lake
Anderson Peak
Stormy Creek
Johnson Pass
Johnson Lake
Trail Creek
Johnson Creek
Alaska Railroad
Trail Creek
Johnson Pass Trail
Upper Trail Lake
to Anchorage
Seward Hwy
9
to Seward
State of Alaska
Lark Mountain
0 1 2 MILES
0 1 2 KM

The Forest Service has designated several backcountry campsites, usually located at the ends of short side trails, all with bear-proof food storage lockers and most with open-air backcountry pit toilets. Good campsites can be found at Johnson Pass above tree line and at the south end of Johnson Lake (mile 11). This trail is popular and gets enough traffic that there is ongoing risk of aesthetic damage from carelessness (see Leave No Trace in the Introduction).

The trail from the Bench Creek bridge to the northern trailhead is closed to motorized vehicles year-round; other parts of the trail are closed to them from May 1 through November 30. The trail is closed to horses from April 1 to June 30. Mountain bikers should avoid the trail until it is sufficiently dry.

### SHORTER AND SEASONAL OPTIONS

As a day hike, walking from the northern trailhead to the Center Creek bridge (4.4 miles roundtrip) or the northern Bench Creek bridge (7.6 miles roundtrip) makes a pleasant day's outing. In winter, the Center Creek valley makes a good longer-adventure ski tour and is closed to snowmachines. Center Creek is entirely off-trail, with some snaking through tight trees required to gain the open upper valley. Stay well away from slopes that could avalanche (see Avalanches in the Introduction). Winter travel on the Johnson Pass Trail between the northern Bench Creek bridge and mile 12, about 2 miles south of Johnson Lake, is not recommended due to avalanche hazard. However, when there is a good freeze ahead of substantial snow, it is possible to bike up to the pass and ice skate on the lakes.

# 14 CRESCENT AND CARTER LAKES TRAVERSE

**DISTANCE:** 17.7 miles point to point
**TIME:** 2–3 days
**ELEVATION GAIN:** 2300 feet
**HIGH POINT:** 1600 feet
**SEASON:** June–October
**SURFACE:** Hardpack, brush, mud
**GRADE:** Rolling with steep segments
**INDIGENOUS LAND:** Dena'ina Athabascan
**MANAGING AGENCY:** Chugach National Forest
**MAPS:** USGS Seward B-7 NW, C-7 SW, C-8 SE
**ONLINE MAP SEARCH:** "crescent lake ak"
**TRAILHEAD GPS:** Crescent Creek 60.502800°N, 149.672020°W
Carter Lake 60.507045°N, 149.445421°W

*Taking in the views at the eastern end of Crescent Lake* (Photo by Marty Welbourn Freeman)

**Hidden in a cluster of mountains north of Kenai Lake and south of the Y where the Sterling and** Seward Highways split is smile-shaped Crescent Lake. A trail at each of the two highways connects to the lake. Both the Crescent Creek and Carter Lake Trails climb to high country right at tree line, where open forests and patches of stunted evergreens give way to areas of tundra and grassland. Eight miles of primitive trail along Crescent Lake's south side connect the two trails into a complete alpine traverse.

The longer, gentler, drier Crescent Creek Trail leads to the west end of Crescent Lake. With more deciduous trees, it makes for a glorious September hike through the golds and reds of autumn. The Carter Lake Trail climbs through rocky switchbacks for quicker access to tree line at Carter Lake and a beautiful, sometimes muddy trek across high wildflower meadows to the east end of Crescent Lake.

The Crescent Creek Trail is especially good for families with children if they have reservations to stay in the US Forest Service cabin at the west end of Crescent Lake. A second cabin awaits through-hikers midway along the lake. Each cabin comes with a rowboat, and fishing for grayling is good. Moose and bears may be spotted in summer, wolverine occasionally in winter.

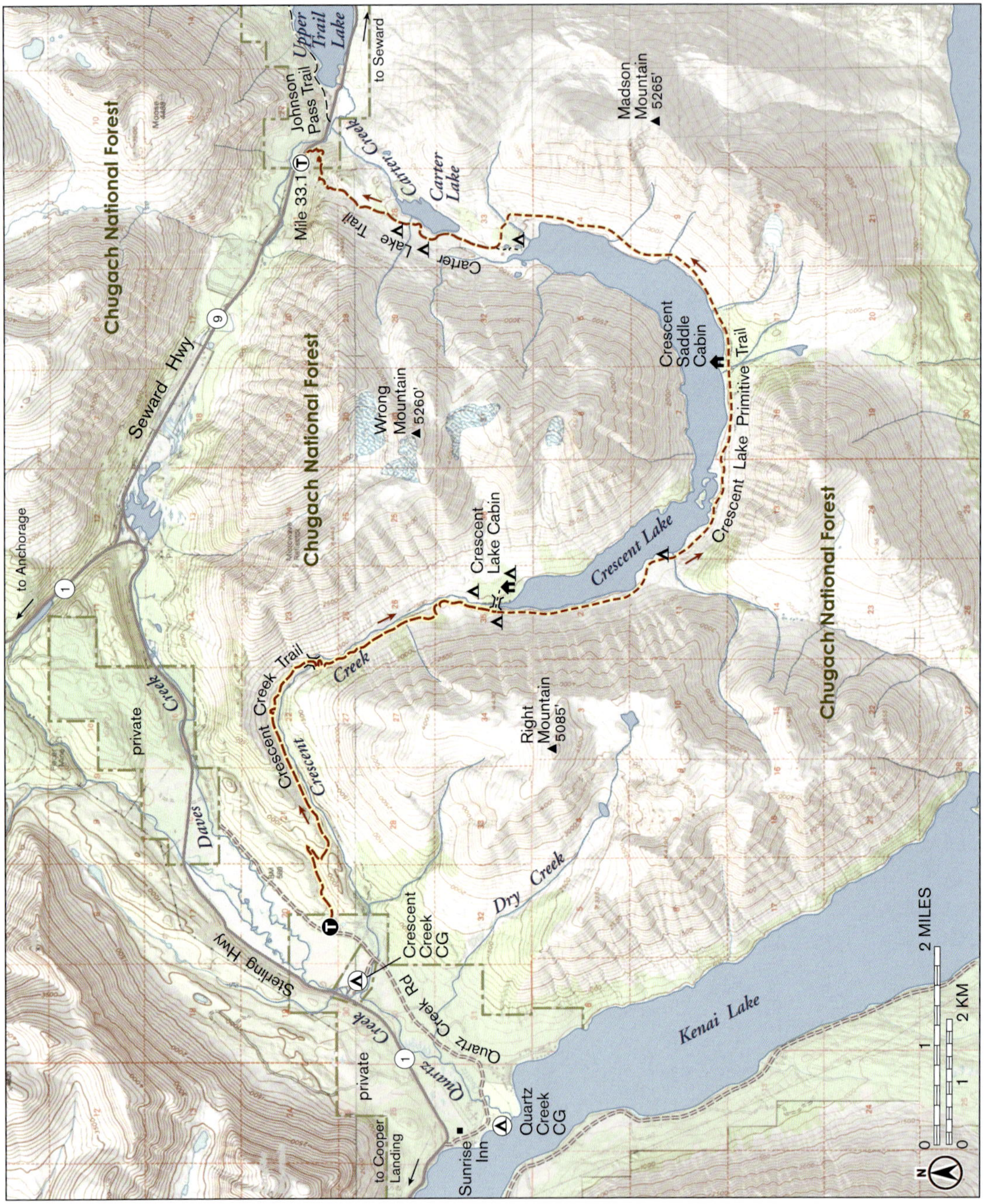
Chugach National Forest
Seward Hwy
to Anchorage
to Seward
Johnson Pass Trail
Upper Trail Lake
Mile 33.1
Carter Creek
Carter Lake
Carter Lake Trail
Madson Mountain 5265'
Wrong Mountain 5260'
Crescent Saddle Cabin
Crescent Lake Primitive Trail
Crescent Lake
Crescent Lake Cabin
Crescent Creek Trail
Crescent Creek
Right Mountain 5085'
private
Daves Creek
Dry Creek
Crescent Creek CG
Sterling Hwy
Quartz Creek Rd
Quartz Creek
Kenai Lake
Quartz Creek CG
Sunrise Inn
to Cooper Landing
0 1 2 MILES
0 1 2 KM
N

## DRIVING DIRECTIONS

This traverse requires a two-car shuttle.

**Crescent Creek trailhead (west).** Search for "crescent creek trailhead ak" online or follow these directions. Drive to mile 44.9 of the Sterling Highway, about 8 miles west of the junction of the Seward and Sterling Highways. Quartz Creek Road begins immediately west of the Sunrise Inn. Follow this road 3.3 miles to the start of the Crescent Creek Trail (marked), 0.5 mile beyond the turn to Crescent Creek Campground.

**Carter Lake trailhead (east).** Search online for "carter lake trail ak," or follow these directions. Drive to mile 33.1 of the Seward Highway. The trail leaves from a marked trailhead parking area on the southwest side of the highway (elevation 500 feet).

## ON THE ROUTE

Hike in either direction. This description starts on the Crescent Creek Trail, which departs directly across the road from the parking area (elevation 590 feet). The path winds through birch and aspen along a tiny stream, climbs over a low ridge, and descends into the Crescent Creek valley. Follow the trail upstream, crossing the creek on a bridge about 3.5 miles in. A second bridge is in a broad, open meadow dotted with trees near the Crescent Lake outlet at 6.2 miles (elevation 1454 feet). Cross in order to reach the Crescent Lake Cabin, 0.2 mile beyond the bridge; make cabin reservations through recreation.gov (see the Resources section). There are designated campsites in this area on both sides of the bridge.

To continue the traverse, stay on the west side of the lake outlet and head south. This trail that connects the Crescent Creek and Carter Lake Trails is called the Crescent Lake Primitive Trail. Because it is primitive, the grass can be quite thick in late summer, and the trail is not always obvious. There is a designated campsite with a bear-proof food box 2.1 miles from the west end of the primitive trail, where a stream enters the lake. The Crescent Saddle Cabin lies farther along the lake below a low point in the ridge, 10.7 miles from the Crescent Creek trailhead and 7 miles from the Carter Lake trailhead. Check with the Forest Service regarding current conditions. Some cautions: The stream by the campsite near the western end of Crescent Lake can be difficult to cross at high water. Toward the east end of the lake, there is an avalanche chute that holds snow late. It is steep, can be icy, and a slip could end in the lake.

Meet the Carter Lake Trail at a junction marked by a rock cairn and a sign, the end of the primitive trail. The left fork reaches the east end of Crescent Lake at a designated campsite in 0.2 mile. Turn right toward Carter Lake and ultimately the Seward Highway, 3.1 miles from here. The trail winds through grassy, gradual terrain, meeting two more designated campsites along Carter Lake. The last 1.5 miles descending on switchbacks to the Seward Highway are the steepest of the trip, but going is pleasant nonetheless. Cross a footbridge to the parking lot and your awaiting car.

The Forest Service has sometimes disallowed camping in overworn spots at the west end of Crescent Lake to allow vegetation to grow back. Please be aware of your impact and try to avoid further damage by using designated campsites whenever possible. Water is readily available at all campsites but must be treated; take a cooking stove. The route as far as the Crescent Lake Cabin is good for mountain bikes but harbors the potential for conflict with hikers. The Carter Lake Trail is too rocky and steep at the beginning and often too muddy beyond to be pleasant for most mountain bikers. Both the Carter Lake and Crescent Creek Trails are closed to motorized vehicles from May 1 to November 30 and are closed to horses from April 1 to June 30 because of soft trail conditions. Mountain bikers should observe the horse prohibitions to prevent trail erosion. The primitive trail (middle section of the traverse) is not recommended for bikes and horses due to rougher trail conditions and overgrowth.

## SHORTER OPTIONS

The Carter Lake Trail makes a great half- or full-day hike because of the early, steep ascent leading to the alpine flatlands. Hike to Carter Lake and back in 4.6 miles with 1150 feet of elevation gain, or venture on to the east shore of Crescent Lake for 6.6 miles roundtrip. Camp overnight at either lake for a two-day, low-mileage option.

The Crescent Creek Trail makes a full-day hike or longer overnight, with the option to stay at Crescent Lake Cabin, at 12.8 miles roundtrip with 1600 feet of elevation gain. An out-and-back overnight from the Carter Lake trailhead to Crescent Saddle Cabin is 14 miles roundtrip.

## SEASONAL OPTIONS

Avalanche terrain makes nearly all of the route hazardous in winter (see Avalanches in the Introduction), and even in spring, the deep, dense snow in avalanche paths melts last, making for slippery footing in places. For those with avalanche knowledge, the Carter Lake Trail makes an excellent snowshoe or ski tour, although climbing skins may be desirable for the initial ascent on skis. Snowmachiners share this winter route, though the steep, icy ascent can be a deterrent. Once past the switchback area, continue across the flats and across frozen Crescent Lake to either cabin, avoiding the most hazardous terrain below steep slopes. On the Crescent Creek end, the Quartz Creek Road plowing stops 1.1 miles before the trailhead, so plan on the additional mileage if tackling that trail in winter.

# 15 GRANDVIEW WHISTLE STOP AND BARTLETT GLACIER

**DISTANCE:** 6 miles roundtrip
**TIME:** 2 days (train ride dictates)
**ELEVATION GAIN:** 750 feet
**HIGH POINT:** 1350 feet
**SEASON:** July–mid-September
**SURFACE:** Hardpack, rocks
**GRADE:** Rolling
**INDIGENOUS LAND:** Dena'ina Athabascan
**MANAGING AGENCY:** Chugach National Forest
**MAP:** USGS Seward C-6
**ONLINE MAP SEARCH:** "bartlett glacier ak"
**TRAILHEAD GPS:** 60.839936°N, 148.981824°W

**Everybody loves a train ride, and what a way to access the roadless backcountry of the north-**east Kenai Peninsula! The Glacier Discovery Trail is a Forest Service work in progress, and the Alaska Railroad's Glacier Discovery Train is the only way to get to it. The train drops hikers off at either of two backcountry whistle-stop platforms: the Spencer Glacier Whistle Stop, which has become reasonably well known and popular, and the Grandview Whistle Stop, which is newer, less well known, and marks the beginning of this sweet little overnight trip. The Forest Service's long-term plan is to connect the two whistle-stop platforms via the Glacier Discovery Trail, extend the trail miles farther, and work with the Alaska Huts Association to establish a hut-to-hut system along the trail.

For now, the Grandview Whistle Stop has a starter trail, which winds through the subalpine zone of lush green rainforest to Bartlett Glacier. At the glacier, leave the green behind. The raw valley walls are newly released from glaciation, and waterfalls and hanging remnant threads of ice decorate sheer mountainsides. Because of the train schedule, most visitors elect to make a quick stop with just enough time to walk a half mile to an overlook of the train and back. Staying overnight allows you to see Bartlett Glacier and experience this country more fully. The beauty of staying overnight is that once the train rolls on down the track, you are left at the high point between Seward and Anchorage, miles away from any road or settlement, in the most glaciated part of the eastern Kenai Peninsula—a truly remote experience requiring little effort. It makes a fine introduction to big-country backpacking for children and a relaxing overnight outing for experienced folks.

## DRIVING DIRECTIONS

This trip starts with an Alaska Railroad train ride. The Glacier Discovery Train starts in Anchorage and proceeds to Girdwood, Portage, Whittier, and back to Portage ("Portage 2nd Stop"); it is possible to start this trip from any of these locations. The least expensive train ticket is from Portage 2nd Stop. Purchase a ticket through alaskarailroad.com, and be sure to choose the "2nd Stop" option. It is not cheap, but passengers may ride back and forth between Spencer and Grandview and stay as many days as desired for the price of the ticket.

To reach the Portage rail platform, search online for "portage depot ak," or follow these directions. Drive to mile 80.3 on the Seward Highway, near the head of Turnagain Arm. Turn east into a gravel parking area with a small concessions building and portable toilets. The train arrives here in early afternoon, loads for a few minutes, and departs for Spencer and Grandview.

## ON THE ROUTE

The Glacier Discovery Train is a touring train. It moves slowly, sometimes stopping for wildlife viewing and generally stops at a river takeout to load rafts, at Spencer where most people get off, and at Grandview. The train may roll south past Grandview for viewing Trail Glacier, which is the headwaters of the Kenai River system, before moving back to Grandview, where it typically stops for about forty minutes. The trail starts here.

The train should follow the same schedule the next day. Be sure to get the correct time the railroad needs you back to board.

*Glacier-scoured rock and Bartlett Glacier valley from the end of the formal trail*

The footpath is a well-built Forest Service trail that winds through hemlock forest, crosses a patch of alder that marks a major winter avalanche path, and traverses open meadows with mountain views in all directions. It also passes four designated campsites, each posted with a sign and located along a short spur trail near a water source. The Forest Service plans to install bear-proof food storage lockers at each site; check with them for updates. Choose a site on the hike in. Safely stash food and then continue on with a day-hiking load. The sites with better views are the two farthest in. Sites more protected are those nearer the train platform.

At 1.6 miles, there is a junction with a sign for the Bartlett Glacier viewpoint to the left and the Bartlett Moraine Trail to the right. The left fork is intended to be the continuing Glacier Discovery Trail in the future. It is built only a few hundred feet to a promontory that affords a good view over the valley below and up into the dramatic Bartlett Glacier side valley. The trail overall is so short—less than 3 miles—the few minutes' detour to this viewpoint is worth it.

The right fork is the continuing trail toward Bartlett Glacier and arguably the best part of the route. It snakes gradually uphill on the divide between two drainages toward an iconic peak and then traverses left below this peak in rockier terrain—the old glacier moraine. New mountain views appear around every bend. Along the way, before reaching the moraine area, the route passes the last two campsites. As the terrain becomes rougher, rock cairns mark the way. The formal trail ends at a prominent, ice-polished rock outcrop, where the entire glacier suddenly comes into view (2.6 miles from the trailhead, elevation 1200 feet).

This is what active deglaciation looks like. Rock and ice fill the view. In the foreground, patches of brush have valiantly gained a toehold, and vegetation takes over the rockiness bit by bit. Compare the current glacier extent in this valley to USGS maps. The rocky terrain and alder clumps have appeared within the time since USGS produced its map data. When the railroad ran steam locomotives through Grandview a century ago, photos show Bartlett Glacier as a hulking behemoth that filled its valley and loomed high over the railroad, barely leaving space for the tracks to be built. Today, the toe of the glacier has retreated a little. Most dramatically, however, the glacier as a whole appears deflated by comparison. The hanging glaciers to either side no longer connect with and feed ice to the main glacier. Bartlett Glacier soon will be cut off from the icefield beyond the pass visible in the distance. It is melting away in place. Go see it while it is still there!

Many people will be content to take in the view and turn back here, but it may be intriguing to continue another third of a mile or so to get a closer look at this landscape. Some hikers may want to mount the glacier and the prominent, rocky, medial moraine that runs like a path up the tongue of ice. Access to this glacier in such a dynamic area could change. Going near the ice for a better view involves rough ground and minor bushwhacking. Descending only slightly, traverse into the valley.

A guide who works this area reported it is possible to hike up the glacier on the central moraine. Intrepid hikers could keep going on this traverse until they are level with the glacier and then could clamber out onto it. Know, however, that this area will continue to hold snow for much of the summer; the snow may hide roaring meltwater streams, holes in the ice, or crevasses, and these dangers may change year to year. Proceeding onto the glacier when the area is totally snow-free and all dangers are visible may be reasonable. But the common advice is that walking on glaciers is not recommended unless the party is properly equipped and trained for glacier travel. Even those proceeding beyond the end of the trail for a closer look should keep their wits about them; the landscape is weird and wild, and once the rock outcrop at trail's end is out of view, paying close attention to landmarks is necessary to return to the trail.

Spend the night in the green meadows or forest at your camp, enjoying the play of light on the landscape and the flights of mist and clouds around the

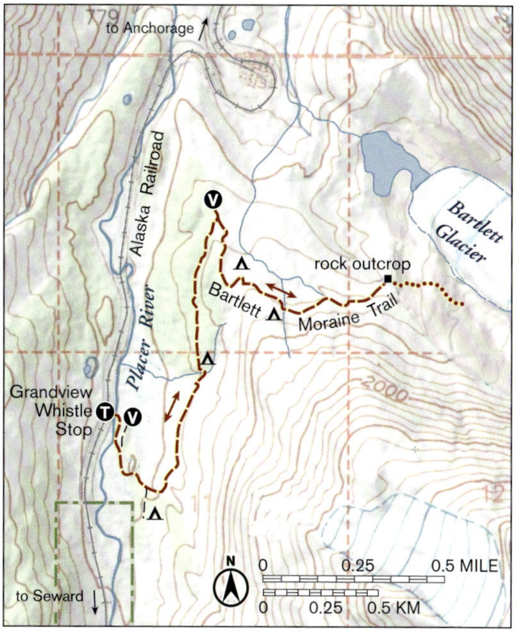

mountaintops. Look for moose and black bears, and find blueberries in season. Be sure to be on time for the afternoon return train. Those who hike back a little early will have time for the 0.3-mile round-trip out a little spur to the tourist overlook platform, which provides grand views of the pass area and waiting train.

*Hanging glaciers seen through scattered hemlock trees from mile 2 of the trail*

Note that Grandview is known for snow in winter. Longtime Anchorage residents fondly remember when the Nordic Skiing Association of Anchorage ran its annual chartered Ski Train to Grandview, and the mounds of snow there that buried all brush and some trees (the Ski Train now goes north to Curry, near Trip 46). Following particularly snowy winters, snow at Grandview sticks around late. In the shadow of trees and on north-facing slopes, deep snow (4 to 8 feet!) could remain into July, even if conditions otherwise are summery and warm. If you are planning a trip in June or early July, check trail and snow conditions with Chugach National Forest's Glacier Ranger District before buying train tickets.

This trail and the railroad corridor are associated with the Iditarod National Historic Trail (see Iditarod Trail and Alaska Long Trail in the Introduction).

## EXTENDING YOUR TRIP

You have paid for the train ticket and might as well get two trips (and glaciers) for the price of one. Get off the train at the Spencer Whistle Stop and explore the Spencer Glacier area. There are backcountry campsites, a group campsite, opportunities for guided rafting and guided hikes on the glacier, and an alpine-elevation Forest Service cabin—Spencer Bench Cabin—that has been in high demand since the moment it opened (reserve through alaskarailroad.com). Spencer is where the Alaska Huts Association has a permit to pursue a multiparty hut. Eventually Lars Spurkland Memorial Hut at Spencer will connect via the planned Glacier Discovery Trail to a hut near Bartlett Glacier.

# 16 MANITOBA MOUNTAIN

**DISTANCE:** 7.2 miles roundtrip
**TIME:** Full day
**ELEVATION GAIN:** 2600 feet
**HIGH POINT:** 3702 feet
**SEASON:** Mid-June–September
**SURFACE:** Hardpack, tundra
**GRADE:** Moderate with steep segments
**INDIGENOUS LAND:** Dena'ina Athabascan
**MANAGING AGENCIES:** Alaska Division of Mining, Land, and Water and Chugach National Forest
**MAPS:** USGS Seward C-7 NW, C-7 NE
**ONLINE MAP SEARCH:** "manitoba ak"
**TRAILHEAD GPS:** 60.669766°N, 149.478919°W

**Manitoba Cabin is a hike-in hut at the base of Manitoba Mountain in historic gold mining coun-**try. The refurbished mining cabin, sleeping yurts, and sauna exude warmth and comfort, and the complex can host several families (reserve at alaskahuts.org). The mountain, too, with its rounded shoulders draped in a tundra blanket, feels comfortable. The distances and elevation gains present a modest challenge compared to many summit hikes, and an old mining road provides easy passage through the forest and brush zone. In July, the area between Manitoba Mountain and an intermediate bump known as Little Manitoba lights up with wildflowers of all sorts. Despite all these signs of comfort, the summit feels like a real mountain—the back side drops steeply to a glacial bowl, Silvertip Peak creates a higher and craggier backdrop across this cirque, and intriguing valleys provide views into the heart of the Kenai Mountains north, south, east, and west.

This is the only trip in the book where hikers may end their day relaxing in a sauna or baking muffins in a hut. Parts of the access trail are associated with the Iditarod National Historic Trail system (see Iditarod Trail and Alaska Long Trail in the Introduction).

## DRIVING DIRECTIONS

Drive to a large, paved pullout at milepost 48 of the Seward Highway. Park at the north end, near the green milepost sign. If you park in another part of this pullout, don't be tempted to walk up other informal paths that head east to adjacent private properties. Find the proper trail at the far north end of the lot, behind the guardrail. There is no parking fee. In winter, carry a good shovel or two in case it is necessary to dig out a parking space or dig out of a berm left by plows.

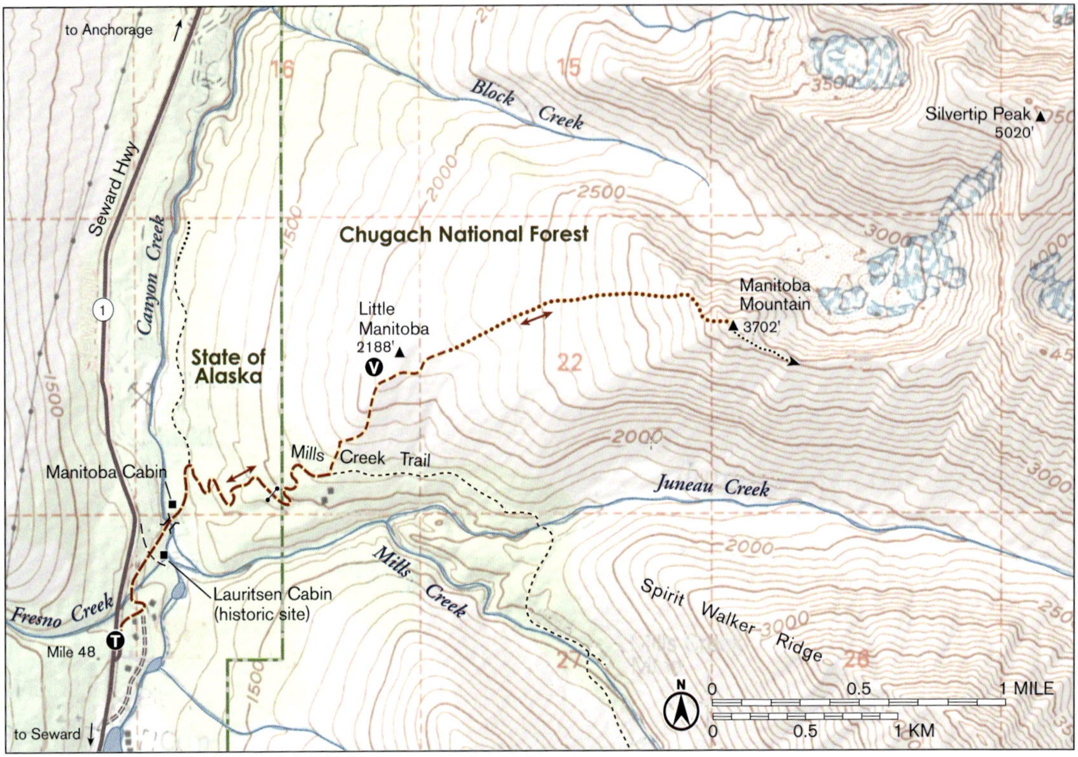


## ON THE ROUTE

The trail begins (elevation 1300 feet) as a gravel ramp that heads diagonally up a 20-foot bluff behind the guardrail, next to the milepost 48 sign. The trailhead itself is not well marked, but way-marking signs for Manitoba Cabin and Manitoba Mountain appear along the first part of the route. This area holds a subtle history. The trail gradually descends along the bluff of Fresno Creek; look over the edge and you may be able to see a grown-over mining ditch. A short way farther along, the trail crosses this ditch on a rock causeway, but the ditch is not obvious, as mature trees grow from it. The footpath intersects a segment of old gravel track that is part of the Iditarod National Historic Trail system (a branch of the main Iditarod Trail). Go left on this old track, perhaps the very track that dog teams and wagons used to deliver mail from the port at Seward to the mining communities of Sunrise and Hope in the early 1900s. Gradually descend to a four-way intersection of mining roads, 0.6 mile from the trailhead. For a brief side trip, consider taking a right turn to reach the Lauritsen Cabin (100 yards down, near the creek, to the left of the track). Lauritsen Cabin was one of the first mining cabins in the area, dating from approximately 1898, and is worth a look.

The main route toward Manitoba Cabin and Manitoba Mountain proceeds straight across the four-way intersection and down to the trail's low point, a steel bridge over Canyon Creek at elevation 1150 feet. The trail here becomes the Mills Creek Trail, a Forest Service easement across state land. Manitoba

Cabin is located across the creek on the bluff above the bridge and dates from the 1930s. Reach it by hiking up the trail beyond the bridge to cabin elevation and then doubling back to the left, 0.7 mile from the trailhead.

When this land still belonged to Chugach National Forest, in the early 2000s, the federal government had invested in rehabilitation of Lauritsen Cabin. The land transferred to the State of Alaska, and Lauritsen and Manitoba Cabins came with it. Lauritsen Cabin is on the National Register of Historic Places and is a tiny, well-crafted, historic treasure but is unused. The state has not maintained it. The nonprofit Alaska Huts Association secured a permit from the state to renovate Manitoba Cabin and make it a hut for public use. It is different from public-use cabins in that it can sleep up to eighteen; provides mattresses, firewood, cookware, and an oven; and comes with a sauna. It is also one of the most accessible walk-in lodging sites in the state and works equally well as a launching spot for hard-core outdoor adventure and as a year-round destination for families with small children or anybody looking for a simple outdoor escape. The hut has a resource book that contains more about the history of the cabin. A wide area around both cabins is covered by mining claims; the land is public and open for use, but the public is not allowed to pan for gold or otherwise mess with or remove minerals or mining equipment.

If you are staying at the hut, drop your gear. Beyond the cabin, the Mills Creek Trail continues as a wide path through a long series of switchbacks that loop through hemlock forest for 1 mile up the hill toward Manitoba Mountain. The trail passes around a gate near the Chugach National Forest property line. Miners with small federal mining claims up Mills Creek have permits to pass through the gate on four-wheelers, but their passage appears to be rare. The switchbacks end where the trail emerges from the forest on a long, straight stretch and where views open in the uphill direction. The trail here continues to ascend gradually and then begins to descend, without substantial turns. At the high point, 1450 feet, look for a smaller trail heading uphill to the left through grass (by July the grass can be quite tall), and turn onto it.

*A camp leader helps kids identify animal tracks near Manitoba Cabin.* (Photo by Avery Wolfe)

*Packing skis in June to pursue lingering snow on Manitoba Mountain*

With the exception of the Mills Creek Trail, this area is closed to any motorized vehicles, but every few years all-terrain vehicles try to follow this grassy trail a ways, so the route may appear as a relatively wide two-track trail or a narrow footpath. Ahead on the uphill horizon is a shoulder of Little Manitoba. Follow the grassy trail up and along the lower edge of a hemlock patch, then up again to an overlook of the Canyon Creek valley, and finally below the high point of Little Manitoba, 2.2 miles from the trailhead (1100 feet of elevation gain). For some people, stopping here or at the overlook is a good, shorter option (and blueberry picking can be great in season). To continue, follow a faint trail, pushing past a couple branches and dropping briefly down to the somewhat-level area between Little Manitoba and the real Manitoba Mountain. A small footpath continues across this area and generally to the northeast and upward, providing ever-better views behind and ever more alpine-style wildflowers. Eventually the path is intermittent and peters out in relatively low vegetation; select the path of least resistance to achieve the ridge above, mentally marking the general route to ensure smoothly reuniting with the trail during the descent.

At the ridge, turn right and follow the ridge crest to a broad summit with views in multiple directions (elevation 3702 feet, 3.6 miles from the trailhead). Enjoy the comfortable summit of Manitoba Mountain and its views of Upper and Lower Summit

Lakes and the steep-sided valleys of Juneau and Mills Creeks where the prospectors found gold. From the top, marvel at the prospectors who rambled over these rugged valleys without maps or GPS (possibly with guidance from Dena'ina residents), and imagine longer treks possible today with a backpack and a miner's fortitude (see Extending Your Trip). But that can wait for another day. For the moment, it's okay to start thinking about those muffins back at the hut.

### EXTENDING YOUR TRIP

Just beyond the Manitoba Mountain summit, the ridge is walkable but narrow. Energetic people have hiked another mile to a three-way junction of ridges, which requires rock scrambling and may not be comfortable for everybody, particularly coming back down. Those who do continue may follow the rim of the cirque north to Silvertip Peak (elevation 5020 feet). Other options nearby include following the Mills Creek Trail beyond the smaller, grassy turnoff to Manitoba Mountain. The Mills Creek Trail disappears at roughly 3.7 miles from the trailhead. It is possible to extend an off-trail hike farther into upper Mills Creek or over Stormy Creek pass to the Johnson Pass Trail (Trip 13), but you will need navigation skills and may face hazardous creek fords. Trekking to the Johnson Pass Trail and out to a trailhead adds about 20 miles beyond the end of Mills Creek Trail (see map for Trip 13).

### SEASONAL OPTIONS

In winter, the Manitoba Mountain route is popular for skinning up and skiing down. Also, the woods near the hut make for great shorter explorations on snowshoes or touring skis, and the looping switchbacks on the Mills Creek Trail can make for some wild sledding. The Mills Creek Trail also is a challenging mountain bike ride when snow-free, and for a brief period in early summer, it is possible to bike up the old mining road, hike up the footpath beyond the switchbacks, and ski the top of the mountain.

# 17 CENTER RIDGE SKI TOUR

**DISTANCE:** 3.6–7 miles roundtrip
**TIME:** Half day to full day
**ELEVATION GAIN:** 1200 feet
**HIGH POINT:** 2200 feet
**SEASON:** December–May
**SURFACE:** Snow
**GRADE:** Rolling with steep segments
**INDIGENOUS LAND:** Dena'ina Athabascan
**MANAGING AGENCY:** Chugach National Forest
**MAP:** USGS Seward D-6 SW
**ONLINE MAP SEARCH:** "tincan creek ak"
**TRAILHEAD GPS:** 60.781977°N, 149.215243°W

**For a delightful ski or snowshoe tour, try Turnagain Pass, which is generally buried in deep snow** during winter and is one of the few places with separate areas designated for skiers and snowmachiners. Winter was meant to be like this—ice crystals glinting in the sunlight or huge flakes falling softly among thick hemlock trees, with a backdrop of towering snowy peaks. The Forest Service has designated the west side of the highway for snowmachines and the east side for nonmotorized winter sports. Enjoy a rolling-terrain day gliding along the scenic alpine hilltops of Center Ridge, or bring out the skate skis in April and May for stellar crust skiing in the basin of Tincan Creek.

## DRIVING DIRECTIONS

Search online for "turnagain pass rest area ak," or follow these directions. To reach the trailhead (elevation 1000 feet), drive to mile 68 of the Seward Highway and turn east into a rest area, which doubles as the trailhead parking lot.

Access to a snowmachiners' pullout is on the west side of the highway, 0.2 mile north. The east side of the Seward Highway from Bench Creek to Ingram Creek, including the Turnagain Pass area, is closed to motorized vehicles year-round.

## ON THE ROUTE

There are several options for skiing. This description focuses on a cross-country tour up Center Ridge, the low hump that divides Tincan and Lyon Creeks, but backcountry skiers and snowboarders with gear for climbing steep slopes have made the higher mountains on either side of Center Ridge some of their favorite destinations. For springtime crust skiing, see Seasonal Options.

Depending on previous ski traffic, the main trail may appear to head to the left as you face away from the highway; this is an alpine-touring route up Tincan Ridge. To access the lower-elevation Center Ridge route, head slightly to the right and away from the highway, descending gently to a bridge over the small gorge of Tincan Creek. Cross the gorge and proceed straight ahead, angling up a broad slope and beneath powerlines. The route bends to the left and heads into the hemlock forest, following small, natural meadows. It bends back to the right, then left again before leveling somewhat and following the base of Center Ridge, which now lies to your left. Snow hangs heavily on the trees, creating myriad imaginary giants and monsters. Look for intermittent markers on tree trunks, imperfectly indicating the route for the first mile or so.

After about a mile, the route swings left and climbs up the base of Center Ridge, ascending through a treeless area to a low spot on the ridge crest. Do not continue into the narrow Lyon Creek valley along the base of the ridge; the slopes on either side of Lyon Creek could avalanche. Check snow stability before climbing the steep, open slope to the ridge. If you are following a track set by skiers with climbing skins, the track likely will be too steep to follow on touring skis without skins. Be prepared to break your own trail, making switchbacks. Mounting the ridge at 1800 feet, a SNOTEL (snowpack weather station) in a small clearing just ahead provides a waypoint. Swing right before the SNOTEL to climb again and begin following the apex of the ridge. Sometimes the established track turns to the right before the SNOTEL site is visible.

Tree line, around elevation 2000 feet and 3.6 miles roundtrip from the parking area, makes a good destination for a shorter day. If time allows, continue

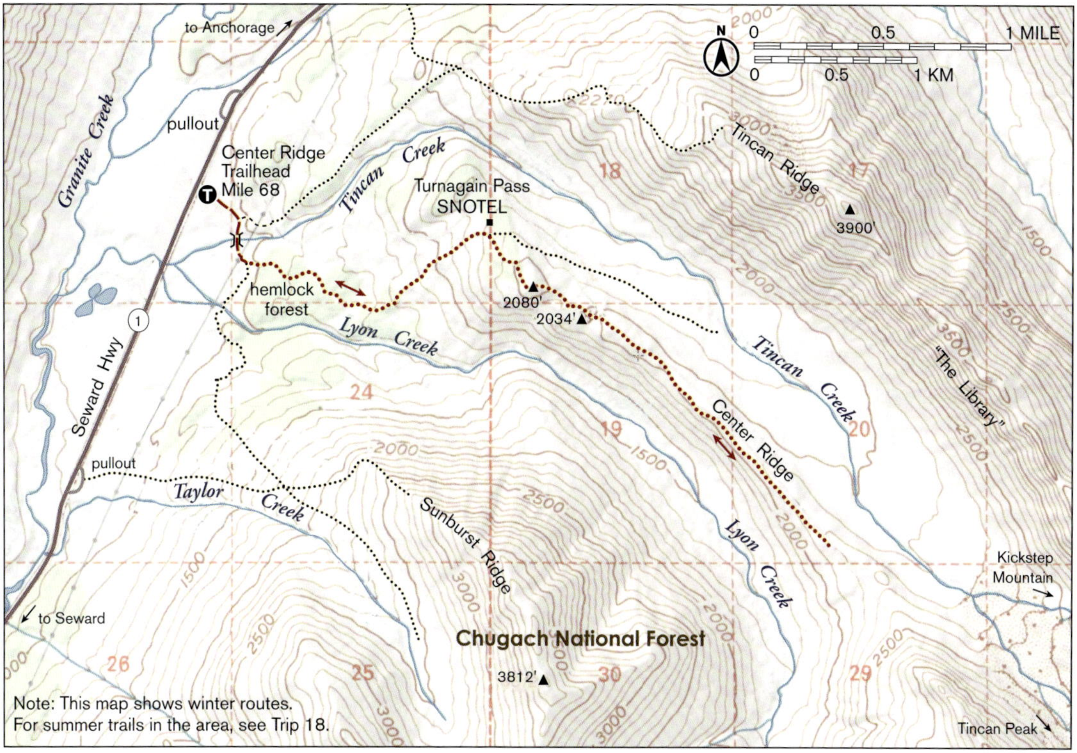


on the crest of this rolling ridge, traversing along the north side of the higher knobs, until the route begins to climb toward a mountain peak, about 7 miles roundtrip. In midwinter the sun seldom reaches Center Ridge, so dress warmly. Fortunately, wind seems to be unusual there. With luck, you may see skiers and snowboarders carving sinuous lines down the southwest face of Tincan Ridge or even the Library, colloquially named for its numerous spines. Jagged white Kickstep Mountain and Tincan Peak rise at the head of Tincan Creek, making for an unforgettable view.

## EXTENDING YOUR TRIP

North of Center Ridge is the much higher Tincan Ridge, a popular destination among backcountry skiers and splitboarders who use climbing skins mounted to their bases to ascend the long, steep approach. The route from the Center Ridge trailhead, which veers left shortly after leaving the parking area, often splits into several skin tracks but converges back to one before the route becomes truly steep around 1600 feet, where it joins another skin track from the north.

On the opposite side of Center Ridge, to the south beyond the point where the Center Ridge route turns into the forest, is a less-used winter route to Taylor Creek and locally named Sunburst Ridge. If there is no previous track, pick your way from meadow to meadow up the hill and into the higher Taylor Creek valley, or mount the base of Sunburst Ridge. The first pullouts on the east side of the

*Center Ridge in April, with the Library, Kickstep Mountain, and Tincan Peak as a backdrop* (Photo by Gretchen Nelson)

highway north and south of Turnagain Pass provide alternate access, respectively, to Tincan Ridge and Sunburst Ridge.

All these routes should be undertaken only by those trained in avalanche risk assessment and rescue. Experienced backcountry skiers have died in avalanches on these slopes. Before venturing into the snowy mountains, take one of many avalanche classes offered to the public each winter (see Avalanches in the Introduction), consult the avalanche forecast (see Chugach National Forest Avalanche Information Center in the Resources section), and invest in the proper gear to keep you and your party safe. Nerding out about snow science in this spectacular setting is, honestly, about as fun as skiing.

## SHORTER OPTIONS

For families with kids and other low-mileage adventurers, even a short trip winding through snow-laden hemlock trees is an excursion into the best that Alaska's winters have to offer. Venture only 0.4 mile into the Center Ridge route to reach the hemlock forest, without steep climbs or avalanche danger. Bring snowshoes or skis. Winding a mile to the base of the steepest climb is reasonable but involves a couple of short hills (2 miles roundtrip).

### SEASONAL OPTIONS

Specifically in April and May, when the sun is strong during the day but the snow's surface refreezes overnight, morning conditions can be great for crust skiing throughout the broad, shallow basin of Tincan Creek. Go early, bring a pair of skate skis, and follow the route described above as far as the final turn near the SNOTEL. It may be pertinent to bring snowshoes for the uphills, but on good crust, people can herringbone, sidestep, walk in their ski boots, and otherwise do what it takes to get up the relatively short, steep segment to the SNOTEL site. From there, follow gaps in the trees generally northward and around the curve of the ridge crest, climbing only slightly, then descending, heading eastward across an open slope on a side-hilling traverse toward Tincan Creek. The 2-mile-long basin is yours to explore. The northeast side of Tincan Creek valley is an avalanche runout zone: even when skiing on the relative flats, snowslides could descend from above, so take avalanche precautions as outlined earlier in this description. If in doubt, err toward Center Ridge and avoid lingering near the steep slopes of Tincan Ridge and the Library.

In summer, a well-used footpath crosses the Tincan Creek bridge, passes a gravel picnic area with a stone monument marking the "Nissman Center Ridge Trail," and continues south to Lyon Creek (unbridged as of this writing). See Trip 18 for an established summer option north from the Center Ridge trailhead. The Center Ridge Trail itself, despite being marked with the stone monument, is not a maintained summer trail and is a rarely trodden bushwhack.

# 18 TURNAGAIN PASS IDITAROD TRAIL

**DISTANCE:** 6.5 miles point to point
**TIME:** Half day to full day
**ELEVATION GAIN:** 500 feet
**HIGH POINT:** 1300 feet
**SEASON:** Late June–September
**SURFACE:** Hardpack
**GRADE:** Rolling with steep segments
**INDIGENOUS LAND:** Dena'ina Athabascan
**MANAGING AGENCY:** Chugach National Forest
**MAP:** USGS Seward D-6 SW
**ONLINE MAP SEARCH:** "turnagain pass ak"
**TRAILHEAD GPS:** Center Ridge 60.781977°N, 149.215243°W
Muskeg Meadows 60.825365°N, 149.124858°W

**Most trails in this book go *up* and back or *up* and over. Few are so mellow as the descending** portion of the commemorative Iditarod National Historic Trail (INHT) at Turnagain Pass. Wending north from Center Ridge, it is a pleasant, scenic, and uncomplicated forest, meadow, and mountain walk that ends some 500 feet lower than it started. This is a point-to-point trip, but hikers (or mountain bikers) can easily modify it as an out-and-back excursion.

After years languishing as a trail missing two important components—bridges at the two biggest stream crossings—the recent installation of these bridges instantly made the trail actually usable. This is another step toward a long-held Forest Service goal of establishing a continuous thread of the INHT from Seward to Girdwood. A mirrored stretch of the INHT from Center Ridge south to the Johnson Pass trailhead is expected to be completed in coming years, promising to extend the hike through Turnagain Pass to 12 miles, with the option to link up to the Johnson Pass Trail (Trip 13) for a total of 35 miles.

*Markers identify this route as the Iditarod Trail.*

## DRIVING DIRECTIONS

A two-car shuttle is required for the recommended route.

**Center Ridge trailhead (south).** Search online for "turnagain pass rest area ak," or follow these directions. Drive to mile 68 of the Seward Highway and turn east into a rest area, which doubles as the trailhead parking lot (elevation 1000 feet).

**Muskeg Meadows trailhead (north).** The northern trailhead is a pullout on the southeast side of the Seward Highway at approximately mile 72.5, also known to winter backcountry recreationalists as the Eddy's pullout. The trail leaves from the north end of the pullout at a gap in the guardrail.

## ON THE ROUTE

Depart the Center Ridge trailhead on a well-used footpath heading east. In 0.1 mile, take the left fork at a sign marking the turn toward mile 72.5 (the Muskeg Meadows trailhead). The trail soon swings north, climbing gradually into the foothills of Tincan Ridge through stands of hemlock and rocky outcrops. The trees sporadically give way to mountain views, with glimpses down to Turnagain Arm. The trail is nicely built; its mellow grading and width make for excellent mountain bike riding and fine walking.

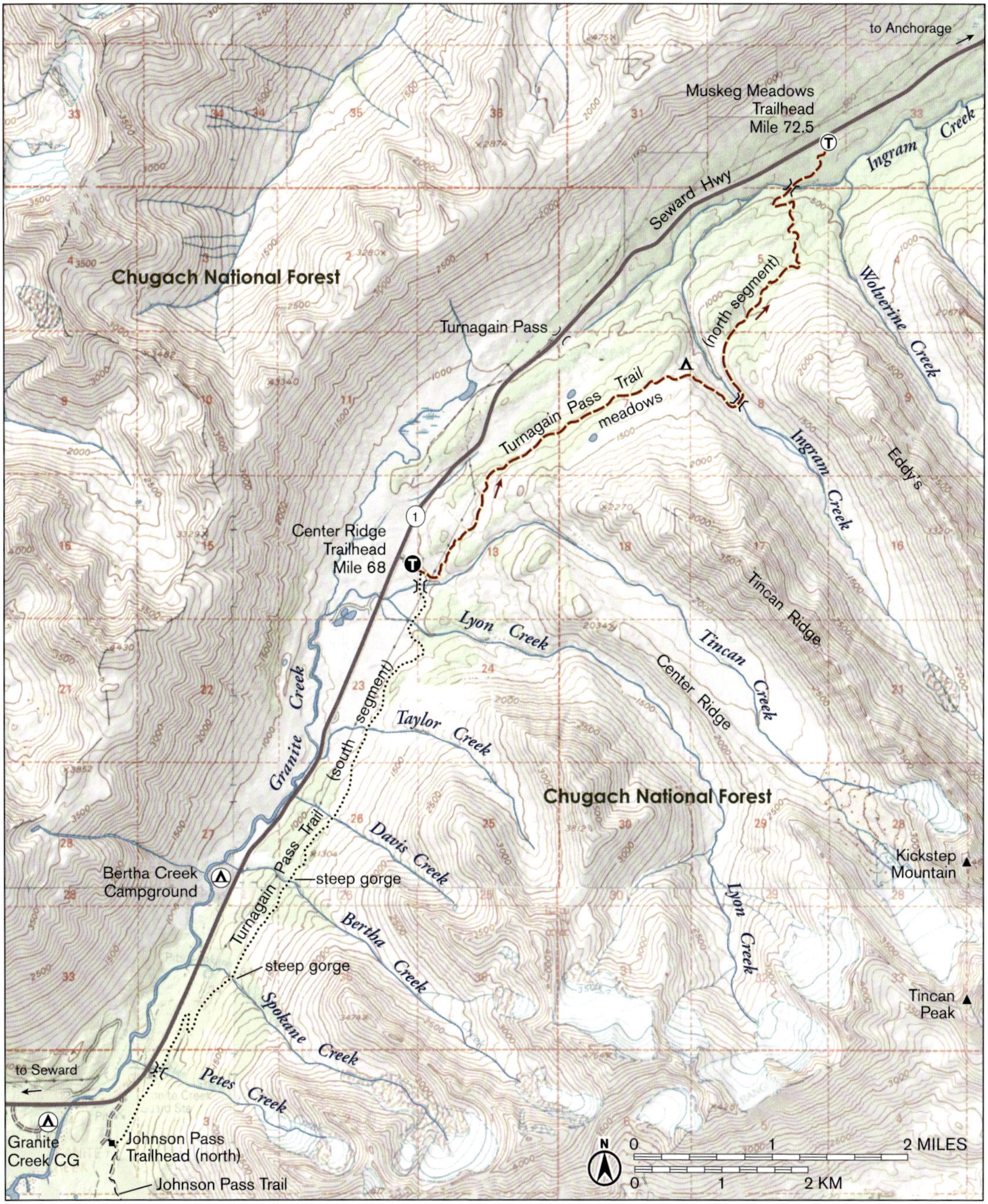
to Anchorage
Muskeg Meadows
Trailhead
Mile 72.5
Seward Hwy
Ingram Creek
Chugach National Forest
Turnagain Pass
(north segment)
Wolverine Creek
Turnagain Pass Trail
meadows
Ingram Creek
Eddy's
Center Ridge
Trailhead
Mile 68
Tincan Ridge
Lyon Creek
Tincan Creek
Center Ridge
Granite Creek
(south segment)
Taylor Creek
Chugach National Forest
Davis Creek
Turnagain Pass Trail
Bertha Creek
Campground
steep gorge
Kickstep
Mountain
Lyon Creek
Bertha Creek
steep gorge
Tincan
Peak
Spokane Creek
to Seward
Petes Creek
Granite
Creek CG
Johnson Pass
Trailhead (north)
Johnson Pass Trail
0 1 2 MILES
0 1 2 KM

After 2.4 miles and slightly more than 300 feet of elevation gain, the trail opens up onto a wet meadow. Primitive camping is possible here, though be careful to pick a dry spot in forest. Blueberry picking can be fruitful in season. From here, the trail swings around the north side of Tincan Ridge. A designated campsite with a bear-proof locker appears as the trail begins descending to Ingram Creek. The bridge across upper Ingram is 3.4 miles from the Center Ridge trailhead (3.1 miles from Muskeg Meadows trailhead), with subalpine views up the narrow valley.

After crossing the bridge, the trail turns back out of the Ingram Creek valley, then drops below tree line again to round the toe of the next ridge to the north, known informally as Eddy's. The remainder of the hike is a forested, meandering descent through the mossy understory with huge hemlocks above. Cyclists likely will appreciate the swooping, curving, and not-too-steep descents. Keep alert for sun-dappled spruce grouse and high-bush blueberries. Several log bridges and boardwalks cross minor drainages, with a second major bridge at the downstream crossing of Ingram Creek, 0.7 mile from the end of the trail at Muskeg Meadows. The final 400 feet of trail crosses a soggy muskeg on a boardwalk, hence the trailhead name, then makes a short climb to the highway pullout at mile 72.5 where your shuttle car awaits. Cyclists may opt to form a loop by riding 4.5 miles back up the highway shoulder.

The segment of the Turnagain Pass Trail south from Center Ridge is built but is missing four key bridges across Lyon, Taylor, Bertha, and Spokane Creeks, with major gorges on the latter two. Substantial alder overgrowth and sketchy workarounds at gorges make this portion not recommendable for now, but the coming years promise sufficient trail work to transform the distance between the Center Ridge and Johnson Pass trailheads into a pleasant, forested 5.5-mile ramble.

## SHORTER OPTION

A 4.8-mile out-and-back hike from the Center Ridge trailhead to the meadows area is a pleasant mosey with mountain views and only 450 feet of elevation gain. Stay at the designated campsite for a short-distance overnight (2.8 mile each way) that kids can tackle.

## SEASONAL OPTIONS

In the winter, this general route makes a good ski tour, though it requires independent routefinding, as the summer trail is not blazed on trees. From each trailhead, the route starts on popular skin tracks set by backcountry skiers headed up Tincan Ridge and Eddy's, but be prepared to break trail in between. Avalanche knowledge and safety gear are important (see Avalanches in the Introduction). See Trip 17 for more ski touring options in the area.

# 19 HOPE COASTAL WALK

**DISTANCE:** Up to 6 miles roundtrip
**TIME:** Half day
**ELEVATION GAIN:** 200 feet
**HIGH POINT:** 50 feet
**SEASON:** May–October

**SURFACE:** Hardpack, roots
**GRADE:** Low angle
**INDIGENOUS LAND:** Dena'ina Athabascan
**MANAGING AGENCIES:** Chugach National Forest and Kenai Peninsula Borough
**MAP:** USGS Seward D-7 NW
**ONLINE MAP SEARCH:** "windy point ak"
**TRAILHEAD GPS:** West 60.924795°N, 149.617137°W; east 60.930238°N, 149.552096°W

**The Kenai Peninsula coastline is not always easy to access, but east of Hope there is a pleasant** forest walk that accesses bluff tops, mudflats, wind-torn rocky outcrops, small grassy estuaries, and beaches of slatey material, gravel, and even sand. On stormier days, the forest provides protection. On nicer days, small beaches invite hanging out on a log or rock in the sunshine or investigating (or making) tracks in the mud. This can be a great trip for families, with multiple opportunities for diversions on different beaches. For those familiar with the Gull Rock Trail, which begins near the end of the Hope Highway, this trail is shorter and has better access to the coast.

This trail is best out-and-back from the western end, but there is a second access point at the eastern end. Problematically, though, there is virtually no parking there. If a driver were willing to meet hikers at the far end or if you were to stash a bike there and ride 3 miles on the Hope Highway back to the car, the hike could be a one-way excursion. Hope Highway traffic is normally fairly quiet, but cyclists should note that there is no shoulder.

## DRIVING DIRECTIONS

The coastal trail makes a good out-and-back walk, and is presented as such, but it does have a trailhead at each end. The primary trailhead is at the western end of the walk. The east end has almost no parking so is best as a pickup or drop-off spot.

To reach the main trailhead, drive the Seward Highway to mile 57.3 and turn north on the Hope Highway (marked with signs for Hope). Drive to mile 15.6, and turn north onto Mathison Drive. After 0.1 mile, turn right on Whiskers Drive. In another 0.2 mile, the road ends at a cul-de-sac. The roads are lined by private properties: some developed, others vacant. The cul-de-sac is on public land owned by the Kenai Peninsula Borough. Note that cul-de-sacs typically are designed for emergency vehicles to turn around, so park carefully and out of the way. If there are several cars, park at wider spots along the roads without blocking any driveway.

The eastern end of the trail is at a communications facility located on Chugach National Forest land. At mile 13.3 of the Hope Highway, along a straightaway, a one-lane driveway leads downhill to a gate. The Forest Service reports that the permit for the communications facility driveway is not exclusive; the public has access to the public lands here. There is space to park only a single vehicle on the driveway near the gate and keep the gate accessible to trucks going to the facility. Note, however, that big vehicles have scant room to turn around, and loose gravel may make backing out a challenge for two-wheel-drive vehicles. Another space or two may be found on the shoulder of the Hope Highway near but not at the driveway. Parking is suboptimum.

Hence the suggestion to hike out and back, stash a bike, or arrange to be met.

## ON THE ROUTE

The trail is informal, apparently built and maintained by local trail enthusiasts. There is no trailhead sign at either end. At the western-end cul-de-sac, the trail begins to the left of a No Camping sign and heads through forest a few yards directly to the coastal bluff. A bench sits on the bluff edge, providing a panorama of Turnagain Arm. The main trail goes to the right along the bluff. A path also leads downhill to the left (see Shortening or Extending Your Trip).

From the bluff-top bench, head right to meander along the high cliff with good ocean views. The trail loses elevation at a switchback en route and later drops a bit more, almost to sea level. Nearly a mile from the start, an accessible beach appears. Bracketed by rocky headlands, this beach has cobbles and also fine material that almost counts as sand. A giant old birch overhangs the beach, and a rope swing invites young and old.

Another 0.2 mile provides access to a small rocky beach adjacent to a grassy marsh with a picturesque low rock headland beyond. From here, there is a succession of about six more small beaches and beach grass areas and a couple of accessible headlands to explore. Each spot has its own aesthetic, with curving tidal channels in the mudflats, trees or rock outcrops for shelter from wind or sun, and open areas where you could bundle up and lean into the air on windy days or tan on those rare still, hot

*One of many varied views from the coast near Hope across Turnagain Arm and Cook Inlet*

days. Between these coastal features, the trail winds through a coastal rainforest mostly of hemlock. Look for interesting mosses and fungi and areas of berry bushes. Notably, the very last beach (a rocky one) appears to have a hard cliffy boundary on the left (west), but poking around will lead to the discovery of a small passage naturally worn through the rock to another beach beyond. Kids and exploratory types will love this. Here and at beaches throughout, be aware of the timing of the tides and the possibility that the water may rise and cut off access.

Beyond the last beach a couple hundred yards, the trail ends at a concrete communications building. Follow its driveway up another couple hundred yards, past a gate, to the hidden bike or waiting ride. Otherwise, from the final beach or any place that looks like a good turnaround spot, head back.

## SHORTENING OR EXTENDING YOUR TRIP

If energy remains after returning to the bench on the bluff, or as a stand-alone mini-hike, consider following the trail to the west from the bluff-top bench. The western route by itself is 1 mile roundtrip, with 100 feet elevation gain. From the bench, the western trail drops downhill and follows the bluff top 0.4 mile to private property signs. Here the trail cuts sharply right and down to the beach. This is the quickest way to a beach from the trailhead and makes a nice walk in its own right. Real sand occurs on parts of the beach here, and the beach is much longer than those beaches to the east, but the big beach is not quite as visually arresting as the nook-and-cranny beaches to the east.

Note that, due to land subsidence in the 1964 Great Alaska Earthquake, perhaps combined with quirks of early land staking in this area, land to the west along this beach shows on borough parcel maps as private land even out on the tidal flats. Coastlines below the high-tide lines normally are public lands throughout Alaska, so there is an inherent unresolved conflict here. The beach is not posted as private; the upland is posted. A five-minute stroll to the west provides a view of Hope, but the beach dead-ends at mud and creek crossings. Just hanging out on the beach where the trail deposits hikers at the base of the bluff and exploring a bit to the east are fine options.

### SEASONAL OPTIONS

Because Hope is on the coast, snow may come and go in winter compared to areas farther inland. Minus the promise of sunbathing, this trail is a good candidate for hiking in winter during periods with little snow cover. It is not suited to skiing or biking.

# 20 BLACKSTONE BAY OVERLOOK

**DISTANCE:** 6 miles roundtrip
**TIME:** Full day
**ELEVATION GAIN:** 2900 feet
**HIGH POINT:** 2900 feet
**SEASON:** July–September
**SURFACE:** Tundra, handholds (scrambling), boulders
**GRADE:** Sustained steep
**INDIGENOUS LAND:** Chugach Sugpiaq (Alutiiq)
**MANAGING AGENCIES:** City of Whittier and Chugach National Forest
**MAPS:** USGS Seward D-5 SE, D-5 SW
**ONLINE MAP SEARCH:** "whittier creek ak"
**TRAILHEAD GPS:** 60.774154°N, 148.673309°W

**Some say if you don't know Prince William Sound, you don't know Southcentral Alaska. This steep** hike accesses the ridgeline above Passage Canal and grants a sweeping view over the crest into a collection of narrow bays, islands, and forests of the sound. There are deep-blue ocean waters, white and translucent-blue glaciers, thick green forests, and silver-gray expanses of bedrock fresh from under the ice. The effects of a changing climate are evident here above the tiny port town of Whittier. In only a decade, what had been a mountaineering route across glaciers has become a reasonable, if difficult, hike without need to set foot on ice. Phillips Cruises has for years advertised its "Twenty-Six Glacier Cruise" out of Whittier, touting that number of glaciers visible in a five-and-a-half-hour boat ride. Here, for a similar time investment, a hiker has "twenty-six glacier views" at the top in one panoramic sweep.

This trail starts on the city's Horsetail Falls Trail and extends beyond it. Do not undertake the full hike beyond the formal trail in iffy weather when clouds are down or may blow in, because it is

*The overlook has sweeping views to the head of Blackstone Bay.*

easy to become disoriented up high, even with a map and compass or GPS device. Expensive rescues have been conducted here because people could not find their way. Also, this route is best from midsummer into fall; the area can receive enormous volumes of snow, especially up high, and it takes a good part of the summer to melt.

## DRIVING DIRECTIONS

Search online for "reservoir road whittier ak," or follow these directions. At mile 78.9 of the Seward Highway, at the head of Turnagain Arm, turn east on the Portage Glacier Highway (a.k.a. Portage Glacier Road). In 6.7 miles, queue up for passage through the 2.5-mile Anton Anderson Memorial Tunnel, a one-lane tunnel that alternates traffic direction every half hour and also is a train tunnel. Search "DOT Whittier Tunnel" online for toll and schedule details. Beyond the tunnel, West Camp Road leads into Whittier.

Entering Whittier, just beyond a bridge, turn right on Whittier Street to cross railroad tracks, and follow Whittier Street 0.6 mile through town to its end at Depot Road. Go straight through the intersection onto Blackstone Road, pass the decrepit concrete monolith called the Buckner Building (designed in World War II to withstand bombing), and immediately turn right onto Shotgun Cove Road (not

*Lunch at the top: bread, cheese, jam, and a view (Photo by Gretchen Nelson)*

marked). In 0.2 mile, turn right on Reservoir Road (marked with a brown Horsetail Falls Trail sign but not a road name). In 0.1 mile, a wide area allows for parking, and a gate is visible just beyond.

Note that because the tunnel lets cars into Whittier in batches, it is likely on nice days that multiple cars will arrive at this trailhead at about the same time. Cove Creek Road makes a loop with Reservoir Road, and parking occurs along both roads. The hike begins beyond the rusty yellow gate. Hikers in this area walk in the immediate watershed of Whittier's drinking water supply; go into town to find a restroom if nature calls.

## ON THE ROUTE

From the car (elevation 100 feet), walk around the gate, follow the reservoir access road a short distance, and find the narrower Horsetail Falls Trail (marked) to the right. If you see large European black slugs, feel free to squish this invasive species, and be sure they don't hitch a ride on your gear up the trail or out of Whittier. The formal trail, with narrow boardwalk segments that volunteers are converting to gravel, ends in 0.9 mile at a wooden viewing platform. Horsetail Falls is not formally identified, and the platform is oriented to look over Whittier and across Passage Canal to Billings Glacier. Falls pour off the convoluted terrain above and behind the platform when snowmelt or rainfall is high.

Beyond the platform, this trip may be thought of in terms of three sections: lower, middle, and upper. Across the wooden platform, the lower section continues on an informal but easily followed social trail (push through a couple of hemlock branches); follow it a short distance downhill before the real uphill begins. The trail is worn in by boots. Footing is not easy in some places, and the trail can be muddy in spots, but it offers a no-bushwhack route to the ridge. A half mile and 600 vertical feet beyond the platform, the trail levels at a small tarn nestled in the tundra—a good spot for a breather, and transition to the middle section.

The worn-in trail peters out about here, and the only route indicators beyond may be small cairns placed intermittently. Unless the social trail extends in the future, only those confident in routefinding and retracing their steps should hike beyond the tarn. The route climbs to truly high, rocky, and somewhat featureless country in which it is possible to become disoriented even on fine-weather days. On days when clouds may roll in and obscure what few landmarks exist, even experienced hikers and climbers should not continue. While it is likely that a route will wear in through the tundra beyond the tarn, soon enough there is only rock.

The middle section commences from the tarn, where the view ahead is up a tundra ramp of sorts, punctuated by low rock outcrops. Avoid terrain that drops off to the left of the ramp toward Cove Creek. Proceed up the ramp, watching for cairns and otherwise keeping toward the base of steep slopes that rise up on the right. Eye these steep slopes for signs of a footpath heading up. Cairns should become more evident near the point where the route turns more steeply up. There may be more than one way up, but the route described here is reasonable and has become the most used. It leads up through green tundra; a faint, worn footpath should be visible. The footing can be slippery. Be cautious, especially coming down. At the top of the slope, the route briefly enters a gully that will require a little use of hands. Hikers then emerge on a broad ridge covered in low tundra and follow a faint trail to the left, ever farther uphill.

The tundra ends at a low rocky escarpment 2.4 miles from the trailhead (elevation 2000 feet). To begin the upper section, go right to descend around the end of this little cliff, then back to the left to continue up a steep, loose rocky path that is barely visible. Look back here to capture all possible visual clues to get back to the escarpment. Above,

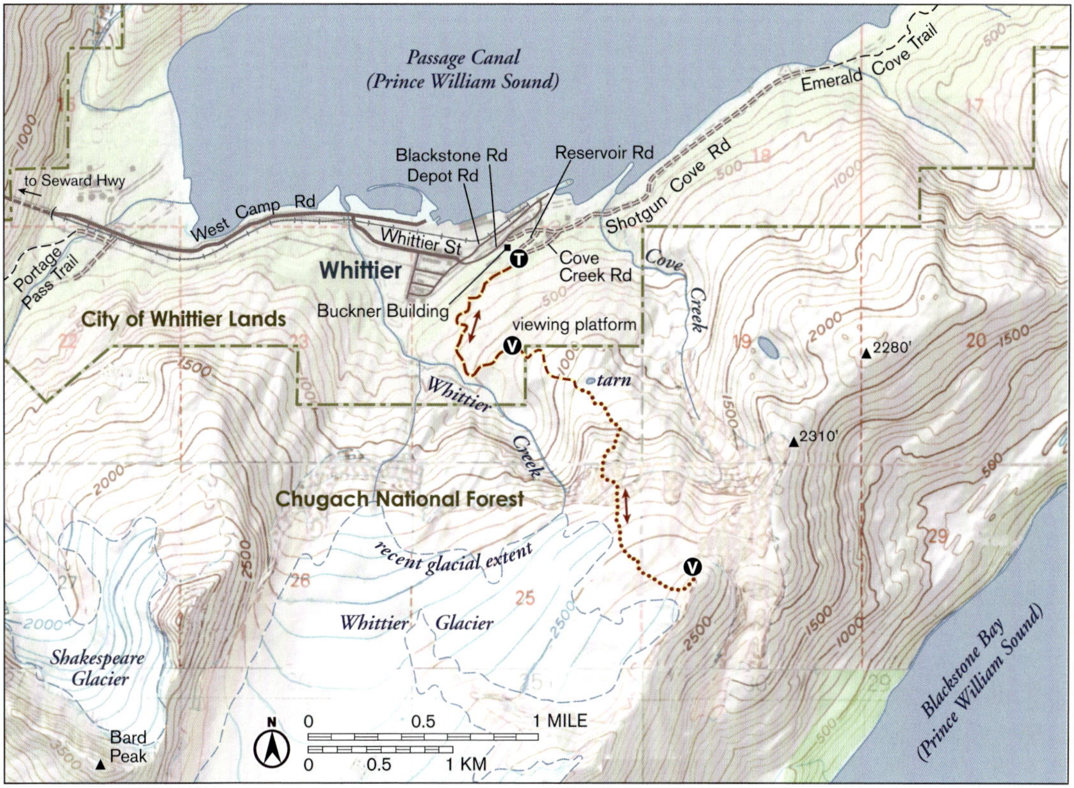

there is no single, obvious route, and it appears few people descend the same way they climbed up. The landscape is vast, endlessly rocky, and generally rounded, so it is not possible to see the destination ridge or easily make out any given path of least resistance. Just clamber upward another 900 vertical feet, erring a bit to the right (south), before arcing back to the left (southeast). By August, when snow has melted, remnants of Whittier Glacier—dead pieces of ice melting away and no longer connected to the rest of the ice sheet—likely will be visible. Earlier in the season, substantial snow persists in this area, and the route will cross angled snowfields; be cautious. Hiking poles or an ice axe and spiky traction devices that slip over your shoes are helpful. After picking through the bedrock outcrops littered with unattached rocks of all sizes, it is a relief finally to ascend to the broad ridge crest, where bits of tundra and tiny flowers reappear and the enormous view of Blackstone Bay opens up.

While the ocean waters you see below are state waters, most of the forest and mountain uplands on the Blackstone Bay side of the ridge are part of the Nellie Juan–College Fiord Wilderness Study Area within Chugach National Forest. Walk a short distance northeast along the ridge to the nearest knob (elevation 2900 feet) for a well-earned snack, and take it all in. The truly ambitious can explore in either direction along the ridge crest and keep the views going for a while.

The routefinding on the descent is just as complicated as it was coming up. Take it slow, look for landmarks, and be willing to backtrack to remain on a comfortable path.

## SHORTER OPTIONS

Hike to the viewing platform (1.8 miles roundtrip, 500 feet elevation gain), or go to the tarn and enjoy the relatively flat tundra meadows (3 miles roundtrip, 1100 feet elevation gain).

OPPOSITE: *Backpackers cross a snow bridge in June near Ship Lake, Trip 27, with Avalanche Mountain beyond.* (Photo by Susan Beesley)

# Anchorage

THE MUNICIPALITY OF ANCHORAGE ENCOMPASSES MUCH MORE THAN THE URBAN-suburban homes of half the state's population: it overlaps almost completely with Chugach State Park and its tundra-covered mountains. Upper Cook Inlet Dena'ina Athabascan people traditionally call this place home, and today Anchorage has the largest Alaska Native population of any community in the state, Native people who hail from all reaches of Alaska. The southern part of the municipality creeps onto the northern edge of the Kenai Peninsula and features some of its flavor in the Girdwood area.

Chugach State Park gets a lot of attention from recreationalists, especially around its edges. While people have walked all the routes and climbed all the peaks, it is still possible, even on a short day hike, to find solitude in this hikers' paradise, with areas forested and alpine, both on-trail and off-trail. Anchorage, as the name implies, has its own coast (and coastal wildlife refuge), which also is worth a visit.

# 21 SKOOKUM GLACIER IN WINTER

**DISTANCE:** 12 miles roundtrip
**TIME:** Full day
**ELEVATION GAIN:** 300 feet
**HIGH POINT:** 250 feet
**SEASON:** February–early May
**SURFACE:** Snow
**GRADE:** Low angle
**INDIGENOUS LAND:** Dena'ina Athabascan
**MANAGING AGENCY:** Chugach National Forest
**MAPS:** USGS Seward C-6 NE, D-6 SE
**ONLINE MAP SEARCH:** "skookum creek ak"
**TRAILHEAD GPS:** 60.819245°N, 148.968480°W

**They say it's not the destination but how you get there that counts. On this substantive ski tour** (sometimes skate skiing, sometimes fat-tire biking), the name "Skookum Glacier" implies it is all about getting to a glacier. And it is. But passage up the Placer River valley and the Skookum Creek valley with Explorer, Byron, and Carpathian Peaks leading skiers on is really the best part of the tour. The succession of ever-steeper, ever-higher summits, combined with other white mountain walls in most directions, creates a circle of splendor, a fine mountain backdrop for a mostly flat tour. The route crosses extensive wetlands—so wet as to be essentially inaccessible in summer. The Skookum Creek valley is isolated by the wetlands, by various drainage channels down low, and by steep, forested mountainsides up higher—except when there is ample snow.

Snow also was the mode for travel on the Iditarod Trail, which followed what is now the route of train tracks (see Iditarod Trail and Alaska Long Trail in the Introduction). The first shipment of gold, more than a half million dollars' worth, left the Iditarod Mining District on dogsleds in December 1911 and passed by here, taking fifty-four days to reach Seward. This part of Chugach National Forest is also open to snowmachines, and on sunny spring-skiing weekends, skiers probably will see and hear them. Mostly, the big country absorbs them.

## DRIVING DIRECTIONS

Drive the Seward Highway to mile 78.9, at the head of Turnagain Arm, and turn east on the Portage Glacier Highway (a.k.a. Portage Glacier Road). Drive 0.3 mile to an electrical substation on the right. This is an informal trailhead; park on the highway shoulder without blocking the substation gate.

## ON THE ROUTE

This is not a marked or groomed trail, but previous skiers will likely have broken trail. The route usually proceeds from the red substation gate or from the highway shoulder just west of the gate. Go around the west side of the substation, picking through a few brush branches to start, and set out generally southward. The route bends a bit to the west toward the railroad tracks before settling into a southerly groove.

This route parallels the tracks at a distance. Trains don't stop easily, and they run over people nationwide every year. Several have died in Alaska. Under no circumstances should people on this route get on and follow the tracks for access.

Nonetheless, the initial part of this route is on Alaska Railroad Corporation (ARRC) property in a 240-acre area set aside for wetland protection (see map). The ARRC is obligated to protect the wetlands here and is highly concerned about safety within the railroad right-of-way proper (100 feet on each side of the tracks). The ARRC cannot encourage skiers and indicated that, technically, people could be cited for trespassing even in the mitigation area. The focus of enforcement is on the tracks. The ARRC also indicated recognition that there are Forest Service facilities and public-use areas on either side of the railroad. Because of other private property, there is no practical way to reach the Skookum Creek valley without crossing the ARRC mitigation land (or crossing the tracks at a right angle; see Alternative Access below). All this is to say, travel far from the tracks, pass through without dallying, and be alert for any change in management that would alter skier access here.

Proceed south, with only a small patch or two of brush to break the ability to kick and glide across wide-open meadows. A few patches of trees and the approaching mountain slopes provide visual variety. Near these slopes, about 2 miles into the tour, the route approaches drainage channels. Conditions are likely to be different every year regarding the freezing of these channels and the cumulative effects of snowfall and wind drifting to cover them. Detouring around these sinuous channels should be possible most of the time.

Another mile, and the route begins to turn the corner into the Skookum Creek valley. Here, about halfway to the glacier, the route passes through an open forest. Snowmachine and skier tracks tend to converge to one to wind through the trees. A set of deep, winding channels draining the north side of the valley presents another potential obstacle. If

*Portions of the trail in Skookum Creek valley pass through an open "ghost forest" of old cottonwood trees.*

you are breaking trail, search for a solid snow bridge to cross just one channel. It may be necessary to climb down and back up to cross the channel. While some snowmachines appear to just hit the gas and jump the chasm, skiers cannot follow their lead, but usually, a route will work out. Some years, conditions may result in no practical way to cross.

In the Skookum Creek valley, the second half of the route passes for a time through meadows and widely spaced cottonwoods—some dead snags and some live. Mountains show continuously through the trees. Enjoy the shadows and light on drifted billows of snow and the brilliance of rimed summits. The grade remains easy until the final half mile; even as the route mounts the final moraine, the grade is only moderate.

The route crests in wide-open terrain with a little elevation, allowing superb views. An exposed ice face visible across a low point makes clear this is, in fact, a glacier. In summer, the lower half of the glacier is mostly gravel covered; likely, it is at its most attractive when buried in snow. The glacier extends almost 5 miles farther up valley, with Carpathian Peak at the head. Skiers have come up only a few hundred feet from sea level; most of the 6000-foot rise of the peak is there before them.

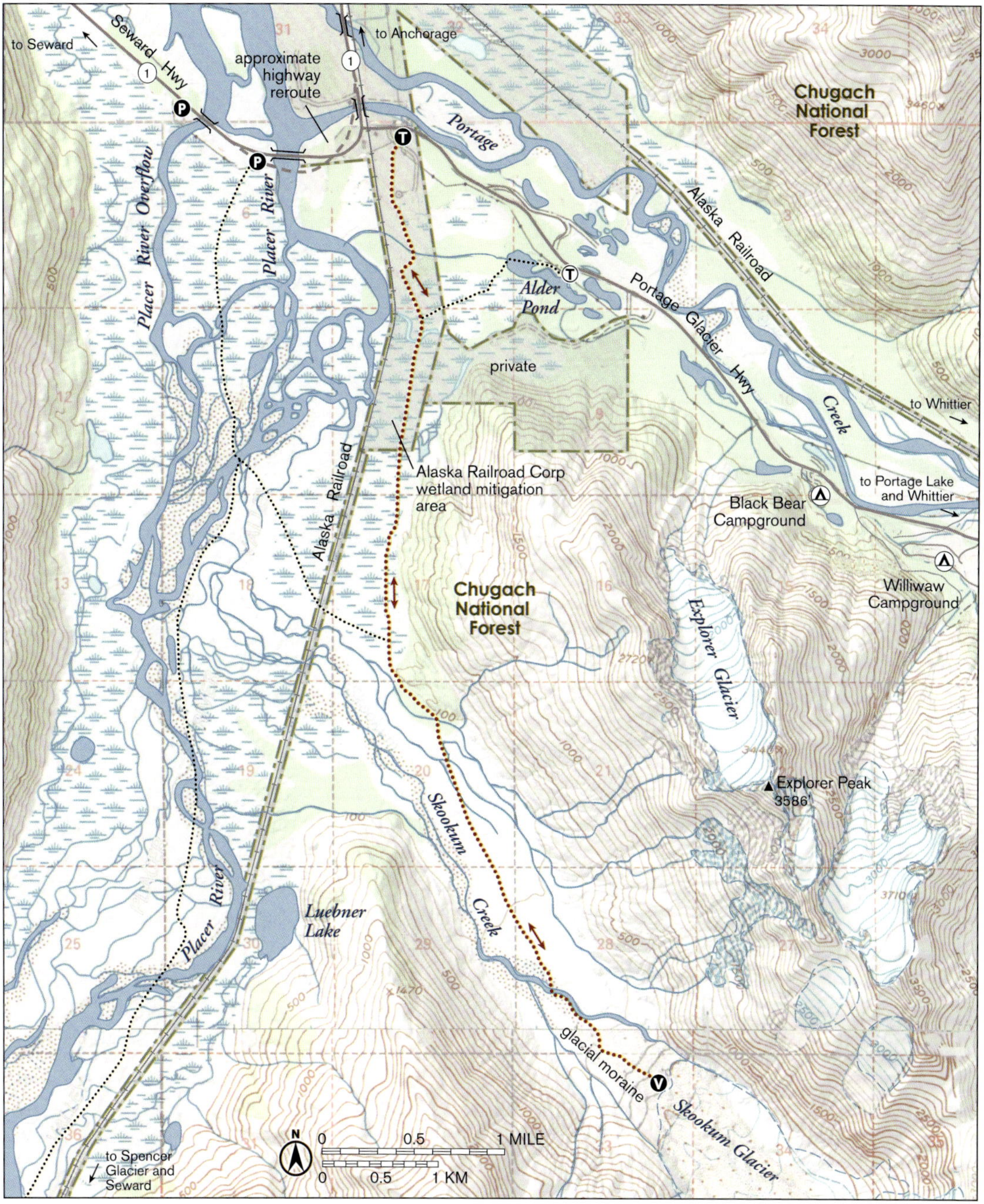
to Seward
Seward Hwy
approximate highway reroute
to Anchorage
Chugach National Forest
Portage
Alaska Railroad
Placer River Overflow
Placer River
Alder Pond
Portage Glacier Hwy
private
Creek
to Whittier
Alaska Railroad Corp wetland mitigation area
to Portage Lake and Whittier
Black Bear Campground
Williwaw Campground
Chugach National Forest
Explorer Glacier
Explorer Peak 3586'
Skookum Creek
Luebner Lake
Placer River
glacial moraine
Skookum Glacier
to Spencer Glacier and Seward
0 0.5 1 MILE
0 0.5 1 KM

Turning the other way, though, it is evident that skiers have come up just enough to gain views back down the length of the valley. The return ski has the subtle advantage of a gravity assist.

## SHORTER OPTIONS

When spring crust is good, a morning of skiing or biking on it is a hoot, even if you do not aim for any particular destination. Good crust days are clear mornings after a good freeze, and on clear days the setting can't be beat. See Alternative Access and Extending Your Trip for other access points and options for skate skiing.

## ALTERNATIVE ACCESS AND EXTENDING YOUR TRIP

To park fully off the highway and start the trip on National Forest land, drive to Alder Pond at mile 1.5 of the Portage Glacier Highway, and use a small spot that usually is plowed. Ski from here west across the pond to its outlet. It is possible to sidestep up a low bank on the south side of the outlet at a thin spot in a band of brush. From there, open skiing through a "ghost forest" of gray trunks leads west and a bit south. Follow previous tracks, or find a route through another band of brush into a treeless, open area and southwest to the route described above, at about the same distance overall. Alternatively, avoid any brush and follow the north side of the Alder Pond drainage more directly west to the route above, adding about 0.2 mile to the roundtrip total. This whole area west and south of Alder Pond has good potential for a smaller ski tour, and for skate skiing when spring crust forms.

The Placer River valley is huge, and it is possible to continue up the main valley to Spencer Glacier, a 21-mile round-trip if you go all the way. Skiers and cyclists often start at pullouts a short distance west of the Portage Glacier Highway—on the west sides of the Placer River Overflow and the Placer River bridges, at Seward Highway mile 77.9 and mile 78.3, respectively. Note that the Seward Highway is undergoing a multiyear construction project, and the big curve at the head of Turnagain Arm will be realigned, approximately as shown on the map. At mile 78.3, recreationalists will pass under the new Placer River bridge to access the valley, and the old highway will function as a driveway. Note that these pullouts are popular with snowmachiners when the area is open to them.

These parking areas provide alternate access for the Skookum Creek valley as well. Ski on National Forest land up the Placer River Valley, then head east, cautiously crossing the railroad tracks without lingering. The ARRC allows nonmotorized traffic to cross the tracks at right angles. On the far side, enter the Skookum side valley.

The trip all the way to Spencer Glacier is reasonable as a day trip only for strong skate skiers and then only when there are good crust conditions. It is reasonable by fat-tire bike when there are solid snowmachine tracks or impeccable crust. When the rivers are adequately frozen, it is possible to ski tour one way to Spencer for a camp-out. The Alaska Huts Association is preparing to build a multiparty hut there, and touring to the hut will make a good outing once it is in place.

In summer, the entire valley is an endless set of wetlands and water channels and is not reasonable for hiking. Spencer is accessible by rail in summer and provides trails, campsites, a Forest Service cabin, and river paddling opportunities. Trip 15 provides information.

# 22 PORTAGE PASS IN WINTER

**DISTANCE:** 7.3 miles roundtrip
**TIME:** Full day
**ELEVATION GAIN:** 480 feet
**HIGH POINT:** 600 feet
**SEASON:** February–April
**SURFACE:** Snow (or ice)
**GRADE:** Low angle, then moderate
**INDIGENOUS LAND:** Dena'ina Athabascan and Chugach Sugpiaq (Alutiiq)
**MANAGING AGENCY:** Chugach National Forest
**MAP:** USGS Seward D-5 SW
**ONLINE MAP SEARCH:** "divide lake ak"
**TRAILHEAD GPS:** 60.783201°N, 148.841091°W

*Trekking across Portage Lake in late winter with views of Bard Peak and Burns Glacier; Portage Pass is near the left edge of this view.* (Photo by Gayle Nienhueser)

**The low point in the mountains between the Kenai Peninsula and the "mainland" is Portage Pass.** On fine late-winter days, people flock across Portage Lake to see Portage Glacier. Relatively few go the short, extra distance to the pass area, which offers a welcome break from the flat expanse of the lake and the feel of a high-peaks ski tour in only 480 feet of elevation gain.

The name is "Portage" because the pass was a route used between the Sugpiaq (Alutiiq) people of Prince William Sound and the Dena'ina people near Cook Inlet for trade and warfare. In historical reports, Old World explorers and early American prospectors recorded crossing miles of glacier instead of miles of lake ice. In 1972 when a previous version of this book was first published, summer hikers from the Whittier side could descend 200 feet from Portage Pass (rather than 600 feet today) and throw rocks at a glacier that loomed above them. The glacier has retreated substantially, leaving a lake some 600 feet deep—hundreds of feet below sea level.

For a body of freshwater located barely 100 feet above the ocean, the setting at Portage Lake feels much higher. Mountain walls of rock and ice rise precipitously from the lake surface, and almost no trees grow along the shore. In winter on the best days, the entire basin is a reflector. Sunlight bounces off the frozen lake surface and back and forth across the valley, backlighting blue shadows with hints of silver. Portage Glacier is big and helps define the high-mountain feel but is visible only from the far end of the lake. The Chugach Mountains meet the Kenai Mountains here, and frequent differences in atmospheric pressure from one side of the mountains to the other can create strong winds. These big blows plume the peaks with windblown crystals, rake and drift the pass area, and can polish the lake ice clean.

Depending on the conditions, the lake could offer passage by ice skates or, with a snowpack, by touring skis, skate skis, snowshoes, boots, or fat-tire bike. This description assumes use of touring skis, but variable conditions make other means better at times. All users should know how to evaluate ice thickness and safety (see Traveling on Ice in the Introduction).

## DRIVING DIRECTIONS

Search online for "begich boggs ak," then see below. Drive to Seward Highway mile 78.8, at the head of Turnagain Arm, and turn east on the Portage Glacier Highway (a.k.a. Portage Glacier Road). This highway goes to Chugach National Forest's primary public facility, the Begich, Boggs Visitor Center, and it goes on through a long tunnel to Whittier. Take an exit to the right at milepost 5 onto Portage Lake Loop toward the visitor center. Drive around the loop counterclockwise 0.6 mile to a parking area overlooking the lake and near the visitor center. Ignore a left turn to a lodge and a right turn for Byron Glacier Road, both closed in winter.

## ON THE ROUTE

Start with a good understanding of recent and forecast weather and likely conditions at the lake. Gather information through wild skating, crust skate skiing, and avalanche center websites (see the Resources section), and search online for a Portage Lake webcam.

If conditions seem right, start on the lakeshore (elevation 120 feet) at the bottom of a curving ramp or set of stairs from the parking lot. In the winter, the ramp and stairs are often buried in snow, with

*People access Portage Glacier by many modes, such as the kicksled shown here. The people in the background could be at risk of icefall.* (Photo by Klara Tamasi)

just handrails showing. To start for the pass, simply ski toward Bard Peak, the prominence punching skyward at the opposite end of the lake.

This routing may diverge from the tracks of others, many of whom aim to see Portage Glacier by the shortest means possible (see Shorter Options). The glacier gawkers' route is slightly to the right, aiming for the Burns Glacier and the jagged creek line that drains it.

Stay away from the lake outlet, lake inlets, or other places where the ice may be thin or damaged. Keep your distance from the potential avalanche and rockfall zones beneath the steep walls along the lake. Get out in the middle where all the mountains are visible and you will likely have more sun. (In darkest midwinter, the mountains mostly block the sun from reaching the surface of the lake.)

To find the pass, proceed across the lake 2.7 miles. Just beyond a prominent, low rock outcrop on the left, a slight rise indicates the shore at the relatively low-angle area draining Divide Lake. The landscape here provides access to the pass without cliffs, but the terrain is rolling in an upward direction. Skiers will need to pick a smart route through this unmarked terrain. No single route is best; the line marked on the map in this

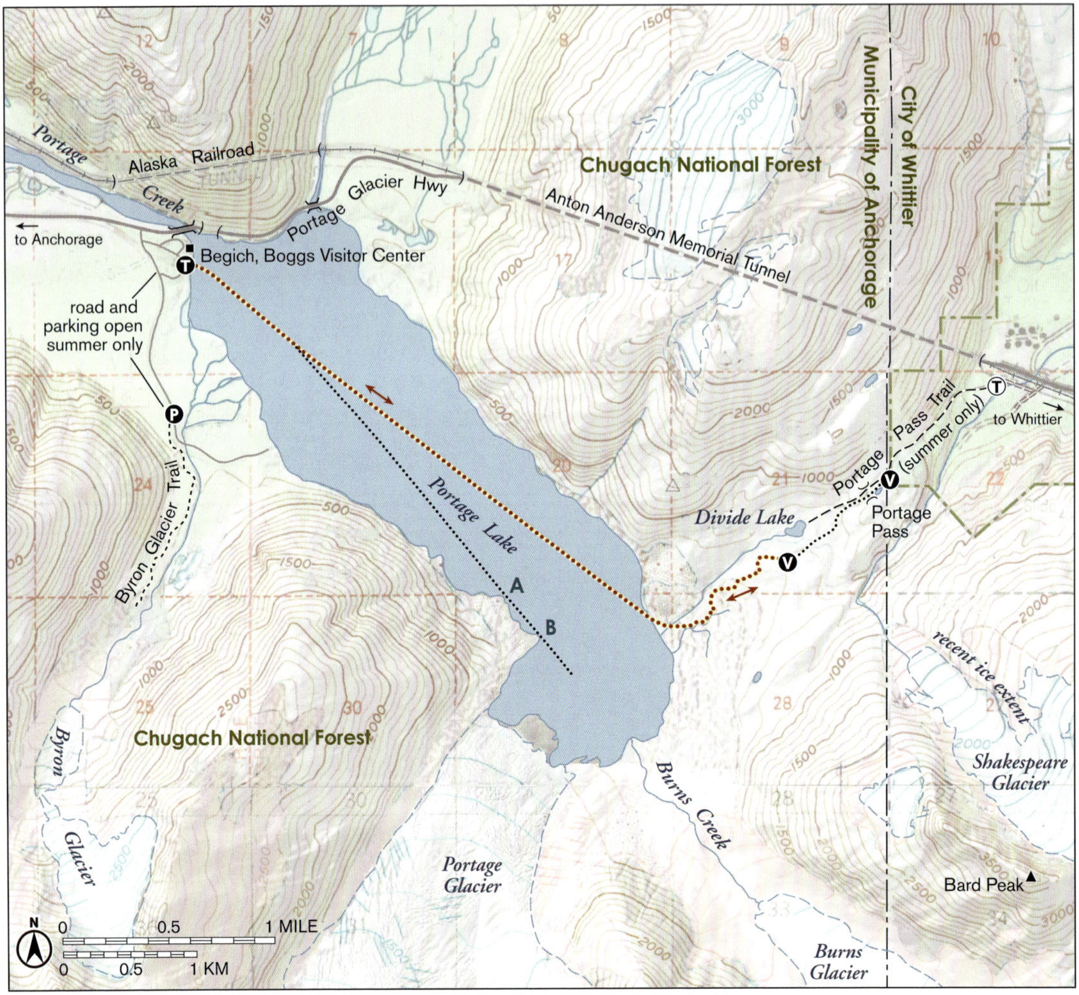


book is probably reasonable in most conditions once a good snowpack is in place to bury brush. The approach to the pass includes short, steep areas where accumulated snow could slide, and some gullies that could be avalanche terrain traps (see Avalanches in the Introduction). For these reasons, it appears unwise to ski directly up the Divide Lake drainage on your left. Instead, look a bit to the right for openings.

The first potential obstacles are the creeks near the lakeshore that can have open water or can create deep channels incised in the snowpack. Pick a route uphill that avoids the need to cross an open channel and that does not force you onto the base of a steep, open slope. You may need to sidestep past a few twigs of brush to get off of lake level and onto the rolling terrain above. Then make looping zigzags uphill, avoiding the widely spaced clumps of trees and brush and aiming for the lower-angle slopes. The terrain is fun, and your route may take you curving around various hills with different microviews in the process.

The route tops out on a little rise at elevation 600 feet, 3.7 miles from the start. This hump overlooks Divide Lake to the north, but the pond is likely to be covered in windblown snow and indiscernible from the surrounding landscape. Across a short stretch of the Divide Lake flats, the crest of the physical divide between Prince William Sound and Turnagain Arm rises just another hundred feet, and from the right angle a far peak pokes up through a gap. Most importantly, this bump overlooks all of Portage Glacier—its full width and length. Compare this to the glacier gawkers' route, which focuses on roughly one-third the full width of the glacier near its northern tip and which loses much of the glacier surface to foreshortening. On good spring crust, skate skiers who don't mind the uphill work can achieve this overlook and then play on the Divide Lake flats, skiing anywhere, taking advantage of the small terrain features, stunted spruce, and other scattered trees as an obstacle course.

Retreat the same way, enjoying the run down but mostly sticking near your up-track to remain on familiar terrain. Back on the lake, detour to the glacier gawkers' route if desired, but see cautions below.

## SHORTER OPTIONS

Plenty of people enjoy shorter visits to the lake for ice skating or skate skiing, depending on conditions. Just doing circles in this steep-walled environment is gratifying.

To ski, hike, fat-bike, or ice skate simply to see the glacier makes a roundtrip of about 5 miles, with no elevation gain. Most people pass close to a couple of small rocky points (A and B on the map), and then turn right when the glacier appears, paralleling the lakeshore toward the northwestern portion of the blue ice face. The best option is to refrain from this turn and not approach the glacier; the view is grand from a little distance.

Consider an account at winterbear.com: A large chunk of ice the full height of the glacier face (60 to 70 feet high at that location) broke off in March 2019 and plunged into the lake. It was a quiet weekday. The author and videographer of the account, reliable outdoorsman Paxson Woelber, reported that his party was on the lake ice a quarter mile from the glacier. The video captures the resulting swells that broke up the lake ice around the people, sending small jets of water up between the cracks and making for an exciting ride. The pans of ice left were large enough to support people for navigation back to the trailhead, but it is an instructive story about the power of the glacier and fragility of "solid" lake ice. The written and photographic account also provides analysis of how much glacial ice fell and photos of the many people who had been at the glacier face the previous weekend. Collapsing glacier ice has killed people nearby at Byron Glacier and at the toe of Exit Glacier (Trip 10).

Distances are hard to gauge on a flat lake surrounded by gargantuan mountain faces. To that end, continuing on a straight course beyond point B toward Burns Creek and Burns Glacier, rather than turning at all toward Portage Glacier, ensures you keep your distance. Is it enough distance to be truly safe? There is no way to know. But staying on that line would put a skier about 0.3 to 0.4 mile from the face of Portage Glacier (as approximated on the accompanying map), not too different from the quarter mile estimated in the winterbear.com account. As long as viewers can still see point A behind point B, they will have at least this separation. And an added benefit is the ability to see the full width of the glacier face instead of focusing solely on the northern portion.

## EXTENDING YOUR TRIP

At the Divide Lake overlook, the notches in the ridge crest to the east will entice some to see over the top to the tiny port town of Whittier on Prince William Sound. To do so adds another 1.4 mile roundtrip from the overlook and 100 feet of elevation gain, for a total roundtrip distance of 8.7 miles. This addition is not included in the recommended route because the final terrain is one step closer to avalanche hazard (see Avalanches in the Introduction). The slopes on either side of the low point are steep enough to avalanche, and the approach to the notch is a bit narrow, which would tend to put skiers who make switchbacks onto the steeper side slopes. It is possible to go straight up to the pass without switchbacks. This extension to the crest is best undertaken only by those educated in avalanche avoidance.

## SEASONAL OPTIONS

In summer, Portage Pass is accessible via a Forest Service trail from the Whittier side. (Going east on the Portage Glacier Highway, exit the Anton Anderson Memorial Tunnel and take the first road to the right, immediately crossing railroad tracks; signs lead a short distance to the Portage Pass trailhead.) The summer trail follows the base of a high, steep slope that presents too much risk to be used in winter. But in summer, to hike up through greenery and salmonberry bushes and be greeted at the top by the ice-white spectacle of the glacier is a treat. At 2 miles roundtrip to the crest area and 4 miles roundtrip to the lake, this hike packs a lot of punch for the effort expended.

Byron Glacier Trail, shown on the map with its parking area, is another short summer excursion amid towering peaks (1.6 miles roundtrip, 100 feet of elevation gain).

# 23 BERRY PASS

**DISTANCE:** 17 miles roundtrip
**TIME:** 2 days
**ELEVATION GAIN:** 1900 feet
**HIGH POINT:** 2000 feet
**SEASON:** June–September
**SURFACE:** Hardpack, water
**GRADE:** Moderate
**INDIGENOUS LAND:** Dena'ina Athabascan
**MANAGING AGENCIES:** Chugach National Forest; Alaska Division of Mining, Land, and Water; Heritage Land Bank (Municipality of Anchorage); and private lease (Alyeska Resort)
**MAPS:** USGS Seward D-6 NE, D-6 NW

**ONLINE MAP SEARCH:** "alyeska ak"
**TRAILHEAD GPS:** 60.969768°N, 149.095174°W

**To crest Berry Pass after 8 miles on the Upper Winner Creek Trail is to enter a new world. The hike** up has its own wonders, rising gradually through big mossy forest, then meadows, and past tumbling streams, but the pass opens the door on a convoluted alpine landscape full of hidey-holes, patches of nodding mountain hemlock, little ponds, and fireweed gardens. And on the other side, rising in counterpoint to the green alpine foreground, is an array of glaciated peaks. You wouldn't know that these are not the highest mountains in Southcentral Alaska. They separate Turnagain Arm from Prince William Sound and jut up high enough to catch all the moist air from the sound, and they wring that moisture out mostly in the form of snow. Glacier-draped year-round, the peaks hold snow late and gather it early. With only patches of trees at Berry Pass, views abound in all directions.

This area has become more popular as people have learned about this trail. Chugach National Forest is in the process of establishing designated backcountry campsites with bear-proof food containers and open-air backcountry toilets in an effort to head off damage to the relatively fragile tundra. This is a great place to practice Leave No Trace principles (see Introduction). Much of this Forest Service trail is on an easement retained when the land around it transferred to the State of Alaska and Municipality of Anchorage.

## DRIVING DIRECTIONS

Search online for "northface road ak," or follow these directions. Drive on the Seward Highway to mile 89.9, and turn toward the mountains on the Alyeska Highway. Follow this road 2.9 miles to a T intersection. Turn left on Arlberg Avenue, and follow it 1.2 miles to the Hotel Alyeska, where there are multiple parking lots on the left. Take the last left turn, for Lot A, on Northface Road (opposite Tram Circle), and park.

Another trailhead, intended principally for Nordic skiing trails (wide gravel paths in summer), also provides access to this trip but has much less parking space. To reach it, proceed to the end of Arlberg Avenue, another 0.3 mile beyond Northface Road. Cyclists trying any of the Winner Creek Trail will want to use this access. See further description below.

## ON THE ROUTE

From the parking lot, make your way along Tram Circle to the actual trailhead for the Winner Creek Trail, beneath the aerial tram. Stepping away from the cleared hotel grounds and ski slopes into the forest is an instant change of scene. This is a stately coniferous forest and a well-maintained Forest Service trail. About a mile along, portions of the neighboring ski trail appear to the left, and there is a marked cross-connection that leads to the alternate trailhead at the very end of Arlberg Avenue. At 1.6 miles, the trail hits a T intersection. Left leads downstream and across Winner Creek (via bridge) and Glacier Creek (via hand-pull tram) and is the commemorative Iditarod Trail, connecting with intermittent trail segments along Crow Creek Road and ultimately with the Crow Pass Trail (Trip 25).

For Berry Pass, however, turn right on the Upper Winner Creek Trail (also the Iditarod Trail) to the headwaters of Winner Creek.

Another mile, and the views begin. There may be options for camping on gravel bars near Winner Creek just after the first real up-valley view (2.6 miles into the trip). The trail pops in and out of trees a few times as it gradually ascends before finally leaving the forest behind. There is good variety as the trail winds through boulders and rocks and crosses several trickles and streams. Some streams have stepping stones, but the chance that you will successfully navigate them while keeping your shoes dry is, well, marginal, depending partly on the water level and partly on your dexterity. With a loaded backpack, it may be best to suck it up and go for wet feet rather than risk slipping. Overall, the trail is a good one, increasing in elevation but often without the grade being strongly evident. There are short, steep stretches, but flatter segments create balance.

The aesthetic appeal of the grand forest gives way to another aesthetic—an open mountain slope with views of the forest below and mountain ridges above. Mixed wildflowers should be good here in July, and wide slopes of fireweed bloom in August. With the pass ahead, the path begins to feel more austere and rocky, but the austerity fades after passing through this brief zone and cresting the pass. This is a friendly pass, padded with tundra that invites a rest. An elf or hobbit might be expected to step out from behind the nearest green hillock.

There are many camping possibilities in the pass area and down the other side on small, flat spots. Use Forest Service designated sites, to be established soon,

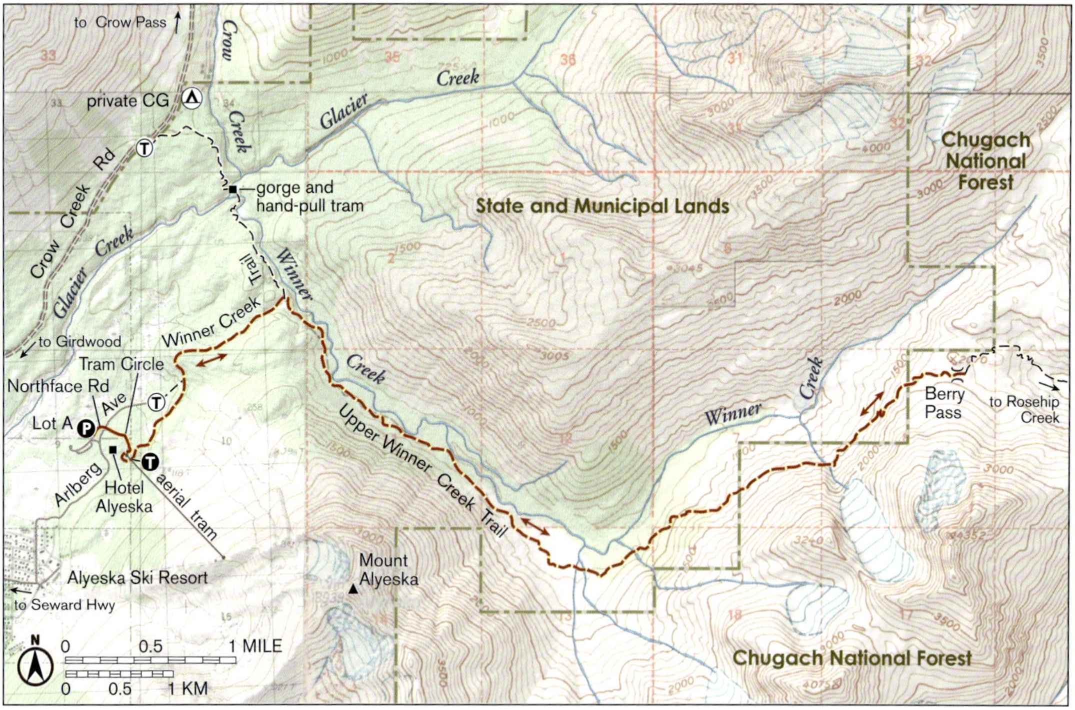

*A tent with a view* (Photo by Gretchen Nelson)

as the first choice to help concentrate impact and preserve the alpine environment. For after-dinner excursions from camp, you could explore a short way either north or south, with the southern direction leading quickly uphill toward high bowls with remnant glaciers—and the promise of ever-better views. Northward is more mellow but has its own interesting new views, reflecting ponds, and the potential for an overlook into the upper Twentymile River valley.

Some mountain bikers use this trail, as do mountain runners and packrafters. This trail is not a good choice in winter because it crosses slopes steep enough to avalanche, and it does not get sunshine. For many cyclists, the climbing on this trail will be difficult, and the downhill poses substantial potential for conflict with hikers, so biking is not highly recommended.

## SHORTER OPTION

The Winner Creek gorge and the Glacier Creek tram make a fun day hike. Follow the trail 1.6 miles to the T intersection, and go left instead of right. It is an additional mile to the Winner Creek gorge, where there is a spray-in-your-face bridge. Across the bridge only a few minutes farther is the canyon of Glacier Creek and a hand-pull tram. It is a 5.5-mile round-trip to take in the tram views and return to the trailhead. Across the gorge, it is possible to connect with Crow Creek Road (mile 2.8) and segments of the continuing Iditarod Trail there.

### EXTENDING YOUR TRIP

The trail from the pass continues approximately 3 miles farther, downhill to Rosehip Creek where it dead-ends for the time being. This is an obvious way to extend your trip. The Forest Service plans to extend the commemorative Iditarod Trail into the Twentymile River valley and to the Seward Highway, likely near highway mile 82 (a total extension of some 15 miles). See Iditarod Trail and Alaska Long Trail in the Introduction. Until the segment is complete, explore the trail toward Rosehip Creek as far as curiosity and fine views take you.

This trail is known as part of a day-trip packrafting loop, starting with the hike over the pass and down to Rosehip Creek, and then bushwhacking to Twentymile River. After inflating a lightweight raft, the trip continues on the water downstream through the vast river marshlands beneath those big peaks to the Seward Highway. It sounds idyllic, and it can be for those who are fit, experienced, and truly prepared. The Forest Service reports that people have seriously underestimated this excursion, and some have needed to be rescued. It is best to packraft with experienced company on summer days with the longest daylight.

## 24 CALIFORNIA CREEK

**DISTANCE:** 7 miles point to point
**TIME:** Full day
**ELEVATION GAIN:** 1450 feet
**HIGH POINT:** 980 feet
**SEASON:** June–early October
**SURFACE:** Hardpack, roots
**GRADE:** Rolling
**INDIGENOUS LAND:** Dena'ina Athabascan
**MANAGING AGENCIES:** Chugach National Forest, Chugach State Park, and Heritage Land Bank (Municipality of Anchorage)
**MAP:** USGS Seward D-6 NW
**ONLINE MAP SEARCH:** "california creek ak"
**TRAILHEAD GPS:** Toadstool Drive 60.945409°N, 149.177880°W
Crow Creek Road 60.967795°N, 149.135239°W

**Many Alaska hikes reach for the stars. They climb steeply, seeking open tundra and ridgetop** vistas. They enter the zone of clouds, wind, and snow associated with the peaks. Few are gentle, sun-dappled, woodsy walks like this California Creek trek near Girdwood. This rainforest walk is perfect for chatting with friends, observing forest details—spruce needles, fungi, bark, leaves, and mosses—and hearing the burbles and cascades of small streams.

But make no mistake: if you prefer steepness, extensions of this modest trip will test your lungs and legs. The featured route combines three separate trails—the Beaver Pond Trail, Abe's Trail, and California Creek Trail—to make a big zig-zagging, point-to-point hike that allows hikers to poke their heads out of the forest for a brief sniff of alpine air at the edge of the forest. If arranging a car shuttle is a pain, you can mix and match the trails for a short or long out-and-back trip.

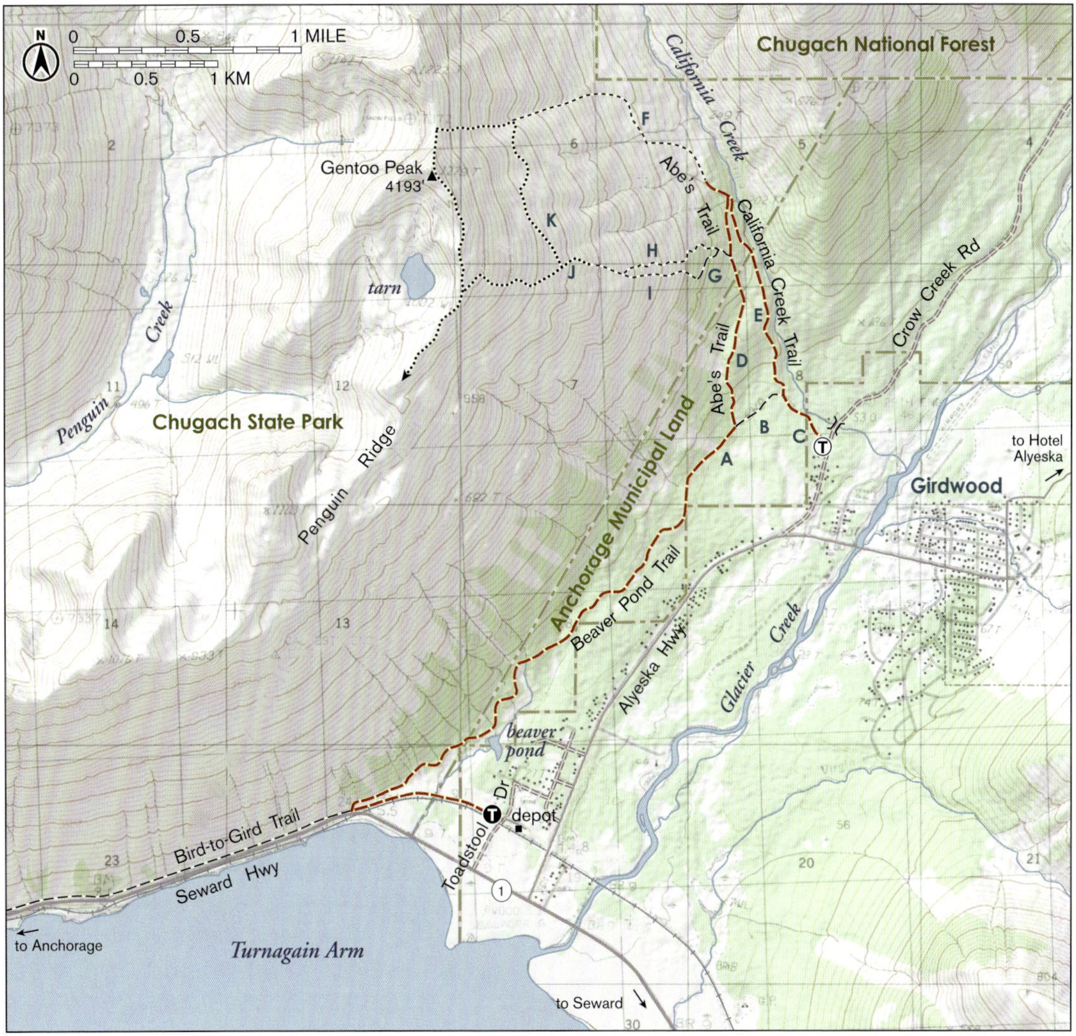

*Evening sun and a good trail surface on the Beaver Pond Trail*

## DRIVING DIRECTIONS

Undertaken as described, this route requires a car shuttle. Out-and-back options are also possible.

**Toadstool Drive trailhead.** Search online for "girdwood depot ak," or follow these directions. On the Seward Highway, drive to milepost 90.2, and turn inland on Toadstool Drive. If you are heading southbound (from Anchorage), watch for a left in the middle of an expansive, grassy salt marsh. It occurs immediately before a Welcome to Girdwood sign. Look also for a sign indicating the Girdwood railroad depot. If you are heading northbound, watch for the first right past the Alyeska Highway junction. Drive 0.2 mile on Toadstool Drive, crossing railroad tracks. The tiny Girdwood depot is to the right; park to the left without blocking a driveway or the paved Bird-to-Gird bike path. Parking is limited here; if necessary, park on wide spots along Toadstool Drive.

**Crow Creek Road trailhead.** From Seward Highway mile 89.9, turn onto Alyeska Highway, and follow it 1.9 miles. As the highway bends to the right, turn left on Crow Creek Road. Follow this paved road 0.4 mile, and park at the bridge over California Creek; there is a small pullout on each side of the road. On the left side, an almost invisible sign on a guardrail post marks the Beaver Pond Trail. Just around the corner up the trail is a much larger, handsome trailhead sign with good information about the trails and area history. Respect private property abutting the trailhead.

## ON THE ROUTE

This description runs south to north. Either direction works. Refer to the map: the trip follows segments A, D, E, and C. Start from the Girdwood depot area, and walk west on the paved path into the salt marsh. This paved section is a half-mile long and should be considered an integral part of the hike, not a prelude to the "real" hike. It provides the best mountain views of the trip and is a distinctly different experience than the rainforest. The marsh attracts waterfowl and raptors and is full of history. The 1964 Great Alaska Earthquake, the second largest ever recorded, dropped the land in this area some 8 feet, inundating a coastal forest and some buildings with salt water at high tide. Most of the rail-side town of Girdwood relocated 2 miles inland. Dead spruce still stand in this marsh, a "ghost forest." This paved trail also parallels the train track, which in this area is the route of the Iditarod Trail (see Iditarod Trail and Alaska Long Trail in the Introduction).

After half a mile, the paved path pinches up against the mountainside. This is the base of Penguin Ridge, and the top is some 4000 feet above. At a wayside with benches and scopes, look for a Beaver Pond Trail signpost, and turn right on a narrow dirt path. The scene quickly changes from one of relatively open marshland to enclosed forest, with enormous Sitka spruce and cottonwood trees. Intermittent views of the marsh and mountains continue, but ultimately the quiet of the forest dominates.

The trees are primarily evergreen—hemlock, with the soft needles and droopy treetops, and two or more kinds of spruce, with sharper, stiffer needles and upright tops. Moss is cast over the forest floor like a rumpled blanket, covering old stumps and logs. The understory is sometimes open, with relatively little growing besides the mosses, and sometimes it is a sea of devil's club, some of them 10 feet tall. Thankfully, maintenance includes trimming.

For a trail implied to be mostly level, as it runs along the base of the mountain, the Beaver Pond Trail has surprising topography. The route rises and falls in short bursts as it twists through the forest and the ancient glacial landscape. This makes it interesting for hikers and fun for mountain bikers, although a multitude of big roots in some places will be a turnoff for many cyclists.

At 1.5 miles from the car, the namesake beaver pond appears, complete with an old beaver dam. At 3.6 miles in, a signpost marks the junction with Abe's Trail. On the way, look for rotting old stumps that have new young trees growing out of them. Notice that some of the biggest, oldest trees have grown thick roots like octopus tentacles that hold the entire tree up out of the ground. It is possible to see daylight beneath some trees. It appears these are places where ancient stumps, once underneath, have finally rotted away entirely. The resilience and succession of the forest is a wonder.

Turn left on Abe's Trail (segment D), which climbs as it wraps around a broad corner in the mountainside terrain and enters the California Creek valley. In this area, a maze of constructed and social trails occurs (see Extending Your Trip). Stay alert for an unmarked fork in the path 0.8 mile along Abe's Trail. The left fork reportedly is a bootlegged mountain bike trail (Segment G) built with real effort but not official authorization. It likely will look like the more-used trail, and it would be easy to pass the continuing Abe's Trail without thinking much of it. However, for this trip, take the right turn to stay on Abe's Trail. The continuing Abe's Trail quickly levels out (in contrast to the mountain bike trail, which climbs through a graceful S turn). Within a quarter mile of this fork, a tiny but formal sign tacked to a tree marks a connection to the California Creek Trail. This crossover is only a couple hundred feet long and is a way to shorten the trip by about 0.8 mile. To persevere to the upper edge of the forest, continue straight and then shortly downhill nearly 100 vertical feet, crossing two streams in close succession. Keep boots dry by hopping carefully.

Immediately beyond the second creek, at the top of a rise, Abe's Trail intersects the upper terminus of the California Creek Trail. There is no sign marking this intersection. Continue uphill on Abe's Trail. From the intersection, it is 0.3 mile and less than 200 vertical feet to the edge of the forest, a small tall-grass meadow, and a chance to see mountains that the big trees mostly have been hiding. This is the recommended turnaround point.

When ready, retreat downhill to the California Creek Trail junction, and take that trail (segment E) instead of Abe's Trail, roughly following the bluff above the creek. California Creek is of moderate size, with a steep gradient, and the sounds of splash and rush accompany hikers. The first part of this descent has a few wet spots, generally avoidable with judicious step placement and small hops. There is a place or two where the trail splits and comes back together, and a few spots where side paths have developed, apparently to get a closer look at the creek. Overall, the main path is easy to follow. It is 1.2 miles back to the Beaver Pond Trail (marked).

For the Crow Creek Road trailhead, turn left (onto segment C), and reach the trailhead in a quarter mile.

## SHORTER OPTIONS

A trip from the Crow Creek Road trailhead using segments C, B, D, E, and back to C makes a nice loop of 3.7 miles (cumulative elevation gain 1180 feet). The Beaver Pond Trail in its entirety from one trailhead to the other (segments A, B, and C) avoids the additional elevation gains of the D and E segments and amounts to 4.1 miles. From north to south, it is downhill overall with minimal intervening elevation gain. Mountain bikers may want to ride the trails one direction and follow the road back to the start to make a loop.

## EXTENDING YOUR TRIP

An out-and-back loop from the Toadstool Drive trailhead, using segments A, D, E, B, and back to A, makes a nice long leg stretcher: 10.4 miles, with 1800 feet of cumulative elevation gain.

Otherwise, the Crow Creek Road trailhead is the launch point for uphill extensions for those who want to bust out of the trees and bust a gut going for those high-alpine views, including those undertaking the full Penguin Ridge traverse. The traverse is a 16-mile ridge "walk" with some 9000 feet of elevation gain over multiple summits. It has a sketchy scramble or two. See Trip 26 for access to the other end of the traverse.

The maze of paths partway along Abe's Trail appears to be the result of construction of the mountain bike trail (segment G) and the result of mountain runners coming and going from the Penguin Ridge traverse (segments F, H, I, and J).

The mountain bike trail is a constructed trail and easy to follow to its sudden terminus. The others are worn in by use. Segment F, the extension of Abe's Trail, is the traditional route to the ridge. Beyond the hemlock forest, it passes through a half-mile alder zone with wet and muddy portions, but the trail has been there for years and is well defined until high in the alpine zone. At that point, it follows a logical line very steeply up a gully to hit the ridge at a col north of Gentoo Peak.

Segments H and I are also as steep as they come and were created by foot traffic only. Both routes work, though neither is great; both involve ducking through alders. Segment I has an ill-defined lower end at the terminus of the mountain bike trail, where there is a giant log to scramble over.

Segment J is above the alders and becomes an overland route without definition as it leaves the last little patches of stunted mountain hemlock. It is likely the social trail will extend uphill over time. From the base of segment J, proceed upward 660 vertical feet to a small topographic bench area and beyond, nearly another 1000 vertical feet, erring somewhat left of directly up. Pass through the upper ends of shallow gullies. As the footing becomes rockier, the overall angle eases, and it is possible to believe the crest ahead may be the actual ridgetop. A shining tarn dominates the view on the other side.

Segment K makes a decent high loop. There is no trail, but it is possible to traverse from segment J at the general elevation of the topographic bench (2750 to 2900 feet) to segment F.

Descending from the ridge for people completing the entire Penguin Ridge traverse apparently is an issue. Traversers often start at Penguin Peak (see Trip 26) and may never have seen the California Creek end. People may be tired and running out of daylight. They see Girdwood below and are tempted to dive off the ridge too early. The traditional and safest descent takes place *after* summiting Gentoo Peak: descend to the col north of the peak and then down the gully (segment F) to pick up Abe's Trail.

The development of the H and I routes opens the possibility of legitimately leaving the ridge early (but not too early!). Pass through the low point on the ridge south of Gentoo Peak, and ascend northward along the ridge until directly east of the tarn. The ridge flattens and creates a sort of off-ramp to the right (east) at about 3700 feet elevation. Leave the ridge crest, traverse out a ways, and then start dropping, reversing the directions above. From the elevation of the topographic bench, flagging may come into view below, tied on the first mountain hemlock branches. Continue down and slightly left between small hemlock patches, and pick up a faint foot trail that drops straight down the outer convexity of the mountainside. Going too far left leads into a gully. Before the trail drops over an edge onto steeper terrain, with a last visible patch of hemlock ahead on the right, segment H diverges to the left. It could be difficult to see in tall grass, and the divergence point could change year to year. Segment I proceeds directly down over the crest and into the alders. Early exit of Penguin Ridge is not recommended if clouds are down on the ridge, as navigating to a visible path may be impossible.

Climbing up any of these routes to the alpine zone leads to grand views of the Girdwood valley, Mount Alyeska, and the big peaks beyond. Hitting the ridge or Gentoo Peak (about 5.6 miles roundtrip) means views of upper Penguin Creek and the tarn. Any of these is a worthy goal that, while very ambitious by most standards, is much more attainable than the entire Penguin Ridge traverse. But, of course, the Penguin beckons.

# 25 CROW PASS TO EAGLE RIVER TRAVERSE

**DISTANCE:** 23 miles point to point

**TIME:** 2–3 days

**ELEVATION GAIN:** 2800 feet northbound, 3400 feet southbound

**HIGH POINT:** 3550 feet

**SEASON:** Mid-June–September
**SURFACE:** Hardpack, roots, water
**GRADE:** Moderate
**INDIGENOUS LAND:** Dena'ina Athabascan
**MANAGING AGENCIES:** Chugach National Forest and Chugach State Park
**MAPS:** USGS Anchorage A-6, A-7
**ONLINE MAP SEARCH:** "crow pass ak"
**TRAILHEAD GPS:** Crow Pass 61.028203°N, 149.116217°W
Eagle River Nature Center 61.234017°N, 149.270939°W

**This hike, over Crow Pass and down upper Eagle River Valley, is the Anchorage area's classic** long trail. It offers gold mine relics, glaciers, enormous peaks, wildflowers, and a serious back-country river ford. Experienced hikers can follow the description below for a two- or three-day point-to-point trip to the Eagle River Nature Center (see Shorter Options for alternatives).

In the early 1900s, the trail over Crow Pass was part of the winter sled trail through the mountains between Turnagain Arm and Knik Arm, en route from Seward to Knik, and thence to Interior goldfields. Today it is a segment of the Iditarod National Historic Trail. Early trail users took pack animals as well as dogsleds over this route, using it alternately with the Indian Valley Trail (Trip 27). Steady use of both trails ended in the early 1920s with regular rail service between Seward and Fairbanks and took off again with recreational use in the 1970s (see Iditarod Trail and Alaska Long Trail in the Introduction).

Today, this is a well-traveled hike popular on long weekends. During the annual Crow Pass Crossing mountain run in July, top athletes manage the trail in three to five hours, despite its obstacles. Described here from south to north, the trail works equally well in either direction. Each end of the trail makes a fine day hike—the Crow Pass Trail to a popular alpine area where there is a Forest Service cabin available for rent in summer (reserveamerica.com), or the Eagle River end to a big river carved through precipitous mountain walls.

## DRIVING DIRECTIONS

Completing the traverse requires a car shuttle. It is 70 miles between trailheads by car. Out-and-back options are good at each end as well.

**Crow Pass trailhead.** Search online for "crow pass trailhead ak," or follow these directions. From Seward Highway mile 89.9, turn onto Alyeska Highway, and follow it 1.9 miles. As the highway bends to the right, turn left on Crow Creek Road. Follow this road, which becomes a minimally maintained gravel road, 5 miles to a bridge. Beyond the bridge, go uphill another mile to the road's end at the trailhead parking area. The trail begins at the far end. On nice-weather days, be sure to park tightly to ensure maximum occupancy; the lot is limited. There is no fee.

**Eagle River Nature Center trailhead.** Search online for "eagle river nature center ak," or follow these directions. Take the Eagle River Loop Road/Hiland Road exit off the Glenn Highway (1.8 miles

*In this reenactment of the cover photo from a previous version of this book, hikers approach Crow Pass from Raven Glacier.* (Photo by Anne Raup)

south of the Eagle River exit, or 7 miles from Muldoon Road in Anchorage). Turn toward the mountains onto E. Eagle River Loop Road. Continue 2.6 miles until the highway crosses Eagle River and comes to a major intersection at Eagle River Road, adjacent to Walmart. Turn right, and proceed 10.8 miles to the road's end at the Eagle River Nature Center. Expect to pay a fee for parking, or buy an annual membership for the nature center; parking here is not included in the state parks annual pass.

## ON THE ROUTE

From the Forest Service's Crow Pass trailhead (elevation 1550 feet), follow an old mining track on foot through switchbacks to brush line. As the trail nears 2500 feet elevation, at 1.7 miles from the parking area, the trail forks (marked). The left-hand fork leads quickly to the ruins of Monarch Mine. Monarch was a hard-rock gold mine that operated from 1906 to 1948. The side trail passes what remains of a mill; above in the cliffs were mine adits. Maintaining elevation, you can walk a path behind the mine ruins into the beautiful canyon through which Crow Creek cascades. Stay on the trails to help prevent erosion and for safety; people have fallen scrambling off the path here. Note that this is not a great place to linger (including sitting to rest or camping), because the Forest Service has determined that

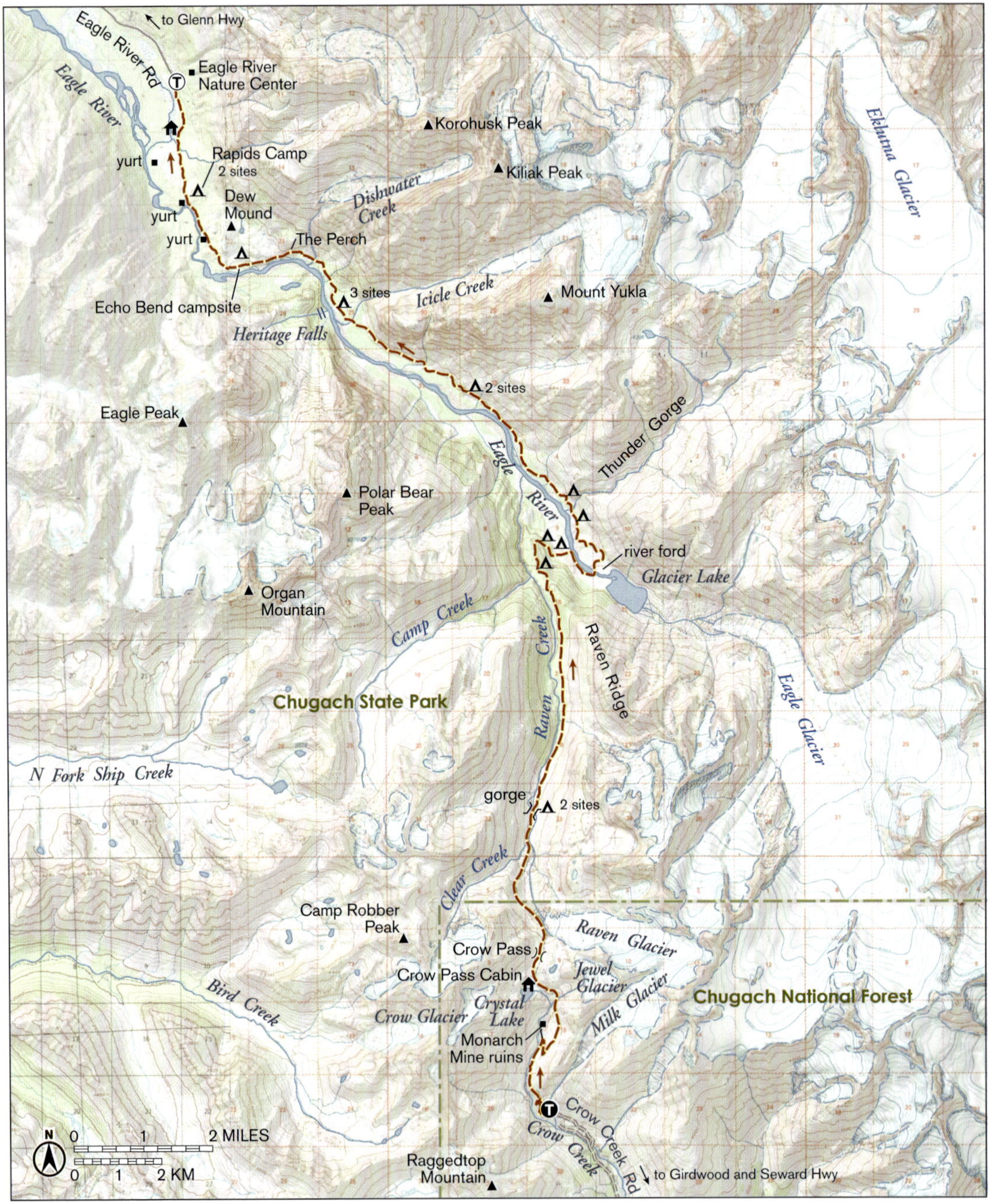

to Glenn Hwy
Eagle River Rd
Eagle River Nature Center
Eagle River
Korohusk Peak
Eklutna Glacier
yurt
Rapids Camp
2 sites
Kiliak Peak
Dishwater Creek
Dew Mound
yurt
yurt
The Perch
Icicle Creek
Mount Yukla
3 sites
Echo Bend campsite
Heritage Falls
2 sites
Eagle Peak
Thunder Gorge
Eagle River
Polar Bear Peak
river ford
Glacier Lake
Organ Mountain
Camp Creek
Raven Creek
Raven Ridge
Chugach State Park
Eagle Glacier
N Fork Ship Creek
gorge
2 sites
Clear Creek
Camp Robber Peak
Raven Glacier
Crow Pass
Jewel Glacier
Crow Pass Cabin
Chugach National Forest
Crystal Lake
Milk Glacier
Bird Creek
Crow Glacier
Monarch Mine ruins
Crow Creek Rd
Crow Creek
0 1 2 MILES
0 1 2 KM
N
Raggedtop Mountain
to Girdwood and Seward Hwy

chemical contamination from the mine remains in the soil and likely in the water.

For the main route to Crow Pass, take the right fork (a switchback) shortly before the mine ruins. Dall sheep are common in the Chugach Mountains near Anchorage, but the trail to the pass is one of the few places where hikers have a good chance of seeing mountain goats. Tell the difference by looking at their coats: sheep tend to look trimmed; goats appear a bit yellower and shaggier. Also, while male Dall sheep horns can curl into a full circle, goat horns stay spiky.

At mile 3, Crow Pass Cabin comes into view. People are not allowed to stay in the cabin during winter and early spring because of avalanche danger on the route up; see Avalanches in the Introduction. The cabin sits near Crystal Lake (elevation 3450 feet), which nestles beneath a steep mountain wall in a rim of wildflowers. This is a splendid destination. For through-hikers, the relatively level ground means the downhill part of the traverse is not far off. Raven Glacier, about a mile farther on, is visible from Crow Pass proper (elevation 3550 feet). Rock cairns provide route direction through the pass where the now-rocky ground does not leave a clear trail impression.

Camping spots abound in the pass area, although snow often persists well into June. Water is available. Campfires are not permitted. Snow showers and strong winds are possible any time of the year, so take warm clothes even on fine summer days.

To continue, follow the trail and giant cairns from the Raven Glacier overlook downhill, passing from Chugach National Forest to Chugach State Park. Note that the park consciously manages its portion of the trail as "primitive." Expect wet feet at Clear Creek, except in the early hiking season when it is possible to cross on a snow bridge. Then cross Raven Creek on a bridge over a gorge. Note the natural stone arch and waterfall. From this point to the Eagle River Nature Center, hikers often sight black bears (see Bears and Other Wildlife in the Introduction).

As the trail loses elevation, the vegetation grows taller. An ocean of fireweed blooms after midsummer to jazz up the color palette, but the profusion of tall vegetation can make it hard to see obstacles in the trail. Where the trail follows the crest of Raven Ridge, there is a view of Eagle Glacier and the area marked for fording Eagle River.

On the river flats, the trail heads up Eagle River Valley toward the glacier to a good river crossing area (elevation 850 feet), which is well marked, half a mile downstream from Glacier Lake. Practice crossing streams before taking on this swift glacial river (see Stream Crossings in the Introduction). Expect at least knee-deep water; people sometimes report hip-deep conditions. Heavy rain and hot days with high glacial melt will cause the water level to rise; if the river is too high to cross safely, camp and wait. Consider preplanning an overnight so as to cross in the morning, when water levels may be lower. It is rare that the river is too high to ford, but people sometimes report the crossing as a challenge. The river crossing is reason to consider not taking a dog.

From the ford, the trail generally parallels the river, passing Thunder Gorge in about a mile. This area can be confusing, with multiple routes that change year to year. All routes ultimately lead the same way, but minor backtracking is to be expected. Commonly, two-day hikers camp at sites near the river ford or Thunder Gorge. From the river crossing, it is about 13 miles to the Eagle River Nature Center. The mountain walls make a fine backdrop along this stretch of trail. Eagle Peak, Polar Bear Peak, and Mount Yukla rise overhead to 7500 feet and are among the most impressive peaks to be found along a trail in Southcentral Alaska. The path through the

*The upper Eagle River portion of the trail is typically surrounded by lush, tall vegetation in July and August.* (Photo by Nikki Navio)

upper valley is narrow and has tricky footing hidden by tall grass. Grades are mostly easy, but the trail along the river is subject to flooding, erosion, and informal rerouting. Hikers should be prepared to navigate around the obstacles nature may present. In one area, the route climbs a short ladder. Rope handholds also occur. Several designated campsites appear along the way (see map). Take a stove for cooking; campfires are permitted only in metal firepits located at some campsites or on the gravel bars of upper Eagle River. Store food safely. Carrying bear-proof canisters is a good idea.

Heritage Falls is visible across the river near Icicle Creek. About 4 miles from the end, the trail takes a high route above the river and descends to a rock outcrop known as The Perch, with a fine view back up the valley. The nature center manages three reservable yurts and a cabin between Echo Bend and the nature center (all within 2 miles of the trailhead; visit ernc.org to reserve). The trail surface continually improves toward the nature center, until a wide gravel path leads through open forest and up the final grade to the trail's end (elevation 500 feet).

If hiking the opposite direction, the first mile or so presents several trail intersections. Follow signs for Crow Pass or the Iditarod Trail. The entire trail is closed to off-road vehicles, including snowmachines. The state park section of the trail is closed to horses and bicycles year-round. The portion in Chugach National Forest is closed to horses from April 1 to June 30 and is too steep to be practical for mountain bikes. Target shooting is prohibited. Contact Chugach State Park for current trail information (see the Resources section).

## SHORTER OPTIONS

The walk to The Perch from the Eagle River end of the trail is an easy introduction to Eagle River Valley. The trailhead is arguably the most spectacular part of the park accessible by car. The walk is on a mostly level trail through a wooded canyon with 6500-foot mountain walls shooting skyward all around. The Perch has great views of Mount Yukla. The trip is 8 miles roundtrip, with 300 feet of elevation gain. A trip to Echo Bend campsite (6.8 miles roundtrip) or Rapids Camp (4 miles roundtrip) is shorter and might be particularly good for families. These outings are good anytime but are especially welcome in early spring or late fall when other hikes are closed by snow. The nature center trail system also includes the Albert Loop Trail, which makes a 3-mile loop partly along river bars, and the Dew Mound Trail, which makes several cross-connections to the Iditarod Trail for loops of various lengths. Check the nature center and park websites.

From the Crow Creek trailhead, Crystal Lake and Crow Pass make a perfect day hike or out-and-back overnight (6 to 7 miles roundtrip, 2100 feet elevation gain). Side trips from the pass include Jewel Glacier to the east and Crow Glacier to the west.

## SEASONAL OPTIONS

In winter, skiing the northern leg of the Albert Loop Trail to the river and then skiing upstream provides open views of the towering mountains. Note, however, that the big peaks cut the sun off entirely for about two months in midwinter, and even in March and April, the sun sets much earlier than in Anchorage. When trail and ice conditions are just right, fat-tire biking or skate skiing on the river is good. The trails are closed to horses, bicycles, and vehicles, except that snowmachines are allowed on the northern Albert Loop Trail access route and downriver from there.

# 26 PENGUIN PEAK

**DISTANCE:** 7.8 miles roundtrip
**TIME:** Full day
**ELEVATION GAIN:** 4280 feet
**HIGH POINT:** 4335 feet
**SEASON:** June–September
**SURFACE:** Hardpack, tundra, rock
**GRADE:** Sustained steep
**INDIGENOUS LAND:** Dena'ina Athabascan
**MANAGING AGENCY:** Chugach State Park, Bird Creek Regional Park
**MAP:** USGS Seward D-7 NE

**ONLINE MAP SEARCH:** "bird creek ak"
**TRAILHEAD GPS:** 60.974020°N, 149.433443°W

**Penguin Ridge is the "other Bird Ridge" and lies east across the Bird Creek valley from its** better-known cousin. The "birds" in the Bird Creek area perhaps started with "crows" at Crow Pass. Around that pass are Raven and Eagle Glaciers, and nearby are Magpie, Camp Robber, and Bird Peaks. These are more or less accepted Alaska birds. How penguins got into the mix is anybody's guess, but you've got to hand it to the early members of the Mountaineering Club of Alaska (MCA)—they used those times when hikers zone out, with their heads down and legs churning, to riff on a good theme and add interesting peak names.

Penguin Peak, the first and highest in a string of penguin-y summits on a long ridge, is one of those steady climbs that provide space for freewheeling thoughts. The route starts in a sea-level forest and passes more than 4000 vertical feet through all the climate and vegetation zones to rocky ridge crests up where the birds soar—although it is unlikely you will see soaring penguins. Hikers are also likely to see fewer people than on the popular Bird Ridge Trail across the valley, but the high-country views to the silver waters of Turnagain Arm and the inner peaks of the Chugach Mountains are just as good. The summit is higher, rockier, and more summit-like without being more complicated.

This hike is notable, too, because the idea for Chugach State Park started on a logging road in the Bird Creek valley. In May 1969, an MCA hike attended by dozens of people celebrated a citizen initiative to prevent further logging in Bird Creek and Indian Creek valleys and brought attention to the recreational potential of the entirety of the Chugach Mountains behind Anchorage. In 1970, spurred by the committee that spun out of that hike, the Alaska legislature designated the park.

## DRIVING DIRECTIONS

Search online for "bird valley trailhead ak," or follow these directions. Drive the Seward Highway to the community of Bird Creek. At mile 100.6, adjacent to the Birdhouse Garage, turn inland on Konikson Road. Follow the narrow, potholed road 0.7 mile past residences, a side street, and a sign for Chugach State Park to a large parking area. Behind a gate, the trail starts on municipal parkland before reaching the state park. There is no parking fee.

## ON THE ROUTE

Because roads already existed in the Bird Creek valley, this is one of the few places in the park that allow motorized recreational vehicles today, so the old road is still almost a road. Beyond the trailhead gate, walk this wide trail, going right at an obvious fork en route. Look for a bear-chewed Penguin Peak Trail signpost on the right 0.6 mile in, and when it appears, leave the old road to follow a narrower footpath uphill.

The trail follows the edge of an avalanche path. For this reason, in years when the avalanches run big, there could be snow here in the early hiking season. Also for this reason, this is a summer route, not a winter or early spring route. Proceed up, mostly in a space between alders and hemlock. Because of avalanches, the forest and brush zone is relatively

*The view from Penguin Peak includes the continuation of Penguin Ridge and a tarn.*

brief. When there has been no recent brush clearing, this portion of the trail could require pushing alder branches aside. This is no place to surprise a bear, so alert wildlife of your presence (see Bears and Other Wildlife in the Introduction).

A couple of areas of damp, exposed bedrock present tricky footing. Under some conditions, the trail may be wet underfoot. Views begin to open up behind, across the lowland forest. It is only about 0.7 mile from the signpost (but already elevation 1450 feet) when the path breaks clear of the woody stuff and enters the low end of a small tundra bowl. A band of hemlocks continues along the right, but avalanches keep the bowl clear for open walking.

The footpath winds through the tundra and over a lip into an upper bowl where the angle eases somewhat, about 2 miles from the car, at 2600 feet. The visible footpath becomes intermittent, but the route is clear enough, following the bottom of the bowl toward a communications structure visible ahead on the ridge crest. Passing some steeper and gravelly ground that is evident on the left, begin to turn upward to the left, aiming for the ridge above. Watch behind; with elevation, the view gradually opens over Turnagain Arm and the Kenai Mountains. Proceeding, a logical route may hit the ridge at elevation 3900 feet, but there is probably no wrong route here. Cresting the ridge provides another sudden new view, across Penguin Creek to Bird Peak and an ocean of other impressive peaks behind it.

Follow the ridge over the nearest summit—a false summit—and on to the next. The going is rocky along the ridgetop. Most hikers will use their hands a couple times. This is fairly standard Chugach

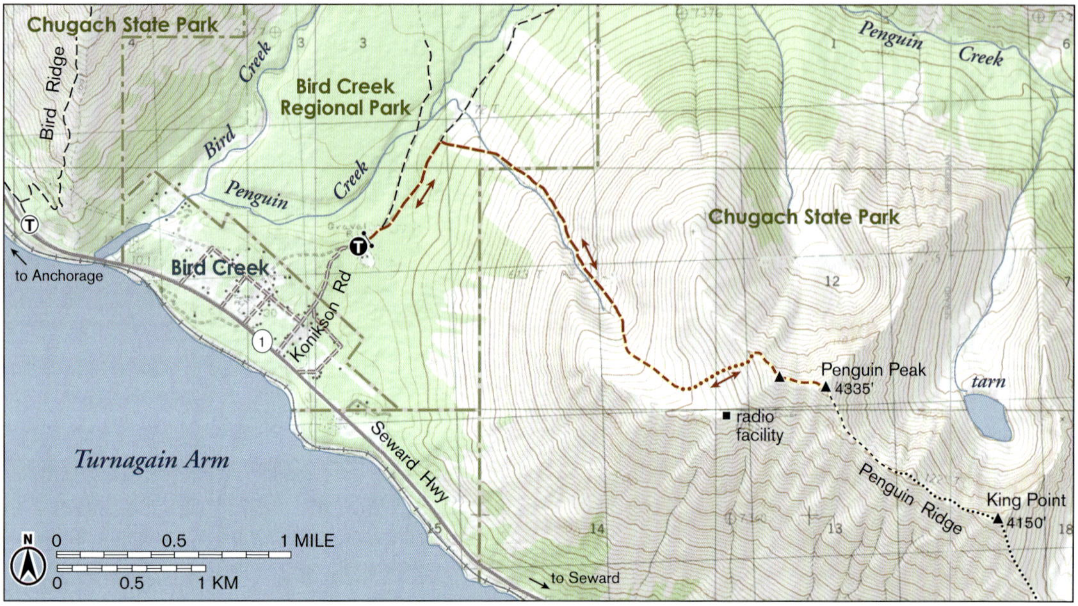


scrambling, but the loose rock and general exposure of the route may cause some to stop at the false summit, saving about a half mile roundtrip. Keep an eye out for sheep on the steep slopes below.

From the Penguin Peak summit (4335 feet), take in the tarn 1700 feet below to the east, the highway and Turnagain Arm waters 4300 feet below to the south, and the big valley of Penguin Creek 3000 feet below to the north. In most directions, the sights occur "below," but the ridge across Penguin Creek sports several spires above 5000 feet, topped by Bird Peak at 5505 feet. To the west stands Bird Ridge, creating an arced skyline, and behind and above it the Suicide Peaks at just over 5000 feet.

The Penguin Peak summit is broad enough for a small group to sit down for a snack (recommended). Admire the ongoing Penguin Ridge, each bump named for another Penguin species: King Point (4150 feet) beyond a sketchy exposed ridge, then Rockhopper Point (3812 feet), Adelie Point (3825 feet), Emperor Point (3576 feet), Crested Peak (3530 feet), Chinstrap Peak (3619 feet), and Gentoo Peak (4196 feet). Elevations and names are as reported by Steve Gruhn, a longtime active member of the MCA, at summitpost.org in his description of Penguin Ridge. Most names come from Vin Hoeman, a storied 1960s-era MCA climber, who apparently was the first to record ascents on this ridge.

Yes, people do push through all those summits to complete the Penguin Ridge traverse to Girdwood, but it is a challenge even for highly experienced and fit mountain runners. Dedicated athletes take eight to twelve hours. See Trip 24 regarding the far end.

Descend the way you came or by minor variations to take in viewpoints along the route.

## SHORTER OPTION

Ascend the trail until the steep grade moderates at the upper bowl (elevation 2000 feet). Survey the tundra-covered ridge enclosing the bowl on its right side (southwest), and pick a spot that looks easy to get to. Hike cross-country up to that spot and take in the view. This will make a hike of 4 miles or slightly more roundtrip, with some 3000 feet of elevation gain, depending on where you hit the ridge.

# 27 GLEN ALPS TO INDIAN VIA SHIP LAKE

**DISTANCE:** 15 miles point to point
**TIME:** 2 days
**ELEVATION GAIN:** 2100 feet southbound, 4700 feet northbound
**HIGH POINT:** 4050 feet
**SEASON:** June–mid-October
**SURFACE:** Hardpack, tundra, mud
**GRADE:** Moderate with steep segments
**INDIGENOUS LAND:** Dena'ina Athabascan
**MANAGING AGENCY:** Chugach State Park
**MAPS:** USGS Anchorage A-7 SW, A-8 SE; Seward D-7 NW
**ONLINE MAP SEARCH:** "indian creek pass ak"
**TRAILHEAD GPS:** Glen Alps 61.103043°N, 149.683046°W
Indian Valley 60.999805°N, 149.499458°W

**This hike combines two old standards—the Powerline Trail from the Glen Alps trailhead and the** Indian Valley Trail—connecting them with a stretch of off-trail hiking in alpine and subalpine tundra. Ship Lake, the literal headwaters of Ship Creek, is the centerpiece to the route, located at the base of 5050-foot Avalanche Mountain, with its almost-perpetual snowy gullies, dark rock, and crenellated ridgelines. The route takes in a high pass above the lake and a lower pass beyond the lake, which means hikers traverse the headwaters of three prominent Anchorage watersheds—Campbell, Ship, and Indian Creeks—with a fine combination of forests and meadows, alpine tundra, and mountain ponds. Hike it either direction, but as presented, it is mostly downhill. This makes a good overnight trip. Very strong hikers and mountain runners confident in routefinding can blitz it in a day. Extend the trip to explore the tundra zone. Out-and-back options from either end make classic trips themselves; see Shorter Options.

## DRIVING DIRECTIONS

Undertaken as described, this route requires a car shuttle. Out-and-back options are also possible.

**Glen Alps trailhead.** Search online for "glen alps trailhead ak," or follow these directions. From the interchange of the Seward Highway and O'Malley

Road in South Anchorage, turn uphill on O'Malley Road. Drive toward the mountains 3.6 miles to the intersection with Hillside Drive. Turn right on Hillside Drive, and continue 1 mile to Upper Huffman Road and a sign for Chugach State Park. Turn left, go 0.6 mile, and turn right on Toilsome Hill Drive (in winter, some combination of studded tires, chains, and four-wheel drive is recommended). This road, which becomes Glen Alps Road, climbs steeply uphill for about 2 miles to the Glen Alps entrance to Chugach State Park (marked). There are two large parking lots; leave your car in either one. Expect to pay a fee for parking.

**Indian Valley trailhead.** Search online for "indian valley trailhead ak," or follow these directions. Take the Seward Highway to the community of Indian. At mile 103.1, turn north onto Boretide Road just west of Indian Creek. After 0.5 mile, take the right fork, and continue another 0.5 mile to the trailhead. Park in a small lot.

## ON THE ROUTE

From Glen Alps (elevation 2500 feet), head out the wide main trail to reach the Powerline Trail, and follow it up valley 2 miles to the German Bridge (kindly installed by the German Club of Anchorage, complete with a bike rack for people who bike here and continue on foot). Cross the bridge to the Hidden Lake Trail, which also is the route to The Ramp and The Wedge, the peaks on either side of Ship Lake Pass at the head of the valley.

The footpath leads to a creek within twenty to thirty minutes. It is actually the confluence of two creeks. This spot can be confusing because people have crossed here and trails are visible on the other side. Instead of crossing, follow the trail that continues upstream a short distance through low shrubs to an obvious crossing spot with stones to step on. Immediately across the stream, the trail forks. There are no markers. Take the right fork. The left fork goes more distinctly uphill following the crest of a bluff or small ridge toward Hidden Lake, with a creek on the left. The right fork (the one you take) winds a bit but settles into an alignment on the bluff above the creek (to hiker's right) that comes from Ship Lake Pass. The trail is obvious most of the way up the valley, but this is an open landscape, soon entirely free of shrubs. Walking in this valley is freedom itself. The brush is behind; the grade is easy; and firm, dry tundra, laced with occasional springs, makes distances seem short. Look for wildflowers in season, ground squirrels, and Dall sheep. Enjoy the smell of heather on a warm, sunny day. Camping is possible in multiple locations; pitch tents well, as the wind can blow hard here. The pass is evident at the head of the valley. Hit it at its low point (4050 feet, just over 5 miles into the hike). Into July, crossing snow patches may be necessary. Ship Lake below is picturesque and inviting.

To proceed with the traverse, drop over the pass, aiming for the lake outlet or the lichen-covered patch downstream of the lake. There is no trail for this steep descent of about 1350 feet.

At the outlet of the lake, a social trail becomes evident. Hop across the creek and follow the trail down valley. It is intermittent, and in a couple of places, there is more than one trail option. With gradual descent, the high-alpine tundra becomes an attractive mix of low tundra, grass meadows, patches of brush, and patches of mountain hemlock. The trail may be difficult to follow in a few places, but it heads eastward at the base of Avalanche Mountain, often right at the toe of the steeper slopes. As the terrain takes the route around a broad bend, the trail leaves the mountain flanks; it picks up a low, linear hump and proceeds

*Ship Lake Pass overlooking the headwaters of Ship Creek, with Avalanche Mountain behind* (Photo by Susan Beesley)

eastward again toward a small tributary of Ship Creek. Very near the tributary, the intermittent trail intersects an extension of the Indian Valley Trail. Turn right toward Indian Creek Pass. Once at the pass, the trail is well defined.

The Indian Creek Pass area is broad and mostly open. However, at 1800 feet elevation, there are extensive patches of hemlock too. The vistas down the big Ship Creek Valley and up to the surrounding peaks and ridges are as pleasing as any, inviting side exploration of the small glacial bowls a few hundred feet above the pass. A low spot on the ridge to the east provides glimpses into another alpine valley with still more bowls, tarns, and peaks and the promise of access to summits, the north end of Bird Ridge, and (with some bushwhacking) the North Fork of Ship Creek.

The trail down Indian Creek is a steady and mostly gradual downhill into bigger timber. This trail is not difficult to follow, but conditions vary depending on maintenance and rainfall. Historically, bridges have been damaged and not always repaired rapidly; wading the tumbling stream may be necessary. The upper part of the trail weaves in and out of trees and grassy meadows (grass can be head-high in the second half of summer), and these parts are particularly picturesque. The forest can include blowdowns. Horses sometimes use this trail, and in wet weather, stretches of tread may be churned and muddy. The trail provides good access, though, through the forest to the Indian Valley trailhead (elevation 250 feet). Camping opportunities below the pass are not great. The descent is about 1600 vertical feet in little more than 5 miles.

If you're starting from the Indian Valley trailhead and proceeding northward, the trail heads out of the parking area and crosses under a powerline. A separate trail (utility access road) follows the powerline across the creek. Be sure to follow the Indian Valley Trail; there should be no immediate creek crossing. Farther up, proceed beyond Indian Creek Pass about a mile until the trail comes very close to the tributary of Ship Creek. The trail passes the eastern end of a low, east-west hump in the terrain. Find an informal trail heading west along this hump, leading intermittently to Ship Lake. From the lake outlet, looking up at Ship Lake Pass, the visible horizon is broad and the low point not distinct. Aim between a lone rock outcrop on the left along the ridge crest and a multiheaded outcrop on the right. It is not necessary to go all the way to the lake to access the pass, but the lake area is an oasis of water, tundra, wildflowers, and rock—and the big face of Avalanche Mountain.

Indian Valley is a good place to spot Dall sheep, but be aware that the valley is open to sheep hunting August 10 to September 30.

## SHORTER OPTIONS

Ship Lake Pass provides access to The Ramp (elevation 5240 feet) and The Wedge (elevation 4660 feet), either of them worthy full-day summit hikes. Either hike amounts to 12.5 miles roundtrip from the Glen Alps trailhead (3200 feet and 2620 feet elevation gain, respectively). Following the Hidden Lake Trail to the lake in a tucked-away bowl is a somewhat mellower hike (10 miles, 1660 feet elevation gain). For those going out and back from the Glen Alps trailhead, mountain bike access to the German Bridge is a great option, providing variety to the trip and speeding up the approach. Bikes are not allowed off the Powerline Trail.

To make a loop from the Glen Alps trailhead via Ship Lake Pass, take a sheep trail south from the pass to traverse behind The Wedge to the next low point on the ridge, and then reconnect cross-country to the Powerline Trail.

## EXTENDING YOUR TRIP

Hiking up the Indian Valley Trail to the pass can be a day hike or an overnight. It is best to spend some time in the pass area, where the world opens up. Note that the ground, while open, is hummocky enough that good flat campsites are scarce at the pass proper.

Experienced off-trail backpackers report successful trips threading through higher passes northeast of Indian Creek Pass, crossing the North Fork of Ship Creek, and exiting the South Fork of Eagle River (Trip 35).

## SEASONAL OPTIONS

An Arctic to Indian ski tour is a classic extended day trip (20-plus miles) for fit and experienced ski tourers. Usually skied in the long daylight days of March and April, it follows Ship Creek from Arctic Valley Road (Trip 34; the trailhead is 4.6 miles from the gate at the bottom of the road) to Indian Creek Pass and on to the Indian Valley trailhead, a route once used by dog-mushing freight haulers as part of what is now the historic Iditarod Trail system (see Iditarod Trail and Alaska Long Trail in the Introduction). While this same route appears enticing as a summer trip when looking at a map, it is principally miles of bushwhacking without a trail, a route that is wet and difficult, and not recommended without snow cover.

# 28 RABBIT CREEK TO MCHUGH CREEK TRAVERSE

**DISTANCE:** 11.5 miles point to point
**TIME:** Full day to 2 days
**ELEVATION GAIN:** 1400 feet
**HIGH POINT:** 3150 feet
**SEASON:** June–September
**SURFACE:** Hardpack, rock
**GRADE:** Moderate
**INDIGENOUS LAND:** Dena'ina Athabascan
**MANAGING AGENCY:** Chugach State Park
**MAPS:** USGS Anchorage A-7 SW, A-8 SE
**ONLINE MAP SEARCH:** "rabbit lake anchorage ak"
**TRAILHEAD GPS:** Rabbit Lake 61.079613°N, 149.678009°W
McHugh Creek 61.018373°N, 149.733044°W

*Day hikers explore the rocky shoreline of Rabbit Lake.*

**Anchorage is known for its fine view of the Chugach front range. Among the most iconic peaks** in that view are the Suicide Peaks, a tall, shapely, well-matched pair with a distinct U-shaped col between them. The peaks stand at the head of Rabbit Creek, and from Anchorage it is the Rabbit Creek valley that provides the slot to that view. The peaks also mark the head of McHugh Creek, which drains to Turnagain Arm about 12 miles south of Anchorage. This Chugach traverse provides the opportunity to walk to the base of those peaks and see them reflected in Rabbit Lake and McHugh Lakes.

You'll walk up one creek and down the other and take in two complete valleys without needing to cross a precipitous pass. The valleys blend into one another at a broad, tundra-and-lichen divide suitable for camping. Hikers transition from the high alpine, where rockiness competes with greenness (and pretty much wins), to a slightly lower and lusher alpine valley—mostly heather and blueberry bushes with patches of low hemlock—to grass meadows, to full forest. Along the way, the focus shifts from those close, muscular Suicide Peaks to far-reaching, serene views across the glistening waters of Turnagain Arm. The variety makes the traverse better than either valley alone, and the traverse is short enough to make a good day trip and long enough to justify camping out. Look for Dall sheep in the high country and black bears at lower elevations.

## DRIVING DIRECTIONS

The traverse requires a car shuttle between trailheads. If you can't arrange a shuttle, the out-and-back trail from either end is satisfying.

**Rabbit Lake trailhead.** Search online for "rabbit lake trailhead ak," or follow these directions. From the Seward Highway, take O'Malley Road, DeArmoun Road, or Rabbit Creek Road east to Hillside Drive, and make your way to a four-way stop where Hillside Drive meets DeArmoun Road. Proceed uphill on Upper DeArmoun Road 0.9 mile to Canyon Road. Turn right and briefly downhill onto Canyon Road, and continue 2.1 miles to the end of pavement, then another 0.6 mile on steep dirt road to a Chugach State Park gate (generally open) with a fee area notice. Proceed another 0.1 mile up a steep hill to a small parking lot on the right. Another parking area occurs at the end of the road, about 0.3 mile farther, where this trip starts. On popular days, the entire road between the two lots can be packed with parked cars.

**McHugh Creek trailhead.** Search online for "mchugh trailhead ak," or follow these directions. Drive to Seward Highway milepost 111.9, and turn toward the mountains into Chugach State Park's McHugh Creek Day Use Area (marked). Drive 0.2 mile uphill, past an open gate and three lower parking lots, to the upper (north) parking lot. Note that the gate is open from 9:00 AM to 9:00 PM daily. If in doubt, park in the lowest lot, outside the gate. Expect to pay a fee to park, even outside the gate.

## ON THE ROUTE

On this route, there is no great expenditure of effort to get to the alpine zone. The Rabbit Lake trailhead is in the alpine, which accounts for its popularity—that and the trail's low gradient. The route follows an old homesteader track up the valley, starting beyond large boulders at the end of the road (elevation 1970 feet). The homesteader's bulldozer created a disturbance in the soils, and alders grew in to fix it, so continuous open views don't materialize for a mile or two.

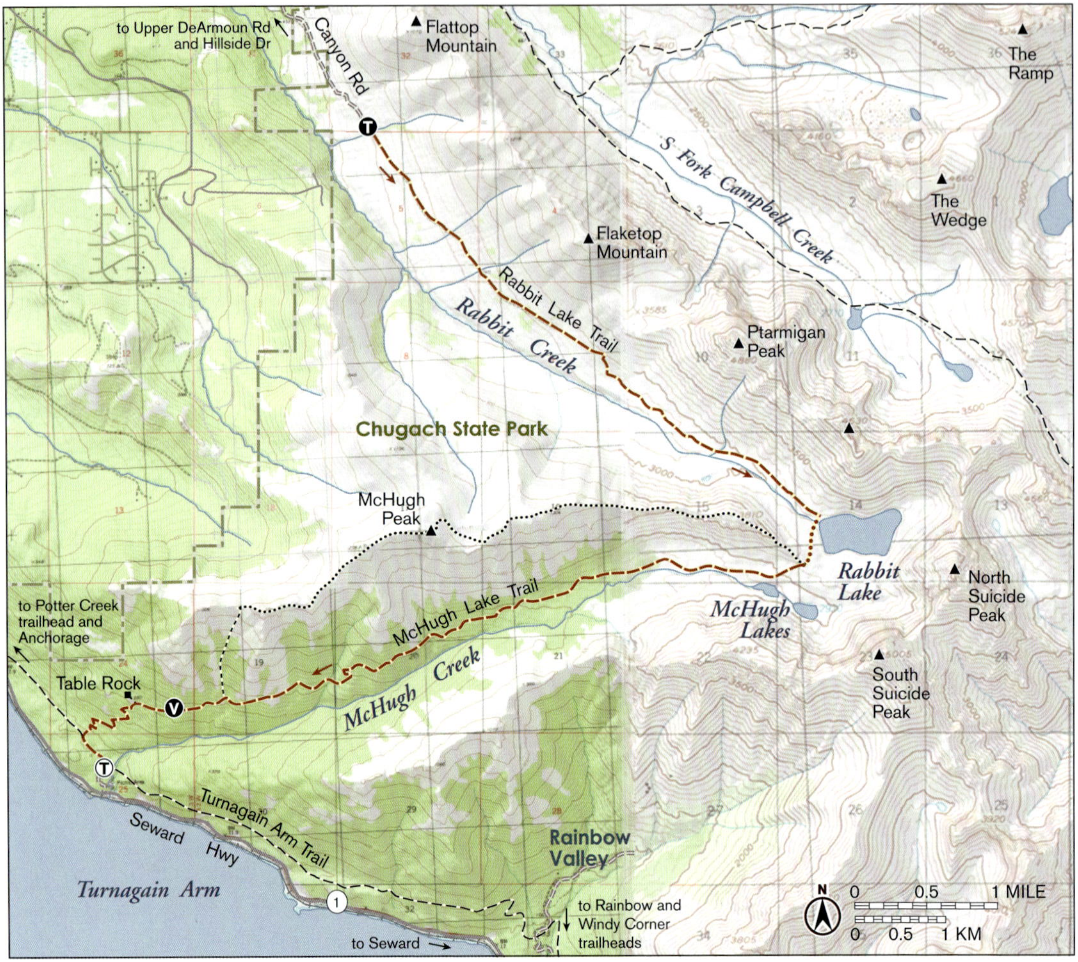


Near trail mile 2, where there is a notch in the left ridge between Flaketop (see Trip 31) and Ptarmigan Peak, the trail goes downhill for a moment, and the view opens upon the upper Rabbit Creek valley: Ptarmigan Peak to the left, McHugh Peak to the right, and North and South Suicide Peaks ahead. The trail is easy to follow and leads directly to the lake, just over a last low rise, 4.4 miles from the trailhead.

Getting to Rabbit Lake is no problem. Going beyond may throw some people off for a moment. At the lake, people have gone in many directions, creating small social trails (such as the one around the lake) but also *not* creating trails as they have dispersed. The land is wide open for walking, so choose any route, but perhaps the best is up and over the low rise to the right (west side) of the lake, rather than along the lakeshore. Angle toward the southwest shoulder of South Suicide Peak and away from Rabbit Lake. A trail starts this way and mostly vanishes for a few minutes in the low tundra and lichen vegetation. Look for large cairns spaced far apart, and look for the McHugh Creek valley opening before you as you top the rise. The trail likely will reappear underfoot without much thinking needed as you pick a logical route toward the valley ahead.

Back on a footpath, two small lakes at the head of McHugh Creek come into view. The descending trail passes near the outlet of the lower lake (about a mile beyond Rabbit Lake). Because the trail does not go directly to these lakes, they see less foot traffic than the larger Rabbit Lake. Camping on this side of the divide may be preferable on days when Rabbit Lake is crowded. The upper McHugh Creek valley is open, flat to rolling, with heather and small patches of mountain hemlock, blueberries in season, and Dall sheep sometimes on the slopes above. The last decent camping, around elevation 2600 feet, is just before the creek drops into a narrow V cut, opposite a low notch in the ridge to the south.

As the creek falls away, the trail continues across the hillside for another 2.5 miles, descending only gradually. Alder shows up where the trail crosses gullies. Five miles from Rabbit Lake, there is an informal, steep, and gravelly side trail up to the right that provides access to McHugh Peak, 1900 vertical feet above. The main trail then carries the hiker down into the forest. A wildfire burned through the McHugh area in 2016, and though some of the burn is visible in the distance, only a small area right at tree line burned near the trail; the forest portion was unaffected. At 5.6 miles from Rabbit Lake, there is a side route to a viewpoint called Table Rock. At 6.5 miles, the trail Ts into the Turnagain Arm Trail. There is a trail sign but no indication of which way goes to the McHugh trailhead. Go left (southeast); the opposite direction goes to the Potter trailhead. A few minutes later, a trail junction sign appears. The Turnagain Arm Trail continues straight ahead toward the Rainbow and Windy Corner trailheads. Take the right turn; it is 0.1 mile to the upper (north) parking lot at the McHugh Creek Day Use Area.

If starting at the McHugh end, access to the Turnagain Arm Trail is prominently marked, but no signs indicate how to get to the McHugh Lake Trail. There is a general map posted at a trailhead kiosk. Hike up the trail to the left of the kiosk and outhouses. After 0.1 mile, go left on the Turnagain Arm Trail toward the Potter trailhead. At 0.4 mile from the McHugh trailhead, the McHugh Lake Trail begins (marked).

### OPTIONS

While not necessarily shorter options, it is common for hikers to make out-and-back trips to the lakes from either trailhead. From the Rabbit Lake trailhead, it is 8.8 miles roundtrip to Rabbit Lake. From the McHugh Creek trailhead, it is about 13 miles roundtrip to McHugh Lakes and 14.2 to Rabbit Lake. Table Rock is a shorter destination from the McHugh trailhead, with Cook Inlet views (2.5 miles roundtrip, with about 1000 feet of elevation gain). Another area with good views occurs within another 0.5 mile.

## 29 WILLIWAW LAKES LOOP

**DISTANCE:** 18.5-mile loop
**TIME:** 2–3 days
**ELEVATION GAIN:** 3800 feet

**HIGH POINT:** 3725 feet
**SEASON:** June–September
**SURFACE:** Hardpack, tundra, rock
**GRADE:** Moderate with steep segments
**INDIGENOUS LAND:** Dena'ina Athabascan
**MANAGING AGENCY:** Chugach State Park
**MAPS:** USGS Anchorage A-7, A-8
**ONLINE MAP SEARCH:** "williwaw lakes ak"
**TRAILHEAD GPS:** Prospect Heights 61.139059°N, 149.710552°W
Glen Alps 61.103043°N, 149.683046°W

**One of the many great things about this trip, among its multiple attractions, is that it is a loop. How** many trips take hikers back to the starting point without repeating miles of terrain they already have seen? This one does. Also, it takes in the South Fork, Middle Fork, and North Fork Campbell Creek valleys, providing a connection with the iconic stream that flows through the lowland city to the Campbell Creek Estuary in South Anchorage. Other pluses: For Anchorage residents and visitors, this fairly big loop is right at hand—no long drive necessary. Most of the trip's miles go by in big, open valleys with continuous mountain views and a lot of time in the cherished alpine tundra. Mountain lakes, always a favorite, come in multiples here, and in several sizes. The trip takes place partly in Chugach State Park's wilderness zone—a management area that comes right up to the edge of Anchorage in the North Fork.

Some routefinding is necessary, but it is within a confined valley where it would be difficult to get truly lost. Expert mountain runners can do this trip in a day, but most people will enjoy it as a two- or three-day backpacking excursion.

## DRIVING DIRECTIONS

Choose from either of two popular park trailheads—Prospect Heights and Glen Alps.

**Prospect Heights trailhead.** Search online for "prospect heights trailhead ak," or follow these directions. From the interchange at the Seward Highway and O'Malley Road in South Anchorage, turn uphill (east) on O'Malley Road. Drive about 3.7 miles to Hillside Drive. Beyond a forced left, turn immediately right onto Upper O'Malley Road. Follow it 0.5 mile to a T intersection. Turn left onto Prospect Drive, and continue 1 mile to a stop sign. Turn left on Sidorof Lane, and proceed 0.1 mile. Then turn right at the Prospect Heights entrance to Chugach State Park. Expect to pay a fee for parking.

**Glen Alps trailhead.** Search online for "glen alps trailhead ak," or follow these directions. From the interchange of the Seward Highway and O'Malley Road in South Anchorage, turn uphill on O'Malley Road. Drive toward the mountains 3.6 miles to the intersection with Hillside Drive. Turn right onto Hillside Drive, and continue 1 mile to Upper Huffman Road and a sign for Chugach State Park. Turn left, and drive 0.6 mile to a three-way intersection. The left turn leads to the Upper Huffman entrance to the park and the Silver Fern Trail, an

*Preparing breakfast on a misty morning in July at one of the upper-elevation Williwaw lakes* (Photo by Hannah Leigh Pratt)

alternate access to the trail system in the Campbell Creek valley. For the Glen Alps entrance, turn right on Toilsome Hill Drive (in winter, some combination of studded tires, chains, and four-wheel drive is recommended). This road, which becomes Glen Alps Road, climbs steeply uphill for about 2 miles to the park entrance (marked; elevation 2200 feet). There are two large parking lots; leave your car in either one. Expect to pay a fee for parking.

## ON THE ROUTE

This trip probably is best from the lower elevation of Prospect Heights, so the description is counterclockwise from there. (See below for notes about access via Glen Alps.)

From the Prospect Heights trailhead (elevation 1050 feet), walk beyond the park kiosk toward a power transmission line. Turn left, and follow the powerline a short way. The wide, main path is an old homesteader road. Follow it over a rise and through a bend to the right, leaving the powerline. Continue downhill to cross the South Fork of Campbell Creek on a bridge (mile 0.9, elevation 950 feet, the loop's low point) and then uphill through a single switchback. At 1.3 miles, find a marked junction for the Middle Fork Loop Trail. Turn right, and follow this trail gradually up through the upper-elevation edges of the forest and through grassy meadows to a bridge over the Middle Fork of Campbell Creek (mile 3.6, elevation 1890 feet). Just beyond, turn left

Chugach State Park
Temptation Peak
Koktoya Peak
Mount Williwaw
Tanaina Peak
Tanaina Lake
West Tanaina Peak
Tikishla Peak
Joint Base Elmendorf-Richardson
Long Lake
Williwaw Lakes
The Ramp
Knoya Peak
Kanchee Peak
North Fork Campbell Creek
Tikishla Creek
O'Malley Peak
Hidden Lake
Middle Fork Campbell Creek
Wolverine Peak
"Football Field"
False Peak
informal trail to military land
A
B
Near Point
Near Point Trail
Williwaw Lakes Trail
Little O'Malley Peak
Chugach State Park
Campbell Creek
Powerline Trail
Middle Fork Loop Trail
South Fork
Wolverine Bowl Trail
Glen Alps
Flattop Mountain
private land
Far North Bicentennial Park
Prospect Heights Trailhead
Sidorof Ln
Prospect Dr
to Hillside Dr
Upper O'Malley Rd
Toilsome Hill Dr
Upper Huffman Rd
0 0.5 1 MILE
0 0.5 1 KM

at a marked junction, and follow the Williwaw Lakes Trail up the Middle Fork valley. The right fork goes to the Glen Alps trailhead.

The continuing route toward Williwaw Lakes has left the forest proper behind and is relatively level at the elevation of mountain hemlock and big, open grass-and-tundra meadows. Ground cover transitions to a variety of mosses and small shrubs. The mountains successively come into view up valley, tall, sharp, and rocky. The north face of O'Malley Peak (5150 feet) and the particularly pointy summit of Mount Williwaw (5445 feet) dominate. The trail may have muddy spots before reaching the lakes.

The Williwaw Lakes, particularly the first of the lakes, make a popular destination in their own right. Once beyond the first lake, trail traffic drops off. The best areas for camping are in the vicinity of the lakes, the pass, and much of the North Fork valley. Note, however, that the lakes area is fragile and, on the Middle Fork side, gets too much use for its own good. The park requires commercial groups to pack out human waste. Others should be diligent about going far from water and common-use areas for toileting. Campfires are not allowed.

The trail climbs more steeply past ponds to a pass. Early in the season, expect to cross snow patches in this area. If you plan to attempt this route in winter, note that the pass approach presents terrain traps and slopes prone to avalanches. Know your risks and how to mitigate them (see Avalanches in the Introduction).

The pass (9.2 miles from the start, elevation 3725 feet) is the route's high point and halfway point. With it comes new views that gradually open to take in the length of the North Fork valley and Long Lake, the largest on the route. Footpaths may be intermittent, particularly along the North Fork of Campbell Creek. Choose either side of Long Lake. Beyond the mile-long lake, the walking is mostly easy, on low, firm tundra. Even where there is no trail, just proceed down the valley. There are small fish in the lakes. Particularly in the upper valley, crossing the creek is easy enough, if desired. There is a string of 5000-foot summits on the north side—Koktoya, Tanaina (the highest at 5266 feet), West Tanaina, and Tikishla Peaks. These rise among the front range's tallest, see little activity, and make for steep scrambles for those so inclined. Tundra camping opportunities are plentiful. Disperse camps to minimize impact to tundra. The upper valley is on military land but is not a designated training area.

As the valley descends, the vegetation inevitably grows taller, and it will become necessary to pay attention to find the easiest route. Luckily, about the time the willows become tall, it is time to exit the valley floor and head again for the heights. Having a good map and paying attention to it in this area are helpful—and critical if the ridge above is in clouds.

To leave the valley, the route aims for the literal low point on the ridge to the left, between Wolverine Peak and Near Point. This low point is marked A on the map. There is another, closer low point (B). On the south bluff above the North Fork and slightly upstream of a confluence with Tikishla Creek, the trail to notch A appears. It becomes better defined slightly higher up the slope. The lower end of this trail winds through grasses and around a patch or two of hemlock. Then it angles upward at a reasonable grade. Climb this trail to notch A. Note that notch B is evident, while notch A is virtually invisible from the valley floor. In truth, gaining the ridge at either low point is fine. The trail to notch B is less defined, crosses several gullies, and requires a direct climb up the final bit, so notch A is preferable.

Once on the ridge, follow a well-worn but rocky trail to Near Point (elevation 3050 feet). The continuing trail heads steeply down the west ridge, back into alder and then forest. At a switchback, the route suddenly meets the upper end of the old homesteader road the trip started on. Follow this trail gently downhill through a scenic forest with views across Anchorage and Cook Inlet. From the switchback at the base of Near Point, it is a mile to the Middle Fork Loop Trail and 2.3 miles to the Prospect Heights trailhead.

If starting from Glen Alps, hike out the main trail from either of the Glen Alps parking lots to the Powerline Trail (0.5 mile). Turn right, proceed about 500 feet down a long, sloping grade, and find a narrower trail to the left (marked). It winds downhill to the South Fork of Campbell Creek, crosses on a bridge, and soon presents another junction: the Little O'Malley Peak Trail to the right, and the Middle Fork Loop Trail to the left. Go left and fairly level to the junction of the Middle Fork Loop Trail and the Williwaw Lakes Trail, discussed above. Please stay on the marked current trails, and let older, muddier, eroded routes grow back in.

It also is possible to get to Williwaw Lakes via a 1200-foot ascent on the Little O'Malley Peak Trail to and across the "Football Field," a high-elevation but low-angle tundra area at the base of O'Malley Peak. An informal trail leads across the ball field and steeply down a rocky gully to the Middle Fork valley, near the first of the Williwaw Lakes. This alternate route is scenic and shorter, but it includes much steeper ground and areas of much rockier footing, and it may expose you to higher mountain wind.

*Enjoying camp below Tikishla Peak in the North Fork Campbell Creek valley*

## SHORTER OPTIONS

A day hike out and back from Glen Alps to the Football Field and Little O'Malley Peak is 4 miles roundtrip with 1400 feet elevation gain to the peak. Hike from Glen Alps to the first of the Williwaw Lakes and back for a substantive day hike (12.4 miles roundtrip, 1000 feet elevation gain). This is a decent overnight backpacking trip for families, with camping at the lakes (recommended) or in limited grassy areas along the Middle Fork Loop Trail. See Trip 32 for a day hike on Near Point.

## SEASONAL OPTIONS

Ski touring from Glen Alps to Williwaw Lakes is pleasant when not too windy. The footpath down to the South Fork of Campbell Creek from Glen Alps is steep and generally packed in enough by boot traffic that many skiers may prefer carrying their skis down. Otherwise, the route is low-angle enough to be accessible to most skiers. Sometimes overflow seeping out of the tundra creates wet and icy spots. Fat-tire bikes are allowed on the Middle Fork Loop Trail in winter and on the Wolverine Bowl and Powerline Trails year-round. Therefore, the complete Middle Fork Loop Trail is accessible by fat bike in winter. It also is a good ski tour loop when there is sufficient soft snow for braking on the downhills. A custom is developing that winter bikers give the Middle Fork Loop Trail a few days after a fresh snowfall—time for skiers to get "first tracks" while allowing the trail to become more packed in and rideable for bikers. The open valley of the upper South Fork of Campbell Creek becomes a popular crust skate-skiing destination during early spring when conditions are right. Access the valley bottom at the Middle Fork Loop Trail bridge from Glen Alps or farther up valley where the Powerline Trail goes near the bluff. It can be a bit of work skate skiing up the valley, but the gentle run back down is a flight of freedom.

# 30 MCHUGH PEAK

**DISTANCE:** 5.6 miles roundtrip
**TIME:** Half day
**ELEVATION GAIN:** 2900 feet
**HIGH POINT:** 4311 feet
**SEASON:** Year-round
**SURFACE:** Hardpack, rocks
**GRADE:** Moderate with steep segments
**INDIGENOUS LAND:** Dena'ina Athabascan
**MANAGING AGENCY:** Chugach State Park
**MAP:** USGS Anchorage A-8 SE
**ONLINE MAP SEARCH:** "mchugh peak ak"
**TRAILHEAD GPS:** 61.072445°N, 149.688429°W

**Among the mountains directly fronting Anchorage, McHugh Peak stands farthest south. From the** northern parts of town, McHugh Peak is where the winter sun rises in the darkest days of winter. It is a peak with a funky summit—a broad, open, easily walkable ridge sweeps up smoothly only to be topped with a jagged, stubby thumb of rock that, while short, is difficult to climb. Most people can handle this satisfying hike along a rolling ridge. The only downside is the limited parking at the trailhead. Officials and public access advocates have been seeking other avenues to McHugh Peak. Stay alert for (and advocate for) new options for getting to this otherwise perfect summer evening hike.

## DRIVING DIRECTIONS

Search online for "bear valley hike ak," or follow these directions. From the Seward Highway in South Anchorage, take the exit for Rabbit Creek Road, and then turn left onto the Old Seward Highway, which becomes Rabbit Creek Road. Proceed uphill about 3 miles. As Rabbit Creek Road curves to the left and levels out, take a right on Clarks Road. Continue following the main road 2 miles (pavement will end; name changes to Kings

*A stroll on McHugh Peak Ridge in August, with a little one along for the ride* (Photo by Gretchen Nelson)

Way Drive; the road will descend and start uphill again).

Turn left onto Snow Bear Drive, then in close succession take a right on Black Bear Drive and a left on Honey Bear Lane. Follow Honey Bear Lane to its end in a small neighborhood. Honey Bear Lane is mostly straight for 0.8 mile and then bends right, ending within 0.2 mile at a cul-de-sac. There is a public parking area for four cars and No Parking signs around the cul-de-sac.

This trailhead is the poster child for contentious trailhead issues with neighboring properties. Hikers should make every effort to foster goodwill instead of problems. The surrounding neighbors are not thrilled with drivers parking randomly, blocking emergency vehicles, and abusing the public right of access here (e.g., partying in the cul-de-sac). Additional parallel parking is available 0.4 mile back along Honey Bear Lane. Any roadside spot that allows 20 feet for traffic to pass and is not marked with official No Parking signs legally can be used for parking, but that kind of clearance is hard to find closer to the trailhead. Park with care, and don't push the legal limits.

## ON THE ROUTE

When the municipality subdivided a larger parcel so owners could form the neighborhood, it created a narrow public access from the Honey Bear Lane cul-de-sac to state park land. The trail starts at the left edge of the parking spaces (elevation 2100 feet). Head out on the trail, here lined with alders, and then up, quickly beyond the brush, toward a knob at the end of McHugh's north ridge. Climb steeply to the knob (elevation near 3200 feet) on a loose gravel trail. While views behind you are good almost right away, the knob presents the first 360-degree views.

Between the knob and the summit plateau lie about 1.5 miles of ridge walking. This is as good as ridge walking gets. The spine rolls along, generally with plenty of width for comfort but just enough rockiness on the crest to make clear this is a real mountain. The route climbs down and then back up through three notches that your thigh muscles will notice. Well into summer, leftover snowdrifts mean walking on snow in some places. The summer snow generally is firm and easy enough. In winter, wind often clears loose snow from the ridgetop or drifts it firmly.

A long ascent followed by a low-angle traverse leads to a broad area below the summit. The last slope starts flat and grows steadily steeper. People usually hit the summit area to the right (west) of the rock nubbin that marks the true high point. The view "over the top" is fine from the base of the rock, stretching southward across the deep McHugh Creek valley, across the green ridge that divides McHugh Creek from Rainbow Creek, to Turnagain Arm and the Kenai Mountains beyond.

It is ironic that this broad, gentle peak ends in a summit that can feel scary. To scramble up the last 60 feet or so, people variously try a slot that opens to the west, which feels like mountaineering, or a route around the north side of the rock thumb and then up where terrain allows. Either way requires use of hands and presents at least a little risk. Once on the outcrop, there is still a last scramble of a few feet to a small sitting spot upon the highest rock (elevation 4311 feet), but many will be plenty happy to leave the highest high point to those not burdened by butterflies in their stomachs. Whichever approach you take, be sure not only to look out at the view but also to look down the slopes toward McHugh Creek and along the east-west ridge—Dall sheep often hang out in the area.

To return, simply backtrack, with all of Anchorage, Cook Inlet and its volcanoes, Mount Susitna, the distant Alaska Range, and the setting sun laid out before you.

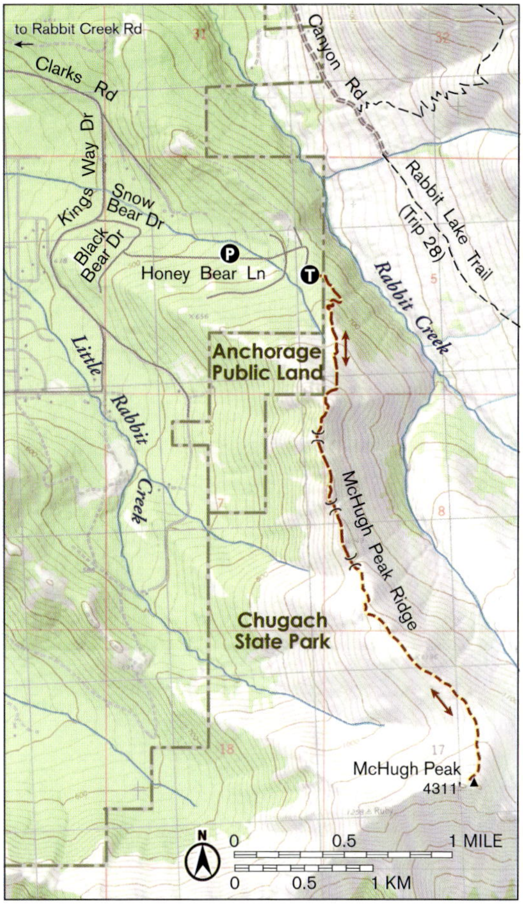

### SHORTER OPTIONS AND VARIATIONS

Hiking to any of the intermediate bumps on the ridge makes a satisfying shorter hike. As an example, the 3300-foot high point just before the first, larger notch in the ridge makes for a 2.4-mile round-trip (1200 feet elevation gain).

Because of private land, there are few other approaches to McHugh Peak from the Anchorage side. Using Trip 28 for access, there are a couple of longer possibilities on the north side (see map for Trip 28). Using the McHugh Creek Trail, the start is near sea level, and the informal side trail to McHugh Peak has sustained-steep grades, making this a much more intensive route. More pleasant, particularly for those camping in the Rabbit Lake area, is a ramble up McHugh Peak's east ridge, a 5-mile roundtrip ridge walk from the lake.

McHugh Peak, more than many others, makes a reasonable hike in winter. Take slip-on spikes for boots. As always in snow season, know what to look for regarding avalanche danger. The initial climb to the first knob certainly is steep enough to avalanche. Often the terrain here is windblown, so there is little snow accumulated, but winter hikers must be fully aware of risks and how to avoid them (see Avalanches in the Introduction).

# 31 FLATTOP RIDGE LOOPS

**DISTANCE:** 6.8-mile loop via Rabbit Creek; 8.8-mile loop via Campbell Creek
**TIME:** Full day
**ELEVATION GAIN:** 2850 feet
**HIGH POINT:** 4488 feet
**SEASON:** Late June–early October
**SURFACE:** Hardpack, rock, handholds (scrambling)
**GRADE:** Moderate with steep segments
**INDIGENOUS LAND:** Dena'ina Athabascan
**MANAGING AGENCY:** Chugach State Park
**MAPS:** USGS Anchorage A-7 SW, A-8 SE
**ONLINE MAP SEARCH:** "flattop ak"
**TRAILHEAD GPS:** Flattop Sunnyside 61.081915°N, 149.681435°W
Glen Alps 61.103043°N, 149.683046°W

**Ask any resident for the most-climbed mountain in Alaska, and they are likely to say Flattop—** despite the sometimes scary scrambling section near the top. With the 2017 addition of the Flattop Sunnyside Trail, a more moderate trail up the back side, the "most-climbed" reputation has only increased. Flattop itself is iconic, but it is just the low end of a long ridge separating the South Fork of Campbell Creek from Rabbit Creek. That ridge includes, in succession, knobs called Peak 2, Peak 3, and Flaketop Mountain. Each is a bit higher and lonelier than the last. Flattop is almost always a social experience, Peak 2 less so. Peak 3 has another section of scrambling and dissuades more folks. Flaketop is quiet, high above it all, with views from mountains to ocean, city to deep wilderness.

Overall this fine rocky ridge ramble is just challenging enough to keep hikers on their toes (and sometimes using their hands) and just easy enough to be hiked in a day. Two exit possibilities tie into the two Flattop trailheads, one in each adjoining valley, and make for a different loop possibility from each trailhead.

## DRIVING DIRECTIONS

Two trailhead parking areas provide for two variations on this ridge-and-valley loop hike.

**Flattop Sunnyside trailhead.** Search online for "flattop sunnyside trail ak," or follow these directions. From the Seward Highway, take O'Malley Road, DeArmoun Road, or Rabbit Creek Road east to Hillside Drive. Follow Hillside Drive to a four-way stop where Hillside Drive meets DeArmoun Road. Proceed uphill on Upper DeArmoun Road 0.9 mile to Canyon Road. Turn right and briefly downhill onto Canyon Road, and continue 2.1 miles to the end of pavement, then another 0.6 mile on a steep dirt road to a Chugach State Park gate (generally open) with a fee area notice. Proceed

*Happy to be on Peak 2, with Flattop behind and Mount Susitna far across Knik Arm*

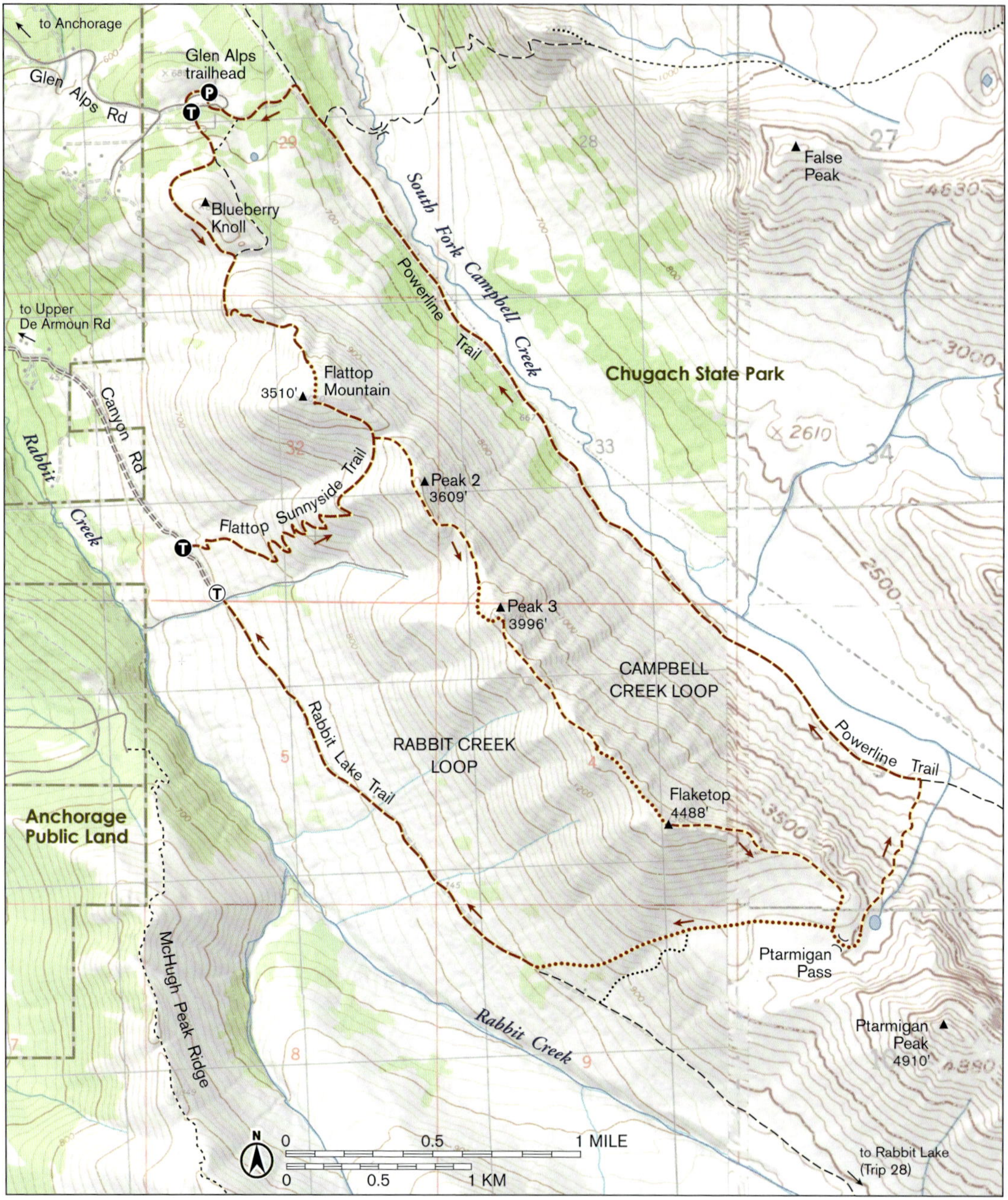
to Anchorage
Glen Alps trailhead
Glen Alps Rd
Blueberry Knoll
to Upper De Armoun Rd
Powerline Trail
South Fork Campbell Creek
Flattop Mountain
3510'
Canyon Rd
Rabbit Creek
Flattop Sunnyside Trail
Peak 2
3609'
Peak 3
3996'
Chugach State Park
False Peak
CAMPBELL CREEK LOOP
RABBIT CREEK LOOP
Rabbit Lake Trail
Flaketop
4488'
Powerline Trail
Anchorage Public Land
Ptarmigan Pass
McHugh Peak Ridge
Rabbit Creek
Ptarmigan Peak
4910'
0 0.5 1 MILE
0 0.5 1 KM
to Rabbit Lake (Trip 28)

another 0.1 mile up a steep hill to a small parking lot on the right. Another parking area occurs at the end of the road, about 0.3 mile farther. On popular days, the entire road between the two lots can be packed with parked cars.

**Glen Alps trailhead.** Search online for "glen alps trailhead ak," or follow these directions. From the interchange of the Seward Highway and O'Malley Road in South Anchorage, turn uphill on O'Malley Road. Drive toward the mountains 3.6 miles to the intersection with Hillside Drive. Turn right onto Hillside Drive, and continue 1 mile to Upper Huffman Road and a sign for Chugach State Park. Turn left, go 0.6 mile, and turn right onto Toilsome Hill Drive (in winter, some combination of studded tires, chains, and four-wheel drive is recommended). This road, which becomes Glen Alps Road, climbs steeply uphill for about 2 miles to the Glen Alps entrance to Chugach State Park (marked). There are two large parking lots; leave your car in either one. Expect to pay a fee for parking.

## ON THE ROUTE

This description focuses first on a loop via the ridgetop and the Rabbit Lake Trail. The other loop starts at Glen Alps, uses the same ridge, and is longer.

### Rabbit Creek Loop

The trailhead parking for the Rabbit Lake Trail is a stretched-out affair over 0.3 mile of road. In this area, several informal and formal trails take off. For clarity, the map shows only the Flattop Sunnyside Trail and Rabbit Lake Trail, which are most pertinent here. Know, however, that on-site, you may see other trails. The first, at the top of the driving grade and just before reaching the first small parking area, is an informal, direct, very steep backside route to Flattop Mountain that features loose rock and scrambling through rocky notches—a little sketchy. Between the two small parking areas, the Flattop Sunnyside Trail takes off uphill at a wood-rail fence. It is a formal park trail. Next is a trail that roughly follows the drainage off Peak 3 and is a way to shortcut this loop with a direct (steep) ascent to that peak. Finally, the Rabbit Lake Trail begins at the far end as a continuation of the road and is the exit for this loop (see also Trip 28).

While this loop can be tackled in either direction, this description starts with the ridge first and ends with the valley leg. Start up the Flattop Sunnyside Trail at the fence (elevation 1930 feet), ascending through multiple long switchbacks, aiming alternately toward Flattop and Peak 3. This area sees so much foot traffic, it is critical to stay on the trail and not cut switchbacks to prevent erosion and scarring of the hillside. Visibility is good, and despite the people, it is possible to see moose and black bears as the trail ascends into alpine tundra, ultimately reaching a notch (elevation 3280 feet) between Flattop and Peak 2. Go left to Flattop (3510 feet) if desired, or turn right to start the ridge-ramble segment of the loop.

A few bigger ascents occur along the ridge, but there are many tiny ascents and descents along the way. The trail to and beyond the rocky top of Peak 2 (3609 feet) is mostly gravelly. Starting up Peak 3, people have gone just to the right of the ridge crest and scrambled upward steeply (the route should become visible as hikers approach it). Others have traversed the long tundra slope that drains toward the trailhead to gain the right-hand skyline and then headed left to the top of Peak 3. Choose either option; expect steep going. Steep snow in June could be reason for extra caution.

Beyond Peak 3 (3996 feet), the ridge is more continually rocky, with intermittent (and fading)

*Hiking the "flaky" ridge crest of Flaketop Mountain, with the South Fork Campbell Creek valley to the left (Photo by Gretchen Nelson)*

segments of visible trail. The trail runs on the crest (or below the crest on the Rabbit Creek side, bypassing outcrops on the top). Multiple small summits and chunks or "flakes" of rock mark the skyline. Go over or around these as seems possible, prudent, and fun. After several "summits," the blocky true summit of Flaketop Mountain (4488 feet) appears, not much different from the others in appearance but less accessible. The views are great throughout, up the South Fork of Campbell Creek and Rabbit Creek to The Ramp, The Wedge, Avalanche Mountain, Ptarmigan Peak, the Suicide Peaks, and many other mountains deeper in the Chugach, and back across Flattop to Anchorage, Cook Inlet, and the perpetually white Alaska Range.

Beyond the high point, continue following the ridgetop descending most of the way toward Ptarmigan Pass. A few scrambling spots are a little dicey and demand attention: scan for better routes if necessary, and use extra caution. The pass (3585 feet) is a deep notch between Flaketop and Ptarmigan Peak. While still high, get a good look at the lay of the land at the pass, because it won't be as evident when you are on it. There are a few loose rocky areas on the descent. Peel off the ridge when the side slope moderates. On the broad, flattish tundra of the pass, there is no one trail. Proceed west, erring to the north side of the flattish area. It doesn't much matter where you descend to the Rabbit Lake Trail, but descending at or immediately north of the most prominent gully is the shortest. In the right conditions, sliding on snow in the gully is a fun way to descend, but judge consequences carefully before risking a slide that goes out of control. The Rabbit Lake Trail is visible below. Once on it, walking is easy. Head down valley to the trailhead, approximately 2 miles. Look up on occasion to admire the dark rocky spine where you were mountain-goating not long ago.

## Campbell Creek Loop

From the Glen Alps trailhead (elevation 2200 feet), follow signs for Flattop Mountain. The main trail circles Blueberry Knoll; choose either side, and then start up Flattop. This trail has been eroded by thousands of hiking boots, sneakers, and even flip-flops. There are long flights of stairs partly eroded out. The hike is steep, but there are natural rest spots along the way. The last part, just below the summit, is particularly steep and rocky along the upper edge of a gully, requiring use of hands for stability. Snow lingers in the gully well into summer. In the early season, the winter's leftover snowdrift (cornice) can be extraordinarily steep at the top and may be unavoidable. Usually other people will have kicked big footholds in the snow. With or without snow, use care in this area. In snow, boots with good tread are highly recommended.

The top of Flattop (elevation 3510 feet) is, in fact, remarkably flat, particularly compared with the last rocky scramble. There is no trail across the top. Proceed southward, aiming toward McHugh Peak Ridge across the valley (well to the right of Peak 2). This bearing to the right allows the hiker to pick up a trail that descends to the southeast. The trail hits the notch between Flattop and Peak 2, and the route continues on the ridge crest, as described above.

Once done with the ridge and at Ptarmigan Pass, go left (roughly north) through the notch, descend past a small tarn, and find an intermittent trail descending steeply to the Powerline Trail visible below. The Powerline Trail descends with the valley but is rolling. After 3.3 miles, at the top of a long rise, signs direct hikers left toward the Glen Alps trailhead, almost 0.5 mile farther.

### SHORTER OPTIONS

For shorter options, hike Flattop Mountain, Peak 2, or Peak 3 and go back the same way. Round-trips starting from the Flattop Sunnyside Trail put Flattop at 3.4 miles with 1580 feet of elevation gain, Peak 2 at 3.2 miles with 1700 feet of gain, and Peak 3 at 4.3 miles with 2300 feet of gain. From Glen Alps, the roundtrip distance to Flattop is 3.4 miles; Peak 2 is 4.4 miles; and Peak 3 is 5.6 miles. Cumulative elevation gain is similar.

### EXTENDING YOUR TRIP

Extend your trip by taking on Ptarmigan Peak (elevation 4910 feet). At the pass, pick up the ridge crest headed east toward Ptarmigan Peak and, after the ridge bends to the right and becomes steeper (when it feels right or becomes necessary), traverse out to the right and then upward to the summit. This is a rugged scrambling climb best for those with good endurance. Hikers do this from either valley and via the pass rather than tacking Ptarmigan Peak on to the entire ridge ramble.

### SEASONAL OPTIONS

Ski touring can be good in either valley. Biking on the Rabbit Lake Trail and Powerline Trail is allowed year-round but is not always good when snow gets deeper. Spring crust skate skiing is popular off the Powerline Trail when conditions allow. Skiers also use the Peak 3 informal trail to ski the gully below the peak in winter and spring; snow-season users should know how to minimize avalanche risk (see Avalanches in the Introduction). Experienced skiers have died in avalanches in the Peak 3 gully and even on the short, steep, north slope that faces Blueberry Knoll just above the Flattop trail—don't underestimate the danger.

# 32 NEAR POINT AND WOLVERINE PEAK LOOP

**DISTANCE:** 10.3-mile loop
**TIME:** Full day
**ELEVATION GAIN:** 4265 feet
**HIGH POINTS:** 4491 feet (Wolverine); 3051 feet (Near Point)
**SEASON:** May–October
**SURFACE:** Hardpack, rocks, tundra
**GRADE:** Moderate with steep segments
**INDIGENOUS LAND:** Dena'ina Athabascan
**MANAGING AGENCY:** Chugach State Park
**MAPS:** USGS Anchorage A-7 NW, A-8 NE
**ONLINE MAP SEARCH:** "wolverine peak ak"
**TRAILHEAD GPS:** Prospect Heights 61.139059°N, 149.710552°W
Basher Drive 61.151542°N, 149.714195°W

**Wolverine Peak stands front and center among the Chugach Mountains as seen from midtown** Anchorage: a broad-shouldered peak with a trail visible from town heading right up the middle. Near Point sits just to the left, like a little brother, not as tall, not as rugged. Typically hiked individually, these two high points use the same trailheads and access. The bigger brother reaches an arm out to the littler—a ridge connecting the two—an option to create a loop.

Whether you tackle the summits as a loop or more traditionally, try them from either Prospect Heights or Basher Drive. The Basher approach runs on a narrow footpath along Campbell Creek Canyon and has a different feel than the more common Prospect Heights route, which crosses the creek upstream of the canyon and follows a wider path that once was a homesteader's road. Both routes take in pleasant forest and then bust out above the trees to attain these rocky summits with wide views over Anchorage and the Susitna Valley, to the northwest, and views southeast into the North Fork of Campbell Creek, a valley defined by a profusion of summits that go on and on.

This description and hike statistics are based on the Prospect Heights approach. The Basher approach makes the loop trip 0.6 mile shorter but involves an extra 300 feet of elevation gain. For out-and-back summit hikes, see Shorter Options.

*On the ridge between Near Point and Wolverine Peak in October, with Tikishla Peak beyond*

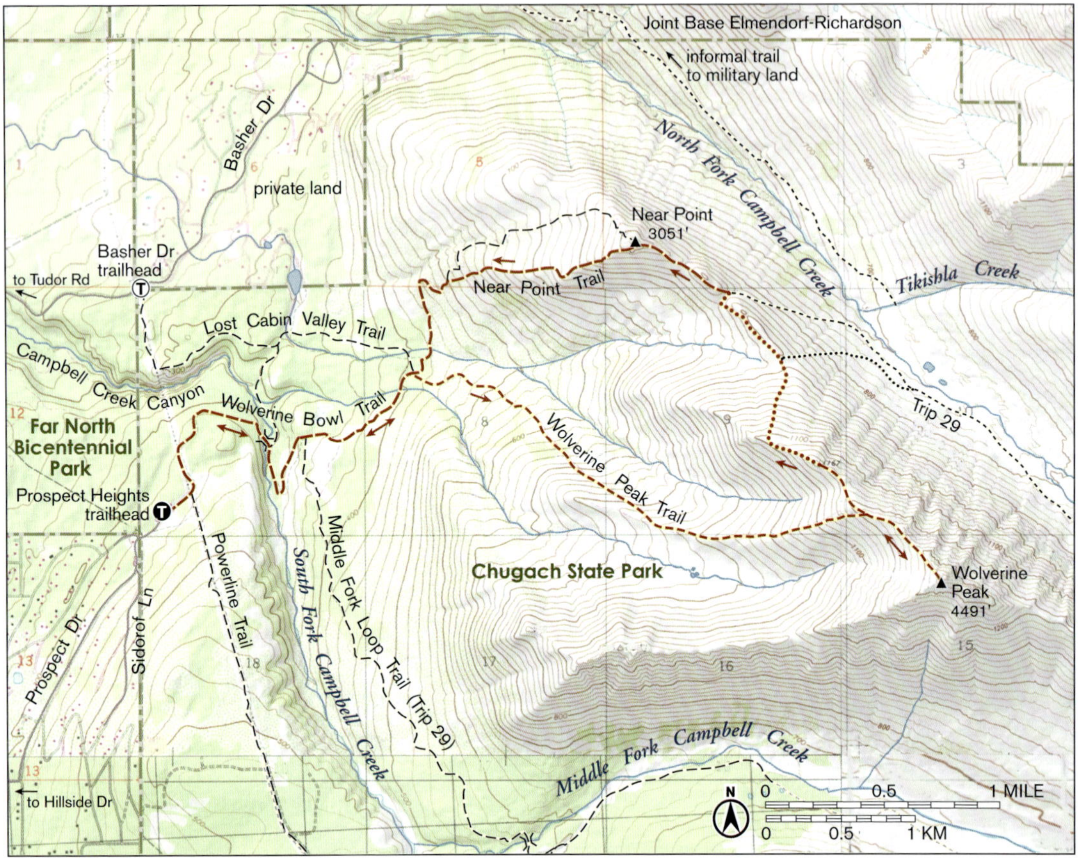


## DRIVING DIRECTIONS

Two trailheads provide access to the same trip. One approach is handy to South Anchorage and the other to East Anchorage.

**Prospect Heights trailhead.** Search online for "prospect heights trailhead ak," or follow these directions. From the interchange of the Seward Highway and O'Malley Road in South Anchorage, turn uphill (east) on O'Malley Road. Drive about 3.7 miles to Hillside Drive. Beyond a forced left, turn immediately right onto Upper O'Malley Road. Follow it 0.5 mile to a T intersection. Turn left onto Prospect Drive, and continue 1 mile to a stop sign. Turn left on Sidorof Lane, and proceed 0.1 mile. Then turn right at the Prospect Heights entrance to Chugach State Park. Expect to pay a fee for parking.

**Basher Drive trailhead.** Search online for "basher drive trailhead ak," or follow these directions. On the eastern portion of Tudor Road in Anchorage, navigate to Campbell Airstrip Road, and turn south. Drive the winding, paved road (name changes to Basher Drive) 3.1 miles through Far North Bicentennial Park to a small Chugach State Park parking area. The free parking lot, minimally marked, is on the right beneath a large power transmission line.

## ON THE ROUTE

From the Prospect Heights trailhead (elevation 1080 feet), the trail heads out straight and almost level beyond a trailhead sign, hits a powerline, and goes left. Over a rise, the main wide route bends right to leave the powerline and descends to the South Fork of Campbell Creek. Follow the main trail across the creek and back up the other side, keeping left at a couple of forks that lead to the Middle Fork of Campbell Creek (see Trip 29). This initial, wider trail leads across the hillside and several small streams to a marked four-way junction at 1.9 miles. The Wolverine Peak Trail goes right and uphill. The Near Point Trail is straight ahead. The left fork is the Lost Cabin Valley Trail, from the Basher Drive trailhead.

Turn right toward Wolverine Peak. The grade increases, and before long the trail narrows. Trees fall away, and soon any stop to catch a breath catches a view too. The longest views, however, always lie behind, so be sure to turn around once in a while. The area where the route transitions from brush to tundra is along north-facing slopes that hold windblown snow later in spring than most of the route and can be a posthole excursion (and potential avalanche hazard) in winter. While this is a true summit excursion, the route never feels cliffy (unless you go looking for cliffs). The trail is well traveled and easy to follow. It mounts a center rib that leads directly to the summit ridge. This rib is a long, steady incline leading from tundra to rock. Look for the twisted remains of an airplane crash to the right partway up.

As the trail approaches the summit, it goes to the right and follows the ridge. The Wolverine Peak summit is now less than 0.5 mile away. It may be just a fraction of a mile, but it still is an ascending fraction. The sudden view deep into the mountains as the trail hits the ridge is a breathtaker and totally different from the flats-and-ocean view behind.

With a last push, the rocky knob of a summit is a satisfying goal (elevation 4491 feet). The drop on the northeast side punctuates the thrill of the view.

To hike the loop, retrace the route on the final ridge, but bypass the trail up the rib, and keep on along the less-traveled portion of the ridge. This is the "arm" reaching out toward Near Point. Traverse over a low knob, and start looking to the right for a steep but straightforward slope down to a reciprocal "arm" reaching out from Near Point. There is no trail here. Head down the steep slope, losing 700 vertical feet in 0.3 mile and landing at the lower ridge. Follow this ridge over tundra and rock bumps and through a couple of notches, climbing back up to the broad top of Near Point (3051 feet). At least two other trails leave the summit of Near Point, one to the northwest, which starts down an open slope, and one to the west-southwest that follows the ridge. Take the ridge, the route farther to the left as you face Anchorage. The other is a bit longer, has a swampy area, and has more potential for confusion.

The ridge descent is steep, with some loose gravel, but straightforward. Follow the most-used trail down to a switchback at tree line, which puts hikers back onto the old homestead road. Follow this gentler grade into the forest, past the Wolverine Peak Trail junction, and on familiar ground back to Prospect Heights trailhead.

To exercise the Basher Drive option, start out of the parking lot (elevation 820 feet), and follow a rollercoaster trail under a powerline. About 0.3 mile in, as the powerline hits the edge of Campbell Creek Canyon and stretches across it, the trail hooks left up a short steep grade and then follows the edge of the canyon. At about 0.8 mile, the trail drops steeply to a small drainage and a trail junction. Go left, and follow the main trail, simply a narrow, worn-in track that can be muddy when wet. It traverses through forest and grassy meadows, with some mountain views ahead and city views behind, until it hits the old homestead road at the base of the Wolverine Peak Trail, 1.6 miles from the car. Proceed to Wolverine Peak by crossing the intersection, or go left to reach Near Point, following the routes described above.

The loop is perfectly good in either direction. Hitting Near Point first is arguably more scenic, because the hiker is facing out on a descent from Wolverine Peak and can better appreciate the views, but this means climbing up the steep slope between Near Point and Wolverine Peak. If you plan to tackle Near Point first, note one spot that some hikers may find confusing: the route reaches the end of the homestead road 0.4 mile from the four-way junction, makes a switchback to the right on a narrower trail, traverses across the slope for a couple hundred feet, and then bends left and uphill to a Y junction. Both ways get to the top, but the right fork is dry and has better views.

### SHORTER OPTIONS

Wolverine Peak as an out-and-back trip is 9.4 miles from Prospect Heights (3700 feet elevation gain). Near Point as an out-and-back excursion from Prospect Heights comes to 6.8 miles (2300 feet elevation gain). Again, either trip is 0.6 mile shorter roundtrip with 300 additional feet of elevation gain from the Basher Drive trailhead.

# 33 ANCHORAGE COASTAL WALK

**DISTANCE:** 5 miles roundtrip
**TIME:** Half day
**ELEVATION GAIN:** 400 feet
**HIGH POINT:** 330 feet
**SEASON:** April–October
**SURFACE:** Hardpack, sand and/or gravel, mud
**MODERATE:** Low angle with a steep segment
**INDIGENOUS LAND:** Dena'ina Athabascan
**MANAGING AGENCIES:** Anchorage Parks and Recreation Department and Alaska Department of Fish and Game (Anchorage Coastal Wildlife Refuge)
**MAP:** USGS Tyonek A-1 NE
**ONLINE MAP SEARCH:** "jodhpur street ak"
**TRAILHEAD GPS:** 61.145942°N, 150.015685°W

**For a city on the coast, named for its access to the ocean, Anchorage is not highly oriented to** the water. But the shoreline provides open vistas across green-and-golden coastal sedges and platinum waters to snow-topped peaks—whitecaps in the foreground, white caps in the background. In summer, listen for the distinctive call of sandhill cranes, a gargling-bugling sound that is one of the loudest and wildest of all bird calls. The Anchorage Coastal Wildlife Refuge encompasses the coastal flats and is the only place these tall, leggy birds regularly nest in the Anchorage area, and even then only a few pairs can be spotted.

Kincaid Park adjoins the refuge. It has an industrial history—military missile site, gravel pit, car dump—and is located adjacent to the state's largest airport and has a motocross track in its southeast corner. Despite this history, the area became Anchorage's premier city park—1400 acres of ski and bike trails, biathlon and archery ranges, the motocross track, and soccer fields, but also hundreds of acres of convoluted glacial topography thick with brush, devil's club, and mature trees where a moose can find a little privacy and feel at home.

The south coast lies protected below a high bluff. Most aircraft traffic to the airport routes in different directions, making this spot often one of the quietest in town—not that there is any sense of being "in town." To reach the quiet coast, this route takes walkers past a large sand dune and the motocross area. It offers high views across the water and intimate views at sea level. The shoreline progresses from productive wetland bird habitat, to cobbles, to real sand.

Although tides are unlikely to cause a problem, it pays to check the tide predictions online or in a tide book to ensure your trip does not overlap with an especially high-tide cycle.

*Windblown beach grass near Point Campbell, with the Kenai Mountains across the water*

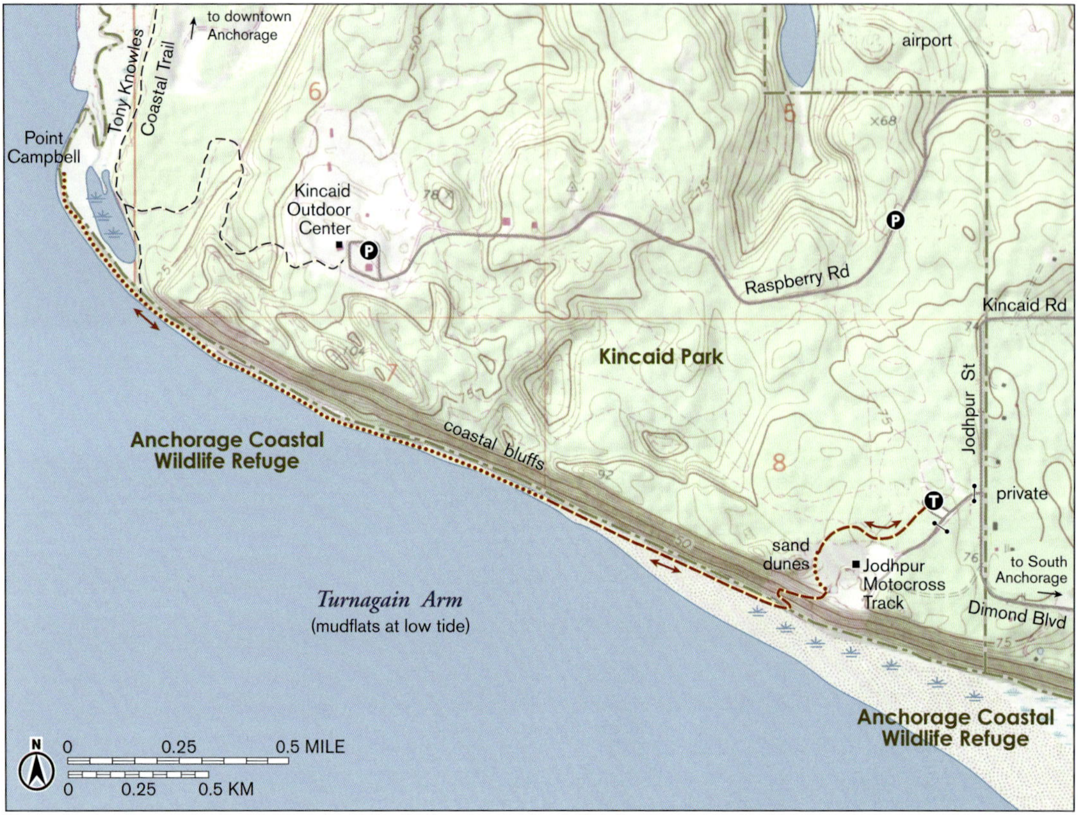


## DRIVING DIRECTIONS

Search online for "jodhpur street ak" or follow these directions. From the Seward Highway interchange at Raspberry Road, go west about 2.3 miles to Sand Lake Road, and turn left. Drive 0.6 mile to Kincaid Road, and turn right. Proceed 1 mile to a forced left on Jodhpur Street. Drive 0.4 mile to the park entrance on the right. Jodhpur Street also connects to the far west end of Dimond Boulevard, which provides alternate access.

This park entrance is gated; the gate is posted as open from 10:00 AM to 9:00 PM daily. If the gate is closed, there is a small area to park outside the gate. Inside the gate, proceed a few hundred feet to the main, paved parking lot. There is no parking fee. Multiple trails depart this parking lot; the featured hike starts at the back left (west) corner of the lot at a singletrack trails sign.

## ON THE ROUTE

Start on a wide, straight path heading southwest through the trees from the parking lot (elevation 260 feet). This path runs to the motocross area fence. Follow a narrower trail to the right along the fence to the open dune area (0.3 mile from the trailhead).

The route passes between the motocross track and the sand dune. The dune attracts kids and families, couples admiring the view, and young people in hammocks. The motocross track attracts people who like speed, jumps, noise, and adrenaline. Somehow, these adjacent areas coexist. The track is closed in winter; from April through October, it is closed Mondays and Tuesdays, open other days from 10:00 AM to 8:30 PM. The time spent on this route adjacent to the track is brief, and usually as soon as hikers drop over the bluff, most sound is gone.

At a hump near the dune, the views start. The Kenai Mountains and the flats of the western Kenai Peninsula lie across the water. There is no defined path through the sandy area at the base of the dune, which rises to the right. Aim for the far end of the motocross fence at the bluff edge.

It is evident from this high vantage that the vegetated coastal marsh below is wider to the left and progressively narrower to the right. This trip descends and heads to the right. Before descending fully, scan for shorebirds, which may be below or to the left. Look for the long necks of sandhill cranes emerging from the beach grasses.

The bluff drops precipitously. Thick beach sedges cover the slope and keep the sand in place. Brown stakes mark a narrow path that angles down the bluff. Please stay on the designated path to minimize erosion. Pass through a couple of switchbacks and in and out of trees, past old cars pushed over the edge (grown over and more curiosity than junk). Emerge at sea level, 0.7 mile from the trailhead, to views across the flats. An informal trail carries hikers onward to the northwest.

Hikers will notice driftwood, including enormous logs, that wind and waves have transported at the highest tides, probably during storms. Unless hikers are out in such a storm, water here should not be an issue. There is no ponding as there is farther east, but the path is right on the edge of damp. With judicious step placement, it usually is possible to pass through here in light hiking shoes without wet feet or ruined shoes, but following an especially high tide or extended rains, waterproof hiking shoes or rubber boots may be the preferred footwear. Enjoy the sheltered place at the interface of the bluff (park) and coastal marsh (refuge). The forested bluff is habitat for moose, bears, lynx, and other critters. The adjoining refuge not only protects waterbirds and their habitat but also provides a corridor for mammals from the mountains. During summer when shorebirds are present, keep dogs leashed or at home. Enjoy breezes in the beach grass and the glint of water.

At about 1.3 miles from the trailhead, the vegetation on the coastal flats gives out, and a cobble beach begins. If the tide is out, the ubiquitous mudflats of Turnagain Arm, with their curving channels and wet reflections, will be close at hand. High tides wet this area more often than the vegetated area you've passed. Some tides come right to the bluff and leave no room to walk, making this a logical turnaround point. Most tide levels, though, leave room for hiking. Wave action takes eroded glacial till from the bluff to the beach. The cobbles stay, and lighter sand particles move farther along. Follow the beach—now without a trail—to find the sand.

Point Campbell is a rounded "point" about a mile farther on (2.5 miles from the trailhead). From there, the bluff line heads north, and new views open up around this corner—Mount Susitna about 50 miles northwest and, on good days, Denali 135 miles north. Wind has created a vegetated linear dune, behind which lies a marshy lagoon. Explore this rich area as much as time allows, or just plop down and run your fingers through what is, in fact, sand.

Point Campbell is also an access point to the beach from the paved Tony Knowles Coastal Trail, so you may well encounter others. It is possible to return to the Jodhpur Street trailhead via the coastal trail and the circuitous network of inland park trails, but returning via the beach is scenic, easier, and more direct. You will now view the coast in reverse, with the Chugach Mountains to the southeast and long views up Turnagain Arm. Returning on the coast provides another opportunity to hear or see the sandhill cranes.

Note that hunting is allowed in the refuge. Waterfowl hunting takes place in fall and generally occurs farther southeast where the marshlands are wider and birds more plentiful, but be cautious.

### SEASONAL OPTIONS

Depending on the freeze-thaw cycle and the tide cycle, winter conditions on the coast can be icy or snowy. The trail down the bluff near the Jodhpur Street entrance is little used in winter and can be wind drifted, but it is possible to carry skis or snowshoes down or to hike in boots if the snow is not deep. Note that the bluff face, 200 to 300 feet high in places, is steep enough to avalanche.

At the end of winter, due to sun action combined with the winter's tidal action, a decent crust commonly forms over the coastal flats. In the best conditions, the entire southern coastal flats can be skate skied or ridden on fat-tire bike. Watch for a few partially or fully open tidal channels and the much larger open channel of Campbell Creek (there is a constructed crossing located at the head of the Campbell Creek Estuary). It is a joy to ski freely, without need for a trail, and snake through driftwood obstacles. The south coast has the advantage of full sun, but the crust typically softens by midday, so skate skiing on crust typically means a morning adventure.

Following are the common access points to the south coast: Oceanview Bluff Park; Carr-Gottstein Park; Campbell Creek Estuary Park; and Kincaid Park, accessed from the Jodhpur Street entrance, as described above. For Oceanview Bluff Park, people generally ski to the northwest; to the southeast is the Rabbit Creek Shooting Park, a.k.a. Rabbit Creek Rifle Range, and it could be dangerous to ski down range. Use the park and access names given to get driving directions online. All locations require carrying skis down the bluff and to a point of open skiing.

# 34 ARCTIC VALLEY RIDGE LOOP

**DISTANCE:** 5.6-mile loop
**TIME:** Half day
**ELEVATION GAIN:** 2450 feet
**HIGH POINTS:** 4134 feet and 4101 feet
**SEASON:** May–October
**SURFACE:** Hardpack, rocks
**GRADE:** Moderate with steep segments
**INDIGENOUS LAND:** Dena'ina Athabascan
**MANAGING AGENCY:** Chugach State Park
**MAPS:** USGS A-7 NW, B-7 SW

**ONLINE MAP SEARCH:** "arctic valley ak"
**TRAILHEAD GPS:** 61.246977°N, 149.535059°W

**Arctic Valley is a simple, peaceful, tundra-covered alpine gem that people can drive into. The** place is popular, but unlike any other Chugach State Park trailhead, there is nearly always parking. Multiple trails fan out, from mellow to steep, and there are two summits to climb, neither of them particularly difficult. There is a downhill ski operation on one ridge and a historic Nike missile site on the other; this is not the wildest country in the park, but you can see the wildest country from here. The view up Ship Creek Valley is into the trailless, undeveloped center of the park—a big forested valley backed by wild mountains. The peaks at the back of the South Fork of Eagle River are equally impressive. Why not spend an afternoon walking the ridges ringing this valley and taking it all in?

Local history is written on these slopes. The Anchorage Ski Club and the military operated ski areas here beginning in 1941. The club still operates the ski area. During the Cold War, the military built the missile site on a mountaintop across from the ski area and, unbeknownst to Anchorage, stocked it with nuclear warheads. The iconic, partially restored white towers look like they could be missile silos but actually contained radar and electronics. The missiles were housed at a less-imposing—but heavily fortified—site just down the ridge. While the army never launched missiles against an enemy from here, it tested them several times—and evacuated all the homesteading families in Eagle River Valley and the South Fork of Eagle River to the army post for an evening of relaxation and entertainment. Hikers with an eagle eye may spot old missile boosters stuck in the soil at a few locations in Arctic Valley and south of the ski area.

## DRIVING DIRECTIONS

Search online for "anchorage ski club ak," or follow these directions. From the Muldoon Road interchange in northeast Anchorage, drive northeast on the Glenn Highway 1.6 miles and take the first exit. This is Arctic Valley Road. Southbound traffic must take the exit for Joint Base Elmendorf–Richardson (JBER) at mile 8.1 of the Glenn Highway and then follow signs to Arctic Valley. Arctic Valley Road turns to gravel within 2 miles and then passes through a gate.

Drive 7.5 miles from the highway exit to the end of the road at Arctic Valley Ski Area. In winter, studded tires, four-wheel drive, or chains may be required for the sometimes-steep ascent. There is ample parking on the left at the end of the road. Expect to pay a parking fee to the nonprofit Anchorage Ski Club that maintains the area (a state park annual pass is not valid here). To return to the Glenn Highway, drivers must use the JBER interchange.

Arctic Valley Road is on JBER, and the military closes the gate at 10:00 PM and opens it at 6:00 AM daily. The military occasionally closes the road midday if training warrants. If in doubt, check with Chugach State Park or JBER (see the Resources section).

## ON THE ROUTE

This trip is a loop and is good either direction. The description runs clockwise. The start of the route may confuse some people because the trail forks

*Hiking along Rendezvous Ridge, with views of the South Fork of Eagle River to the left and Ship Creek to the right* (Photo by Nikki Navio)

may not be marked. The idea is to head up the main valley well to the left (north) side of the creek past two bridges to a broad, tundra-covered gully and then take a steeper trail up it to the ridge.

From the trailhead (elevation 2600 feet), the trail goes gradually uphill beyond the information kiosk. It starts wide on an old military cut. At the end of the initial straight stretch, near a ski area light, look for a narrower footpath to the right heading into the main valley, and follow it. Pass by an intersection that leads down to a bridge. A short distance later, at a fork 0.6 mile from the trailhead, go left again to stay left of the creek (the right fork leads to another bridge). Look for old missile boosters uphill on your left. When the trail turns left and heads up into the gully, take it. It is steep but pleasant, with wildflowers early in the season and blueberries later on. Near the ridgetop, look for rock ptarmigan.

The route tops out at a broad low spot on the ridge, and views open to the north, toward Denali in the distance and Eagle River in the foreground. Hikers can see across the southern ridge as well. Turn right, and follow the ridgeline in a rolling fashion toward the summit of Mount Gordon Lyon. Mr. Lyon was a military engineer who helped design the missile site, which is visible at fairly close range behind you as you start along the ridgetop. Although the visible trail is intermittent on the ridge, it is a straightforward hike to the rocky peak (mile 2, elevation 4134 feet). This is the high point of the loop. You may be able to see cracks from the November 2018 earthquake that show the summit was beginning to come apart. Perhaps after the next big shaker, this no longer will be the high point of the loop.

Backtrack a short distance from the summit, and follow a trail angling down about 700 vertical feet to a pass (elevation 3460 feet). Beyond the low point, follow the trail back up steeply, cutting behind (east of) Rendezvous Peak to a notch in the ridge. Hook back to the right to scramble northward up the ridge on a gravelly path to the second summit of the day (mile 3.4, elevation 4101 feet), only a few feet shorter than the first. A rock windbreak on top makes for a good lunch spot if the wind is blowing. Backtrack from the summit, and continue now along the southern ridge.

The ski lift towers on the ridge are a strange attraction. Look, but leave them alone. Progressing westward, the views into the Ship Creek Valley are unobstructed and are some of the finest and most accessible in the park. The route mostly descends, with a couple of small rises to break things up. Some segments drop steeply. The trail becomes a cat track, once used to deliver fuel to a ski lift powered by an engine on the top. On an unlucky day, a loaded fuel truck rolled off the ridge, killing the driver. The truck and tanks still lie on the south-facing slope below in the bushes.

The military removed its lift and lodge at the west end of the ridge in 2003. The ski slope has grown

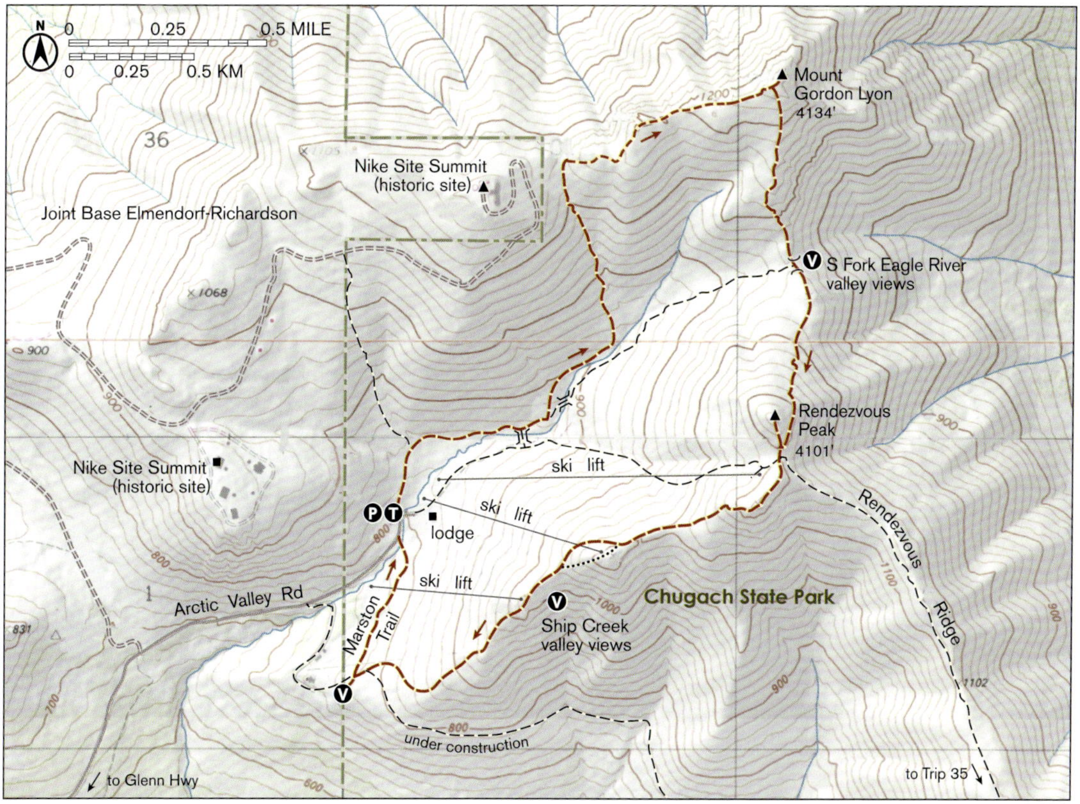

*The author's brother on Rendezvous Peak, his first summit, circa 1970* (Photo by Nancy Simmerman)

over in a patch of alders that the trail passes through before arriving at a four-way trail junction. The left turn is a quick jaunt beyond the alders to a viewing platform with benches made from old lift chairs. Straight ahead leads to military land. Go right on the Marston Trail to return to the trailhead. Note that the trail emerges onto Arctic Valley Road, and the last few hundred feet back to the trailhead kiosk will be on the road.

Arctic Valley is popular for blueberries in late summer—so popular that it is best to count on not finding any berries within easy reach of the parking area. But the advantage of this ridge ramble is that it takes hikers beyond the reach of many pickers, where a little poking around off-trail may be literally fruitful.

Because Arctic Valley Road is on military land and subject to military control, civilian travel may be restricted occasionally for military training or for security, but such closures are rare. Arctic Valley Ski Area buildings and equipment are the private property of the nonprofit ski club. Please respect this property. The area is closed to off-road vehicles year-round.

Those intrigued by the area's military history may take an occasionally scheduled tour of the missile installation by searching online for Friends of Nike Site Summit. Otherwise, the facilities are fenced and off-limits. The land around them is military land closed to the general public.

## SHORTER OPTIONS

Either Rendezvous Peak or Mount Gordon Lyon makes a perfect first summit, initiating little hikers to the joys of topping out. These out-and-back trips are short enough for kids, both in distance and elevation, and adults will enjoy the pleasant, uncomplicated climbs and the views. Start as stated above, go 0.6 mile to a fork in the trail, and go right, crossing the second bridge. Proceed up the center of the valley to the pass between Mount Gordon Lyon and Rendezvous Peak. For Rendezvous Peak, follow the trail to the right described above, up the back side of the peak. For Mount Gordon Lyon, go left. Either route amounts to 4 miles roundtrip, with about 1500 feet of elevation gain.

## EXTENDING YOUR TRIP

The loop as described finishes on the Marston Trail. As this book was going to print, an extension of the Marston Trail had been funded but not yet constructed. The alignment, shown in part on the map in the book, will connect to Hunter Pass, 3.8 miles from the trailhead (and to Trip 35 in another mile, providing an alternative to the overcrowded trailhead for that trip). It features great views of Ship Creek Valley, is more protected from wind than the ridgetops, and makes for a great afternoon outing, since it faces south and west. The extension should pass several sites with old missile boosters. And, for more ridge walking, you can incorporate it into a loop by returning from Hunter Pass 2 miles along a fine ridge crest to the notch south of Rendezvous Peak.

### SEASONAL OPTIONS

In winter, when snow conditions are good, the trip to the pass can be fun on cross-country skis. It is necessary to stay on the left side of the valley and out of the way of the downhill ski area. If going anywhere beyond the pass in winter, stay on wind-scoured ridges to minimize avalanche hazard. People have triggered multiple avalanches, particularly on slopes overlooking the South Fork of Eagle River (see Avalanches in the Introduction).

# 35 SOUTH FORK VALLEY TRAIL AND EWE VALLEY OVERLOOK

**DISTANCE:** 21 miles roundtrip
**TIME:** 3 days
**ELEVATION GAIN:** 3650 feet
**HIGH POINT:** 4724 feet
**SEASON:** June–September
**SURFACE:** Hardpack, tundra, boulders
**GRADE:** Moderate with steep segments
**INDIGENOUS LAND:** Dena'ina Athabascan
**MANAGING AGENCY:** Chugach State Park
**MAPS:** USGS Anchorage A-7 NE, A-7 NW
**ONLINE MAP SEARCH:** "south fork valley trail ak"
**TRAILHEAD GPS:** 61.232547°N, 149.455597°W

**The South Fork of Eagle River valley goes places. This trip takes hikers to the edge—to an over-**look of little-known Ewe Valley, where intriguing off-route exploration of the deepest heart of Chugach State Park is at hand. This trip proceeds to Symphony Lake to set a camp, uses day two to explore the overlook area high behind Symphony Lake, and heads back to the car on day three. Strong packers could complete this route in a single overnight.

Eagle and Symphony Lakes are sizable mountain lakes in different hues set among alpine tundra and boulders beneath some of the park's higher, pointier, steeper peaks. They make this valley a favorite. While the typical trip at the South Fork of Eagle River is a day hike (included as part of this route), going with overnight gear extends the range beyond commonly used trails and into some rugged but truly satisfying hiking with a bonus of high-mountain tarns and silvery rivulets. Parts of this route have no trail, but it is a reasonable trek for confident hikers. For those who are good with maps, can plot their way, and are comfortable dealing with the unforeseen, going beyond opens several possible bigger off-trail trips. None, however, is likely to be more scenic than this trek to a broad, tundra-covered ridgetop and its overlooks.

## DRIVING DIRECTIONS

Search online for "symphony lake trailhead ak," or follow these directions. From the Glenn Highway, take the Eagle River Loop Road/Hiland Road exit near mile 11.4, and go toward the mountains on Eagle River Loop Road. A stoplight appears immediately; turn right at the light on Hiland Road. Drive 7.2 miles up this curving, paved road to the edge of the alpine zone, and turn right on S. Creek Road. A brown state park sign marks the way. In 0.4 mile, turn right on W. River Drive. The trailhead parking lot appears within 0.1 mile on the left.

This park entrance has become extraordinarily popular, and the lot routinely fills. Overflow cars park on the edge of W. River Drive. This is also a residential access street, and tension has reportedly run high among neighbors who have to put up with disrespectful trail users. Ensure there is good visibility for residents turning in and out of driveways, and keep noise down and dogs leashed. See "Trailheadiquette" in the Introduction.

## ON THE ROUTE

The trail to Eagle Lake is straightforward. It is wide and well built as it heads gently uphill to gain an old lateral moraine and follows the moraine about 1.5 miles, providing views across the entire valley from well up on the valley's side wall. While the trail is below tree line, the spruce are mostly widely spaced and short; the views begin immediately. The trail begins to descend to the valley floor at about mile 1.7 and crosses the South Fork of Eagle River on a bridge at mile 2.2. It continues as a narrower path to and along the opposite side of the valley. The route has only minor ups and downs, accounting in part for its popularity.

There are several side trails that lead to interesting variations (see Shorter Options below). At and beyond the bridge, patches of mud may occur after wet weather, but the trail largely remains good to the outlet of Eagle Lake. The last fifteen to twenty minutes of this segment of trail become rockier, but the trail skirts around the edges of a true boulder field.

At mile 4.8, a bridge appears at the outlet of Eagle Lake, a long, narrow water body with a powdery blue-green color from the silt of Flute Glacier at its headwaters. Across the bridge, the trail disappears into the boulder field. Turn immediately right beyond the bridge and then left toward the high center of the boulder field. Look for bits of worn dirt to indicate where boots have passed. The trail passes immediately to the right of a clump of tall willows visible ahead. Symphony Lake comes into view 0.5 mile beyond the bridge.

From here, this description is a recommended route. Mix and match your tundra explorations as you see fit. The aim of this trip is to enter the high country behind Symphony Lake. To do so with minimal risk of wet feet, aim for a trail around the right (west) side of the lake. Other trails go onto the crest of the hill that divides the two lakes, past a weathered hexagonal ruin, and around the east side of Symphony Lake.

*Lakes in tones of blue, from left to right: Tarn #1, Symphony Lake, and Eagle Lake*

To go around the west side, proceed down a small draw toward Symphony Lake. Near the shore, cut right along the lake. Step carefully through another boulder field, without much evidence of a trail, to the lake's outlet. Large timbers lie across the rocks to create an informal bridge. Beyond the outlet, follow a narrow trail along the western shore.

The trail on this side is narrower and less used than the trail on the east (thanks to those boulders). It passes only three obvious informal tent sites. But it has a key advantage: it avoids the need to wade the inlet upstream of Symphony Lake.

Camp where you can (there are several more options on the east side of the lake), and admire mountain reflections in the lake. Because these campsites are close to the lake, go inland a good way for toileting. Human waste has become a problem in this popular area with limited camping spots. Carry a bear-proof food canister because the trees are too short to hang food. If you camp on the east side, in the morning you may prefer to wade the inlet stream immediately upstream of the lake (typically easy) rather than hike back to the boulder field.

Upstream of the lake about 1000 feet, the west-side trail angles up and left across a steep section of slope and may become intermittent after it levels out. There are parallel trails here. If you need to, hike uphill 200 feet with little sign of a trail to find the other trail heading up valley. While these trails are informal and braided, the routes go the

same general direction, coalescing and paralleling a little drainage that leads up to a tundra cirque and an attractive tarn we will call Tarn 1.

The tarn (elevation 3430 feet) invites a snack break, but camping here is not recommended; the area is fragile. Be mindful of Leave No Trace practices (see Introduction). From the tarn's outlet, facing south, inspect the terrain up to the right (west)—you may wish to descend there. The ascent trail mounts a rib to the left (southeast) of the tarn and follows this rib with minimal complication and ever-improving views to the broad ridge crest 1000 feet above. Another picturesque tarn (Tarn 2) appears below on the far side of the rib.

The narrow rib gives way at about 4250 feet elevation to an open tundra slope that is easy walking but has few identifiable features. Take note of the lay of the land behind you and the spot to get back on the rib, in case clouds blow in. The broad ridge crest heading southeast is rolling but mostly not rocky.

Hike up and left a mile to the far southeastern end of the rolling ridgetop. It's a thrill to sidle along the edge of a big drop into a cirque to the north. At the far end, a rock buttress provides an airy view into the upper end of Ewe Valley, where there is a rock glacier at the base of Mount Ewe (6293 feet). This overlook (A on the map, elevation 4675 feet) is 2.8 miles from the upstream end of Symphony Lake. Ewe Valley drains into the North Fork of Ship Creek, which in turn flows to the main stem of Ship Creek. Parts of the two Ship Creek valleys are visible from the ridge.

Head back toward the rib, varying your route as you wish. Eagle and Symphony Lakes are key parts of the view when facing north. Then hike up and south to a notch between two peaklets on the ridge (we'll call them East and West). Walk through the gap to rocky knobs (overlook B on the map) southwest of East point. Besides the views into wild valleys, Ship Lake (Trip 27) may be visible if the light is right, glinting beyond the back sides of The Ramp and Mount Williwaw, mountains normally seen from Anchorage. There are ways to proceed off-trail into Ewe Valley and the valley of the North Fork of Ship Creek to explore; see Extending Your Trip below.

To return to camp, you can retreat the way you came, which is shortest and most straightforward. But to make a small adventure loop, follow the ridge over West point and downward to circle around Tarn 1. Midway down the ridge, a cliffy bit interrupts the ridge-crest walk. It is easy enough to pick your way steeply off the crest to the right for a few minutes to avoid this rock band, then turn left and sidehill back toward the ridgetop. Here, pick up a sheep trail that cuts down to the right below a rock outcrop. Continue on the sheep trail as it traverses across a steep but not frightening slope high above Tarn 1. The trail peters out, but hike on a few yards to a tundra-covered rib. Follow the rib (no trail) to a logical point above the outlet of Tarn 1, and descend a final steep slope to the outlet. There, rejoin the trail you ascended, and follow it back down to camp at Symphony Lake. Going to both overlooks and descending via the loop creates a trip of 7 miles from the upper end of Symphony Lake on day two. Take a leisurely hike out to the car on day three.

## SHORTER AND SEASONAL OPTIONS

From the trailhead for the South Fork Valley Trail, several options make good day hikes:

Mile 0.3: Hunter Pass cutoff, marked. This short, steep, eroded trail goes to a notch in the ridge above and gains the ridge crest, connecting northward to Trip 34 and Arctic Valley if desired.

Mile 1.7: Rendezvous Ridge junction, marked. This informal trail goes to a second notch in the ridge above and allows for a loop back to the Hunter Pass cutoff (5 miles roundtrip from the trailhead).

Mile 2.7: Hanging Valley Trail junction, not marked. This informal trail takes off to the left 0.5 mile beyond the South Fork bridge, as the main trail turns and heads up valley. The side trail climbs into a hanging valley, leading to a high mountain lake and—via a steep climb through wildflowers—to Eagle River Overlook, a high point (elevation 5138 feet) with views into the main fork of Eagle River. The Eagle River Overlook hike is 13 miles roundtrip.

In winter, people hike, ski, or snowshoe the South Fork Valley Trail, but the initial climb from the trailhead may dissuade many skiers. The slopes and gullies above the trail could avalanche under certain conditions; use caution. See Avalanches in the Introduction.

*Fireweed in August at the Eagle Lake bridge, with Triangle Peak in the background*

## EXTENDING YOUR TRIP

Overlook A is essentially at the base of the last pitch of steep hiking to reach the summit of Triangle Peak (elevation 5495 feet). The ascent is rocky underfoot but straightforward. People have traversed the peak and descended into the headwaters of the Symphony Lake drainage and followed the creek back to the lake.

The overlook area allows access to the North Fork of Ship Creek. Hike to West point, and head down the southwest ridge (rib). Hikers may need to push aside a few willows or alders to get into the bottom of the North Fork, but aiming up valley avoids substantive bushwhacking.

Ewe Valley provides many camping opportunities. The North Fork of Ship Creek has a trail that heads upstream toward Grizzly Bear Lake. Camping is good in the upper valley. Across the North Fork of Ship Creek, people report finding their way through a series of passes to Indian Creek Pass (see Trip 27), with some bushwhacking likely necessary. These are substantive backcountry trips off the beaten path, wonderful to try for those who are fully prepared.

Finally, it is possible to proceed around either side of Eagle Lake to the flat valley beyond for camping or up a steep headwall or two to the toe of Flute Glacier.

# 36 PETERS CREEK WINTER TOUR

**DISTANCE:** 6.3 miles roundtrip
**TIME:** Half day
**ELEVATION GAIN:** 790 feet
**HIGH POINT:** 1670 feet
**SEASON:** November–April
**SURFACE:** Snow
**GRADE:** Rolling
**INDIGENOUS LAND:** Dena'ina Athabascan
**MANAGING AGENCY:** Chugach State Park
**MAP:** USGS Anchorage B-7 NE
**ONLINE MAP SEARCH:** "peters creek valley trail ak"
**TRAILHEAD GPS:** 61.397351°N, 149.412501°W

**On a winter day, especially once the light has returned, try a tour on skis, on foot, or on snow-**shoes to Fourmile Creek, where a terrace and opening in the trees overlook a forested valley backed by a brilliant-white mountain landscape. Peters Creek is one of the deep valleys of Chugach State Park, extending about 16 miles from the trailhead. Tributary names along the valley are mile markers—Fourmile, Sixmile, Sevenmile, and Ninemile Creeks. Prospectors before 1920, or later homesteaders, must have named these based on some lower trailhead. Today, Fourmile Creek is about 3 miles in, a good distance for a tour. Advantages of coming to this forested valley in winter are that it puts you in the mountains without real risk of avalanche, the trees protect you from wind, and the lack of leaves means the sun can get in.

In part because the trail once was a road, the route is wide and is one of the places where the park allows snowmachines when snow cover is adequate. Sometimes you may be breaking trail, and other times you may be on a relatively wide trail broken by snowmachiners. Motorized traffic does not appear to be heavy, so the risk of too much noise is low. Bicycles are allowed on the first 5 miles year-round. At 1.7 miles in, the nonmotorized trail diverges from the motorized trail; the Fourmile Creek destination is in a nonmotorized area. A long, skinny loop adds variety.

## DRIVING DIRECTIONS

Search online for "malcolm drive ak," or follow these directions. On the Glenn Highway northeast of downtown Anchorage, take the Peters Creek exit (about milepost 22). Turn southeast toward the mountains on Ski Road, and drive 0.8 mile to a T intersection at Whaley Avenue. Turn right (west) away from the mountains. The road immediately bends left and becomes Chugach Park Drive. Follow Chugach Park Drive 1 mile through a couple of steep grades. Turn left on Kullberg Drive, and go 0.1 mile. Turn right on Sullins Drive, and proceed 0.7

mile through sharp bends to Malcolm Drive. Turn right on Malcolm Drive. The trailhead is 0.2 mile straight ahead, where Malcolm Drive bends to the left.

Parking is little more than a wide spot in the road, accommodating a handful of cars. On busy days, cars park parallel along the road. A private driveway is adjacent to the trailhead; take care not to block it. In fact, the first portion of the trail passes through undeveloped private land. Stay on designated trails, and be respectful of neighbors near the trailhead (keep noise down, stay out of the road, and keep dogs leashed).

## ON THE ROUTE

There are no houses in the Peters Creek valley, except at the trailhead, and no development except for the old homestead road that now serves as a trail. It is the wildest forested valley in the park.

From the trailhead, the old road rolls in a rising fashion for 1.5 miles. The grades are moderate, requiring skiers to set their edges into the snow going up (herringbone) and down (snowplow). One grade about 0.4 mile in is the steepest—okay going up but a little dicey on the descent; some may wish to walk this one. Between the upgrades are flatter spots and mild downhills. Snow conditions will make a big

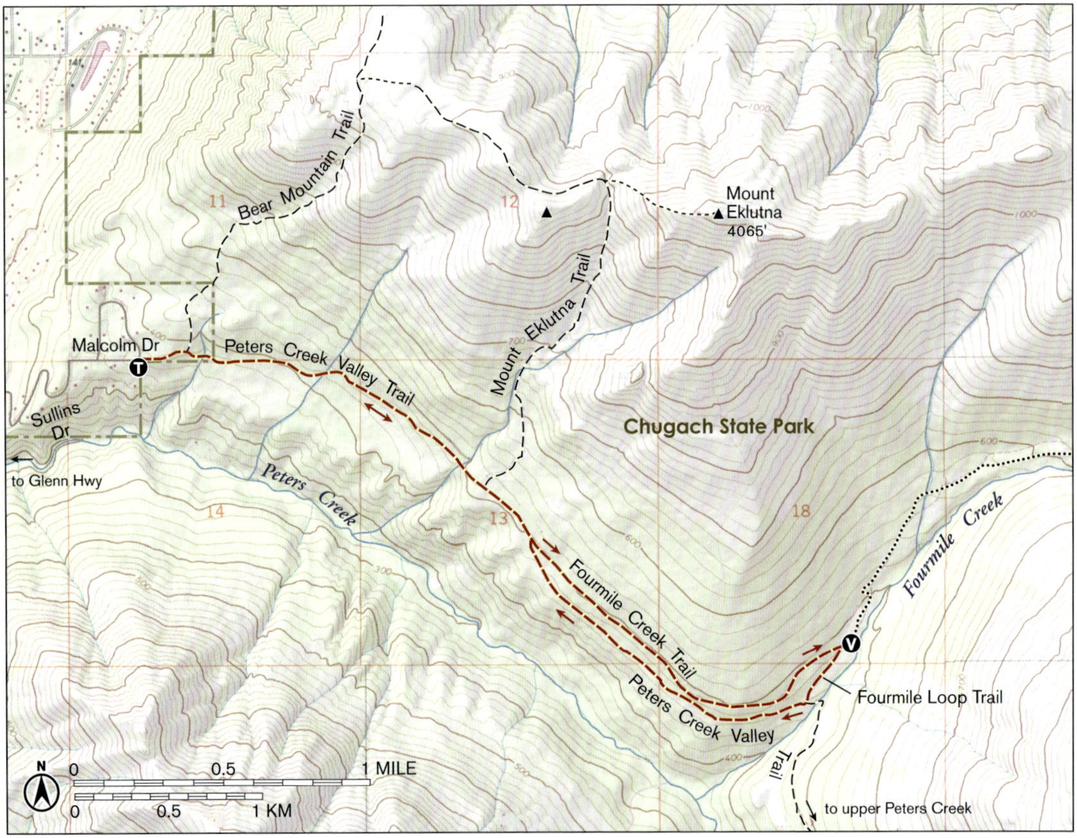

*Skiing toward Peeking Mountain on the Peters Creek Trail in March*

difference: when the trail is soft, the route will be most forgiving for skiing. When unbroken, it could be perfect for snowshoeing. When icy, don't bother trying to ski this route; use slip-on metal spikes over your boots, and hike it.

Only 0.2 mile in, while still passing through private property, a smaller trail takes off uphill. This steep, mostly summer route heads to "Bear Mountain," a rolling alpine plateau that looks from the lowlands like a summit. The route gets some use in winter, but portions are steep enough to avalanche. At 1.4 miles, the Mount Eklutna Trail takes off uphill. This, too, is a mostly summer route (see Seasonal Options) and crosses areas at risk of avalanche in winter. Near this junction is the high point of the route (1670 feet). As the trail begins to descend, look for views 10 miles up Peters Creek to Peeking Mountain—the same mountain that "peeks" over the front range in vistas from Anchorage. (Original author Helen Nienhueser named it when her children were small as "Peekaboo Peak," a name the US Board of Geographic Names deemed too frivolous and adjusted for greater formality.)

The Fourmile Creek Trail junction (marked) appears at 1.7 miles. The Fourmile Creek Trail is really the continuation of the old main road, and the Peters Creek Valley Trail diverges to the right. Using one of these trails on the way into the valley and the other coming back creates the loop portion of the trip. The two trails run parallel at different elevations, but the character of the vegetation alongside each and the views at gaps are different, making the loop desirable. For now, stay straight ahead to take the Fourmile Creek Trail, which rises pleasantly and descends gently a couple of times as it enters the side drainage of Fourmile Creek. A last descent glides into a flat, open clearing—an old homestead site, the cabin removed. To the southeast is a bluff above Fourmile Creek, which has places of open water even in winter. To the southwest is a big open view, with the forested hillside dropping away below the clearing and an impressive snowy mountain ridge rising up on the far side of Peters Creek. Timed right, the sun streams in here, making a good lunch spot. To the north and northeast are the near ridges of Mount Eklutna and the Fourmile Creek valley, rising shiny white above the dark branches of spruce, birch, willow, and cottonwood. The valley of Fourmile Creek curves enticingly out of sight, and likely someone will have broken a trail in that direction (see Extending Your Trip).

This area serves as wildlife habitat and as a place for people to enjoy because the Alaska office of The Conservation Fund was instrumental in brokering a deal to buy up large homesteads and donate the land to Chugach State Park, removing the crumbling cabin and retaining the trails.

The Fourmile Loop Trail (marked) takes off where you entered the clearing. Follow this zippy, rolling downhill a quarter mile to the Peters Creek Valley Trail, turn right, and follow this trail to close the loop. Then follow the trail you started on back to the trailhead.

### EXTENDING YOUR TRIP

Ski or snowshoe up the Fourmile Creek valley, following or diverging from skier or moose trails, and generally climbing at moderate grades to stay on terraces north of the creek. Ski to the end of an old track, approximately as shown on the USGS map, where a small bluff provides a natural break point (elevation 2040 feet) and views. This is at the second drainage bowl on the left. This extension adds about 2.8 miles, for a total of 9.1 miles roundtrip. Locations farther up valley or on open mountain slopes above the trees are prone to avalanche and should be avoided by those not equipped and trained; see Avalanches in the Introduction. Of course, there is the entirety of the Peters Creek valley to explore as well.

### SEASONAL OPTIONS

In summer, the alpine beckons. Connect the Bear Mountain and Mount Eklutna Trails as a loop for a rugged ridge ramble. The full loop plus an out-and-back spur to the Mount Eklutna summit (elevation 4065 feet) amounts to 6.5 miles, with 3250 feet of cumulative elevation gain. The Peters Creek Valley Trail can be hard to follow in some areas because it is minimally maintained and gets overgrown, but it warrants exploration as access to a fine, big valley.

## 37 EKLUTNA LAKE BIKEPACKING

**DISTANCE:** Up to 26 miles roundtrip
**TIME:** 2 days
**ELEVATION GAIN:** Up to 800 feet

**HIGH POINT:** 600 feet
**SEASON:** Late May–September
**SURFACE:** Hardpack
**GRADE:** Rolling
**INDIGENOUS LAND:** Dena'ina Athabascan
**MANAGING AGENCY:** Chugach State Park
**MAP:** USGS Anchorage B-6
**ONLINE MAP SEARCH:** "eklutna lake ak"
**TRAILHEAD GPS:** 61.409444°N, 149.135761°W

**The Dena'ina name for Eklutna Lake is *Idlu Bena*. By far the largest lake in Chugach State Park,** *Idlu Bena* is Anchorage's water source and produces hydroelectric power, and the current main trail was first a military access road. The water treatment plant and hydroelectric plant are located well away from the lake; despite these industrial uses, the lake is best known for its turquoise waters that compose the foreground in views of Chugach State Park's highest peaks and for its endless, year-round outdoor recreation potential. Less known is that the power and water supply projects that have given Anchorage a boost have cut off the water needed to sustain wild salmon runs in the Eklutna River.

Eklutna Village likely was sited near the mouth of the river by the ancestors of current Dena'ina residents because the river supported all five species of salmon, a staple food source. A project spearheaded by The Conservation Fund, Native Village of Eklutna, and Eklutna Inc. removed an unused dam in 2018. Eliminating the dam, which was well downstream of the lake, reestablished the free flow of water, promising that salmon will eventually spawn once again along the length of the Eklutna River. Continuing work is meant to ensure that adequate water drains into the river to support the fish. It is possible that, one day, migrating salmon will inhabit *Idlu Bena*.

Because the Eklutna Lakeside Trail is an old military road, it is suited to wheeled travel. This is one of the routes in Chugach State Park where mountain bikes are allowed and the only one truly long enough to encourage overnight bikepacking. While perfectly walkable as well, the 9- to 12-mile distance to good camping and the hardpack of the old gravel road is better suited to cycling than backpacking. The route is wide enough to tow a trailer full of gear or kids, and it is great for families with children too small to power themselves and for preteen and teenaged kids to enjoy pedaling—all in a valley in which sheer peaks frame the experience.

## DRIVING DIRECTIONS

Searching online for "eklutna water treatment plant" will guide drivers partway up Eklutna Lake Road; continue to the end of the road, or follow these directions.

Drive the Glenn Highway to the Eklutna exit, about 26 miles from downtown Anchorage or 16 miles from Palmer. Turn toward the mountains, and then immediately turn right onto the Old Glenn Highway. In 0.4 mile, turn left onto Eklutna Lake

*Looking toward the head of Eklutna Lake, or* Idlu Bena, *from the Lakeside Trail* (Photo by Anne Raup)

Road (signed for Eklutna Lake), and follow this paved but narrow and winding road 9 miles into the mountains. At 9 miles, pass a park entrance station (no longer used; instead, pay state park fees at kiosks in parking areas). From here, the next couple of turns are for overflow and main campground entrances; pass these. At 0.5 mile from the park entrance station, turn right and park in a large parking complex.

## ON THE ROUTE

On a bike (or on foot), exit the southeast corner of the parking complex, cross a bridge, and turn right to start the Eklutna Lakeside Trail. A wide main trail (old gravel road) follows the lakeshore more than 8 miles to the far end of the lake and another 5-plus miles beyond. This trail is open to off-road motorized vehicles Sunday through Wednesday each week. A smaller trail occurs intermittently and runs parallel, closer to the lake. It is closed to motorized vehicles and preferred for cycling, whether it is a motorized day or not, because the lake views are better and the grades generally a little flatter. However, waves from the lake have continually eaten into portions of the smaller trail, a trend likely to continue. Cyclists and hikers have made a few small detours inland, where there are roots and some mud. Because of the erosion and detours, portions of the smaller trail are too narrow for a trailer, and even people who are not towing a trailer will likely end up pushing their bikes a time or two. The wider main trail is always an option.

Otherwise, the route is straightforward, with minimal chance for confusion. The park generally has posted signs at intersections of the two parallel trails. The route has mostly minor ups and downs and passes through forest with many views across the lake. There may be puddles, but bridges or culverts mean no creek fords.

Cycling into the valley, the "B" peaks command attention: Bold Peak (7522 feet), east of the lake; Benign Peak (7235 feet), west of Eklutna Glacier; and Bashful Peak (the tallest peak in the park at 8005 feet), visible up the East Fork of the Eklutna River after riding about 10.5 miles. Rising 6000 to 7000 feet from the lake surface, these are world-class mountains, yet the trail along the lake is a fairly flat way to enjoy them.

Beyond the end of the lake, about 8.5 miles in, the trail hits a junction. Go right, and ride about a third of a mile to the lakeshore. The route passes an informal gravel airstrip sometimes used by small-plane pilots for their own recreation adventures. The area near the lake is suitable for camping but is not a formal campground. However, at the south end of the airstrip there is a designated camping area with a bear-proof food container and outhouse. Take-offs and landings are rare enough that they are an interesting highlight rather than an annoyance, and whether you camp near the lake or in the camping area, it is possible to use the bear-proof food storage container installed at the campground.

Other places to unload your bike for an overnight include two more state park campsites a little farther out the main trail: Eklutna Alex Campground, about 0.4 mile past the junction, and Kanchee Campground, about 2.4 miles beyond the junction or about 11 miles total from the trailhead. The three small backcountry campgrounds do not require reservations. There are also two public-use cabins, which are available by reservation: Yuditna Cabin is 3 miles from the trailhead, and Serenity Falls Hut is about 12 miles from the trailhead and 3.5 miles beyond the junction for Bold Airstrip Campground. Note that the trail approaching (and beyond) Serenity Falls Hut is a bit more difficult, with a gradual uphill gradient and a looser, rocky surface to negotiate. Yuditna Cabin is a standard state park cabin, with bunks for four to six. Serenity Falls Hut is larger, with bunks for thirteen. Reserve cabins through alaskastateparks.reserveamerica.com. It may be necessary to reserve space in Serenity Falls Hut directly with state parks; for instructions, search online for "reserve serenity falls."

*Serenity Falls Hut is the largest reservable cabin in Eklutna Valley.* (Photo by Mark Wedekind)

The area where people recreate around Eklutna Lake, while managed by Chugach State Park, is owned by Eklutna Inc., a village Native corporation established by the Alaska Native Claims Settlement Act. By formal agreement, the Native corporation allowed management of its lands here as a park. It is thanks to this agreement that Southcentral Alaska residents and visitors have the opportunity to play outdoors in this valley.

## EXTENDING YOUR TRIP

Wherever you camp, it is possible to explore farther. The main trail bridges the Eklutna River to its west side near Serenity Falls Hut, and ends a mile later. A narrow footpath continues beyond, but Eklutna Glacier has receded such that it is no longer visible from the west side of the river and is hard to access on the other side. Experienced mountaineers equipped for crevasse rescue trek across the glacier to Crow Pass (Trip 25), a trip called the Eklutna Traverse. There are three tiny mountaineering huts along the way, maintained by the Mountaineering Club of Alaska. Most traverses occur during spring skiing season, when snow and ice make the glacier approach easier. In summer, informal trails through the woods in the vicinity of Serenity Falls Hut lead up the east side of the river a ways (be respectful of anybody who has rented the hut). However, the toe of the glacier lies 2.5 miles upstream of the hut through a winding, rocky, and wet canyon. For most, the best glacier viewing option is Trip 38.

The East Fork of the Eklutna River also bears exploring. A foot trail leaves the main trail at mile 10.5, where the wider track crosses the East Fork bridge. While the path may fade out, the valley is walkable for 6.5 miles or more, beneath Bashful Peak and its lofty neighbors.

## SEASONAL OPTIONS

In snow season, when the ice is adequately thick, Eklutna Lake itself becomes the preferred travel surface instead of the Eklutna Lakeside Trail (see Winter Modes and Traveling on Ice in the Introduction). The head of the lake or the snow-covered river bars upstream of the lake are favorite crust skate-skiing destinations in early spring. When skiing out from the trailhead (or paddling out), be aware that nice-weather days often are accompanied by wind from the north. The joyous feeling of heading out downwind may mean a hard slog against the wind coming back. Paddlers should keep in mind that wind and waves change quickly on mountain lakes.

Eklutna Lake includes the Kokanee Cabin on its western side, approximately opposite mile 5 on the Eklutna Lakeside Trail, at the bend in the lake. Kokanee Cabin, named for landlocked salmon that swim in the lake, is accessible by paddle or electric boat motor in summer. That is, there is no trail on the western side of the lake. Kokanee Cabin is accessible across the lake ice via touring skis or snowshoes or, when conditions are right, by ice skates, skate skis, or fat-tire bike. Near the trailhead for the Eklutna Lakeside Trail is the large, drive-in Eklutna Lake Campground and the drive-in Dolly Varden and Rainbow Trout Cabins. All cabins are open in winter, but the drive-in cabins require a short walk or ski when snow closes the driveways. Reserve these cabins through alaskastateparks.reserveamerica.com.

A park concessionaire, located across the bridge from the parking lot, rents bicycles and kayaks (see the Resources section for contact information).

to Glenn Hwy
to Pepper Peak
Twin Peaks Trail
Eklutna Lake Rd
Eklutna River
Eklutna Lake CG
Dolly Varden and Rainbow Trout cabins
Eklutna Lakeside Trail (Trips 37 and 38)
Yuditna Cabin
Eklutna Lake
Kokanee Cabin
Eklutna Lake (Idlu Bena)
Bold Creek
Bold Ridge Trail (Trip 38)
Bold Ridge
4456'
5281'
Hunter Creek Pass
Eklutna Lakeside Trail (Trip 37)
Bold Peak 7522'
Thunderbird Creek
Bold Airstrip Campground
Eklutna Alex Campground
Thunderbird Peak 6575'
Eklutna River
Kanchee Campground
Chugach State Park
Peters Creek
Serenity Falls Hut
East Fork Eklutna River
Benign Peak 7235'
The Mitre 6650'
recent ice extent
Eklutna Glacier
0 1 2 MILES
0 1 2 KM

# 38 BOLD RIDGE OVERLOOK BIKE TO HIKE

**DISTANCE:** 15.5 miles roundtrip (10 miles biking, 5.5 miles hiking)
**TIME:** Full day
**ELEVATION GAIN:** 2850 feet
**HIGH POINT:** 3650 feet
**SEASON:** Mid-June–mid-September
**SURFACE:** Hardpack
**GRADE:** Moderate with steep segments (hiking); rolling (biking)
**INDIGENOUS LAND:** Dena'ina Athabascan
**MANAGING AGENCY:** Chugach State Park
**MAP:** USGS Anchorage B-6
**ONLINE MAP SEARCH:** "eklutna lake ak"
**TRAILHEAD GPS:** 61.409444°N, 149.135761°W

**From the northern end of Eklutna Lake, Bold Peak stands alone and visually centered over the** water. The mountain's north face holds snow virtually year-round. At 7522 feet, it is twice as tall as Flattop Mountain and other well-known points on the Anchorage skyline. It is robust, high, and—well—bold, the first big mountain among a series of high peaks that come into view beyond the bend in Eklutna Lake. For those who want to get up close to Bold and see the big view from a high vantage, a sturdy but pleasant uphill hike to alpine views starts at mile 5 of the Eklutna Lakeside Trail. A ridgetop overlook takes in all of shimmering Eklutna Lake, Eklutna Glacier, and many of the highest peaks of Chugach State Park. The Eklutna Lakeside Trail is a mostly gentle prelude to the Bold Ridge Trail. Why not bike the flat part and hike the "up" part to add a little variety?

Few places lend themselves so obviously to this combination of biking and hiking. Cycling speeds up the lakeside portion and makes this trip achievable in a day. Of course, it is good entirely on foot, but the 15.5-mile total distance may be off-putting as a walking-only excursion. It is a perfect day trip for those staying overnight at Yuditna Cabin because the out-and-back distance from the cabin is about 9.5 miles, and a cabin near a lake is always a good place to unwind after a hoof into the mountains. The map for this trip appears in Trip 37.

## DRIVING DIRECTIONS

Searching online for "eklutna water treatment plant" will take drivers partway up Eklutna Lake Road; continue to the end of the road, or follow these directions.

Drive the Glenn Highway to the Eklutna exit, about 26 miles from downtown Anchorage or 16 miles from Palmer. Turn toward the mountains, and then immediately turn right onto the Old Glenn

*Bold Ridge overlook area, with upper Eklutna Glacier visible* (Photo by Gretchen Nelson)

Highway. In 0.4 mile, turn left onto Eklutna Lake Road (signed for Eklutna Lake), and follow this paved but narrow and winding road 9 miles into the mountains. At 9 miles, pass a park entrance station (no longer used; instead, pay state park fees at kiosks in parking areas). From here, the next couple of turns are for overflow and main campground entrances; pass these. At 0.5 mile from the park entrance station, turn right and park in a large parking complex.

## ON THE ROUTE

Pedal to the southeast corner of the parking lot and a bridge. Cross it and turn toward the lake to start the gravel Eklutna Lakeside Trail. This portion is straightforward, and the cycling in most places is easy enough to allow you to look around at the lake and mountains. While virtually all cyclists will use mountain bikes or fat-tire bikes, the Eklutna Lakeside Trail can be negotiated by gravel bikes and even road bikes. Note that a narrower trail closer to the lake appears intermittently and is the way most cyclists go. It may have a couple of challenging spots. Follow the Eklutna Lakeside Trail to a bridge over Bold Creek, just past mile 5. Beyond the bridge a few yards, look for a sign for the Bold Ridge Trail on the left. Hide your bikes in the woods, or lock them to stout alders just up the first grade. They are not allowed on the hiking trail.

The trail uphill is an old vehicle track cut by the military back when it used Eklutna Lake as a training area. Alders encroached over the years, but most of the route has been cleared of brush since, creating a pleasant, wooded walk to the alpine zone. Because the builders created the route for vehicles, the trail occasionally zigzags through switchbacks and, while always pushing upward, is never too steep. As the trail approaches the bluff cut by Bold Creek, the roar of the stream becomes evident. As the trail angles away, the woods fall quiet. With elevation, gaps provide small views back toward the lake, promising even better things to come.

As the trail breaks into alpine vegetation, angled meadows extend to either side of the trail. This section is not always cleared of brush, and the "trail" may be a ribbon of brush in some segments. People have developed routes on one side or the other of the brush, and the expansive feeling of looking out across the meadows is far better than walking in the tunnel of alders.

The trail leaves the last of the trees behind and enters the Bold Peak valley, framed on the right by Bold Ridge. An old excavation may be visible to the right, grown over with tundra plants, and a few minutes later, a small, unidentified concrete foundation appears. In this area, for those questioning their resolve to push farther on, it is possible to traverse to the right and gradually uphill across the tundra, rounding the end of the ridge, until good views appear.

The main trail mounts a low morainal ridge and follows its crest about half a mile, with improving views ahead. Then the moraine ends, and the most obvious trail goes to the right and up onto tundra-covered Bold Ridge, where the lake, glacier, and surrounding sheer, sharp, pointy mountains suddenly burst into view. The overlook makes an obvious destination and turnaround spot. The rounded tundra ridgetop invites napping if the sun is out. Return the same way.

## EXTENDING YOUR TRIP

If you still have energy, walk the heights nearly a mile farther to point 4456 for an in-your-face view of Bold Peak. From here, a return option is to descend the steep, tundra-covered east slope of the ridge to the Bold Peak valley and follow the valley floor back to the moraine. Another fine alternative, instead of going to the ridge at all, is to continue to the head of the valley. At the end of the moraine, go left and downhill a bit on a faint footpath instead of up to Bold Ridge. Go a mile or more along the low-angle valley floor to the glacial moraine at the head of the valley and to a different bold view of the north face of Bold Peak. Camping is possible in this area. Note that the stream shown on the USGS maps draining the valley is partially underground, limiting access to water. The stream runs on the surface at the head of the valley near the gravel moraine though. Snow patches may be viable water sources well into June.

Those who camp out may have time to climb the steep scree slope at the head of the valley to Hunter Creek Pass (elevation 4850 feet), then follow the ridge left to point 5281. There are good views into the relatively inaccessible Hunter Creek drainage and the mountain wilderness rising behind it. For a loop tour of the valley, follow the northwest ridge from point 5281 back toward the lower end of the valley, descend as desired to the valley, and then hike back up to the trail on the moraine. Bold Peak itself should be attempted only by experienced climbers. Trip 37 presents other options in the Eklutna Lake area.

OPPOSITE: *The footpath leading up Fairangel Creek toward the Talkeetna Mine site, Trip 42*

# Mat-Su

THE MATANUSKA-SUSITNA (MAT-SU) BOROUGH ENCOMPASSES THE DRAINAGES OF THE MATAnuska and Susitna Rivers. The Susitna Valley has broad, flat, and forested lowlands, including many canoeable lakes, fishable streams, and state recreation areas. The Matanuska Valley is narrower, with dramatic mountain sidewalls. The Talkeetna Mountains dominate and provide a mountain environment different—more granitic and blocky—than the peaks in the Anchorage or Kenai sections. To the north, the Alaska Range and Denali (20,310 feet) create a natural boundary for the Mat-Su area, and hikes in Denali State Park provide spectacular views of the big, white peaks. The Susitna Valley is mostly homeland of the Dena'ina Athabascan people. To the east, up the Matanuska Valley, traversable drainages lead deep into the Talkeetna Mountains where the Nelchina caribou herd roams. The Matanuska Valley is the homeland of Ahtna Athabascans.

# 39 RABBIT SLOUGH IN WINTER

**DISTANCE:** 10 miles roundtrip
**TIME:** Half day (longer if hiking)
**ELEVATION GAIN:** Less than 10 feet
**HIGH POINT:** 16 feet
**SEASON:** October–March
**SURFACE:** Snow, ice
**GRADE:** Low angle
**INDIGENOUS LAND:** Dena'ina Athabascan
**MANAGING AGENCY:** Palmer Hay Flats State Game Refuge
**MAPS:** USGS Anchorage B-7 NE, C-7 SE
**ONLINE MAP SEARCH:** "rabbit slough ak"
**TRAILHEAD GPS:** 61.534272°N, 149.267839°W

**This trip follows a sinuous, frozen waterway and is flat-out the flattest trip in this book. It has** become a classic winter route for wild skating, fat-tire biking, ski touring, or hiking, depending on fickle ice and snow conditions. "Flat" in this landscape is like a big snow-scoop shovel, with a truly flat base, a wide-open edge on one side, and a big rim curving around the other edges. In this case, the open edge is to the southwest, toward Knik Arm, and the rim is the ring of mountains hemming in the north, east, and south sides—Talkeetna Mountains to the north, Matanuska Peak

OPPOSITE: *New Year's Day on Nordic blades at Rabbit Slough, with Pioneer Peak and Twin Peaks beyond* (Photo by John Pearce)

to the northeast, Pioneer Peak and the Twin Peaks to the southeast. Winter enthusiasts proceed out a winding ribbon of ice (often snow covered), leaving trees behind, until they stand (or skate figure eights) in the vastness of the frozen flats, agog at the mountain views. This route does not have a maintained trail. When the area is covered in snow, a trail develops from use. Otherwise, the plan is to simply *follow the ice*.

Because of nearby open water at the mouth of the Knik and Matanuska Rivers, low fog is common and can add an ethereal wispiness to the views. Tendrils of vapor come and go, rise and settle, playing with the light and unveiling peaks and ridges at unexpected moments, and the moisture adorns branches and grasses with sparkling hoarfrost.

The beauty of this trip is that the slough leads just the right distance—about 5 miles—to a lake-wetland complex. This is Duck Lake. When not covered in snow, it has more than 10 miles of shoreline to explore on skates, dodging in and out of patches of reeds, with ample space to play in the open center. This lake is a common destination, but skating out only partway has

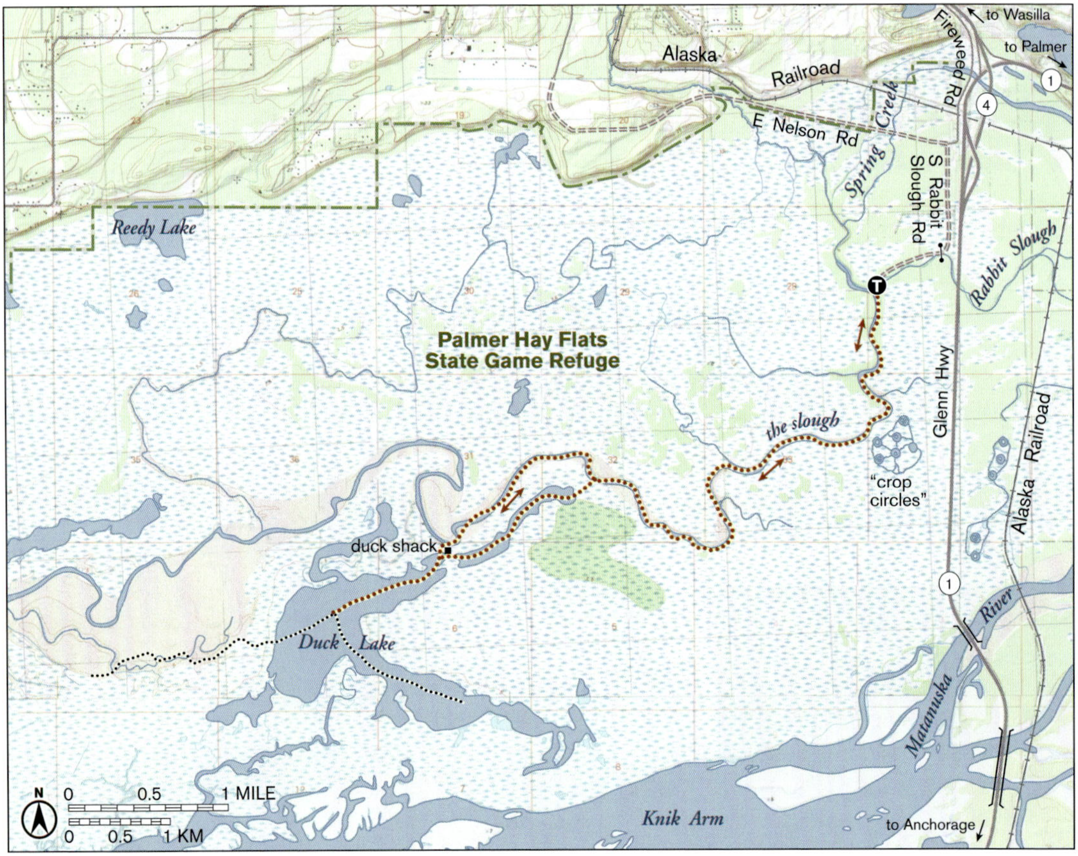

all the view advantages and, of course, is shorter. Most common for wild skating are Nordic skates, which have long blades and a free heel, like Olympic speed skates, but which clip in and out of standard skate-skiing boots. They are more comfortable than many typical skates, partly because the long blade rides over ice imperfections, and partly because of the boot. They aren't required though. Hockey skates and figure skates are fun too. Nordic skates may be rented in Anchorage at Alaska Mountaineering and Hiking (see the Resources section).

Some of this area, known generally as Palmer Hay Flats, was once agricultural, but the land dropped in the 1964 Great Alaska Earthquake just enough to make whatever was dry land into wetland. Birds appreciate it in summer, and moose year-round, such that the State of Alaska has designated it a wildlife refuge. In winter, moose are common, and myriad smaller tracks in the snow indicate the activity of other four-legged critters.

When the ice is hard and smooth for wild skating, or when the right amount of snow has fallen and adhered to the ice so that bikers with fat, studded tires can move well, the slough sees traffic. When the ice is cracked or rough, or when the snow is too deep or wind-crusted, the route sits and waits for better conditions, or becomes a hike. The ice changes through the winter, sometimes collapsing, sometimes reflooding and refreezing with tides or runoff, sometimes hot-mopped by a warm wind and rain to create a fresh ice surface. This changeability can be good for renewing bumpy or cracked ice to skateable condition, but it is possible to break through if the ice is not thick enough or to plow into a wet spot where water has welled up through a crack. Go cautiously until you are confident you understand conditions (see also Winter Modes and Traveling on Ice in the Introduction). The NordicSkate-SouthCentral Alaska Facebook page has good safety tips and conditions reports.

## DRIVING DIRECTIONS

Drive the Parks Highway to the Trunk Road exit, a mile west of the Parks Highway interchange with the Glenn Highway. Find a roundabout at the southwest (ocean) side of the bridge over the Parks Highway. In the roundabout, there is a brown sign for Rabbit Slough. Proceeding carefully, exit the roundabout, heading southeast (toward Anchorage) on E. Fireweed Road. This turn is immediately before the highway on-ramp.

E. Fireweed Road is a frontage road along the Parks Highway and then the Glenn Highway. Follow it 1.4 miles to its end, drive through a little dogleg at E. Nelson Road, and continue parallel to the Glenn Highway on S. Rabbit Slough Road another 0.7 mile to the road's end at a turnaround, gate, and Palmer Hay Flats State Game Refuge sign. It is 0.5 mile through the open gate and down a narrow, winding dirt road to a sizable parking lot located where Rabbit Slough runs into a larger stream.

## ON THE ROUTE

There is some confusion about the official name of the waterway that is the route for this trip. USGS maps show Spring Creek and Wasilla Creek upstream of the parking lot but also show Wasilla Creek joining the same waterway many miles downstream. The same map shows Rabbit Slough entering the larger waterway at the parking lot. At its lower end, the slough is called Palmer Slough. Most outdoor enthusiasts refer

*Thin fog and drifted snow in the Duck Lake area* (Photo by Anne Raup)

to this trip as Rabbit Slough. Call it what you will, we refer to it as "the slough" from here on.

From the trailhead, skate or ski south (downstream) on the widest channel. It also is possible to go upstream a ways, and some people explore the smaller Rabbit Slough inlet, which parallels the entrance road. The main route, however, goes downstream along a channel initially lined with large cottonwood trees, some birch, and brush. Winter leaflessness allows for views.

An etiquette note: skiing, walking, or biking on the slough when it is barely snow covered has potential to ruin the slough for ice skaters. There is a particular joy in ice skating through a light skim of snow. In these conditions, skaters will appreciate the efforts of all other users to stay to the sides—ideally one side—and pack down the snow only there. That way, ice skaters can still enjoy the light snow or the ice itself when a windy day clears off the unpacked snow.

At about 1.1 miles, as the slough quits its initial winding run to the south and heads west, some have reported fun exploring odd "crop circles" just to the southeast. These are small channels and islands in a vaguely circular pattern, reportedly created as habitat enhancement for waterfowl. The nearest is about 100 yards southeast (walking required).

About 2 miles in along the slough, taller brush gives way to low wetland vegetation barely poking through the snow, and the views open up. On this circuitous slough, you skate toward the sun at one point and follow your shadow at another. An advantage is that the views change continually.

If the ice is solid and clear without snow cover, and perhaps particularly early in the season, skaters may peer through the ice and see waving plant life, fish, or even a muskrat.

At about 3.8 miles, if there is snow, a cycling or ski trail typically leaves the slough at a point where the waterway bends to due north. The side trail heads west-southwest about 800 feet to a narrow, linear pond. This pond almost connects skateably with the Duck Lake complex. Most ice skaters continue on the slough to access the larger lake more directly.

For the next access to the lake, look for the first duck shack on the left, at about mile 5 on the slough, at the *next* point that the channel bends north. Bushes in this area could screen the duck shack, a rough little building, but there are a couple of other manmade items visible along the streambank to alert people of the turn. (There are several permitted cabins, or duck-hunting shacks, in the refuge.) If there is snow, the main packed trail likely will leave the slough at this point. A key feature of Nordic skates is that they make use of skate-skiing boots and bindings, so the skater can easily step off the blades and walk in the boots to the lake, where ice skating may resume. People with regular ice skates will want to carry guards to protect their blades, or spare shoes. Proceed past the shack without disturbing anything. It is about 450 feet to Duck Lake.

The lake is amorphous and without crisp edges, inviting exploration. Vistas are unimpeded by terrain or trees. Mountains appear even out to the west—the open edge of the shovel—where stand the distant, pointy outline of Mount Spurr and the lower, rounded crest of Mount Susitna.

After taking it all in and skating or exploring until you are content but not quite exhausted, return as you came, or make a small loop out of the two exits from the slough. Remember, it is all uphill on the way back (elevation gain fewer than 10 feet in 5 miles).

## OPTIONS AND SEASONAL VARIATIONS

The obvious shorter option is to proceed on the slough only as far as desired. As noted, 2 miles (4 roundtrip) gets into good viewing territory. Pick a bend and call it the turnaround point.

Cyclists and skiers with energy to extend their tours can continue west in the right conditions on a wetland extension of the Duck Lake complex or on the slough. Another 2 miles is reasonable when ice is firm and snow is shallow or well crusted—up to 16 miles roundtrip. Eventually tidal guts (channels that flood and drain with the tides) will impede the way, and the ice will become poor or dangerous. Cyclists and skiers sometimes lay tracks up other little side channels and through open areas.

In summer, the slough is canoeable. This can be outstanding birding territory during spring and fall migrations and in summer when some birds are nesting. The refuge is a migratory stopover and has been denoted an Important Bird Area by BirdLife International and the National Audubon Society. The slough also is fishable. Anglers mainly cast for silver salmon during a weekend-only, daytime-only silvers fishery starting in mid-June. Motors are limited to three horsepower on the slough during the weekend fishery. Refuge managers advise paddlers to consult tide tables (noaa.gov) because canoers working against the current at low tide may have trouble returning. Planning ahead, paddlers may benefit from the incoming tide to get back to the trailhead. Also, be aware that waterfowl hunting occurs in this area in the fall.

# 40 LAZY MOUNTAIN LOOP

**DISTANCE:** 8.5-mile loop
**TIME:** Full day
**ELEVATION GAIN:** 3300 feet
**HIGH POINT:** 3740 feet
**SEASON:** Late May–mid-October
**SURFACE:** Hardpack, roots
**GRADE:** Moderate with steep segments
**INDIGENOUS LAND:** Dena'ina and Ahtna Athabascan
**MANAGING AGENCIES:** Matanuska-Susitna Borough and the Alaska Division of Mining, Land, and Water
**MAP:** USGS Anchorage C-6 SE
**ONLINE MAP SEARCH:** "lazy mountain trail ak"
**TRAILHEAD GPS:** Matanuska Peak 61.599360°N, 149.000034°W
Lazy Mountain 61.611054°N, 149.015420°W

**Lazy Mountain is a popular afternoon or after-work hike near Palmer, that reaches a good height** (elevation 3740 feet) in short order. The hike provides great views into the Chugach Mountains, particularly of Matanuska Peak. Out across the silvery, winding Matanuska River and surrounding flatlands, are farmland and lakes near Palmer and Butte, with Knik Arm in the distance. The Talkeetna Mountains across the broad Matanuska Valley serve as a rugged backdrop. Most people hike out and back, but a network of trails provides for a perfect loop opportunity. The Morgan Horse Trail at low elevation and Southside Trail up high complete the loop. The southern combination of Matanuska Peak and Southside Trails may be the best route—for variety of views, terrain, and ground cover and possibility of solitude.

## DRIVING DIRECTIONS

Lazy Mountain has several approaches from two trailheads. The Matanuska Peak trailhead is also known as the McRoberts Creek trailhead and has few parking spots. The Lazy Mountain trailhead has much more space and requires a fee.

**Matanuska Peak trailhead.** Search online for "mcroberts creek trailhead ak," or follow these directions. Drive on the Glenn Highway to Palmer, and turn east on Arctic Avenue. Go through Palmer and beyond, crossing the Matanuska River. Arctic Avenue becomes the Old Glenn Highway; follow it to E. Smith Road at mile 15.5 (mileposts begin at the opposite end). This junction is 2.8 miles from the Glenn Highway. (From Anchorage, the Old Glenn Highway is also accessible from the Knik River/Old Glenn exit on the Glenn Highway.) Go straight on E. Smith Road for 1.5 miles (ignore N. Smith Road, which jogs off at a right angle after 0.5 mile). Online directions may use Smith Drive for the desired

*Matanuska Peak and the McRoberts Creek valley from Lazy Mountain in October*

route. The road you want to follow dead-ends at the trailhead. Kendy Circle and Harmony Avenue extend left and right. There is no parking fee.

**Lazy Mountain trailhead.** Search online for "lazy mountain trailhead ak," or follow these directions. From the Glenn Highway, get on the Old Glenn Highway, as stated above. Drive to mile 16. A brown sign for the Lazy Mountain trailhead indicates the turn onto Clark-Wolverine Road. Proceed 0.7 mile to a T intersection at E. Huntley Road, and turn right. Follow E. Huntley Road 1 mile to a Y intersection. Go right and downhill on Mountain Trail Circle. The road ends in 0.2 mile at a Matanuska-Susitna Borough trailhead with a parking fee; annual state park passes do not apply here.

## ON THE ROUTE

Approach this loop from either trailhead and hike it in either direction. Because the Matanuska Peak trailhead is at the lowest elevation, this description starts describes a counterclockwise loop from there.

The Matanuska Peak Trail starts (elevation 525 feet) as a wide easement between homes and across Eklutna Native Corporation land. Within about two minutes, the trail crosses the Morgan Horse Trail, which will be the final part of this loop. At this point, continue straight on the Matanuska Peak Trail. A couple of minutes later, as the wide track and easement continue straight ahead up a steep gravelly slope, a sign marks the Matanuska Peak Trail veering left. The trail enters state land and climbs steadily, sometimes quite steeply, through forest for a mile. The borough has marked this trail with numbered brown stakes starting at the trailhead and proceeding as multi-digit numbers, apparently marking distance in feet. The turn away from the easement is at marker 1400. About a mile in, between markers 5000 and 6000, views through the trees appear, both

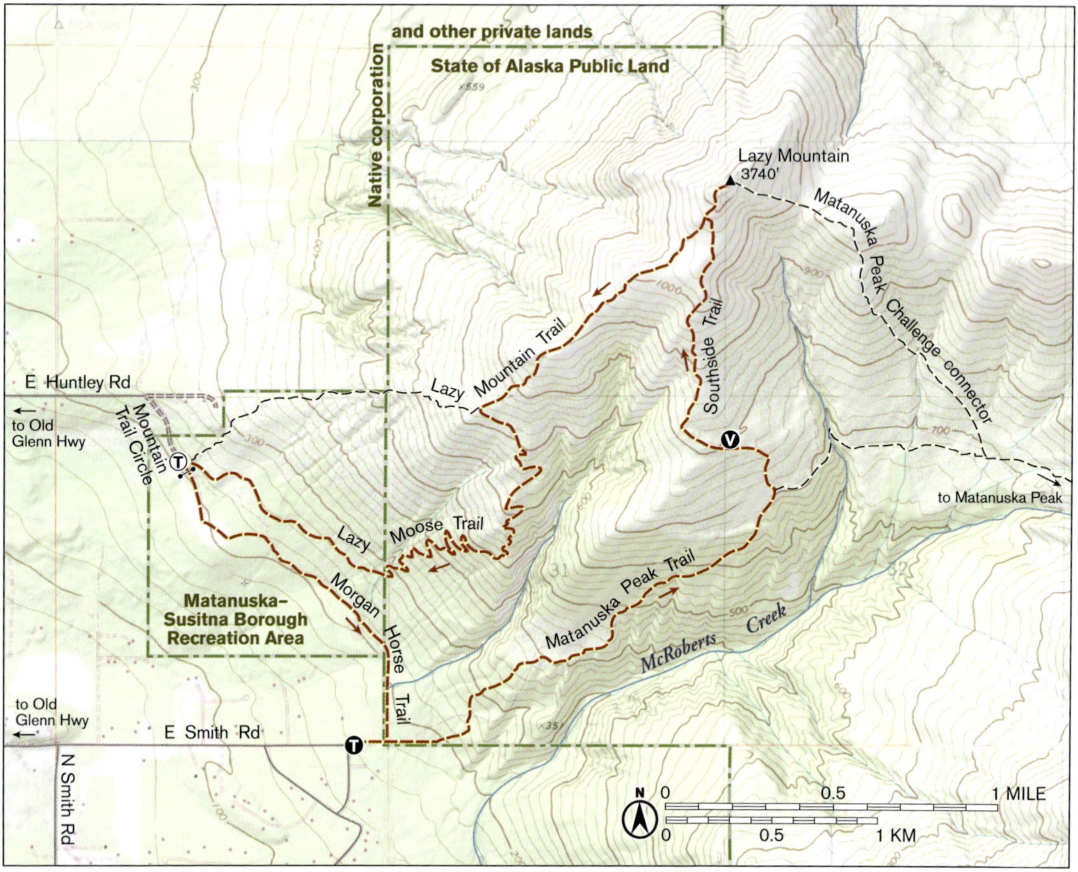


ahead to Matanuska Peak and behind to the rocky knob called Bodenburg Butte, which rises from the Matanuska Valley flats.

At mile 1.7 (elevation 2300 feet), just beyond marker 9200, the trail breaks into a small opening where there stands an informal tripod of sticks dragged in from the surrounding woods. The Southside Trail (not otherwise marked) takes off uphill to the left, while the Matanuska Peak Trail continues ahead and actually descends for a short distance. Go left at the tripod, leaving the other trail for another day (see Extending Your Trip).

The Southside Trail quickly leaves the last trees and brush behind as it aims for the top of one of Lazy Mountain's ridges. The views show up everywhere. Once on the rounded crest of the ridge (0.3 mile from the tripod), find a place to sit and ogle the scenery (and rest; it has been a lot of ascending). The humpy-bump ridge that runs east from Lazy Mountain to Matanuska Peak is in view. The valley draining from Matanuska Peak via McRoberts Creek is laid out in tundra and rock at its upper extent, all grassy below in its middle segment, and incised and forested in its lower reaches. Some grand high peaks of the inner Chugach Mountains push into the view beyond the Knik River (to the southeast).

From here, you can imagine the grueling Matanuska Peak Challenge, an annual mountain-running competition. It climbs the Lazy Mountain Trail, passes over the summit and down along the ridge toward Matanuska Peak, and then comes down off the side of the ridge through the grass to the Matanuska Peak Trail. It then heads up that trail and, after ascending a steep, rocky jumble, reaches the Matanuska Peak summit—and then reverses the entire route. Winners knock out these 14 miles and 8600 feet of elevation gain in barely three hours.

Proceed up the rounded ridge toward Lazy Mountain, with views off both sides. It is a mile or so from the overlook to the summit. About 0.2 mile below the summit, the Southside Trail intersects the Lazy Mountain Trail, the junction marked by two large cairns but no sign. Proceed uphill to the peak, where a flagpole is bolted to the rock. The last few yards are on a narrower rocky ridge than anything encountered so far. A protected area below the flag and actual summit may count as the top for many, because the last scramble to the true top (mile 3.2, elevation 3740 feet) may be uncomfortable.

After a celebratory snack and gulp of water, head back downhill a few minutes to the junction with two cairns. To complete the loop, go right, now on the Lazy Mountain Trail. After following the ridge down on a good trail for most of a mile from the summit (past two picnic tables 0.8 mile apart), the Lazy Moose Trail junction will appear to the left, with a signpost. Either trail gets to the destination, but the Lazy Moose, at 2.6 miles long from

*On the Matanuska Peak Trail in September* (Photo courtesy of Nikki Navio)

this point to the Lazy Mountain trailhead, is more scenic in its upper half, gentler on the knees, and less slippery when wet. Also, the borough only maintains the Lazy Moose Trail. Go left to follow it.

The trail winds through open meadows past widely spaced large birch trees and provides views in several directions. The upper part is as pleasant as a trail can get. Deeper into the forest below, there are several switchbacks in more convoluted terrain and a long traverse—easy enough but unremarkable. The Lazy Moose Trail joins the Lazy Mountain Trail a few yards above the Lazy Mountain parking lot. Popping out of the trees into the parking lot, look left for the upper end of the Morgan Horse Trail (marked), behind a gate and past an outhouse.

Walk through calm forest on a wider path, ignoring side trails in this area. Go a mile to the Matanuska Peak Trail. Turn right, retracing your steps on the final few yards to the trailhead.

### SHORTER AND SEASONAL OPTIONS

The original Lazy Mountain Trail is the most direct route to the high ridges (2.7 miles from Lazy Mountain trailhead to the summit; 5.4 miles roundtrip). The picnic tables make decent destinations short of the summit. They lie at mile 1.1 and 1.9 via the Lazy Mountain Trail and at mile 2.4 and 3.2 via the Lazy Moose Trail. The overlook on the Southside Trail is 2 miles from the Matanuska Peak trailhead (4 miles roundtrip, 2130 feet elevation gain).

Often, hikers keep the Lazy Mountain Trail packed in during winter. Metal spike creepers for traction are a good idea. The borough grooms a ski loop off the Morgan Horse Trail.

### EXTENDING YOUR TRIP

Follow the Matanuska Peak Trail to the summit of Matanuska Peak (elevation 6093 feet) 11 miles roundtrip, with 5500 feet of elevation gain. The trail portion is straightforward. The last steep ascent includes large blocks of rock.

Make a larger Lazy Mountain loop by following the Matanuska Peak Trail farther up the valley, then hook back to the left on the small connector track used for the Matanuska Peak Challenge. It is not marked. The Matanuska Peak Trail continues past this junction through a small drainage (usually dry) where brown marker 13700 stands and where the trail makes an abrupt, short switchback. If you get to this point, backtrack a short distance to find the connector trail. Hike up it, across a steep gully to the ridge, and up again along the ridge to Lazy Mountain, and then hike down the Lazy Moose Trail (8.2-mile loop, 3500 feet elevation gain) or the route of your choice.

# 41 HATCHER PASS TO GOVERNMENT PEAK TRAVERSE

**DISTANCE:** 7.2 miles point to point
**TIME:** Full day
**ELEVATION GAIN:** 2360 feet
**HIGH POINT:** 4811 feet
**SEASON:** July–September

*Admiring the ridge route ahead with Government Peak in the background on the left*

**SURFACE:** Rock, tundra, hardpack
**GRADE:** Moderate with steep segments
**INDIGENOUS LAND:** Dena'ina Athabascan
**MANAGING AGENCIES:** Alaska Division of Parks and Outdoor Recreation and Matanuska-Susitna Borough
**MAPS:** USGS Anchorage C-7 NE, D-7 SE
**ONLINE MAP SEARCH:** "hatcher pass ak"
**TRAILHEAD GPS:** Government Peak 61.705289°N, 149.277549°W
Hatcher Pass 61.768007°N, 149.316350°W

**Like a foldable ruler, this high traverse measures its distance in an unfolding series of zigzags** along a surprisingly walkable ridgetop, linking two popular trailheads with a comparatively lonely segment full of expansive views but mostly empty of people. It links Hatcher Pass proper (a low point on the ridge) with the Government Peak Recreation Area. Choose a direction: hike from Hatcher Pass out to the edge of the mountains, which overall loses elevation and provides views

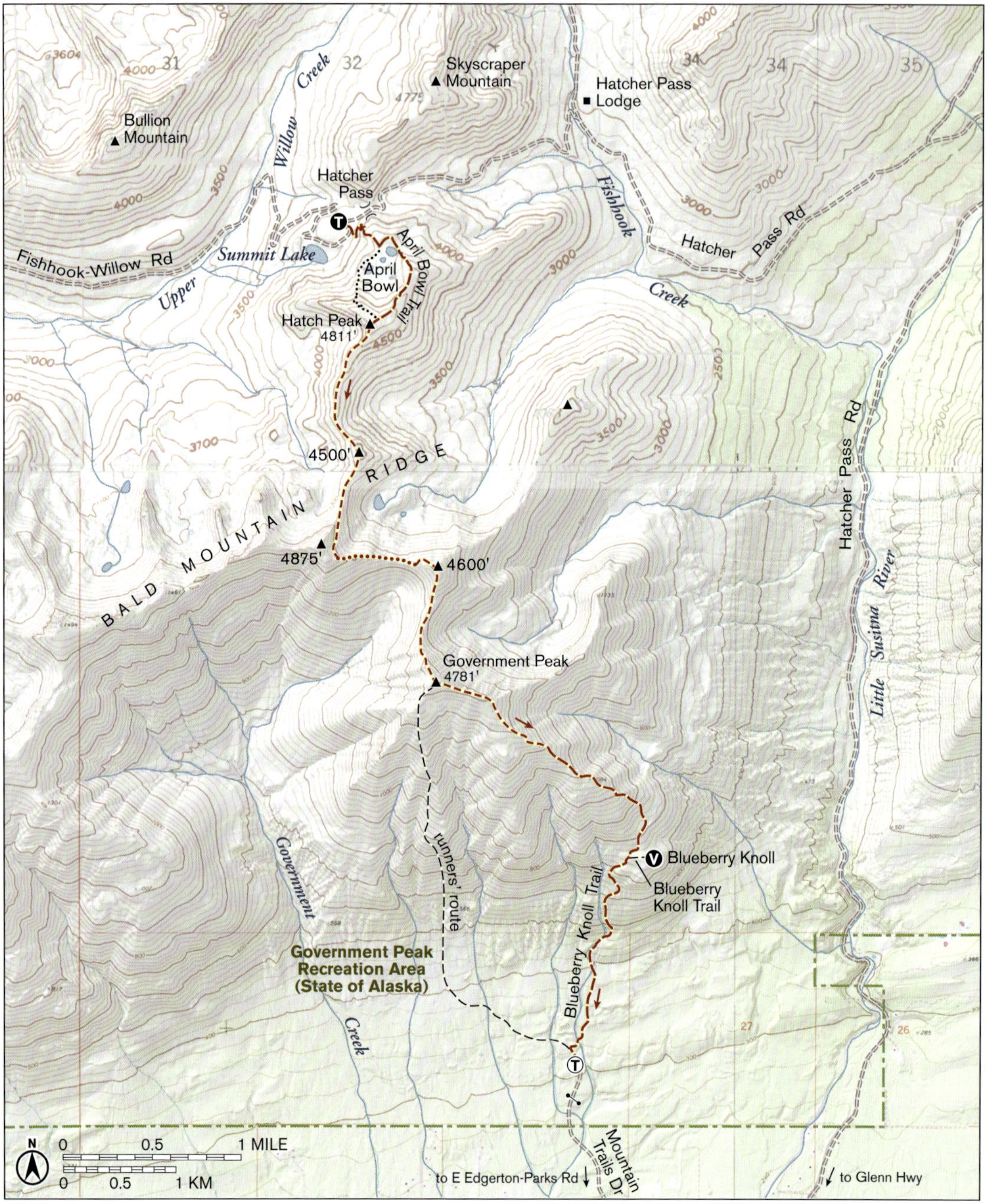
Skyscraper Mountain
Hatcher Pass Lodge
Bullion Mountain
Willow Creek
Hatcher Pass
Fishhook Creek
Hatcher Pass Rd
Fishhook-Willow Rd
Summit Lake
Upper
April Bowl
April Bowl Trail
Hatch Peak 4811'
4500'
BALD MOUNTAIN RIDGE
4875'
4600'
Government Peak 4781'
Little Susitna River
Blueberry Knoll
Blueberry Knoll Trail
runners' route
Government Creek
Government Peak Recreation Area (State of Alaska)
Mountain Trails Dr
to E Edgerton-Parks Rd
to Glenn Hwy
0 0.5 1 MILE
0 0.5 1 KM

first of the mountains and then of Southcentral Alaska's primary farmlands, or hike the opposite direction, which starts with a big climb of Government Peak and then leads the winded walker into unfolding views of the inner Talkeetna Mountains, with Denali rising up in the distance on a clear day. This description runs from Hatcher Pass south to Government Peak.

## DRIVING DIRECTIONS

This traverse requires a car shuttle. The driving distance between the two trailheads is about 13 miles, or 25 minutes each way. Out-and-back options are also good. Search online for "hatcher pass ak" and "government peak recreation area ak," or follow these directions.

To reach the general area, get on Trunk Road at its interchange with the Parks Highway (about a mile northwest of the Parks Highway interchange with the Glenn Highway), and follow it about 6 miles north to its terminus at Palmer-Fishhook Road (informally called Hatcher Pass Road). Go left. This intersection is at mile 2.7 of Palmer-Fishhook Road.

**Government Peak Recreation Area.** Go to milepost 7 of Palmer-Fishhook Road, and turn left on E. Edgerton-Parks Road (marked). Proceed 1 mile, and turn right on N. Mountain Trails Drive. The road terminates in another 0.9 mile, after passing through a gate, at the recreation area parking lot and trailhead. There is a borough parking fee; annual state park passes do not apply. The gate closes at 9:00 PM in winter. Plan accordingly.

**Hatcher Pass trailhead.** Keep following the paved Hatcher Pass Road past E. Edgerton-Parks Road and into the mountains (the formal name changes from Palmer-Fishhook Road to Fishhook-Willow Road). Watch for mileposts. At mile 17.3, well into the alpine zone, a junction appears on the left, marked with signs for Hatcher Pass and Summit Lake. This gravel road is the continuing Fishhook-Willow Road. Follow it to the Summit Lake State Recreation Site and Hatcher Pass proper. On summer days with decent weather, expect a congregation of people and cars near the pass. Ideally, park just west of the pass marker at a parking area and overlook. There is no fee for parking. Parking spaces are limited. The unpaved Hatcher Pass segment of Fishhook-Willow Road is closed to street vehicles from sometime in October, when snow shuts it down, until crews bust through the last drifts, almost always by July 4.

## ON THE ROUTE

On foot, start up the switchbacks of the April Bowl Trail, across the road from the Hatcher Pass parking and overlook area. After the initial switchbacks, the grade moderates, and the trail circles around and above several turquoise mountain tarns in April Bowl, a favorite backcountry ski area in winter. The trail is on a ridge crest with expansive views; snow remains on parts of the route well into July. About a mile in, the route tops Hatch Peak (elevation 4811 feet), the high point. To this point, the trail is popular on decent-weather days. Most people return the way they came. Some make a loop by descending the northwest ridge and a northern spur to the tarns. On the Hatch Peak summit, face away from the tarns; Government Peak is visible in the distance beyond a crooked ridge at nearly the same elevation. Proceed southward down this ridge.

Another mile brings the first jogs in the ridge. As the ridge angles left and up toward a rocky summit, it is possible, at the first flatter spot, to cut across the slope to the next low point and avoid climbing up and over. However, the top, at mile 2 (elevation 4550 feet), is pleasant and view-worthy.

The next incline is intimidating—a rocky ridge spine that looks like it could require ropes. It may not actually, but avoid it by hiking up tundra almost to the base of the rocky segment and then traversing out to the left. A faint and intermittent path is visible on this tundra-and-rock cross slope. Looking ahead, choose a route to regain the ridge while minimizing any crossing of snow. If there is too much snow for comfort here, consider descending to the left and reclimbing to a lower point farther along the ridge. Another summit (elevation 4600 feet) marks the final jog and final high point before reaching Government Peak; there is some fine tundra ridge walking in this segment with no visible trail.

Government Peak, at elevation 4781 feet and about 4 miles into the hike, has an odd summit marker and a "building" the size of a closet cabled down just below the summit. A mountain runners' race route comes up the ridge beyond the building. Top runners ascend the steep, 3-mile, 3700-foot climb from the Government Peak trailhead area in less than fifty minutes. Visible from the top of Government Peak are the Little Susitna Valley (location of the Gold-Mint Trail), Gold Cord Lake tucked in a rocky cirque, Palmer and Wasilla, Anchorage farther off, and Denali.

The hikers' route down to the Government Peak trailhead is on the east ridge, well to the left of the runners' route. The descent of 3700 vertical feet is never too steep, but it never lets up either. It is marked loosely with cairns, posts, and, farther down, brown stakes. Because the ridgetop is broad in some areas, the initial part of the descent, where there is little vegetation (and therefore only a faint path), could be difficult to discern in misty or foggy conditions, particularly for those new to the traverse. In addition to the markers, carefully look for compacted soil in the lichen and tundra to see where people have passed. Farther down, the route is obvious through ever-taller berry bushes, wildflowers, and ultimately trees. Blueberry Knoll becomes visible and is on a short spur trail. A picnic table invites a rest with a great view and makes a perfect out-and-back destination from the Government Peak trailhead.

Ultimately, the trail drops through forest into a maze of ski and mountain bike trails, but the hiking trail continues across the other trails and is generally easy to follow. Along the correct route, there are some signs for the Blueberry Knoll Trail, or BBK, that are oriented for people ascending.

To start at the Government Peak trailhead, from the parking lot, go to the trailhead information kiosk to the left of an outhouse. Walk past the kiosk, turn right on a wide grassy ski trail, and then turn immediately left on a narrower hiking trail marked "Blueberry Knoll, 1.5 miles, 1500 vertical."

## SHORTER OPTIONS

There are several ways to achieve shorter day trips and avoid the car shuttle: April Bowl tarns from Hatcher Pass: 1.3 miles roundtrip, 450 feet elevation gain; Hatch Peak from Hatcher Pass: 2.3 miles roundtrip, 1000 feet elevation gain; Blueberry Knoll from the Government Peak trailhead: 3 miles roundtrip, 1500 feet elevation gain; Government Peak summit from the Government Peak trailhead: 6.2 miles roundtrip, 3700 feet elevation gain. The mountain bike and walking trails at the Government Peak trailhead are also an option.

## SEASONAL OPTIONS

In winter, the Mat-Su Ski Club grooms a beautiful network of trails at the Government Peak

Recreation Area and near Independence Mine. Winter parking near Hatcher Pass is located at the end of the plowed pavement, just beyond the summer turnoff to Hatcher Pass. Backcountry skiers fan out from this parking area, including skiing up to Hatch Peak and April Bowl. Off the groomed winter trails, the mountain slopes are subject to avalanches (see Avalanches in the Introduction).

# 42 TALKEETNA MINE

**DISTANCE:** 6.2 miles roundtrip
**TIME:** Half day or longer
**ELEVATION GAIN:** 1800 feet
**HIGH POINT:** 4150 feet
**SEASON:** July–September
**SURFACE:** Hardpack, boulders, tundra
**GRADE:** Moderate with steep segments
**INDIGENOUS LAND:** Dena'ina Athabascan
**MANAGING AGENCIES:** Alaska Division of Parks and Outdoor Recreation
**MAPS:** USGS Anchorage D-6 SW, D-7 SE
**ONLINE MAP SEARCH:** "fairangel creek ak"
**TRAILHEAD GPS:** 61.801298°N, 149.201194°W

**The arêtes, cirques, cols, couloirs, and gendarmes surrounding the Talkeetna Mine route are** enough to make a person speak French. The mine is labeled on USGS maps with a location high above Fairangel Creek in a small, hidden glacial bowl (and nowhere near the town of Talkeetna). The edge of this hanging valley provides grand views of The Pinnacle and other granite horns (gendarmes) and knifelike ridges (arêtes), and of the ponds and streams of Fairangel and Archangel Creeks shining in green lowlands. The bowl and slopes leading to it are a short but steep walk into history, complete with a modest mine adit (horizontal underground excavation) that will make you wonder at the determination and strength of miners a century ago. This trip shares part of the trail to Fairangel Lakes, and the two destinations may be easily combined. Besides appreciating its mining history, look for blueberries in season and rock climbers on crags.

## DRIVING DIRECTIONS

Search online for "archangel road ak," or follow these directions. From the Parks Highway, take the Trunk Road exit. (It is about a mile northwest of the Parks Highway interchange with the Glenn Highway.) Follow Trunk Road about 6 miles north to its terminus at Palmer-Fishhook Road (informally called Hatcher Pass Road). Go left. About 7 miles farther on, well into the mountains, the road makes a hard switchback at the Gold-Mint trailhead and becomes steeper. Continue another 0.7 mile to Archangel Road on the right, across from a pullout marked as a fee area.

Take Archangel Road, on a good gravel surface, 2.2 miles to a parking area, again marked as a fee area (expect to pay a fee, or purchase an annual state park pass). The main parking is just before the road crosses a bridge over Archangel Creek. Park here, or, with a higher-clearance vehicle and a little moxie, proceed on a very rough and unmaintained road 0.1 mile to the Reed Lakes trailhead on the right (or beyond).

## ON THE ROUTE

The following describes the trip from the Archangel Creek bridge (elevation 2400 feet) on Archangel Road, but plenty of people drive farther up the incredibly rough old road beyond the bridge and park in little informal pullouts.

The old road makes a better walking trail than driving surface, and walking allows time to view the mountain scenery. Some use knobby-tire bikes for this first section. Continue past the Reed Lakes trailhead and up the valley. Approximately 1.8 miles from the Archangel Creek bridge, a rusted metal gate appears across the road. A much narrower footpath up Fairangel Creek takes off on the left. It is unmarked and hard to find. Other little trails have developed that may distract. To find the correct path, as the gate first comes into view, look for a large, white, double-knob boulder in the ditch on the right (uphill) side of the road. The narrow, unmarked footpath starts about 50 feet beyond the boulder on the left side of the road (elevation 3150 feet). Look for a lone willow taller than the other, smaller bushes lining the road; a mostly invisible trail cuts through the brush immediately to the right of this tree. Look for cut stubs of branches on the tree and possibly a small cairn along the road edge. If you have passed these landmarks, proceed to the gate, and backtrack about 65 to 70 long steps (65-plus yards) to find them.

From this point, hikers have only 1.3 miles (but still 1100 feet of climbing) to reach the Talkeetna Mine bowl. The route, while relatively short, is partly off-trail. Study the map and make the best of it. The following description is for those who like detail.

From the road, push through the initial few feet of willows, and head down a somewhat rutted boot-width track. This leads to a crossing of upper Archangel Creek, accomplished by stepping across closely spaced boulders. Continue on a good, worn-in trail. It becomes evident, at an old bench cut in a side slope grown over with moss, that the route partly follows a historic mining track.

With head-turning spires rising on three sides and mostly level walking, the trail leads 0.6 mile toward a small pond in Fairangel Creek, crosses the creek on stones just upstream of the pond, then climbs steeply through a gap between a massive rock outcrop on the left and a less massive outcrop on the right. Footing can be tricky here. The original mining access trail followed the slope above to the right, over the top of the less massive outcrop, but a critical portion of that trail disappeared in a landslide. The current trail gets the job done and begins to pass remnants of mining history, such as a section of flattened, rusted water pipes.

Beyond a second section of water pipes and after crossing a pair of old cables, the trail grade moderates, and the gap begins to open to a small valley. Look for a fork in the trail. This fork is not on the map, because of scale, but it is where the dashed trail becomes a dotted route. The forks quickly rejoin, but take the right fork; it leads closest to the adjacent creek, which flows largely under rocks at this point. To get to the Talkeetna Mine bowl, leave the Fairangel

*Ambling along Fairangel Creek*

Lakes Trail where it is closest to the creek, and proceed cross-country.

Cross the creek from south to north on stones. Then follow a tundra ramp uphill and to the left (northwest). The objective is to skirt around rock outcrops above.

Beyond the initial ramp, proceed almost level for a short distance to the edge of a field of boulders. Turn uphill along the edge of the boulders and then arc to the right (east), essentially completing a broad switchback.

Look for a large, rounded rock outcrop ahead (east), and aim to the right of it, passing through a gap in bedrock. Continue gradually upward to another crossing of the two cables and to a rusted-out old cookstove sitting on the tundra (1 mile from Archangel Road, 3750 feet elevation).

The cookstove likely sits at the location of miners' quarters. Mining reportedly began at Talkeetna Mine in 1910, with more extensive tunneling, a tram (the cables), and milling principally in the 1917–1923 era. At the stove, carefully survey the nearby terrain

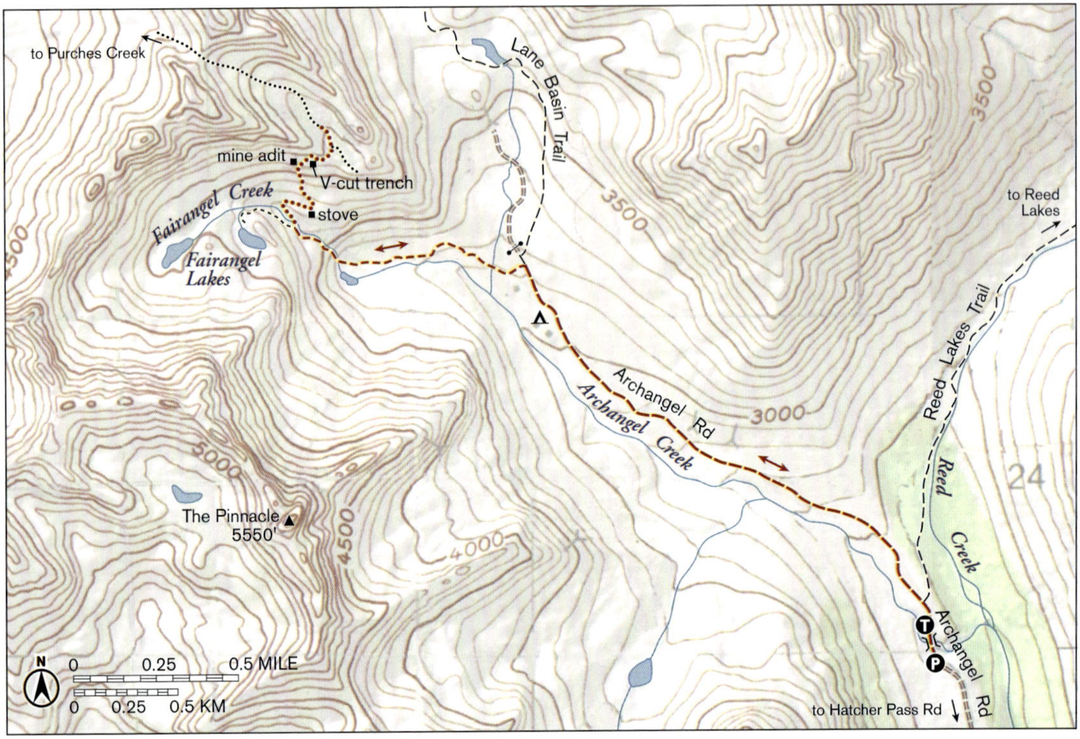


to pick up the old mining trail, visible as a narrow bench cut in the earth but completely overgrown with low tundra plants. It curves uphill around the base of a tundra hump and leads away from the stove. Imagine miners coming and going from a cabin on this path.

Follow the old trail uphill around the curve. The trail almost immediately hooks left and trends uphill to the left (northwest) with occasional short zigzags. Where it traverses across the top of rock slabs, it soon intersects the two cables again.

At this point, the most obvious route proceeds at the same grade into some low willow brush growing in the old trail, but the discerning eye may pick out a steeper, historic trail climbing toward the base of a rock outcrop on the right. For an interesting diversion, look for a short adit under this outcrop at the top of the steeper trail.

From the cables, the best way to continue to the Talkeetna Mine bowl is to go up the steeper trail a few steps and then, before the adit comes into view, head upward off-trail to the right of the rock outcrop, picking the path of least resistance while arcing slightly left until essentially on top of the outcrop.

From a more level stance well above the adit, find an old V-cut trench proceeding uphill (now to the northeast), and follow it. A bit of old path beyond the trench leads to a low point in the mellow tundra-and-rock ridge that separates the high Talkeetna Mine bowl from the Fairangel Creek valley.

Pass through the low point. The hanging valley of Talkeetna Mine opens to the right and left (1.3 miles from Archangel Road, 3.1 miles from Archangel Creek bridge; elevation 4150 feet). Remnants of an old mining water intake and metal pipeline appear as curiosities in the base of the lower bowl, these likely dating from efforts in the 1970s.

From here, there are several options. Sit in the tundra and simply admire the views. Proceed up or down the ridge a short way. Descend slightly into the base of the hanging valley and explore up and down the stream. Miners reportedly explored the far wall of the valley, a notion reinforced by evidence of more old trail cutting up the slope; there may be other historic excavations to find. Hikers willing to lug an overnight pack up here will find camping opportunities at the lower end of the bowl, and water. For most people, this valley makes a fine place for a snack break before returning the way they hiked up.

A large area extending from Fairangel Lakes, across the Talkeetna Mine bowl, and into the Archangel Creek valley near the gate is a collection of patented private mining claims. Hikers and rock climbers have used the trail up Fairangel Creek and the route to the Talkeetna Mine area and surrounding crags for decades without problem or closure. However, hikers should be respectful of private land, should not disturb mining artifacts or minerals, and should remain alert for any change in the status of these lands.

## EXTENDING YOUR TRIP

At the upper end of the Talkeetna Mine valley is a bouldery cirque (upper bowl) backed by a col (high mountain pass) that allows a narrow view of (or rugged passage to) the headwaters of Purches Creek. Both sides of the col require long stretches of boulder hopping (or walking on steep snow earlier in the season), and this route is only for those confident in their footing on such terrain.

From higher elevations above the mine adit, both of the Fairangel Lakes are visible across the Fairangel Creek valley. On the return trip, a detour up the continuing trail to visit the lakes up close adds only a little extra distance and time to the overall hike.

## SEASONAL OPTIONS

In winter, Archangel Road is closed to cars, and the Mat-Su Ski Club maintains it for cross-country skiing. Park in the pullout across from the beginning of the road (a state park fee area), and follow the wide ski trail, generally groomed for both classic and skate skiing, as far as the gate, 4 miles. The terrain is rolling at first, with a long, steady uphill over the second half. Beginner skiers will find the long grade very challenging. The downhill run on this big grade is a hoot for expert skiers but can be gripping for those who aren't. Off-trail skiing opportunities abound, but the mountain slopes are avalanche terrain, and skiers off the groomed trail should be trained in avalanche safety (see Avalanches in the Introduction). Snowmachines are allowed to cross the ski trail, use portions of these valleys off-trail, and share use of the trail beyond the Archangel Creek bridge. See Seasonal Options in Trip 41 for more.

*Looking out from the opening of an old mine adit*

# 43 REED LAKES

**DISTANCE:** 9.1 miles roundtrip
**TIME:** Full day to 2 days
**ELEVATION GAIN:** 2100 feet
**HIGH POINT:** 4270 feet
**SEASON:** July–September
**SURFACE:** Hardpack, boulders
**GRADE:** Moderate with steep segments
**INDIGENOUS LAND:** Dena'ina Athabascan
**MANAGING AGENCIES:** Alaska Division of Parks and Outdoor Recreation and Alaska Division of Mining, Land, and Water
**MAP:** USGS Anchorage D-6 SW
**ONLINE MAP SEARCH:** "upper reed lake ak"
**TRAILHEAD GPS:** 61.801060°N, 149.201317°W

**At the foot of towering granite spires reminiscent of the High Sierra, plunging cascades feed two** alpine pools, the Reed Lakes. On the edge of the vast wilderness of the Talkeetna Mountains, this mountain world is unlike any other in Southcentral Alaska. Enjoy boulder hopping and tundra lounging. Brave a dip into frigid cyan-blue waters, too pristine to pass up. Watch for marmots, ground squirrels, pikas, ptarmigan, northern shrikes, and golden eagles.

## DRIVING DIRECTIONS

Search online for "archangel road ak," or follow these directions. From the Parks Highway, take the Trunk Road exit. (This is about a mile northwest of the Parks Highway interchange with the Glenn Highway.) Follow Trunk Road about 6 miles north to its terminus at Palmer-Fishhook Road (informally called Hatcher Pass Road). Go left. About 7 miles farther on, well into the mountains, the road makes a hard switchback at the Gold-Mint trailhead and becomes steeper. Continue another 0.7 mile to Archangel Road on the right, across from a pullout marked as a fee area.

Take Archangel Road, on a good gravel surface, 2.2 miles to a parking area, again marked as a fee area (expect to pay a fee, or purchase an annual state park season pass). The main parking is just before the road crosses a bridge over Archangel Creek. Park here, or, with a higher-clearance vehicle, proceed on a very rough, unmaintained road 0.1 mile to the Reed Lakes trailhead on the right.

## ON THE ROUTE

From the parking fee area south of the Archangel Creek bridge (elevation 2400 feet), walk along Archangel Road for 0.2 mile to the Reed Lakes trailhead on the right. Begin by walking the old Snowbird Mine road 1.5 miles to its end at the site of the old Snowbird Mine village. Building foundations and other scraps of history are buried in the brush here.

*Upper Reed Lake framed by the Talkeetna Mountains' granite spires* (Photo by Shawn Horning)

The mine itself was high on the mountainside to the northwest up Glacier Creek. From the historic village site, Lower Reed Lake is about 2 miles away, and Upper Reed Lake about 1 mile beyond that.

The Reed Creek valley is not obvious. While the main valley appears to head back to the right (northeast), Reed Creek comes down more steeply from the north; look for cascades partway up. From the end of the old road, follow a footpath to Glacier Creek, and cross it on a bridge. Then immediately cross two braided channels of Reed Creek in quick succession. The main trail heads left up Reed Creek after crossing.

The trail climbs uphill in switchbacks first painstakingly set by the youth group British Exploring Society as a service project. The project included replanting the old, direct trail that was eroding badly. Trail crews similarly put in extensive effort recently to fix erosion caused by switchback-cutters in this area. Please do not cut corners and create further erosion on this popular trail.

The trail contours left below the hilltop to an area of granite boulders. Boulder hopping is necessary, a difficult task for less-steady hikers, young children, and dogs (though children may also find the boulder playground motivating). Beyond the boulder field,

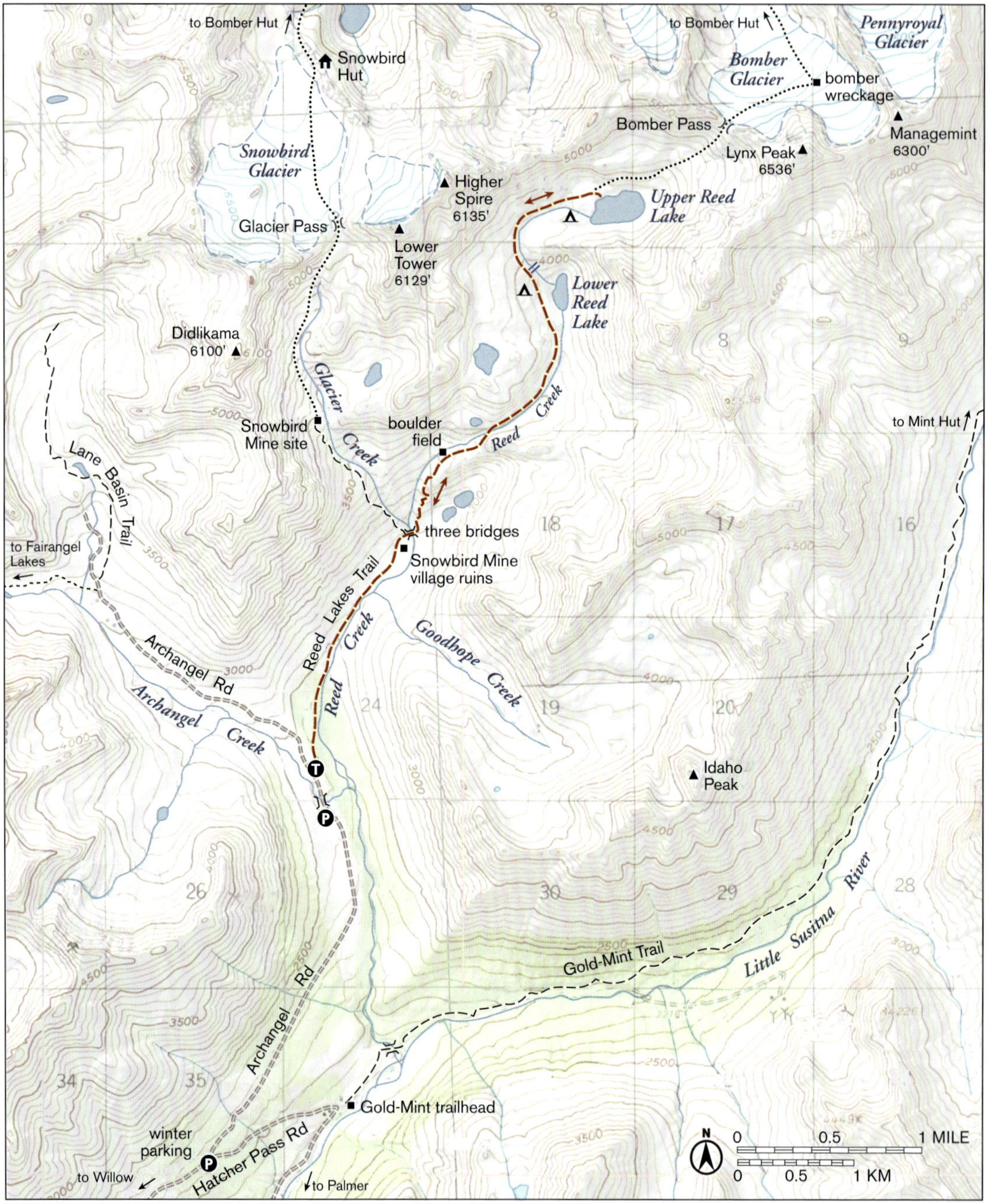
to Bomber Hut
Snowbird Hut
to Bomber Hut
Pennyroyal Glacier
Bomber Glacier
bomber wreckage
Bomber Pass
Managemint 6300'
Lynx Peak 6536'
Snowbird Glacier
Higher Spire 6135'
Upper Reed Lake
Glacier Pass
Lower Tower 6129'
Lower Reed Lake
Didlikama 6100'
Glacier Creek
Reed Creek
Snowbird Mine site
boulder field
to Mint Hut
Lane Basin Trail
three bridges
to Fairangel Lakes
Snowbird Mine village ruins
Reed Lakes Trail
Reed Creek
Goodhope Creek
Archangel Rd
Archangel Creek
Reed
Idaho Peak
Little Susitna River
Gold-Mint Trail
Archangel Rd
Gold-Mint trailhead
winter parking
Hatcher Pass Rd
to Willow
to Palmer
N
0 0.5 1 MILE
0 0.5 1 KM

follow sparkling Reed Creek through grassy meadows and past small, clear pools that reflect the surrounding mountains. Cross on boulders to the north side of the creek as you approach these pools. The aqua beauty that is Lower Reed Lake lies 200 vertical feet above (at elevation 3750 feet), although the trail stays high on the left above the lake upon reaching it. Beyond, a waterfall cascades over rock slabs.

To reach Upper Reed Lake (elevation 4250 feet), a mile from the lower lake, skirt the falls to the left, crossing rocks and grassy meadows. Beyond a shallow pond, the vivid upper lake appears at the base of Lynx Peak (elevation 6536 feet). Granite spires and sheer faces rise high above talus and glaciers. The lakes are often ice covered into July, and ice forms again by mid-September. Nonetheless, hardy types dip in these chilly waters on hot days. Use the designated campsites with gravel tent pads and latrines at the lakes to minimize impact to the tundra.

## SHORTER OPTIONS

Lower Reed Lake is about 7 miles roundtrip. From the Snowbird Mine village ruins on the way to Reed Lakes, the hanging valley of Glacier Creek makes a nice alternate hike, leading up an impressively steep path to the flattened buildings of Snowbird Mine (0.8 mile; 5 miles roundtrip from the trailhead) and beyond (without a trail) to an overlook of the Snowbird Glacier (roughly 2 miles; 7.5 miles roundtrip). Flat spots for camping can be found along the way.

## EXTENDING YOUR TRIP

Experienced hikers with knowledge of glacier travel may continue on from Upper Reed Lake to Bomber Hut, a trailless route that scales the wall of talus northeast of the lake to Bomber Pass, drops onto Bomber Glacier, and descends to Bomber Hut, a minimalist cabin maintained by the Mountaineering Club of Alaska (MCA). The glacier was the crash site of a US Air Force bomber on a training mission in the 1950s, hence the name. The wreckage is visible still from the pass above the Upper Reed Lake, though scaling steep talus for that view alone is a slog. Crossing the glacier should only be attempted with hefty ice spikes underfoot. A round-trip from Archangel Road to Bomber Hut with a curiosity stop at the bomber wreckage is roughly 15 miles.

For an even more epic trek, MCA's Mint Hut at the head of the Little Susitna Valley and American Alpine Club's Snowbird Hut at Snowbird Glacier can bookend a stop at Bomber Hut for a three-night, hut-to-hut route known as the Bomber Traverse. A detailed route map is available from winterbear.com; you can purchase a hard copy or download it free. If you stay at a hut, please make a donation to the organization that maintains it (see the Resources section).

## SEASONAL OPTIONS

The Mat-Su Ski Club grooms Archangel Road in winter, making it a popular destination for Nordic skiers (see Seasonal Options in Trip 42 for details). For a leisurely backcountry ski or snowshoe tour, turn off the groomed Archangel Road at the Reed Lakes trailhead to travel over gently rolling terrain to the old Snowbird Mine village site, a logical destination before the trail gets steep (7.8 miles roundtrip from winter parking at the start of Archangel Road). Snowmachiners use a route paralleling parts of Archangel Road and are allowed in the lower end of Reed Creek valley but are prohibited past Goodhope Creek.

The Gold-Mint Trail also offers ski touring in a nonmotorized area, although the trailhead can be noisy with snowmachiners heading toward Hatcher Pass. Farther up the road toward Hatcher Pass are more winter opportunities; see Seasonal Options in Trip 41 for details.

The huts mentioned in Extending Your Trip are popular winter destinations for skiers with alpine touring gear but require planning, navigation, and avalanche skills (see Avalanches in the Introduction) and careful glacier crossings for Snowbird and Bomber Huts.

# 44 NANCY LAKES CANOE LOOP

**DISTANCE:** 8-mile loop
**TIME:** Full day to 2 days
**ELEVATION GAIN:** 400 feet
**HIGH POINT:** 270 feet
**SEASON:** Mid-May–early October
**SURFACE:** Water, hardpack, roots
**GRADE:** Low angle
**INDIGENOUS LAND:** Dena'ina Athabascan
**MANAGING AGENCY:** Nancy Lake State Recreation Area
**MAPS:** USGS Tyonek C-1 NE; for Little Susitna River, Tyonek C-1 SE and Anchorage C-8 NW, C-8 SW
**ONLINE MAP SEARCH:** "lynx lake ak"
**TRAILHEAD GPS:** 61.674856°N, 150.094141°W

**Nancy Lake State Recreation Area covers a landscape formed by glaciers and long since grown** up in mature lowland forest. It is a place of rolling low hills, dozens of lakes and ponds, and woodsy tranquility. The Lynx Lake Loop described here, through a chain of fourteen forest-rimmed lakes, is a microcosm of voyageur canoeing on the Great Lakes and big rivers of Canada in the 1700s—here, the lakes come small, the portages short. The whole thing is possible in a day, but the loop makes a good overnight trip, and there are other lakes to explore to make a multiday trip if desired (see Extending Your Trip).

On the loop, reasonably good trails make the twelve overland portages manageable (one connection is by water channel). The trailhead for each portage is marked. Loons dot the lakes, moose and bears occasionally use the portages, and fishing is good in several of the lakes. Some of these waters warm up enough for swimming, and at least a couple of times, intrepid wetsuited swimmers have swum the whole loop.

Historic Dena'ina village sites occur a short distance east and west of this loop in the Nancy Lake and Red Shirt Lake areas. Shem Pete, a preeminent elder who contributed extensively to a recorded understanding of Dena'ina place names, territory, and practices before he died in 1989, grew up here. He was born in the late 1890s, just as white prospectors started exploring the Susitna Valley. According to the Cook Inlet Historical Society, he was of the Nulchina clan of

*Canoe portage in June* (Photo by Gretchen Nelson)

the Susitnuht'ana band, which was one of three groupings of Dena'ina who formed the Upper Cook Inlet Dena'ina Athabascans. A lake adjacent to the loop is named for him, and this trip is an opportunity to experience the area in which he grew up and imagine what life might have been like. Although the old villages near these lakes are no longer visible, Dena'ina people still live throughout the upper Cook Inlet area.

Canoes may be rented online through Tippecanoe Rentals and can be waiting for you at the trailhead (see the Resources section).

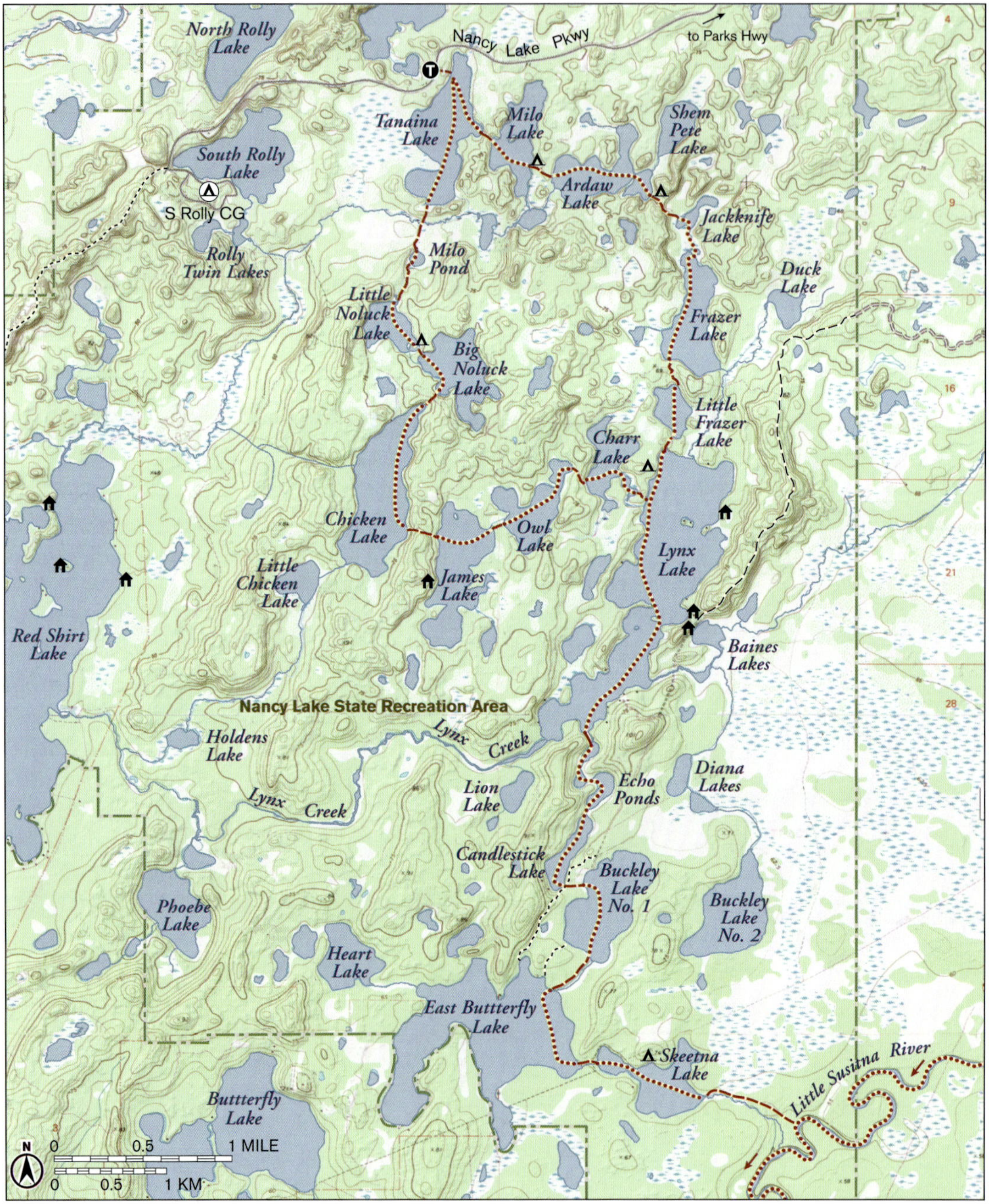

Nancy Lake Pkwy
to Parks Hwy
North Rolly Lake
South Rolly Lake
S Rolly CG
Rolly Twin Lakes
Tanaina Lake
Milo Lake
Shem Pete Lake
Ardaw Lake
Jackknife Lake
Milo Pond
Duck Lake
Little Noluck Lake
Big Noluck Lake
Frazer Lake
Little Frazer Lake
Charr Lake
Chicken Lake
Owl Lake
Lynx Lake
Little Chicken Lake
James Lake
Red Shirt Lake
Baines Lakes
Nancy Lake State Recreation Area
Lynx Creek
Holdens Lake
Diana Lakes
Echo Ponds
Lion Lake
Candlestick Lake
Buckley Lake No. 1
Buckley Lake No. 2
Phoebe Lake
Heart Lake
East Buttterfly Lake
Skeetna Lake
Little Susitna River
Buttterfly Lake
0 0.5 1 MILE
0 0.5 1 KM

## DRIVING DIRECTIONS

Search online for "lynx lake ak" or follow these directions. Take the Parks Highway to mile 67.2 near the community of Willow. Turn west onto Nancy Lake Parkway. Find a self-serve fee station at mile 1.3 (a ranger station is here also) and another at mile 2.2. Choose one, and pay a fee for parking and camping (unless you have an annual state park pass). Drive a total of 4.6 miles from the Parks Highway, and turn left into the driveway for the canoe trailhead (marked). The parking lot, with outhouses, is a short distance from Tanaina Lake.

## ON THE ROUTE

The USGS maps listed above or a Nancy Lake State Recreation Area brochure map will aid in finding portages. The brochure map is available on the recreation area website and at state park offices. Make the loop in either direction. Going first by way of Milo Pond, in a counterclockwise direction as described here, puts the longest portages at the beginning of the trip. Begin by paddling to the south end of Tanaina Lake and portaging to Milo *Pond*. Note that the second lake in the opposite direction is Milo *Lake*. Milo Pond is ridiculously small, but it gets you through your first two lakes quickly.

All of the portages are a quarter mile or less, and most are considerably shorter. They are marked by orange, diamond-shaped signs. Boardwalks cover most wet spots, but rubber boots are desirable at lake edges. Several portages require carrying the canoe uphill. The connection between Frazer and Jackknife Lakes is by water.

The best camping spots are at designated campsites: between Little Noluck and Big Noluck Lakes (a little over an hour from the trailhead); on the northwest corner of Lynx Lake (a little over four hours from the trailhead via Milo Pond and a little over two hours via Milo Lake); and at either end of Ardaw Lake (roughly an hour from the trailhead via Milo Lake). Each of these campsite areas has an outhouse; some have bear-proof food lockers and tent platforms; most are run-down but serviceable. There are also four public-use cabins on the Lynx Lake Loop: one at James Lake and three on Lynx Lake. Make cabin reservations through alaskastateparks.reserveamerica.com.

All of the lakes except Lynx Lake are surrounded by public land. Lynx Lake has some private land and private cabins around it, and on this lake camping is permitted only at the designated campsites and cabins. Floatplanes and boats with outboard motors are allowed on Lynx Lake but not on the other lakes.

Bring binoculars for watching birds and spotting portage markers. A head net and mosquito repellent are good to have for the portages, particularly in June. To ensure availability and access to the locked canoes at the trailhead, it is best to arrange the rental ahead of time. However, there is a canoe rental office near the boat launch at the South Rolly Campground, and it is generally staffed during summer. Early and late in the season, when the campground still is closed, Tippecanoe may operate out of Willow. Early and late season are fine times to explore these lakes, with less dense vegetation and fewer bugs.

## TRIP OPTIONS

Several variations on the standard loop trip are possible. Paddling out and back as far as desired can make a fine short option. For example, the portage east to Milo Lake is short and provides the quickest access to a campsite (1.6 miles roundtrip). The portages south to the two Noluck Lakes may yield good trout fishing, as the Department of Fish and Game stocks these two lakes (3.5 miles roundtrip).

Or extend the trip by heading south from Lynx Lake through six lakes and then returning via the same route. There is a campsite (somewhat overgrown) on Skeetna Lake. It is also possible to enter the canoe system via the Little Susitna River. Access is from mile 57 on the Parks Highway. It takes four to five hours on the river to reach the portage for Skeetna Lake (marked). The river portion requires more canoeing experience than do the lakes. The river is open to powerboats.

In addition to cabins on the Lynx Lake Loop, Nancy Lake State Recreation Area offers other public-use cabins and two drive-in campgrounds. See the state park website for information.

### SEASONAL OPTIONS

When the lakes freeze solid before the snow falls, they offer the opportunity for ice skating, including overnight ice-skating trips. Take a light plastic sled for gear, and reserve a cabin for a novel weekend. Nordic skates are ideal for this trip because it is easy to clip out of the blades and walk the portages in the boots (see Winter Modes in the Introduction).

In winter, 10 miles of maintained cross-country ski trails loop through the rolling, lake-dotted country north of Nancy Lake Parkway. The area north of the parkway is closed to snowmachines. The state park website has a map of the ski trails. The winter trailhead is at mile 2.2 of the parkway; the road is not plowed in winter beyond this point. There are several cabins nearby.

# 45 PETERS HILLS

**DISTANCE:** 15.6 miles roundtrip
**TIME:** 2–3 days
**ELEVATION GAIN:** 3100 feet
**HIGH POINT:** 3929 feet
**SEASON:** July–September
**SURFACE:** Tundra, bushes (low), hardpack
**GRADE:** Rolling with steep segments
**INDIGENOUS LAND:** Dena'ina and Ahtna Athabascan
**MANAGING AGENCIES:** Alaska Division of Mining, Land, and Water and Denali State Park
**MAP:** USGS Talkeetna C-2
**ONLINE MAP SEARCH:** "peters hills ak"
**TRAILHEAD GPS:** 62.508580°N, 150.775430°W

**The majestic white mountain called Denali looms over Peters Hills from 40 miles away, making its** presence felt whether or not it is visible. When Denali is out, the views of it and its consorts, Mount Foraker and Mount Hunter, are superb. Famed Alaska artist Sydney Laurence painted many of his canvases of Denali from just below Long Point, the destination of this trip. When Denali is shrouded with clouds, you may still be able to see the Kanikula and Tokositna Glaciers and the jagged black peaks of the Tokosha Mountains—and there is always the chance of glimpsing Denali later in the trip. No matter what the weather, this route offers wonderful walking on rolling ridges, great camping beside alpine lakes, blueberries and low-bush cranberries in season, and the possibility of glimpsing a grizzly bear or wolf. The hike is particularly scenic in early September when the rich reds and golds of autumn foliage are at their best. Beginning in late August, the area is also popular with hunters, particularly on weekends, and many hunters use all-terrain vehicles (ATVs) near the beginning of this hike.

A few cautions: much of this cross-country hike does not follow a formal trail. The first part follows an ATV trail through brush, but it peters out and eventually disappears. There is not a developed trailhead or signs, and the trail is not maintained. Finding the point where the ATV trail leaves the road can be challenging. Some off-trail experience is necessary to ensure that you can find the best route and your way back to your car. A map and compass along with a GPS device or app (and the ability to use them) are essential in the event that the clouds settle on these hills, as they often do.

*Scouting for a tent site near the trail among the lower lakes of Peters Hills*

## DRIVING DIRECTIONS

Search online for "forks roadhouse ak," then follow these directions. At mile 114.8 of the Parks Highway, turn west onto Petersville Road at the tiny community of Trapper Creek. The Peters Hills trailhead is 30.5 miles away. The first 9.4 miles of the Petersville Road are paved, and the next 9 miles to the Forks Roadhouse are fairly good gravel. At the Forks Roadhouse, bear right. From this point the road is less maintained and may have mudholes during spring and early summer. When the road is dry, usually by July, cars with normal clearance should have no trouble reaching the trailhead, 12 miles north of the Forks Roadhouse. Allow one and a half hours to drive the 30.5 miles from Trapper Creek. Contact the Alaska Department of Transportation for road conditions (see the Resources section).

To find the trailhead, watch for the buildings of the Petersville placer mine about 11 miles north of the Roadhouse, in the bottom of a small valley. Drive 1 mile farther and find a rutted, gravelly ATV track heading uphill on the right side of the road. This is the trailhead. Look for an open gravel area to the left of Petersville Road a few yards past the ATV track. Park here (elevation 1825 feet).

## ON THE ROUTE

On foot, follow the rutted ATV trail that leaves Petersville Road, heading uphill. It bends to the left and follows the dry crest of a low ridge, then makes a broad U-turn to the right and traverses a hillside. This arc makes an end run around a small drainage and is pleasant walking. A less-defined track makes a muddy shortcut across the drainage. Along the arc, a few short side trails lead left to minor lookout points; keep right and on the main ATV trail. Rounding the arc, the trail climbs a short hill and heads northeast. It then loses and regains less than

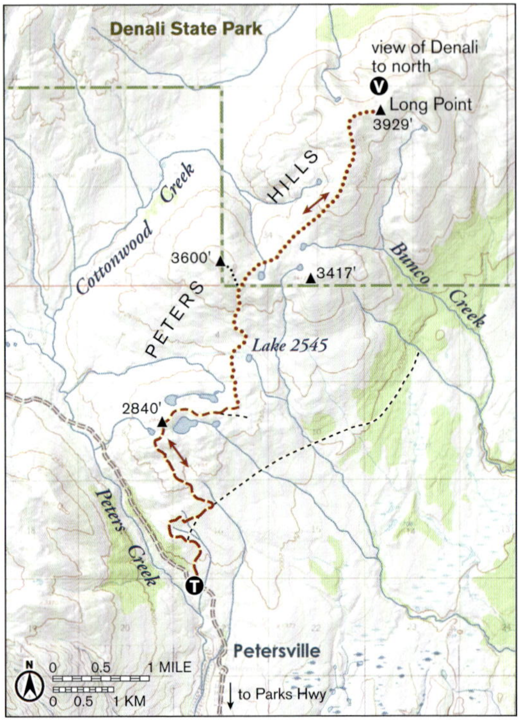


100 feet to cross a small creek. You may have to bushwhack short distances around mud puddles.

After 1.5 miles, follow the dominant, well-worn ATV track as it curves left to head uphill while another overgrown track continues straight. After the turn, hike about a mile northwest up a long ridge. New ATV trails are continually being created. If in doubt, stay on the low ridge heading northwest, paralleling the stream a ways off on your right. At 2.5 miles from the trailhead, the first small pond comes into view. Continue following the visible ATV trail as it skirts to the right of the pond and begins weaving through a collection of small lakes. At 2.7 miles from the trailhead, reach point 2840, which offers a wonderful view of Denali and makes a good destination for a day hike. From there, continue on the ridge north of the lake that is east of point 2840.

Follow this ridge past the outlet of the lake as shown on the map, heading east and still following a fading ATV trail. The lakes north and south of this ridge offer good camping opportunities.

The intermittent ATV trail continues east past the last lake, dropping about 100 feet to a viewpoint. Those heading toward Long Point should instead veer left off the faint track before losing altitude, contouring northeast around the eastern end of the nearly dry, heart-shaped lake. Hikers may pick up a worn footpath for a few hundred feet, but otherwise, the rest of the route does not follow a trail. Head north cross-country along a low, rolling ridge, then cross the willow-strewn valley at the highest point to avoid marshy ground. A small lake in the valley, labeled 2545 on USGS maps, drains southeast, as shown on the accompanying map, contrary to the USGS indication. The easiest route is west of this lake. Next, undertake the steepest climb of the trip toward point 3600, following dry-looking, brownish patches on its south face. Head for the broad top of this peak as an option, summiting at 5.5 miles from the trailhead, or contour to the right before summiting to reach a saddle at about 3400 feet. Scattered lakes at this elevation present alpine camping spots and possible views of Denali to the north.

From here, the route to Long Point is a comparatively easy, gently rising 2.5-mile walk. Follow the tundra-covered ridge northeast as far as time permits. Sunlight, clouds, and storms sweeping through the mountains to the north are hypnotic. Watch the sunset, sunrise, or the northern lights play with the continent's highest peak.

There is plenty of water, but take a stove for cooking. Most of the ridge lies in Denali State Park, which is closed to ATVs.

### SHORTER OPTIONS

The first viewpoint, point 2840, is an easier objective at 5.4 miles roundtrip from the trailhead and 1200 feet of elevation gain, and does not require cross-country routefinding. This spot offers a wonderful view of Denali and makes a good destination for a day hike. The numerous surrounding lakes provide hospitable campsites for an overnight trip.

Point 3600, on the boundary of Denali State Park, is the next closest Denali viewpoint, with vistas of the Kanikula and Tokositna Glaciers spreading from the foothills. A trip to this broad summit totals 11 miles roundtrip with 2400 feet of elevation gain. Nearby lakes offer alpine camping.

# 46 K'ESUGI AND CURRY RIDGES

**DISTANCE:** 37 miles point to point; 48 miles with the Curry Ridge Trail
**TIME:** 3–5 days; 4–6 days with the Curry Ridge Trail
**ELEVATION GAIN:** 6100 feet southbound, 8300 feet with the Curry Ridge Trail
**HIGH POINTS:** 3550 feet (K'esugi Ridge); 2750 feet (Curry Ridge)
**SEASON:** June–September
**SURFACE:** Hardpack, roots, water
**GRADE:** Rolling with steep segments
**INDIGENOUS LAND:** Dena'ina Athabascan and Western Ahtna Athabascan

**MANAGING AGENCY:** Denali State Park
**MAPS:** USGS Talkeetna Mountains C-6, D-6; Talkeetna C-1
**ONLINE MAP SEARCH:** "kesugi" (no apostrophe)
**TRAILHEAD GPS:** Little Coal Creek 62.891420°N, 149.746693°W
K'esugi Ken 62.592538°N, 150.223587°W

**With superlatives in scenery, landform, weather, and physical challenge, the K'esugi Ridge Trail** has long captured the diversity of Southcentral Alaska backpacking on an extended route. Now the route stretches even farther, encompassing adjacent Curry Ridge to become the longest formal hiking trail in Alaska. Park rangers historically have recommended hiking the trail from north to south. The description below covers the full traverse (48 miles) and adopts this norm. Day trips and shorter overnights are good options as well. Note that the Curry Ridge portion is still under construction at the time of publication.

Trending north–south between the Alaska Range and the Talkeetna Mountains, K'esugi and Curry Ridges offer miles of walking on alpine tundra along their broad, rolling tops. This ridge system is the central feature of Denali State Park. The hike comes complete with wee tundra flowers, outrageous rock formations, shining tarns, and tumbling streams. It is not only an alpine ridge though. The traverse drops into stands of beautiful old birch trees, open cottonwood groves, and spruce forests. On clear days, none of these features, fine as they are, will likely gain hikers' attention as much as the view of the towering dark cliffs of Moose's Tooth and the brilliant ice peaks of Denali, the highest point in North America at 20,310 feet. The view of these summits is

*A pond on K'esugi Ridge reflects Denali, Mount Hunter, and other peaks of the Alaska Range.* (Photo by Gretchen Nelson)

## POINTS OF INTEREST ON K'ESUGI AND CURRY RIDGES

| NUMBER ON MAP | POINT OF INTEREST | APPROXIMATE MILEAGE | |
|---|---|---|---|
| | | CUMULATIVE | FROM PREVIOUS |
| 1 | **Little Coal Creek trailhead** | 0 | 0 |
| 2 | **Ermine Hill Trail junction** | 14 | 14 |
| 3 | **Cascade Trail junction** | 25 | 11 |
| 4 | **Ten-Mile Hill junction (Curry Ridge Trail)** | 27 | 2 |
| 5 | **Troublesome Creek ford** | 31 | 4 |
| 6 | **Curry Lookout** | 40 | 9 |
| 7 | **Loop trail junction (Lake 1787 and Rocky Knob)** | 45 | 5 |
| 8 | **K'esugi Ken Campground trailhead (Curry Ridge Trail)** | 48 | 3 |
| | **SIDE TRAILS** | **MILEAGE** | |
| 9 | **Ermine Hill Trail** | 4 | |
| 10 | **Cascade Trail (via the Byers Lake trailhead)** | 4 | |
| 11 | **Upper Troublesome Creek Trail** | 10 | |

**Notes:** The Curry Ridge Trail from points 4 to 6 was under construction at the time of publication; see trip description for details, and confirm current status with Denali State Park. The Upper Troublesome Creek Trail (point 11) technically extends from the Parks Highway through Ten-Mile Hill to the Cascade Trail; mileage is based on the junction with the Curry Ridge Trail.

arguably best from these ridges, which offer the right combination of elevation (up to nearly 3600 feet) and setback (some 40 miles) to allow views between and over lesser peaks and into the heart of the Alaska Range. Denali presents a particularly dramatic profile from this vantage.

The Curry Ridge part of the trail, at this writing, is halfway constructed. The section noted on the map as "tentative" is the *planned* route—laid out in the field but still taking shape as a physical trail. No part of the tentative segment is expected to open until construction is complete. The construction schedule or route may change.

This new part of the route adds 17.5 miles of trail, and it gets back to the roots of hiking adventure in this area. Beginning in 1923, decades before Parks Highway construction, railroad passengers would stop to hike up the east side of Curry Ridge and look over the top from the Curry Lookout to the Alaska Range. The lookout, a small, hexagonal shelter on the National Register of Historic Places, sits on this ridge, but there has been no formal trail on Curry Ridge for decades. The new Curry Ridge Trail will make this area accessible again and is expected to be popular. Search "kesugi trails" within dnr.alaska.gov for updates on the new segment.

### DRIVING DIRECTIONS

This point-to-point trek requires a car shuttle or another way to get to a second trailhead. With just one car, leave it at one of the larger trailheads (K'esugi Ken or Byers Lake), and actively solicit a ride from motorists stopped at those spots (including the Veterans Memorial adjacent to Byers Lake), or hitchhike on the highway. Another option is a formal shuttle (for a fee) run by Denali Southside River Guides, a park concessionaire based at Talkeetna (search online).

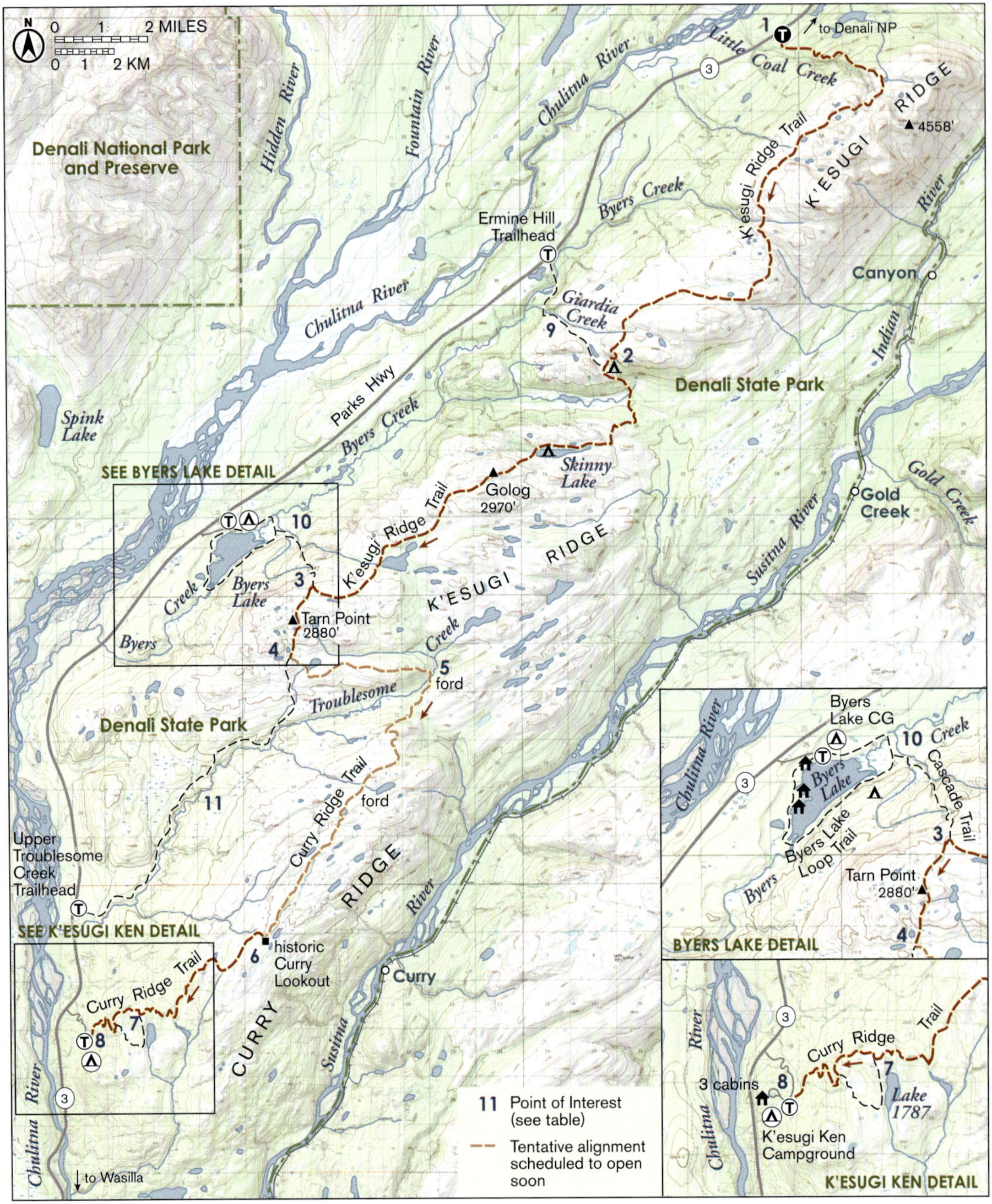

0 1 2 MILES
0 1 2 KM
Denali National Park and Preserve
Hidden River
Fountain River
Chulitna River
Little Coal Creek
to Denali NP
K'ESUGI RIDGE
4558'
K'esugi Ridge Trail
Byers Creek
Ermine Hill Trailhead
Canyon
Giardia Creek
Indian River
Denali State Park
Parks Hwy
Spink Lake
Skinny Lake
Golog 2970'
SEE BYERS LAKE DETAIL
Gold Creek
Susitna River
Byers Lake
Tarn Point 2880'
Troublesome Creek
ford
Curry Ridge Trail
CURRY RIDGE
Upper Troublesome Creek Trailhead
SEE K'ESUGI KEN DETAIL
historic Curry Lookout
Curry
to Wasilla
11 Point of Interest (see table)
Tentative alignment scheduled to open soon
BYERS LAKE DETAIL
Byers Lake CG
Cascade Trail
Byers Lake Loop Trail
K'ESUGI KEN DETAIL
3 cabins
Lake 1787
K'esugi Ken Campground

Use the bold terms below to find driving directions online. "Kesugi Ken Campground" may get you close but not accurately display the final approach.

**Little Coal Creek trailhead.** To reach the trail's northernmost access, follow the Parks Highway to the Little Coal Creek trailhead (marked, on the east side) at mile 163.9.

**Ermine Hill trailhead.** The Ermine Hill Trail begins at a pullout on the east side of the Parks Highway at mile 156.4. Trailhead information is posted at the pullout and on a sign a few dozen yards into the woods.

**Byers Lake.** Byers Lake Campground is at mile 146.9. The trail is accessible from the campground loop and from a boat launch. The launch area, near the campground entrance, has parking for people who are not camping and is marked as the trailhead on the map. There is additional parking farther west at Public-Use Cabin Number 1, which connects via a trail paralleling the lakeshore. Note that the Veterans Memorial has a separate driveway off the highway less than 0.1 mile north.

**Upper Troublesome Creek trailhead.** The Upper Troublesome Creek Trail begins on the east side of the Parks Highway at mile 137.6. Don't be confused by the Lower Troublesome pullout across the highway at mile 137.2.

**K'esugi Ken Campground.** The Curry Ridge Trail southern terminus is at K'esugi Ken Campground, located at Parks Highway mile 135.4 and 1.3 miles up a winding, paved road (elevation 900 feet). Internal trails from the campground, a parking lot, and an interpretive center lead to the Curry Ridge Trail. Follow signs.

## ON THE ROUTE

These ridges may offer the promise of a perfect adventure, but that perfection comes at a steep price. Five routes from the Parks Highway to the ridgetop are evenly spaced for abbreviated traverses, but all include an extended ascent. Additionally, except at the north end, the ridge-crest trail tends to climb over high points rather than traversing around them. It winds through the best visual features even if that means greater effort. The trail can be wet in spots, and it historically has been characterized by taking grades head-on instead of using switchbacks (Alaska State Parks has been working over several years to create lower grades). Also, weather can be a challenge. Sections of the trail at the highest elevations are nearly indecipherable without the many cairns placed along the way. In foggy, rainy, windy weather, picking out these rock piles from the backdrop of natural stone can be impossible. It is imperative to carry good topographic maps and a compass and/or a reliable GPS unit or app. Know how to use them, and be prepared to turn around or sit tight and

*Cairns mark the way on the K'esugi Ridge Trail in the high country south of Skinny Lake.* (Photo by Gretchen Nelson)

wait when the weather is poor. Troublesome Creek and Byers Creek and Lake can attract bears from mid-July to early September when salmon reach the creeks. The park rerouted the Upper Troublesome Creek Trail to minimize chances for interactions, and the back side of Byers Lake and its outlet can be avoided, but hikers should be particularly alert in these areas. The accompanying table lists points of interest, keyed to the map, and basic mileage.

From the Little Coal Creek trailhead (elevation 1350 feet), the trail climbs out of the trees in about 1.5 miles and continues uphill for a total ascent of 2200 feet to the high point on the entire traverse at 3550 feet. The ridge itself goes to rocky summits 1000 feet higher. Ready access to water is lacking along much of this initial ascent. Beyond the trail's high point, the route is level for several miles along the western edge of the ridge—prime view territory—before climbing again, this time along the eastern edge. Camping spots with good views and water are plentiful, but this segment of the route has sustained exposure to weather conditions. The Ermine Hill Trail junction is in a somewhat protected depression near a lake, where there is a simple designated campsite.

The segment of the ridge trail from the Ermine Hill Trail junction to the Cascade Trail (Byers Lake) junction has perhaps the greatest variety, but if you have just come up the Ermine Hill Trail, you'll be chagrined to know that the route toward Byers Lake only stays high for a short distance before dropping steeply 900 feet to forest and wetlands, only to ascend again. Camping is poor for at least 3 miles through the lowland.

From the wet lowland, the route ascends over granite slabs and outcrops, passing by Skinny Lake and over a rounded, 2970-foot summit called Golog. There are first-come, first-served tent platforms toward the western end of Skinny Lake. The rolling route continually makes new views of the big peaks across the valley and provides camping options west of Golog. The junction with the Cascade Trail is over the edge of the ridge a bit on the western side, above Byers Lake.

The segment from the Cascade Trail junction toward Troublesome Creek climbs back up and over 2880-foot Tarn Point. The route to Tarn Point sees day-use traffic from Byers Lake via the Cascade Trail (see Shorter Options). Beyond, the route historically has been least used. The new Curry Ridge Trail, which branches off a short distance beyond Tarn Point at Ten-Mile Hill, is likely to change use patterns in this area. The description from this point on only applies once the new trail is open to public use.

The Curry Ridge Trail diverges to the east, descending toward the upper reaches of Troublesome Creek, which divides K'esugi Ridge from Curry Ridge. Trail designers selected a ford site at this stream. Because of its ridgetop orientation, the K'esugi portion does not cross more than small streams that hikers usually can step over. The Curry segment, however, presents three notable crossings without bridges. Troublesome Creek is the first and largest. It has a rocky bottom and should be no more than knee-deep during most water conditions (see Stream Crossings in the Introduction). South of the ford, the route climbs slowly through about 3 miles of thinning forest and brush back to high-alpine country on Curry Ridge, with two more stream crossings en route that have stepping stones. An intense rainstorm could produce a short-term flood on any of the three. In these (luckily rare) instances, wait for the water to recede.

Beyond, it is then a rolling, 7-mile alpine jaunt, with 360-degree views, past lakes and over the Curry segment's high point (2750 feet), before beginning a descent. The Curry Lookout is at elevation 2575

*Backpacking through rock formations north of Ermine Hill Trail* (Photo by Gretchen Nelson)

feet, and the trail then begins to enter patches of brush and trees, but with ample views. At 3 miles from the southern trailhead, there is an option for a loop near Lake 1787. From Curry Lookout, the final descending trail has been in place, is not "tentative," and is popular. The traverse ends at K'esugi Ken Campground (elevation 900 feet).

On any part of the trail system, hikers should be prepared for mud, eroded areas, slippery and rocky footing, snow crossings, minor stream fords, and—in forest areas—blown-down trees. That said, the park has typically kept up maintenance on this trail. Mostly, finding drinking water is not a problem. During the latter half of hot summers, some ponds at upper elevations dry up entirely and others shrink dramatically and cannot be counted on as a water source.

A Denali State Park ranger station at the K'esugi Ken complex provides trail information for the entire trail in summer. It may be worth stopping in even if hiking the northern segments to pick up a brochure with a map or draw the route from posted maps onto your USGS maps and to learn about recent trail conditions. The state park office at Finger Lake, near Palmer (see Mat-Su/Copper Basin Area Office in the Resources section) may also provide information.

Byers Lake and K'esugi Ken Campgrounds feature tent and RV camping and six popular walk-in and drive-in public-use cabins—reservable through

## MILES BETWEEN TRAILHEADS

| TRAILHEAD | LITTLE COAL CREEK | ERMINE HILL | BYERS LAKE/ CASCADE TRAIL | UPPER TROUBLESOME CREEK |
|---|---|---|---|---|
| **K'esugi Ken Campground** | 48 | 38 | 27 | 31 |
| **Upper Troublesome Creek** | 37 | 27 | 16 | 0 |
| **Byers Lake/Cascade Trail** | 29 | 19 | 0 | |
| **Ermine Hill** | 18 | 0 | | |

**Note:** See trip description for cautions about the trail from K'esugi Ken Campground, part of which was under construction at the time of publication.

alaskastateparks.reserveamerica.com. The cabins are available year-round.

### SHORTER OPTIONS

A day hike from Byers Lake to Tarn Point via the Cascade Trail is nearly 10 miles roundtrip (2500 feet elevation gain), a good activity for those staying at Byers Lake.

Or from K'esugi Ken Campground, hike to Lake 1787 near tree line (6 miles roundtrip, 1000 feet elevation gain). There is a loop trail with good views from the high point, known as Rocky Knob, adjacent to the lake. Camping is not permitted within a half mile of the lake. An extended day hike is possible from K'esugi Ken Campground to the Curry Lookout and back (16 miles roundtrip, 1700 feet elevation gain).

As indicated above, the full traverse may be shortened in various configurations. The "Miles Between Trailheads" table presents approximate mileage for all trailhead-to-trailhead options. Historically, the most common shorter traverses have been via the Little Coal Creek or Ermine Hill trailheads to Byers Lake. The new Curry Ridge Trail creates a traverse from Byers Lake to K'esugi Ken Campground (27 miles).

The three intermediate side trails are as follows:

**Ermine Hill Trail.** The Ermine Hill Trail (trailhead elevation 1375 feet) winds through the woods at the base of the ridge for about 1.5 miles before crossing Giardia Creek and mounting the ridge side in switchbacks. This route provides one of the easiest accesses to alpine country, with about 1000 vertical feet from the trailhead.

**Byers Lake Loop Trail and Cascade Trail.** The Byers Lake Loop Trail (trailhead elevation 850 feet) encircles the lake in about 5 miles, is flat, and combines woodland and shoreline scenery. It leads to the Cascade Trail (marked), which climbs past a waterfall about 1700 vertical feet to the ridge-crest trail.

**Upper Troublesome Creek Trail.** The Upper Troublesome Creek Trail (trailhead elevation 650 feet) climbs gradually through a beautiful forested valley, different from the other routes. The trail generally parallels the creek, which carves its way through granite pillars and buttresses. The stream is loud; be diligent in letting wildlife know you are coming, particularly in the second half of summer when salmon in the creek may attract bears. The forested portion is best for transit and not for camping. Before reaching Ten-Mile Hill, the path breaks out of the narrow valley into open views. This trail historically has been less used than the others, and parts of it may be difficult to follow once grass is tall.

The trailheads each provide for a reasonable out-and-back day hike to alpine country, except for the Upper Troublesome Creek Trail, which does not clearly break to alpine for nearly 9 miles.

# 47 HICKS CREEK AND CHITNA PASS

**DISTANCE:** 48 miles point to point
**TIME:** 4 days or more
**ELEVATION GAIN:** 5300 feet
**HIGH POINT:** 4700 feet
**SEASON:** Late June–August
**SURFACE:** Hardpack, mud, tundra
**GRADE:** Rolling with steep segments
**INDIGENOUS LAND:** Western Ahtna Athabascan
**MANAGING AGENCIES:** Alaska Division of Mining, Land, and Water; US Bureau of Land Management and Matanuska-Susitna Borough easements on private lands
**MAPS:** USGS Anchorage D-2, D-3, D-4
**ONLINE MAP SEARCH:** "chitna pass ak"
**TRAILHEAD GPS:** Hicks Creek 61.802734°N, 147.865044°W
Purinton Creek 61.804667°N, 148.085482°W

**The eastern Talkeetna Mountains are a wilderness of peaks, tundra, alpine valleys, clear moun-**tain streams, and braided caribou trails. Visitors to this vast area may see members of the Nelchina caribou herd. The trip over Chitna Pass is nearly circular and follows unmaintained trails. It mostly traverses subalpine country and river bars without extensive forests to block the views. The country is expansive, huge even, and hikers feel small. Using the trails as access and topographic maps as a guide, many other trips are possible.

Ahtna people used routes in these valleys for travel and trade and likely showed explorers and prospectors their routes. According to old-timers, prospectors traveled parts of this trail in the early 1900s. The route took them from Knik (which was accessible by ship from Seattle in summer) up the Matanuska River and Boulder Creek, over Chitna Pass, and along Caribou Creek to Alfred Creek (see Trip 49). Their destinations were gold prospects and mines on Alfred and Albert Creeks. Today, many of these routes are all-terrain vehicle (ATV) trails used primarily by hunters in late summer and fall. The route described here starts on an ATV trail known as the Pinochle Creek or Hicks Creek Trail and ends on an ATV trail known as the Purinton Creek Trail, connecting them with a partly off-trail route over Chitna Pass.

Previous versions of this book have been apologetic about ATVs and muddy trails on this route. But this epic trip is one of the longest and certainly one of the wildest hikes in the book, with a satisfying variety of terrain and views. While the trails do sometimes have boot-sucking muck and present a visual mess in these stretches, they make it possible to trek deep into the backcountry.

*Mount Monarch, the highest of the Talkeetna Mountains in the area, is a great side trip.* (Photo by Gary Snyder)

A four-day trip here means averaging 12 miles per day, which would be a lot without trails. For most, the big country and views of the spectacular Chugach and Talkeetna Mountains make up for the mud. It is probably best to plan this trip in midsummer, when conditions are usually driest and there is less use of the trails by ATVs.

This route is not for novices. The USGS maps are essential, and help is far away. Do not go unless your party includes someone good at reading topographic maps. Experienced backpackers in good condition will find that these routes lead to delightful country. In addition to caribou, watch for moose, black bears, grizzly (brown) bears, Dall sheep, wolves, and coyotes.

## DRIVING DIRECTIONS

The circuit requires a car shuttle or arrangements to be dropped off or picked up.

**Pinochle Creek (Hicks Creek) Trail.** Take the Glenn Highway to mile 99.4, 0.1 mile east of a large pullout on the north side of the highway. Turn north onto Pinochle Lane, and drive 0.5 mile to a poorly marked ATV trailhead on the north side of the road. Park across the road just past the trailhead in an area defined by boulders.

**Purinton Creek Trail.** A large roadside gravel pullout at mile 90.7 of the Glenn Highway is the western trailhead. The trail winds uphill from the eastern end of the pullout, near a trailhead information kiosk.

## ON THE ROUTE

To complete the full trip, follow the ATV trail north of the Pinochle Creek trailhead (elevation 1776 feet). The trail starts up the Pinochle Creek drainage and soon climbs through tree line to a 3150-foot pass and the Hicks Creek drainage. Camping is possible in the pass area, with small streams crossing the route just before and after the broad pass. The trail over the pass is good, although the lower ground on either side is rutted and often mucky. The north side of the pass is muddy even in dry weather.

Within 1.5 miles beyond the pass, the trail descends steeply to Hicks Creek, at 2950 feet. An off-trail side trip from the creek heads northwest to a small alpine lake (elevation 5000 feet) 3.5 miles away, where there is good camping. Use maps to find your way there. Mount Monarch (7108 feet), towering above the lake, is the highest in the area and is a steep but uncomplicated climb with a dramatic summit.

The main trail continues to Hicks Lake. Camping is possible, particularly near the south end of the lake. Watch for muskrats and swans in the water. Beyond Hicks Lake, the ATV trail becomes drier. It crosses an indistinct 3300-foot divide, then follows a rocky route down Divide Creek to Caribou Creek at 2800 feet elevation, about 4 miles from Hicks Lake.

Follow the trail as it goes left up the south side of Caribou Creek. Good campsites occur along river bars. Nearly 2 miles after leaving Divide Creek, follow the most distinct route as it climbs the bank to avoid cliffs and winds along higher ground roughly paralleling the creek (another track continues up the creek's gravel bars). Beyond a small ravine and upstream of the junction of Chitna and Caribou Creeks, the trail forks. Follow the right branch steeply down to Chitna Creek (the left fork climbs to an old mining camp).

Chitna Creek is swift but usually not deep or difficult to cross. The trail up the opposite bank goes up two distinct levels. Follow it up the second rise, which tops out on a vegetated ridge crest. Along this little ridge, at the trail's high point and as the ATV trail begins to descend north toward Caribou Creek, look for a narrow footpath headed west, following the Chitna Creek valley upstream. To zone out here and blindly follow the wider trail will create a whole different and possibly very long adventure deep in the Talkeetna Mountains.

The "trail" up the Chitna Creek valley is a blend of human and animal trails. There is more than one track, and the trails diverge and merge, but the route does continue nearly to Chitna Pass and is worth following. Take forks that generally maintain elevation rather than descending toward the creek. About 2.5 miles from Caribou Creek, turn northwest up a tributary of Chitna Creek toward Chitna Pass. Map-reading skills are essential to find this drainage that leads to the pass, because the trail disappears here for a while in patchy head-high willows. Two separate creek channels come down this one valley, but only the larger ravine farther to the west shows as a creek on the USGS map. You may not find much water in the smaller ravine, but the two parallel ravines indicate that this is the correct valley

Caribou Creek
Divide Creek
Hicks Lake
Pinochle Creek (Hicks Creek) Trail
Hicks Creek
old mining camp
Chitina Creek
Chitina Pass
TALKEETNA MOUNTAINS
Mount Monarch 7108'
alpine lake
Boulder Creek
East Boulder Creek
State of Alaska Public Land
ANTHRACITE RIDGE
Purinton Creek
Purinton Creek Trail
private
mostly private land ownership
Glenn Hwy
Pinochle Ln
Pinochle Creek
1
to Glennallen
Lion Head
Matanuska Glacier
Matanuska River
Long Lake
potential highway reroute
to Anchorage
0 1 2 MILES
0 1 2 KM

to ascend. Make your way uphill between these two channels, following whatever shreds of caribou trail you can. Soon enough, they coalesce again into a more solid trail.

At 3700 feet, the vegetation changes from brush to open tundra. A gradual 2.5-mile climb to Chitna Pass (elevation 4700 feet) traverses fine country for camping and exploring. The trail fades in and out, but the walking is not difficult. Camping in this area and scaling nearby 6000-foot peaks is tempting. There is water but no firewood.

Chitna Pass is a notch in the mountains but provides almost flat passage. Southwest of the pass, the route parallels a small creek, and a well-defined footpath reappears. Follow it to nearly level ground (camping is possible in this area) and a bend to the left. A short time later, about 2 miles from the pass, the stream plunges into a small canyon. In that area, the trail climbs a little bluff to leave the creek and traverses out to the right as the creek falls away below. The footpath here is good and descends nearly 1000 feet to Boulder Creek, mostly following a ridge crest. (It does not drop steeply to Boulder Creek directly west of Chitna Pass as the USGS map shows.) This is a well-placed trail. The views from high on the tundra ridge of broad peaks streaked with color, waterfalls, and the broad river bars up and down Boulder Creek make the whole trip worthwhile.

Four miles from Chitna Pass, the well-defined trail ends when it enters the Boulder Creek gravel bars. The standard is to walk these open gravel boulevards, splashing back and forth across the braided channels—by far the easiest mode of travel. At higher water, cross Boulder Creek once and stay on the northwest side where stretches of ATV trail alternate with occasional stretches of bushwhacking. Following the southeast riverbank requires scrambling over bluffs and bushwhacking, necessary if Boulder Creek is flooding. Camping generally is good on the river bars. Rocks swept down over the ages come in every color. Be prepared to backtrack to seek out the best channel-crossing sites. Sites where ATVs have crossed are not necessarily safest for hikers.

From the point the foot trail hits the river bars, it is 11 miles to Anthracite Ridge. The crest of Anthracite Ridge drops steeply to the riverbank. Find the Purinton Creek Trail on the east bank of Boulder Creek right at the base of the ridge. Follow this trail south, then east to the Glenn Highway. This rolling segment has some large wet holes created by ATVs, particularly where it leaves Boulder Creek,

*Boulder Creek contains rocks in a rainbow of colors.*

*Approaching Chitna Pass on the path of caribou*

but generally the walking is good. It is tempting to think of this as the home stretch and try to hustle through it, but there are places to camp and rest, and it is a worthwhile place to spend time. On a clear day, the entire 9-plus-mile approach to the Purinton Creek trailhead presents a spectacular panorama of the Chugach Mountains across the Matanuska Valley. The trail has signs and markers as it approaches the trailhead (elevation 2300 feet) to help trail users avoid private property.

The two ends of the trail could be reasonable for strong, adventurous mountain bikers in dry conditions. Each end climbs substantially and has at least one long steep climb that is likely to require tough stints of pushing the bike. Each eventually becomes too wet for reasonable cycling. Much more of the route can be used for ski touring, either for day trips from either trailhead or as a several-day trip for experienced skiers and winter campers. The segment of the loop between Caribou Creek and Boulder Creek is too steep and avalanche-prone to make the whole route work in winter. The segments near the trailheads are likely to be packed by snowmachines. In midwinter be prepared for temperatures down to –30°F.

# 48 LION HEAD

**DISTANCE:** 2.3 miles roundtrip
**TIME:** Half day (or less)
**ELEVATION GAIN:** 1100 feet
**HIGH POINT:** 3185 feet
**SEASON:** June–September
**SURFACE:** Hardpack, boulders, mud
**GRADE:** Rolling with steep segments
**INDIGENOUS LAND:** Western Ahtna Athabascan
**MANAGING AGENCY:** Private (AT&T)
**MAP:** USGS Anchorage D-2 SW
**ONLINE MAP SEARCH:** "lion head ak"
**TRAILHEAD GPS:** 61.790274°N, 147.678657°W

**It is an iconic image on the Alaska highway system: drivers headed west on a Glenn Highway** straightaway out of the big, broad country of Eureka Summit feel the mountains closing in to form the Matanuska Valley, and they see there, guarding the headwaters, a sphinxlike lion, reclined, holding its head up. A chunk of rock left behind as glaciers retreated, Lion Head occupies the ground between the Chugach Mountains to the south and the Talkeetna Mountains to the north. On a sunny autumn day with new snow on the high peaks and aspen leaves burning yellow in the lowlands, it's hard to resist the urge to check out the view of the Matanuska Glacier and multiple perpetually white peaks above 10,000 feet in the inner Chugach Mountains.

The way up Lion Head is short but by no means easy. A trail of sorts is worn in, but steep grades, slippery surfaces, and rockiness all combine to make it more challenging. The entirety of Lion Head is on land owned by AT&T for communications facilities, and AT&T requests that all hikers call them to log in and out. You may not have phone service in this remote location, unless you are an AT&T mobile customer. Call AT&T's office in Anchorage before you hike from a place with known phone service: (907) 264-8363, or (800) 252-7521.

## DRIVING DIRECTIONS

Search online for "lion head ak" or follow these directions. Drive the Glenn Highway to mile 105.8, and turn south toward Lion Head onto a gravel access road. For drivers headed east away from Anchorage and Palmer, be alert for the turn after passing Glacier View School. Traffic heading west will be climbing out of the Caribou Creek drainage, and the driveway will suddenly appear. In either case, there is a short gap in the guardrail on the outside of the curve at the crest of a hill. Go cautiously to ensure you make the turn. Almost immediately, a gate blocks the access road. Park along the road or in an adjacent, higher pullout area. The walk begins at the gate.

*Admiring Matanuska Glacier from the summit of Lion Head*

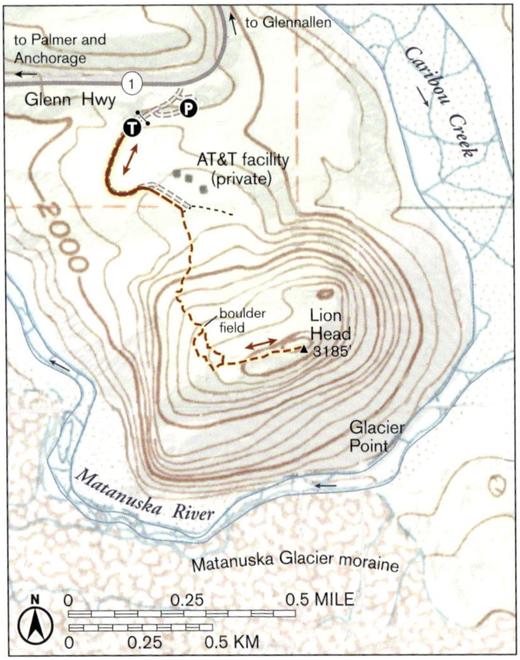


## ON THE ROUTE

After calling AT&T to log in, slip around the gate (elevation 2100 feet), and walk up the access road and around a bend. As the grade flattens and the communications buildings come into view, go right on a smaller offshoot road, which may be marked with a small pile of rocks. It is possible to miss the initial turn and end up alongside the buildings with an apparent trail straight ahead (southeast); this is *not* the main trail. If you are next to the buildings, go to the third building and tower, turn hard right, and head away from the buildings (southwest) to find the most-used route. At the top of a modest grade, look for two additional rock piles marking the footpath into the woods, away from the buildings and toward Lion Head.

This trail heads briefly downhill into a patch of trees, then breaks into the open and heads uphill on a track that can be muddy and slippery, with some awkward step-ups. Expect some minor brush; it might come in handy to hold on to. En route, breaks in trees give improving views. At a crest, there is a first view of the toe of Matanuska Glacier. Just beyond, 0.8 mile from the gate, the trail enters a boulder field with two options: a steeper route that goes approximately straight up the boulders and continues more directly to the ridge crest, requiring use of hands, or a route that exits the top right side of the boulder field and continues up at a more modest grade. Ultimately, the routes rejoin on the "summit" ridge (1 mile in, elevation 2950 feet), and the whole glacier comes into view, framed nicely by clusters of conifers.

Follow the rocky ridge crest or a trail just below the crest to the high point, 3185 feet. This knob feels like a real summit, even though the hike up is barely a mile long. Up the glacier 20 miles stands a wall of peaks draped in ice and reaching above 10,000 and 11,000 feet high. These unnamed peaks wring snow out of moist ocean air from Prince William Sound, generating the Matanuska Glacier on the north side and the Harvard Glacier at the head of College Fjord on the south side.

While the ridge near the summit feels relatively safe and can accommodate several parties, be cautious. Toward the glacier (south side), the ridge initially drops off at a modest angle, but there is an edge, and it marks a long drop. A fall would be fatal. Similarly, the back side (north) has crumbled away over eons, leaving boulder fields below a smaller set of cliffs. Cracks in the rock and tundra near the summit are evidence of freeze-thaw action that levers the solid rock apart. Stay back from cracks and from the edge. Also, the Grand Canyon effect has potential to occur on this ridge: people posing for photos with their backs to the view step off an edge. Oops. Instead, descend the trail.

Upon departure, call AT&T again as soon as you have cell service. AT&T says if they don't hear back, they will assume people still are out on Lion Head and may need help.

# 49 BELANGER PASS LOOP

**DISTANCE:** 17-mile loop
**TIME:** 2–3 days
**ELEVATION GAIN:** 4000 feet
**HIGH POINT:** 4500 feet
**SEASON:** June–September
**SURFACE:** Hardpack, bushes (low), mud
**GRADE:** Rolling with steep segments
**INDIGENOUS LAND:** Western Ahtna Athabascan
**MANAGING AGENCY:** Alaska Division of Mining, Land, and Water
**MAPS:** USGS Anchorage D-1 NW, D-2 NE
**ONLINE MAP SEARCH:** "belanger pass ak"
**TRAILHEAD GPS:** 61.919203°N, 147.328353°W

**A network of trails spreading from Belanger Pass provides access into the backcountry of the Talkeetna Mountains,** inhabited primarily by caribou, sheep, miners, and—during the last part of summer—hunters. A 17-mile loop stringing together ridges and valleys makes for a sizable two-night trip, described here. The route easily breaks into smaller loops (see Shorter Options) to accommodate shorter backpacking trips or ambitious day hiking. In late June, watch for the Nelchina caribou herd migration through this area. Look for sheep, black bears, grizzlies, coyotes, wolves, and other wildlife anytime. In season, there are blueberries and the gamut of Alaska wildflowers. All options are rugged and require routefinding skills and backcountry experience.

The Chickaloon–Knik–Nelchina Trail system, which includes this area, is a route originally used by the Ahtna people for hundreds of years as they traded goods between Dena'ina people on Knik Arm and the Ahtna Nenn' (homeland) in the Copper River Basin. In the early 1900s, prospectors traveled from Knik Arm via the Chickaloon–Knik–Nelchina Trail, which then provided access to gold mines on Alfred and Albert Creeks before there was a Glenn Highway. When the price of gold was deregulated in the mid-1970s, mining activity began again, and the Alfred Creek valley contains an operation that may still be active.

Note that sections of the all-terrain vehicle (ATV) trails this route follows can be very muddy, particularly in the fall when the weather is wetter and the hunter traffic is higher, churning up the surface. The ATV trail network in this area provides good backcountry access for die-hard mountain bikers, but the routes are only pleasant bicycling when at their driest.

## DRIVING DIRECTIONS

Search online for "belanger pass ak" or follow these directions. Drive to Glenn Highway mile 123.5, and turn north at a sign for N. Startup Road. A sign labeled "Trail" indicates the turn. Follow the road 1.3 miles to its junction with a substantial ATV track known as Squaw Creek Trail, which leads to the Belanger Pass Trail. A sign notes the left turn to the trails, as well as a private subdivision straight ahead. Because of deep mudholes, the ATV track is not drivable by street vehicles much beyond the junction. Park on the roadside but out of the way of through traffic. Respect private land along the ATV trail by sticking to the trail and complying with signs.

## ON THE ROUTE

A better name for Squaw Creek Trail is *Xelt'aats'i Na' Tene*, meaning "water lily river trail" in Ahtna Athabascan (the term "squaw" is a racial slur). Start your hike heading southwest on Xelt'aats'i Na' Tene for 0.3 mile to the signed junction with Belanger Pass Trail; turn right. The Belanger Pass Trail, also an ATV track, winds its way uphill, gaining nearly 1400 feet in about 2.5 miles. Just before cresting the pass, an intersecting gravel track departs left up the hillside to the ridge of Syncline Mountain, good fodder for day hikers, promising grand views (see Shorter Options). For this route, continue straight on, soon reaching a four-way intersection at the high point of the pass, 4370 feet. The left branch heads down to Pass Creek, for those completing the loop in a clockwise direction. A second branch leads right on the aptly named Ridge Trail, the counterclockwise route. The third branch, farther to the right, is a short spur trail to a magnificent viewpoint overlooking the vast valley to the

*Ridge walking along an escarpment, with Pass Creek valley to the left*

south and the Chugach Mountains beyond, picnic table included. This description takes you counterclockwise.

Start up the Ridge Trail to the right along a gentle, rolling crest with a well-worn ATV track to lead the way. This is easy high-country walking with views looking back into vast, wild valleys. After continuing this way for 3.2 miles from the four-way junction, the ATV track comes to a small, flat spot (where ATVs have turned around) and takes a sudden dive off the ridge to the right into the Crooked Creek valley. Instead, drop off the ridge to the left, leaving the track and beginning the cross-country portion of the route.

This middle portion of the hike is entirely without an established trail, though plentiful animal paths ease travel through low bushes. Make use of these worn treads, but don't let them lead you astray. Hike down the hillside through tussocky grasses and boggy patches, aiming to the left of a bump ahead and toward a gravely mountain face across the valley. In a half mile, the terrain levels out near a small pond, a possible, though bushy, camping spot about 6.5 miles from the trailhead. Immediately thereafter,

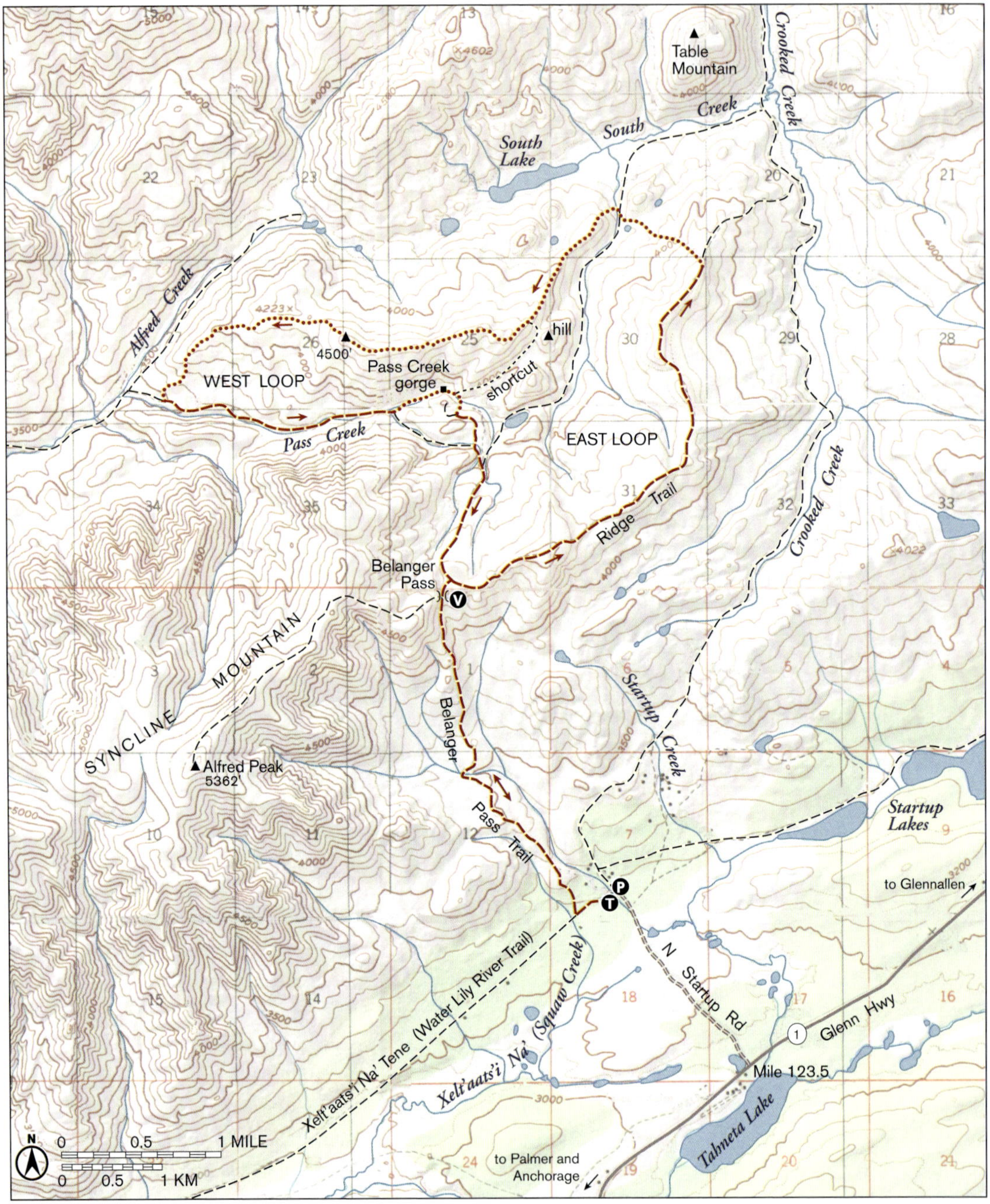
Table Mountain
Crooked Creek
South Creek
South Lake
Alfred Creek
WEST LOOP
4500'
Pass Creek gorge
shortcut
hill
EAST LOOP
Pass Creek
Ridge Trail
Belanger Pass
SYNCLINE MOUNTAIN
Alfred Peak 5362'
Belanger Pass Trail
Startup Creek
Startup Lakes
to Glennallen
N Startup Rd
Glenn Hwy
Mile 123.5
Tahneta Lake
Xelt'aats'i Na' Tene (Water Lily River Trail)
Xelt'aats'i Na' (Squaw Creek)
to Palmer and Anchorage
0 0.5 1 MILE
0 0.5 1 KM

descend to the valley floor where an ATV track follows a stream flowing north into South Creek. This area presents a few more camping options. A flat patch next to the ATV trail is promising; motor traffic here appears to be scarce, but be prepared for vehicles to pass. Alternatively, a rocky bench overhanging the creek on the west side is hospitable. South Lake looks tempting on a map but is a vast, brushy marshland in reality. High-quality, level campsites are hard to come by on this route; make the most of your options.

To continue, make a short, steep climb from the creekside onto the toe of the ridge overlooking South Lake. Thus begins a nearly 4-mile ridge walk without water that passes through a brush zone at either end but consists of rock-and-tundra footing for most of the way. Simply follow the crest of the ridge west. About a mile after leaving the creek, there is an opportunity to shortcut the larger loop and head directly back to Belanger Pass, creating a smaller loop described in Shorter Options. To continue on the full route, keep following the ridge as it becomes increasingly rocky, forming an escarpment that drops dramatically toward South Lake. Admire the sheep and caribou trails that impressively traverse this topography, and look for raptors soaring here. After 2.3 miles of ridge walking and 9 miles from the trailhead, at an elevation of 4500 feet, the ridge hits a rocky precipice that prevents continuing straight. Swing to the right around the cliff, beginning a steep descent.

The next 1.5 miles is unavoidable hip-high brush—almost bushwhacking—that can be soaking in rainy weather, although animal paths make the going easier. Continue to follow the broad crest of the ridge nearly to its toe, looking for a small bump to the left. Drop through a low point and briefly back up over the bump, looking for moderate enough grade to drop to the valley floor of Pass Creek and the ATV trail.

There are workable campsites near the confluence of Pass and Alfred Creeks. Look for brush-free benches on the south bank of Pass Creek, though wet feet are necessary for crossing here. Flat spots can also be found at the acute angle formed by the ATV tracks along the two creeks. Vehicles are more likely to pass here at any time, however, and in early summer this junction may remain covered in ice and snow. To continue back to Belanger Pass along Pass Creek, head east and upstream along a muddy ATV trail. The route crosses Pass Creek several times and then generally follows it on the north side. The easiest option is to follow the track and walk in wet boots.

About 1.8 miles from the confluence of Pass and Alfred Creeks, the valley splits around a topographic knob. The ATV trail goes to the right of the knob along one branch of the creek, but you can follow the main branch of Pass Creek straight ahead on an off-trail route through a small gorge that is scenic and exploratory (following the ATV trail to the right may be slightly easier going). To take the recommended gorge route, follow the creek ahead, hugging the right hillside to avoid wet feet. As the creek begins to turn right and the banks become more canyon-like, follow an increasingly well-worn animal trail through bushes, criss-crossing the creek where necessary. The bushes open up into the boulder-lined gorge, which is prime habitat for pikas. Immediately after passing through a pinch point, half a mile since leaving the ATV trail, climb up the grassy hillside on the right of the creek to an obvious ATV track. Turn left onto the track, following it around a bend to a junction with the primary Pass Creek ATV trail. Turn left again, rejoining the main route as it climbs south back to Belanger Pass. Proceed over the pass to return to the trailhead.

## SHORTER OPTIONS

For day hikers, a round-trip to the viewpoint at Belanger Pass is 5.7 miles with 1400 feet of elevation gain, up a possibly muddy ATV track the whole way. The views of the Chugach Mountains to the south are superb.

For peak baggers, Alfred Peak on the Syncline Mountain ridge is 9.8 miles roundtrip with 2500 feet of elevation gain. To get there, take the gravel track to the left just before reaching Belanger Pass from the south side, and follow this ATV trail along the ridge to the peak. Continuing along the 7-mile ridgetop makes a tempting extended day for quick hikers and mountain runners.

For those wanting a shorter loop, a cross-country shortcut (shown on the map) from the ridge south of South Lake directly to Belanger Pass creates two smaller loops from the lobes of the main route. The west loop is 14.5 miles, 2900 feet elevation gain, and includes the more "wild" ridge walk. The east loop is 12.8 miles, 3200 feet elevation gain, and is pleasant in that it cuts out most of the brushy going and features the tamer Ridge Trail ATV track. To complete the 0.8-mile shortcut, hike to a point at 4300 feet on the ridge south of South Lake where there is a notable hill adjacent to the southeast (the shortcut is mentioned under On the Route above). There is a small saddle between the ridge and adjacent hill; it is just west of a rocky spine on the ridge. Hike down to the saddle on braided animal trails, then head southwest down the valley still on animal trails toward the lowlands of Pass Creek. The going is relatively easy, if boggy in spots; hikers can avoid wet feet altogether by choosing animal paths that hug the right hillside. Step over Pass Creek at the rocky gorge, then climb the grassy opposing slope to an ATV track. Turn left onto the track, following it around a bend to a junction with the primary Pass Creek ATV trail. Turn left again, rejoining the main route as it climbs south to Belanger Pass.

OPPOSITE: *Looking down the Strelna Creek drainage from Dixie Pass, Trip 51, in September* (Photo by Lang Van Dommelen)

# Copper Basin

THE EASTERNMOST PORTION OF SOUTHCENTRAL ALASKA ENCOMPASSES THE COPPER RIVER Basin and Valdez. Ahtna Athabascan people have lived in communities along the Copper River for eons, in the broad area between the high white Wrangell Mountain volcanoes and the glaciated peaks of the Chugach Mountains. These mountains drain to the sea via the Copper River and provide an avenue for a strong run of salmon. Here is an inland climate hotter in summer and colder in winter than the more moderate climates nearer the coast, with scrubbier but extensive boreal forest. The southern edge of this area, near Valdez, circles back to Prince William Sound, with its dense green rainforest coast and waterways backed by jutting mountains, the home environment of the maritime Chugach Sugpiaq (Alutiiq) culture. Wrangell–St. Elias National Park and Preserve provides samples of inland rugged mountain hiking, and Valdez promises coastal and rainforest walks. Thompson Pass is an alpine wonder that combines elevation with a touch of coastal influence.

# 50 MENTASTA MOUNTAINS LOOP

**DISTANCE:** 22-mile loop
**TIME:** 3 days
**ELEVATION GAIN:** 3050 feet
**HIGH POINT:** 6050 feet
**SEASON:** June–August
**SURFACE:** Tundra, sand and/or gravel, water
**GRADE:** Moderate with steep segments
**INDIGENOUS LAND:** Upper Ahtna Athabascan
**AGENCY:** Wrangell–St. Elias National Park and Preserve
**MAP:** USGS Nabesna C-5
**ONLINE MAP SEARCH:** "mentasta mountains ak"
**TRAILHEAD GPS:** Trail Creek 62.523001°N, 143.222709°W
Lost Creek 62.513050°N, 143.177295°W

**Near the northern edge of Wrangell–St. Elias National Park and Preserve, in a far corner of the** Southcentral region of Alaska, two creeks flow south off the Mentasta Mountains, join a larger waterway, and then arc northward. This "Southcentral" water escapes through a gap in the mountains and heads north into Interior Alaska's Tanana River. These waters ultimately flow to the Bering Sea at the Yukon Delta. Back at the headwaters in the Mentasta Mountains, a 6000-foot pass divides Lost Creek and Trail Creek, a gap traversable on foot. This is the only trip in the book in a watershed that does not drain south to the Gulf of Alaska.

Lost Creek and Trail Creek have carved valleys that make a fine, if mostly trailless and often rocky, trekking route into and out of the peaks. Both streams cross the quiet Nabesna Road 1.8 miles from each other, making an attractive closed loop possible. Much of the walking is on gravel bars or easy tundra, but hikers may encounter brief stretches of tussocks or willows, and they likely will wade several braided river channels. There is no one trail, though in places all-terrain vehicles (ATVs), sheep, or previous hikers have worn in segments. Routefinding skills and the ability to read a topographic map are essential. Watch for Dall sheep, caribou, wolves, bears, moose, pikas, lynx, and glimpses of the high, perpetually white Wrangell Mountains to the south.

## DRIVING DIRECTIONS

Search online for "mentasta mountains ak" or follow these directions. Take the Tok Cutoff (Glenn Highway) to mile 59.8 near Slana, and turn southeast onto the gravel Nabesna Road. Distances in these directions are measured from this intersection. Go to mile 0.2, and turn right on the access road to the National Park Service's Slana Ranger Station, which has information on road conditions (it is worth stopping to check). Return to Nabesna Road, and drive to Trail Creek (mile 29) and, if possible, Lost Creek (mile 30.8). There are no bridges over these creeks, and water levels affect whether cars can pass. The stream channels often change across wide gravel

*Above Lost Creek in the Mentasta Mountains in midsummer* (Photo by Steve Cleary)

Noyes Mountain
8147'
MENTASTA
MOUNTAINS
Section 28
Trail Creek
Wrangell-St. Elias National Preserve
constricted area
Peggy Lake
Soda Lake Trail
Creek
to Tok Cutoff
Trail
Lost
Big Grayling Lake Trail
Nabesna Rd
Kendesnii Campground
Creek
Chalk Creek
Big Grayling Lake
Twin Lakes
Jack Lake
Jack
Creek
Graves
Wrangell-St. Elias National Park
0 0.5 1 MILE
0 0.5 1 KM

bars, and mileage could vary by more than a tenth of a mile. Either stream could have too much water to drive through, but either could be completely dry, especially Trail Creek.

About 0.2 mile beyond Lost Creek is the informal trailhead for the Big Grayling Lake Trail on the left. There is good camping here (but no facilities) and a place to leave a car off the road, but the safest option, particularly for those in smaller vehicles, is to leave the car on the west side of Trail Creek, because the creeks could rise and block your return. Park along the road well away from the river and out of the way of traffic.

## ON THE ROUTE

The description here runs counterclockwise. The trip works equally well the other direction. From Trail Creek (elevation 3150 feet), hike first along the road 1.8 miles to Lost Creek. The hike away from the road most likely will start up the Lost Creek gravel bars. But, if you choose to park at Lost Creek, you may want to start on the Big Grayling Lake Trail (an ATV trail). This trail heads north through brush and in 0.4 mile emerges on the gravel bar. In a few hundred yards, you may follow the ATV trail back into the woods for perhaps another ten minutes, roughly paralleling the stream, before returning to the gravel bar. About 1.7 miles from the road, the main ATV trail heads east toward Big Grayling Lake. This time, stay on the gravel bar, and do not follow the trail to the lake.

The route follows Lost Creek almost to the pass. Until entering the mountains, the route mostly follows the gravel bars. Sometimes you may find yourself on the low terrace above the creek walking through scattered dwarf birch and willow on animal trails. Ultimately, as you enter the mountains, the best route is on the west side of the stream. Hikers usually can ford the creek. While unlikely to be noticed, the Soda Creek Trail (an ATV trail) takes off to the east before reaching the mountains and may make for intriguing explorations another day.

A short way into the mountains, Lost Creek flows out of a steep-sided cut not suited to walking. There is a route around this cut on the west side of the creek that heads steeply up almost 300 feet onto a bench where the walking is good, with intermittent bits of trail. The route on the east is passable but requires side-hilling.

On the west, a rolling and discontinuous bench system parallels the stream for about 1.5 miles. At one point, a ravine seems to force a descent, but it is possible to cross it on tundra just above a dramatic gorge and continue along the bench well above Lost Creek. Drop back to Lost Creek beyond the ravine where convenient, and proceed upstream as the mountains press in and form a sort of canyon. At this point, approaching elevation 4500 feet, it is best to cross back to the east side of the creek. Camping spots are scarce at this point in the circuit, but they do exist.

Finding the route out of the canyon area and to the pass is the trickiest part of the hike, especially if visibility is poor. Consult a topographic map. Several streams come together out of several small canyons; follow the one that leads north into Section 28 on the USGS map and then forks. Multiple crossings of the stream you are following may be necessary. When you round a bend to the right and the canyon opens up a bit (entering Section 28), a steeper stream fork comes in from the left, and the main valley continues to the right at a shallower grade. Creating the divide between these forks is a steep, vegetated hill. The best walking to the pass is at the top of the hill. Mounting the slope directly between the two

*Camp near Trail Creek* (Photo by Steve Cleary)

forks appears best, but continuing up the right fork a short distance until you see a notch on the left side allows less-steep access toward the pass, if desired. Once you are above these creeks, in a sort of mountain bowl, the views are fine and the walking good. Camping is possible, although it may be necessary to walk for water. Head to the back left part of this bowl and find the pass, where slatey-gray gravel and rust-colored gravel meet at a distinct line.

The northwest side of the pass drops to a valley that leads about 2 miles to Trail Creek. The descent from the pass requires crossing steep scree and likely a snow patch or two. This slope may make some uneasy, but there are sheep trails. From the pass, the visible sheep trail to the right is best. The trail to the left eventually runs into rock bands (good for nimble sheep but not hikers). The broad, partially vegetated hump of a rock glacier in the valley bottom makes good walking, but stay toward the left (south) side to bypass an active ice face toward the right side. Find your way off the rock glacier, and follow tundra bluffs above a pleasant stream back into the land of willows, knee-high grass, and wildflowers. As you approach the Trail Creek valley, depending on your exact route and the weather, the high white Wrangell Mountains may appear in the distance. These include Mount Sanford and Mount Blackburn, both of which top 16,000 feet. Camping is good in the general area where the small stream joins Trail Creek.

To complete the loop, follow Trail Creek—narrower in some spots than Lost Creek, and with brushy islands—nearly 7 miles. There is a trail along Trail Creek, but it is intermittent. Find the route that offers the best walking. Often it will be gravel bars, sometimes an ATV trail. Sometimes (especially in the lower stretches) you will face a choice between willow-bashing for a short stretch or wading across the creek. Neither option should be particularly difficult.

Before or after the trip, a stay at the park's Kendesnii Campground at Twin Lakes, mile 27.8 of Nabesna Road, is handy and pleasant.

Note that the Trails Illustrated map "Wrangell–St. Elias National Park and Preserve" covers this area, but the scale is insufficient to make the map useful for navigation. Hunting is allowed in the preserve; sheep season generally begins August 10, and moose season, August 20.

## EXTENDING YOUR TRIP

Experienced mountaineers can climb Noyes Mountain (8147 feet) from the pass. The green tundra of upper Trail Creek invites exploration upstream and perhaps over a pass into other drainages.

Along Nabesna Road are other trails and two reservable public-use cabins. Most people who come to this area have to travel a long distance, so make the most of it. Check the National Park Service website for a Nabesna Road Guide and other options, including the Skookum Volcano Trail near the end of the road.

# 51 DIXIE PASS

**DISTANCE:** 17.6 miles roundtrip
**TIME:** 3–4 days
**ELEVATION GAIN:** 3730 feet
**HIGH POINT:** 5190 feet
**SEASON:** Late June–early September
**SURFACE:** Hardpack, water, brush (high)
**GRADE:** Moderate with steep segments
**INDIGENOUS LAND:** Lower Ahtna Athabascan
**MANAGING AGENCY:** Wrangell–St. Elias National Park
**MAPS:** USGS McCarthy C-8; Valdez C-1
**ONLINE MAP SEARCH:** "dixie pass ak"
**TRAILHEAD GPS:** 61.552423°N, 144.052799°W

**Dixie Pass is one of the few backcountry trips in the Wrangell Mountains that can be done without** an airplane, yet it offers a microcosm of Wrangell backcountry, with stream fords, gravel bar hiking, and a mountain pass. The pass area offers the chance for views of massive, glacier-covered, 14,163-foot Mount Wrangell and of 16,390-foot Mount Blackburn. The hike follows crystal-clear Strelna Creek along successively smaller branches until it disappears at its source just below the pass. The countryside is wild, rugged, big, and beautiful, changing from open spruce and willow forest at lower elevations to willow-covered gravel bars somewhat higher, and then becoming alpine tundra below the pass. Watch for bears, moose, Dall sheep, ground squirrels, and ptarmigan.

Although the hike is not long, it is on unmaintained trails and not easy. Part of the route has only intermittent animal trails, and hikers must choose between walking the gravel bars, crossing and

recrossing the stream, or following animal trails through thick willow. Map-reading and routefinding skills are necessary to find the pass. Despite these challenges, the trip is popular with Alaska visitors because it is one of the few readily accessible routes in Wrangell–St. Elias National Park.

## DRIVING DIRECTIONS

Search online for "nugget creek trail ak," then follow these directions.

Drive to mile 82.5 of the Richardson Highway (32.5 miles south of Glennallen). Turn east onto the Edgerton Highway, and continue 34 miles to Chitina Village (*Tsedi Na'* in Ahtna). Expect no gas or groceries beyond here. Follow the main road through Chitina as it becomes mostly gravel and crosses the Copper River bridge. From the east side of the Copper River bridge, drive about 13 miles on the gravel McCarthy Road to Kotsina/Nugget Creek Road on the left, across from the grassy Strelna airstrip. A mostly obscured railroad wheel at the junction is painted to mark the way "to Kuskulana Nugget Creek." (Local residents have erected their own mileposts on McCarthy Road; Kotsina/Nugget Creek Road is at mile 14.4 by this measurement.)

Follow the rough, unpaved Kotsina/Nugget Creek Road 2.5 miles to the intersection of the Nugget Creek and Kotsina all-terrain vehicle (ATV) trails. This intersection is easily identified by the ford of Strelna Creek on the Nugget Creek ATV trail just past the intersection. Two-wheel-drive and low-slung cars should park here for a fee, paid to the Chitina Native Corporation, which owns the private land on which this junction occurs. There is a cylindrical container for payments. Four-wheel-drive vehicles with enough clearance can continue on the Kotsina ATV trail, though the road is heavily rutted and dicey. By four-wheel-drive or by foot, continue another 1.3 miles to the Dixie Pass trailhead, where a smattering of clearings can hold eight to ten cars.

## ON THE ROUTE

The trail to Dixie Pass, a narrow footpath on the east side of the clearing, is marked by a sign stating (erroneously) that the pass is 10 miles away. The route winds through open woods of spruce and willow on a good trail for the first 2.1 miles. After descending to Strelna Creek, where the first reasonable camp spots appear, the trail veers northward to follow the creek through much denser forest. The trail in this stretch is more difficult to walk, as it is sometimes blocked by a fallen tree or heads steeply uphill to avoid a cliff.

Around 4.4 miles from the trailhead, just after passing a large, informal campsite with space for multiple tents, the trail reaches the confluence of the west and east forks of Strelna Creek, the first major confluence. The route follows the east fork. Cross the west fork above the confluence where the water is generally less than knee-deep and not too difficult to cross. Wearing boots or other shoes is advisable. Worn tread on either side of the crossing will help identify the route.

The next 3 miles up the east fork is the most difficult part of the trip. There is a trail of sorts on the north (left) side of the creek for the first half mile, though some may prefer to walk the creek bed. Cross the creek to the southeast (right) bank when the trail pinches out at a cliff 4.9 miles from the trailhead. The route for roughly 2 miles beyond

OPPOSITE: *Wading through Strelna Creek canyon in low water conditions* (Photo by Lang Van Dommelen)

Wrangell-St. Elias Wilderness
Rock Creek
wilderness boundary
Elliott Creek
5770'
Dixie Pass
Iron Mountain 6657'
Tributary B
canyon
5658'
West Fork
Tributary A
private inholdings
East Fork
Wrangell-St. Elias National Park
Kotsina Trail
4878'
Strelna Creek
private inholdings
Dry Creek
Nugget Creek Trail
alternate parking
Kuskulana River
private inholdings
Creek Rd
Kotsina/Nugget
to Chitina
Strelna Creek
McCarthy Rd
to McCarthy
0 0.5 1 MILE
0 0.5 1 KM

the initial cliff is on gravel bars or intermittent animal trails through scrub willow, and it is necessary to cross the creek several times. It may be possible to cross on rocks, depending on the water level, but it is best to embrace wet feet. There is a grassy tent site at 5.5 miles and gravel bar camping at 5.8 miles into the trip.

Some of the many tributary creeks are not shown on topographic maps, which can make pinpointing your location difficult. The first major tributary of the east fork (Tributary A on the map) is 6 miles from the trailhead; the path leads clearly up the northwest side of the left fork from this confluence. About a mile beyond, the creek goes through a canyon for about 100 feet. Choose between scrambling up the steep hillside to the east to get around the canyon or walking in the creek if the water level is low enough. Neither is easy. In the canyon, the water is very cold, and in one place hikers must clamber over a boulder overhung by a cliff to avoid a deep pool. Though tricky, the canyon is also a highlight of the trip.

Beyond the canyon, the valley widens into a broad gravel bar dotted with willow and laced with dwarf fireweed (elevation 3600 feet). This popular campsite could become overused. Practice Leave No Trace principles (see the Introduction), particularly because careless toileting could affect water quality. The second tributary (Tributary B on the map) comes in at the north end of the gravel bar, 7.4 miles from the trailhead.

To reach the pass, 1.4 miles farther, follow the obvious trail heading uphill between the two forks of the creek. (The left branch of the creek leads to the pass but goes through another canyon as a waterfall.) When the trail becomes faint above the last willows, the route splits into high and low routes, with both options leading back to the same trail, although the paths are intermittent from this point on. For the final 900-foot climb to the pass, choose to walk up a lingering snowpack over the creek, or traverse steeply up to parallel the creek on one side or the other on faint trails. There are beautiful views from Dixie Pass—of Strelna Creek drainage and the Chugach Mountains to the south, of Rock Creek valley and peaks reaching to 7500 feet to the north, and on clear days, glimpses of snowy Mounts Wrangell and Blackburn. For the best views by far, push on to point 5770, a short, steep climb along the ridge to the northwest.

Camping at Dixie Pass itself is not recommended, as the pass is an animal route, may feature strong winds, and lacks a good water source. One option is to camp partway down the Rock Creek valley on the north side of the pass. There are many workable campsites on gravel bars along the entire route, allowing hikers to set their own pace. Strong, fast, experienced backcountry hikers can do this trip in two days. Leisurely hikers may prefer four days.

## EXTENDING YOUR TRIP

The Nugget Creek ATV trail, an old mining road, makes a rugged backcountry mountain bike trip or hike. It is 30 miles roundtrip and leads to a public-use cabin on the east side of Nugget Creek (reservations online through the National Park Service), the rubble-covered base of the Kuskulana Glacier, and views of Mount Blackburn. The first several miles of the old road can be muddy and difficult, especially with a loaded bicycle. After that the trail is higher, drier, and easier. There are several creeks to ford. The trail gains roughly 900 feet of elevation in 15 miles. Most bicyclists should allow two days, plus time to explore. The Kotsina ATV trail beyond the Dixie Pass trailhead can also be biked or hiked. Contact the National Park Service for more information (see the Resources section).

# 52 JUMBO MINE AND ROOT GLACIER TRAIL

**DISTANCE:** 12.1 miles roundtrip
**TIME:** 1.5 days (half day for Root Glacier, full day for Jumbo Mine)
**ELEVATION GAIN:** 4000 feet
**HIGH POINT:** 5700 feet
**SEASON:** June–September
**SURFACE:** Hardpack, rocks, gravel
**GRADE:** Sustained steep (Jumbo Mine), rolling (Root Glacier)
**INDIGENOUS LAND:** Lower Ahtna Athabascan
**MANAGING AGENCY:** Wrangell–St. Elias National Park and Preserve
**MAPS:** USGS McCarthy B-6 NE, C-6 SE, C-5 SW, B-5 NW
**ONLINE MAP SEARCH:** "kennicott ak"
**TRAILHEAD GPS:** 61.481049°N, 142.885275°W

**Historic buildings of the Kennecott Copper Corporation and the nearby, once-boisterous town of** McCarthy sit beside the Kennicott Glacier. High above, on precipitous mountain slopes, mines once disgorged precious blue-green ore onto aerial trams to be transported to the mill 4000 feet below. Abandoned wagon roads leading to three of the mines, Jumbo, Bonanza, and Erie, are trails into history. While several trails depart from Kennicott, this itinerary recommends an overnight at the Jumbo Creek camping area with a side trip to Root Glacier, then a rewarding uphill day hike the next day for lunch among castle-like peaks surrounding the site of Jumbo Mine.

The Lower Ahtna people controlled the copper resources in the Chitina River basin for centuries, leveraging the metal as a valuable trade commodity. Later, at the turn of the twentieth century, white settlers exploited the hospitality of the Ahtna to find and seize control of copper deposits, leading to mining across the region at a massive scale. Five Kennecott mines tapped a total of 4.6 million tons of copper ore, much of it highly profitable chalcocite (nearly 80 percent copper by weight). Producing 591,000 tons of copper and 900,000 ounces of silver, it was one of the richest mining operations in history for its scale. A honeycomb of more than 70 miles of layered tunnels connects the five mines: Erie, Jumbo, Glacier, Bonanza, and Mother Lode. When the mines closed in 1938, the towns of Kennicott and McCarthy died. Through the years, Alaskans who prefer a more remote lifestyle have been reclaiming the settlements. With the area's designation as Wrangell–St. Elias National Preserve, tourists began to visit the area in summertime. The preserve also spurred protection and renovation of historic buildings. Sixty miles of gravel access road discourage some visitors, to the benefit of those who do take this trip.

## DRIVING DIRECTIONS

Search online for "mccarthy ak," then follow these directions. Drive to mile 82.5 of the Richardson Highway (32.5 miles south of Glennallen). Turn east onto the Edgerton Highway, and continue 34 miles to Chitina Village (*Tsedi Na'* in Ahtna). Expect no gas or groceries beyond here. Follow the main road through Chitina as it becomes mostly gravel and crosses the Copper River bridge.

The 59-mile, primitive gravel McCarthy Road begins here and follows the bed of the old Copper River and Northwestern Railway, which carried ore from Kennicott to Cordova from 1911 to 1938. The road is not recommended for large camper vehicles or trailers. Allow two and a half hours to drive the

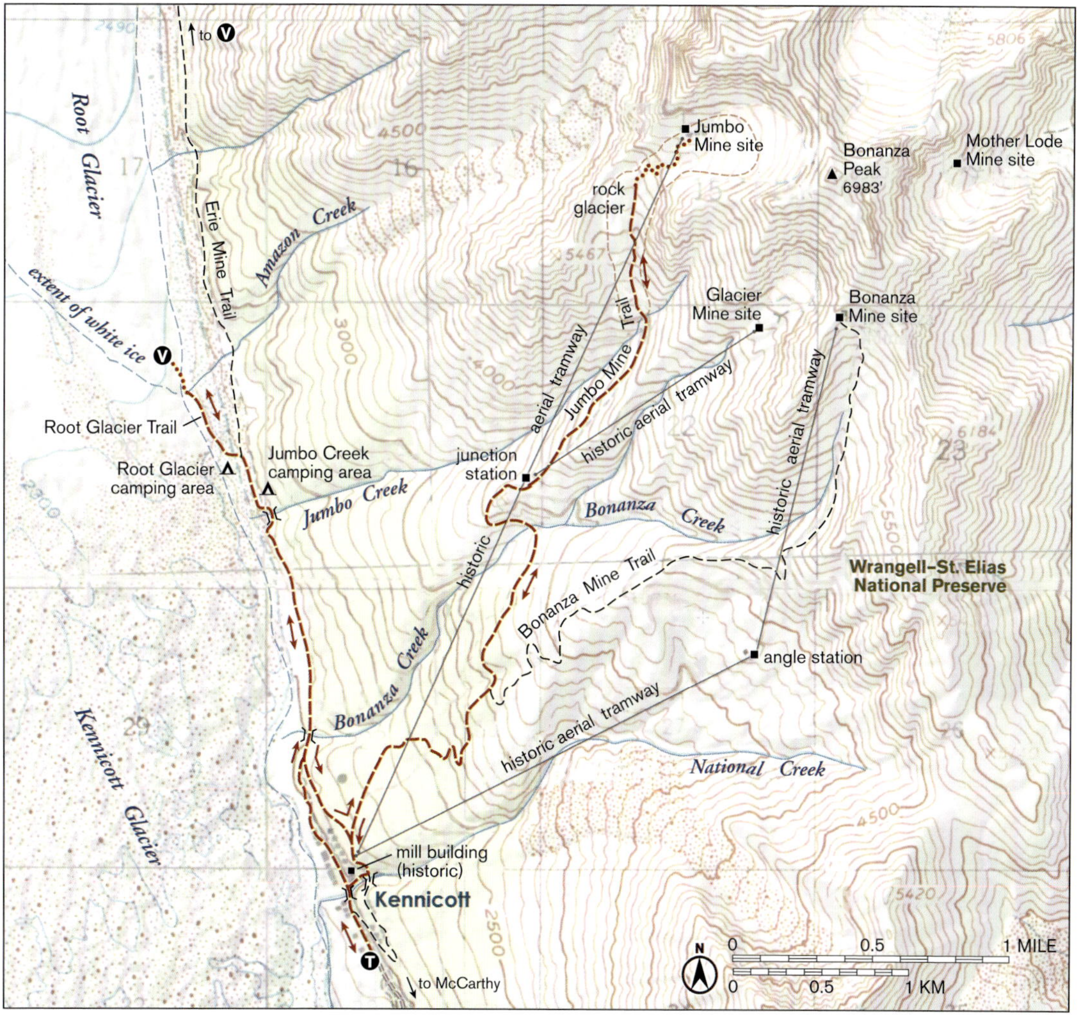

*The trek from Kennicott to the white ice of Root Glacier and nearby campsites is easier than the steep Jumbo Mine Trail.* (Photo by Gretchen Nelson)

rough road, and be prepared for flat tires. The road terminates at the Kennicott River. There is no public bridge for cars (some residents use a private bridge with a seasonal pass at high cost). Park at the river for overnight stays, for a fee, or park near the National Park Service Day Use Area 0.7 mile before the river, and walk the last bit. An alternate access to McCarthy is to fly to the airstrip just outside of town.

Cross the Kennicott River on the footbridge and walk or bike the gravel road east, up a small rise, to an intersection at the McCarthy–Kennicott Historical Museum. This old red railroad depot is well worth a visit. The left fork of the road goes to Kennicott, 4 miles away. The right fork leads quickly into McCarthy. To reach the trailhead, take a ground shuttle north from the museum to Kennicott. Several shuttles operate between the footbridge, McCarthy, and Kennicott; inquire at the riverside parking lot or in town. Walking or bicycling the road to Kennicott is another option, on a trail that parallels the road near glacial moraines.

## ON THE ROUTE

From the shuttle stop in Kennicott, the effective trailhead for this trip, cross the bridge over National Creek and proceed on flat ground on the main street through town (elevation 2000 feet). Follow this old wagon road 0.8 mile through the collection of historic buildings to a junction with trail signs and a restroom. The options from this junction are to head straight along Kennicott Glacier toward the Root Glacier Trail (a spur off the Erie Mine Trail) or take a hard turn on a four-wheel-drive track uphill toward Jumbo and Bonanza Mines. For now, continue straight.

The walk toward Root Glacier, also known as the White Ice Trail, is on an easy, mostly level footpath with great glacier and mountain views. Almost immediately, the trail crosses Bonanza Creek on a plank bridge. Nearly a mile from the junction, the trail jogs uphill to cross Jumbo Creek on a footbridge. Shortly after Jumbo Creek, at 1.7 miles from the trailhead, there are two separate tent sites with a shared bear-proof food storage locker and outhouse. Although there is an outhouse, campers must supply their own toilet paper and pack out bathroom trash. This is the first possible place to camp. About 0.2 mile farther is the turn to Root Glacier, which flows into Kennicott Glacier below you.

The spur trail to the glacier has been rerouted from time to time. Follow signs toward Root Glacier. A few hundred feet along the descent to the glacial moraine is another food storage locker and several surrounding tent sites. In late June, blue lupine grace the trailside and frame the glacier and mountains in the distance. Stop along the trail or at the edge of the white ice (2.3 miles from the shuttle stop) to enjoy the view of Root Glacier's Stairway Icefall to the north and the majestic white mountains: Mount Blackburn (16,390 feet) and Regal Mountain (13,845 feet). For walking on the glacier, crampons and an ice axe are recommended; the ice can be slippery and, with occasional water holes and bottomless tubes eroded from the ice, dangerous. A guided trip can be arranged in Kennicott or McCarthy and includes the use of crampons and an ice axe. Return to spend the evening at your camp, resting for the more strenuous day hike to Jumbo Mine tomorrow.

In the morning, backtrack to the trail junction just north of Kennicott. If you are carrying heavy overnight gear that you don't want to haul uphill, consider stashing a pack with rangers at the Kennecott Visitor Center, or find another bear-proof solution. From the junction, head uphill on a clear four-wheel-drive track toward Jumbo and Bonanza Mines. Turn left and uphill at the first major switchback, where another fork continues straight to the top of the mill building, the centerpiece of Kennicott. Above this point and to Bonanza Creek, there is some private land; stay on the trail. Watch for all-terrain vehicle traffic, both from tourist groups and private residents, as you continue on the clear main route at a steady climb. After 1.4 miles, reach another signed junction: the right fork heads to Bonanza Mine; take the left fork to Jumbo Mine.

The first part of the way to Jumbo Mine is an old wagon track. It appears the park occasionally clears encroaching alders. The trail crosses Bonanza Creek 0.6 mile after leaving the last fork, necessitating wet feet, then travels through alder tunnels with occasional clearings featuring wild columbine. On the ridge between Bonanza and Jumbo Creeks is the aging post-and-beam junction station building, an intersection of two aerial tramways that once carried supplies up to and ore down from Jumbo Mine and neighboring Glacier Mine. Look carefully for a spur trail leading left through the alders to the junction station and the nearby operator's house.

Back on the main trail approaching Jumbo Creek, scree slides cover the route, and it is necessary to cross short stretches of steep scree slope. At about 4700 feet, the trail climbs up a massive rock glacier. If you want to camp up here, there is water and a possible campsite at the lower end of the rock glacier.

Follow the remnants of the old track up the rocky footing, or pick your own way where no track is visible, bearing right into a high cirque below Bonanza Peak (elevation 6983 feet). As you climb, notice rocks underfoot shot through with blue-green veins, telltale of the coveted copper, and tramway cables slicing the sky above. On a topographic bench along the north side of the high cirque, 4 miles from the start of the uphill climb and at elevation 5700 feet, with luck, you will find relics from the old mine.

On the way down, take a shortcut from the final switchback to reach the top of the mill building, a nice overlook, then continue straight past it to pick up a trail that descends along the north side of National Creek to reach the heart of Kennicott. Be sure to spend some time exploring the historic mill town before catching the shuttle back. Walking tours are worthwhile, and the Kennicott Glacier Lodge is filled with memorabilia. Ask about the two spellings of Kennicott. For more relics and old photographs, visit the McCarthy Lodge, built in the early 1900s. Rent bicycles or arrange commercial raft trips at the river. If you camp near McCarthy, find a spot near the Kennicott River. Clear Creek, which you cross as you walk into McCarthy, supplies drinking water to residents; be careful not to contaminate it. Please remember that all structures and land in McCarthy and some in Kennicott are privately owned—do not enter buildings, take relics, or use old lumber for firewood.

*Castlelike formations near Jumbo Mine provide a backdrop for the historic junction station.*

## SHORTER OPTIONS

A stroll through Kennicott is enough of a destination in itself. To get off the main wagon road, a roughly 1-mile loop leads uphill on a sinuous switchback past historic cottages on the south side of National Creek, then crosses a charming bridge before descending along the north side of the creek. Stop to look out at the top of the mill building.

Root Glacier alone makes a 4.6-mile day hike from the shuttle stop to white ice and back. Jumbo Mine alone is a 9.6-mile roundtrip day hike from the shuttle stop. Bonanza Mine, on a relatively straightforward uphill route similar to Jumbo, is roughly 9 miles roundtrip.

The Erie Mine Trail continues past the Root Glacier cutoff, paralleling the glacier's edge along moraine. The trail culminates where mine cables cross the trail and a historic bunkhouse is visible 3000 feet above on the hillside, but it does not reach the mine itself. Views up valley are well worth the roughly 8 miles roundtrip from Kennicott.

## EXTENDING YOUR TRIP

Donoho Basin is the green peninsula of land caught between the flowing Kennicott and Root Glaciers. To get there requires crossing the full width of Root Glacier from Kennicott; education and confidence in glacier travel are essential. There are two designated National Park Service campsites with food storage lockers, one at each of the two lakes in the basin. A backpacking trip of two to four days or more is possible as an independent or guided trip (see the Resources section). Groups of eight or more must register with the Park Service; see their website for more information.

# 53 MOONLIGHT ODYSSEY AT THOMPSON PASS

**DISTANCE:** 6 miles roundtrip
**TIME:** Half day
**ELEVATION GAIN:** 2000 feet
**HIGH POINT:** 4400 feet
**SEASON:** Late June–September
**SURFACE:** Tundra, snow, rocks
**GRADE:** Moderate with steep segments
**INDIGENOUS LAND:** Chugach Sugpiaq (Alutiiq) and Lower Ahtna Athabascan
**MANAGING AGENCY:** Alaska Division of Mining, Land, and Water
**MAP:** USGS Valdez A-5
**ONLINE MAP SEARCH:** "thompson pass ak"
**TRAILHEAD GPS:** 61.127016°N, 145.728433°W

**Sunrise at Thompson Pass is a time to gaze out across gaping valleys, savoring sun-kissed glacial** bowls speared through with rocky spires. This pass, a larger-than-life highway route through the Chugach Mountains east of Valdez, is beloved by backcountry skiers and snowmachiners for its record-breaking snows in winter, though most people experience it through their windshields as a particularly scenic section of the Richardson Highway. Pulling over to hike from the highway, or maybe even camp for the night, allows remarkably quick access to rolling tundra terraces dotted with alpine lakes. This out-and-back route follows a natural bench from the highway near the pass, then turns up a gully to Moonlight Basin and climbs to the ridge next to Odyssey peak for views of Worthington Glacier on the other side.

## DRIVING DIRECTIONS

Search online for "thompson pass ak," or follow these directions. Parking for this route is a highway pullout 0.1 mile south of milepost 26 on the Richardson Highway, 26 miles from Valdez and 89 miles from Glennallen. Heading southbound, look for a steep rock cut forming the highway bed at the pass itself and, shortly after the cut, a large gravel pullout on the right. Park here.

*Rambling cross-country with the Chugach Mountains for company*

## ON THE ROUTE

After parking, cautiously cross the highway to the northeast shoulder, then walk the shoulder uphill toward the pass about a hundred yards, searching on the right for a gravel four-wheel-drive track that intersects the highway (elevation 2700 feet) shortly after a guardrail starts on the left shoulder. The track is not well used but is apparent; in early season it likely will be partially obscured by snow. Follow this track to the right and up a moderate grade, then slightly downhill. When the track takes a hard turn to the left, 0.2 mile from the highway, continue straight (east), striking out cross-country without a trail.

From here, the route follows terraces of rolling tundra along the bases of Little Odyssey and Odyssey peaks. Traverse east along these terraces between tiny lakes, being careful not to lose or gain much altitude. This terrace zone offers big-time tundra camping within even the first mile from the trailhead, featuring the kind of mountain views that other trips in this book take multiday uphill treks to reach. Easy access to alpine areas is hard to beat for families with kids and other short-distance hikers. Children will enjoy exploring the spongy tundra and shallow lakes.

To continue to the Worthington Glacier viewpoint, pick your way east along the bench, pressing on through minor, unavoidable patches of knee-high brush. About 1.6 miles from the highway, hop across a small creek that drains from a steep gully between Little Odyssey and Odyssey peaks. Roughly 2 miles into the trip, reach a more substantial stream in a gully leading up to Moonlight Basin. Turn left without crossing the stream, and follow the bank steeply upward. Some sections of the bank consist of steep, rocky talus, but it is not necessary to walk on lingering snow over the stream and risk collapse of snow bridges. After about half a mile of climbing up, the drainage opens into Moonlight Basin, elevation 3600 feet, leveling out temporarily. Cross the stream where it is shallow in the basin, keeping an eye out for rock ptarmigan that call this zone home.

Look up at the ridge above the basin to the north where a broad, high pass stretches between Odyssey to the left and Goodwills, as it is known to skiers, to the right. The left and right notches of this pass are lowest, but direct routes to either are prohibitively steep. Instead, aim for the center of the pass, circling right to avoid the steepest snow and talus and seeking out rock or vegetation for the most secure footing. Near the crest of the ridge, traverse slightly left to the viewpoint. Clamber up the last rocky spine to 4400 feet, 3 miles from the trailhead, and look out over a precipitous drop to the Ptarmigan Creek valley below and Worthington Glacier hanging high in the mountains beyond. The Richardson Highway is visible below, as well as the clear-cut of the Trans-Alaska Pipeline carrying crude oil toward the end of its journey from Prudhoe Bay to Port Valdez. Picture the scene in winter, when skiers hike up and swoosh down the snow-blanketed slopes to your right or ski laps in Moonlight Basin behind you.

When following the route back down from Moonlight Basin, remember to turn right to catch the bench when you begin seeing knee-high willow brush again, at a point where the stream breaks briefly into channels. As you near the west end of the bench and crest a small rise approaching the lakes, look out for the four-wheel-drive track coming over the hill in the distance, your passage back to the highway.

## TRIP OPTIONS

Prime camping with a view is possible with as little as 1 mile of moderate hiking from the parking pullout, a great opportunity for families and other short-distance hikers to spend time in the alpine.

Many hikers will be ready to retrace their steps down from the viewpoint, but the most

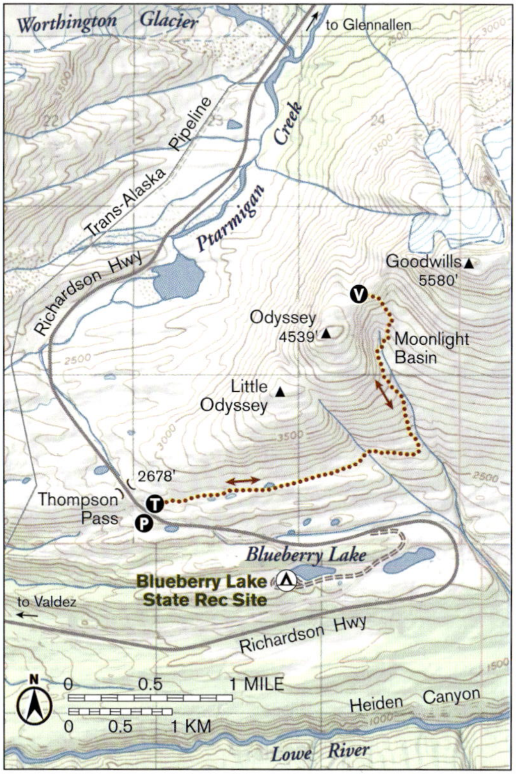

adventurous may want to branch off the route to further explore the ridge toward Odyssey. If you are day hiking but staying in the area for the night, a State Parks campground run by the Valdez Adventure Alliance is located at Blueberry Lake State Recreation Site, 1.5 highway miles southbound from the parking pullout.

## SEASONAL OPTIONS

Thompson Pass is a world-class backcountry ski destination. Avalanche gear and education are necessities (see Avalanches in the Introduction). The common skin track for Moonlight Basin departs from a pullout at the hairpin switchback on the Richardson Highway and heads north along the drainage into the basin.

# 54 HISTORIC VALDEZ TRAIL

**DISTANCE:** 8.3 miles roundtrip
**TIME:** Full day
**ELEVATION GAIN:** 2050 feet
**HIGH POINT:** 950 feet
**SEASON:** Mid-May–mid-October
**SURFACE:** Hardpack, roots
**GRADE:** Rolling with steep segments
**INDIGENOUS LAND:** Chugach Sugpiaq (Alutiiq)
**MANAGING AGENCIES:** Alaska Division of Mining, Land, and Water and the City of Valdez
**MAP:** USGS Valdez A-6 SE
**ONLINE MAP SEARCH:** "keystone canyon ak"
**TRAILHEAD GPS:** 61.061433°N, 145.939051°W

**Take a walk into history through Keystone Canyon, along a critical portion of the route used by** seekers of gold more than one hundred years ago. The cliffy canyon of the Lowe River was an impediment to access through the mountains to the Copper River country, but early settlers persevered. Today, the Historic Valdez Trail climbs moderately above the south end of Keystone Canyon and then traverses the west side of the canyon several hundred feet above the Lowe River. After the initial climb at the south end, it is mostly an easy walk on a gently rolling trail through a thick forest of Sitka spruce with occasional glimpses of spectacular waterfalls plunging down canyon walls and misty mountains looming overhead. An access point at Bridal Veil Falls allows for shorter excursions, and extensions are possible too.

This trail, built in 1899 by the US Army, offered the first glacier-free, year-round route from an ice-free port to Alaska's Interior that did not involve passing through Canada. At first, it was a pack trail for horses and dogs. A telegraph line connecting Eagle (Fort Egbert) and Valdez came next. In 1905, work began on widening part of the trail so wagons could use it, and by 1916, the first adventurous motorists used the road. When the Richardson Highway was built in the bottom of the canyon after World War II, alders reclaimed the historic trail. A small group of dedicated volunteers reopened the trail, and the City of Valdez maintains it.

## DRIVING DIRECTIONS

Seaqrch online for "keystone canyon ak," or follow these directions. Drive to mile 11.9 of the Richardson Highway (about 16 miles from downtown Valdez), and turn north on Old Richardson Highway Loop. A "Pack Trail of 1899" sign announces this turn for northbound traffic. From the intersection, drive 0.3 mile to find a small pullout on the right for parking. The trail, marked, is on the left a couple hundred feet farther along. The east end of the Old Richardson Highway Loop is at mile 12.4 of the Richardson Highway. The parking pullout lies about 0.4 mile from that intersection.

Richardson Highway mileposts are associated with the original Valdez townsite, which was heavily damaged during the 1964 Great Alaska Earthquake. Add about 4 miles if you are measuring from present-day Valdez (the intersection of Pioneer Drive and the Richardson Highway).

## ON THE ROUTE

This description assumes that hikers start at the southern trailhead. The initial section of the trail is known as the Pack Trail. Volunteers cleared this section using only hand tools, to keep alive the original spirit of 1899. For 0.6 mile the trail climbs through coastal rainforest of Sitka spruce and northern hemlock laced with devil's club, dwarf dogwood, and ferns. The tall trees, providing some shelter, make this a good hike for a rainy day. Some of the Sitka spruce are 3 feet in diameter, large for Southcentral Alaska, and may be two hundred years old. Interpretive signs along the way tell the trail's history. After the trail levels, it crosses a small stream where trail-building efforts more than one hundred years old show in the rockwork.

Yes, those black piles in the trail are bear scat, so remember to make noise. Openings in the forest provide occasional views of the Lowe River valley, Meteorite Mountain (6565 feet) to the south, and Keystone Canyon and its waterfalls.

After 1.3 miles, the trail begins to descend gradually to Horsetail Falls Creek. It crosses the stream on a small footbridge, and then heads down valley with the roar of Horsetail Falls below. The vegetation changes

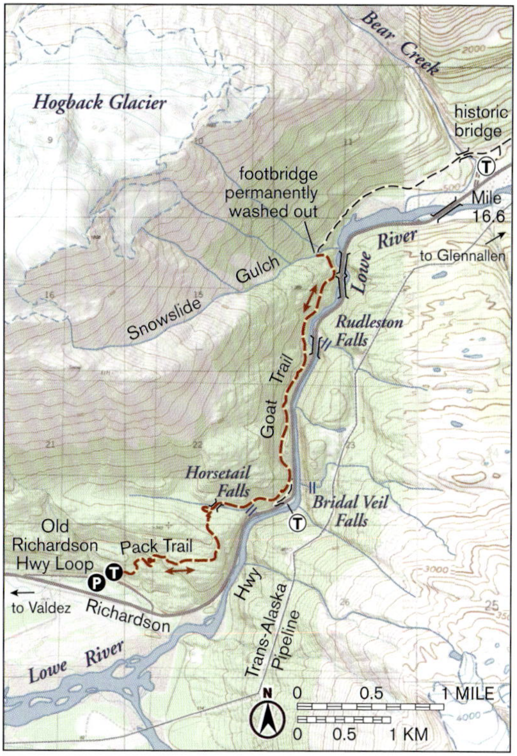

in this area, losing the hemlock and adding more birch, currants, and salmonberry. The trail appears to be brushed annually, but if it has not been by midsummer, this segment could be overgrown.

As the trail descends toward Bridal Veil Falls, across the Lowe River canyon, it reaches a short, steep downhill section with footing more difficult than previous parts of the trail. The tall falls are visible in a couple of different locations in this area.

Approximately 2.3 miles from the trailhead, the Pack Trail reaches an intersection with the wagon road that was built partly on top of the original trail. This section is known as the Goat Trail. A side trail to the right leads 0.2 mile to the intermediate parking lot at Bridal Veil Falls.

To continue the hike, bear left onto the Goat Trail. Parts of this segment are wider and more open than the Pack Trail, allowing views of rocky cliffs and cloud-swathed, snow-streaked mountains above as the sound of Bridal Veil Falls fades behind. Later, alder and tall grasses crowd the view. Look for the occasional old telegraph pole or length of wire; in a couple of spots, telegraph wire could trip unwary hikers. Parts of the trail hug the sheer, flower-studded cliffs. In one place, the trail traverses a ledge with a steep drop-off. Though the path is good, there is some exposure—and good views of a historic tunnel below and another waterfall.

About 1.8 miles from the intersection with the Pack Trail (4.2 from the start), the Goat Trail reaches Snowslide Gulch where large, dramatic avalanches often leave snow lingering well into July and sometimes all summer. A footbridge fell victim to an avalanche, so for all practical purposes, this is the end of the trip (but see Extending Your Trip). Boulders and small islands split the tumbling, splashing waters of Snowslide Gulch, and wildflowers add color. The gulch provides open mountain views. Sit for a few minutes to take it all in, and then head back the way you came.

Contact the Valdez Parks and Recreation Department for information on current conditions (see the Resources section).

## SHORTER OPTIONS

A roundtrip hike from the Bridal Veil Falls parking lot to Snowslide Gulch runs 4 miles, with 850 feet of elevation gain. The Bridal Veil Falls pullout and trailhead are at mile 13.7 of the Richardson Highway, on the west side. Walk southeast on a path paralleling the highway for 500 feet. The path then doubles back to head uphill.

## EXTENDING YOUR TRIP

On the north side of the washed-out bridge over Snowslide Gulch, the old wagon road continues 2.7 miles up the Lowe River valley, and hikers may access it at two highway locations:

**Mile 16.6, at Bear Creek.** Access is via a narrow gravel track that is nearly impossible to see. From the eastern end of the highway bridge over the Lowe River, it is 0.2 mile farther east to this turn, just northeast of buildings on the opposite side of the highway. The track dives steeply off the shoulder and disappears into tall brush. A trail sign may be mostly hidden in vegetation. The narrow track ends in 0.1 mile at the hillside; find the access trail on the right. It is marked by a sign on a tree, but midsummer vegetation may hide the sign. There is limited space to park and turn around.

**Mile 18.** The trail begins at a large pullout on the north side of the highway with a defining feature

OPPOSITE: *Meteorite Mountain in July with the Lowe River and Richardson Highway below*

*Spruce grouse in camouflage along the trail*

that has stood the test of time: an old pay phone standing by itself. Find the trail about 50 yards west of the phone.

At Snowslide Gulch, there is a small chance conditions will allow hikers to cross the stream and continue without driving to another trailhead. In early summer it may be possible to cross the gulch on leftover hard-packed snow. Use extreme caution: evaluate the snow thickness, the amount of water underneath, and where you would land if you broke through. Later, depending on water level, it may be possible to wade. It is usually not deep, but this high-gradient stream has a lot of energy splashing through boulders; don't count on being able to cross.

The segment between Bear Creek and Snowslide Gulch is 1.2 miles. A narrow side trail leads from the informal Bear Creek trailhead to the old wagon road. About 100 yards to the left, a historic steel bridge, constructed by the army during World War II, provides a crossing of Bear Creek for hikers.

Heading east from Bear Creek, the trail follows the old wagon road for another 1.5 miles through woods of cottonwood, alder, and Sitka spruce. Wild cucumber, fireweed, goatsbeard, and cow parsnip join the devil's club and grasses lining this part of the trail, known locally as the Dutch Flats segment.

The City of Valdez reports another segment of historic pack trail is open to hiking, leading from Richardson Highway mile 25.7, just below the crest of Thompson Pass, to mile 19.9. This route passes through open alpine areas near Thompson Pass and descends through the alder zone to forest.

It appears the segments described in this section get less use and may get less maintenance than the primary Pack Trail and Goat Trail route through Keystone Canyon.

# 55 SHOUP BAY TRAIL

**DISTANCE:** 2 miles roundtrip
**TIME:** Less than half day
**ELEVATION GAIN:** 250 feet
**HIGH POINT:** 50 feet
**SEASON:** Mid-May–October
**SURFACE:** Bog, sand and/or gravel, brush (high)
**GRADE:** Low angle
**INDIGENOUS LAND:** Chugach Sugpiaq (Alutiiq)

**MANAGING AGENCIES:** Valdez Adventure Alliance and the City of Valdez
**MAP:** USGS Valdez A-7
**ONLINE MAP SEARCH:** "front street valdez"
**TRAILHEAD GPS:** 61.135969°N, 146.390115°W

**A primitive trail, built by Alaska State Parks and maintained by the Valdez Adventure Alliance,** leads hikers to a stunning beach stroll along Port Valdez. Enjoy access to the shore while basking in views of fjord-like mountainsides rising from the water to their glacial apices. Originally, this trail ventured 10 miles one way across rugged terrain to three public-use cabins and campsites on the shores of Shoup Bay, but most of the trail has since grown impassable. (The three public-use cabins are, however, still reservable and accessible by water; check with the Valdez Adventure Alliance for reservation information and water taxi recommendations.) Hikers may still make it as far as the Gold Creek campsite (3.5 miles one way) in May and early June, before thick vegetation grows in. Due to maintenance unpredictabilities, the focus here is on the reliable, local-favorite part of the trail: the simple joy of an out-and-back hike to the beach.

## DRIVING DIRECTIONS

Search online for "shoup trail park valdez ak," or follow these directions. Follow the Richardson Highway west through Valdez as it turns into Egan Drive. Continue straight to Mineral Creek, about 1 mile past Hazelet Avenue. Cross the creek, and follow Egan Drive until it ends at Front Street in a little over a block. A parking lot and trailhead bulletin board are on the left, along with a small playground and restroom.

## ON THE ROUTE

The first mile or so of the trail is wide, relatively level, and quite easy. Begin hiking on a wooded path, quickly encountering high alders that volunteer crews frequently battle back; consider leaving a donation at the trailhead kiosk. After crossing a bridge, the trail becomes muddy in places; waterproof hiking boots or even rubber boots may be appropriate. In less than a mile, reach a broad, wildflower-dotted salt-marsh meadow and great views of Port Valdez. In winter, fat-tire bicyclists reach these flats on a groomed snow trail. In summer, boardwalks and small bridges help hikers skirt the marsh to the right, but the path may flood here depending on weather.

*Salmonberries ripening along the Shoup Bay Trail in early July*

*Port Valdez and the Chugach Mountains serve as a grand setting for hikers and boaters alike.*

After slightly more than 1 mile of hiking, follow a short side trail on the left to the gravel beach. Stopping here makes a fine destination. Day boaters land on this beach from Valdez Harbor by kayak, packraft, and motor to enjoy their picnics alongside hikers. While snacking, look south across Port Valdez to the Trans-Alaska Pipeline terminal, the end point and control center for 800 miles of 48-inch pipe carrying crude oil from the north coast to the south coast of Alaska, Prudhoe Bay to Valdez. Note the massive storage tanks on land and oil tankers that may be docked and filling.

## EXTENDING YOUR TRIP

To prolong the hike, a few options are possible. Strolling west along the beach is an obvious good choice, as the surface is wide and gravelly, and the gentle curve of the coast reveals a rock outcropping 0.5 mile down the shoreline from the beach access as the stopping point. Even at moderately high tide, hikers can enjoyably pick their way over rocky footing this far. Up to the rock outcrop, there is low risk of getting truly cut off by the tide; the worst case is an uphill battle with the tall, dense bushes that separate the beach from the parallel trail above.

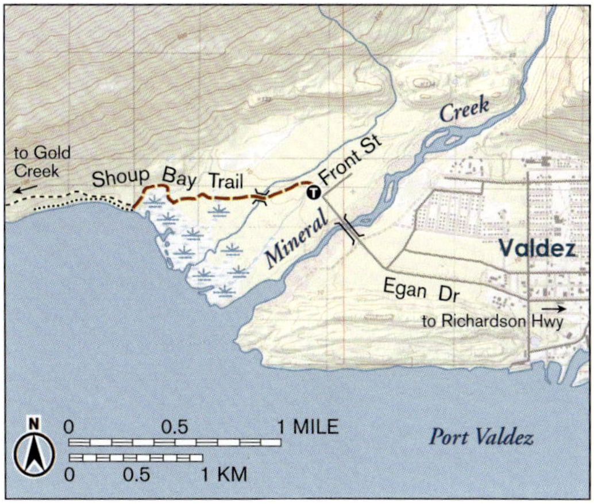


Another option is to return to the main trail and forge on past the beach access point. The trail narrows and may at times be overgrown and wet in rainy weather. Beware of cow parsnip and stinging nettles, although those willing to brave the bushes may be rewarded with salmonberries mixed in with the less pleasant plants. Do consider turning around to avoid injury when footing becomes both obscured and uneven, or when bear sign is prevalent—surprising a bear foraging in the thick bushes on a narrow trail is dangerous (see Bears and Other Wildlife in the Introduction).

In early season or after rounds of trail maintenance, hikers may have a clear way on the Shoup Bay Trail to the broad, green, fan-shaped delta of Gold Creek, 3.5 miles from the trailhead, where a campsite with a latrine and food storage locker is available. Be aware, though, that while the way may be more clear, hiking very early in the season presents avalanche danger as the trail follows the base of a steep mountainside. Only choose this adventure after researching current conditions; check with the Valdez Parks and Recreation Department or Valdez Adventure Alliance (see the Resources section) for trail status and maps.

# Acknowledgments

Special thanks to Gretchen Nelson, wife and mother of the authors, who put her heart into supporting her people and this project.

## PROFESSIONAL EXPERTISE

We aren't experts on every subject in this book. Thanks for filling in the gaps: Gary Lee Brown, mining history; Polly Hessing, Alaska Department of Fish and Game (retired), bear behavior; Brentwood "Hig" Higman, Ground Truth Alaska, Tutka Backdoor Trail; Eeva Latosuo, Alaska Pacific University, avalanches; Dick Mylius, Alaska Department of Natural Resources (retired), ANILCA trainer; Pat Owens, Mat-Su Borough (retired), lands and access; Derek and Catriona Reynolds, Cycle Logical Homer, bicycle maintenance; Melissa Shaginoff, artist, activist, and Alaska Pacific University Art Galleries curator, Indigenous land acknowledgment; Dorn Van Dommelen, University of Alaska Anchorage, geography and maps.

## PHOTO CONTRIBUTORS

Special thanks to Anne Raup, *Anchorage Daily News* photo editor, for advice as well as her own photos. Other generous contributors: PJ Bell, Susan Beesley, Imee Sudaria Casalamitao, Jessa and Joe Casquejo, Mike Chavez, Steve Cleary, Rob Clark, Tami Hamler, Taylor Horne, Shawn Horning, Nikki Navio, Marty Freeman, Gretchen Nelson, Mark Miner, Gayle and Helen Nienhueser, Hannah Pratt, John Pearce, Cody Priest, Nancy Simmerman, Gary Snyder, Henry Stevens, Klara Tamasi, Kjerstin and Joe Thomas, Jessica Tolentino, Lang Van Dommelen, Mark Wedekind, Denny Wells, Avery Wolfe, Dave Wolfe, Duncan Wright.

## FEET ON THE GROUND

Many others joined us on the trail, allowed us to pick their brains about recent adventures, or offered us places to stay or gear to use. Thanks to Anne and Dan Billman, Bob Butera, Rob Clark, Steve Cleary, Amy Dalton, Cami and Mark Dalton, Marty Freeman, Sally Gibert, Julie and Mike Graham, Tami Hamler, Chism Henry, Austin Hess, Shawn Horning, Peter Johnson, Brian Litmans, Alan McCutcheon, Eleanor McMahon, Jeanne and Mark Larsen, Lizzy Iandoli Miner, Mark Miner, Ian Moore, Ginny and Ted Moore, Jack Mosby, Helen and Gayle Nienhueser, Doug and Helen O'Harra, Ariana O'Harra, Cooper Parish, Chuck 'Kent Waite' Pratt, Hannah Pratt, Anne Raup, Jim Renkert, Victor Shen, Carla and Tony Slaton-Barker, Dick and Liska Snyder, Gary Snyder, Bill Spencer, Tucker and Ginger Spohr, Karmen Staveland, Kjerstin and Joe Thomas, Gabe Travis/Interior Trails, Joan Trarostino, Dorn Van Dommelen, Clyde Vicary, Mark Wedekind, Duncan Wright, Annika Wolfe, Avery Wolfe.

## LAND MANAGERS

Managers of parks, forests, and other lands generously spent time confirming details, plans, and

*A Dall sheep in the Chugach front range, with Anchorage in the background* (Photo by Hannah Leigh Pratt)

status of trail projects. Thanks to Jack Blackwell, Alaska Division of Parks and Outdoor Recreation (DPOR), Kenai Peninsula Area; Will Brennan, Chugach National Forest (CNF), Glacier Ranger District; Ben Corwin, Chugach State Park; Justin DiPaola, Denali State Park; Jesse Labinski, CNF, Seward Ranger District; Stuart Leidner, DPOR, Mat-Su Area; Irene Lindquist, CNF, Seward Ranger District; Diane Milliard, Wrangell–St. Elias National Park and Preserve; Marcie Roberston, City of Valdez; Jason Stancil, CNF, Glacier Ranger District; Andy Schidner, Lanette Oliver, Jonathan Goold, Valdez Adventure Alliance.

## BOOK PRODUCTION AND PUBLISHING

The crew at Mountaineers Books was forever friendly, helpful, and professional in keeping this fiftieth anniversary incarnation on track for the actual anniversary. Thanks to Kate Rogers, Janet Kimball, Laura Shauger, Jennifer Kepler, Ben Pease, McKenzie Long, and the rest of the Mountaineers Books team.

# Glossary

**alpenglow** A usually pinkish, sometimes golden light on mountainsides when the sun is low. Usually applied to sunset light, but the same effect occurs at sunrise.

**alpine** The mountain life zone above tree line, dominated by low-growing tundra plants. See also *subalpine*

**blowdown** A tree blown down by wind. Blowdowns block trails and make travel difficult.

**bushwhack** To brush past, push through, or proceed by climbing upon plant material, generally involving use of the hands. Walking through knee-high to waist-high bushes may count as bushwhacking if passage is impeded. Bushwhacking generally involves no trail or only a faint trail. Walking through head-high grass, ferns, cow parsnip, and the like generally is not considered bushwhacking but could be if passage were substantially impeded or devil's club were present.

**cairn** A small or large pile of rocks to mark the way or mark a summit.

**cirque** A glacier-carved mountain bowl, sometimes containing a tarn.

**climbing skins** Cloth strips that are fur-like on one side and adhesive on the other and stick to the bases of backcountry skis or splitboards. The directionality of the fibers allows users to glide forward over snow but stick before sliding backward, aiding travel up steep slopes.

**col** On a high ridge, a low point between two peaks.

**cornice** A windblown accumulation of usually dense snow built up on the lee side of a ridge or other edge. Cornices are subject to breaking off under their own weight or the weight of a skier or hiker and creating an avalanche.

**dryas** A low evergreen plant of mountainous arctic and subarctic regions, often with a white flower. The plants can form cushions of greenery in otherwise bare-looking soils.

**escarpment** A cliff or bluff face, typically where a relatively low-angle area drops suddenly to a lower-elevation area.

**glissade** To slide, generally in control, on feet or butt on the snow. Not to be confused with "avalanche," which is a slide of a mass of snow that can take trees, rocks, and people with it, causing death and destruction, and in which people are not in control.

**moraine** Mixed sand, gravel, and boulders deposited by a glacier. Lateral moraines occur along the sides of a valley glacier. Medial moraines form where glaciers come together. Recessional and terminal moraines form across the front (toe) of a glacier when it recedes.

**packraft** A lightweight, high-tech, inflatable watercraft meant for easy carrying in the backcountry, used primarily for floating along or across rivers in combination with hiking.

**portage** A short trail connecting two lakes or other bodies of water, on which to carry a boat and gear from one to the other. It can also mean the act of hiking, often carrying a boat and gear, between bodies of water or around an area impassable on the water.

**posthole** To plunge with each step deep into the snow surface while walking. Postholing is taxing compared to walking on a firm snow surface or a trail.

**rime** Frost accumulated on the sides of steep rock, trees, poles, or towers by fog freezing to the windward surface and thickening into the wind.

**saddle** A pass or low point between hilltops or peaks; similar to *col* but generally broader, lower, or less steep.

**scree** A field or channel of loose small rock on a slope. Because the rock moves underfoot, a scree slope is difficult to climb but sometimes fun to plunge down.

**skin track** The usually steep track in snow left by skiers using climbing skins on their skis. See *climbing skins*.

**social trail** A trail created almost entirely by passage of people's feet; not a professionally designed and built trail. Social trails may be indistinguishable from moose or sheep trails, may go straight up grades rather than angle across them, and are more likely to be wet underfoot. Many social trails are as good as any formal trail, but many are prone to erosion and are not considered sustainable trails.

**subalpine** The transition life zone between forested mountainsides and alpine tundra; the few trees that survive at this elevation can grow smaller and twisted due to fierce winds. See also *alpine*.

**talus** A field or area of blocky rocks and sometimes boulders, generally on a slope or forming a slope. While individual rocks may be tippy, talus does not generally move en masse like scree.

**tarn** A mountain lake left after retreat of a glacier, usually in a cirque.

**tussocks** Compact, unstable, boot-sized wads of vegetation, often closely spaced and elevated above wet ground, that can make for tricky walking.

# Resources

Physical addresses are listed where they are useful. Social media handles are provided only for accounts that were active at the time of publication.

## ALASKA NATIVE ENTITIES

These Alaska Native entities are near trips in this book and offer information on history and culture. Some statewide Native organizations and resources on Indigenous land acknowledgment are also listed.

**Ahtna, Inc.**
ahtna.com
Regional Native corporation centered on Copper River drainage

**Alaska Federation of Natives**
nativefederation.org
@nativefed
Statewide tribal advocacy organization

**Alaska Native Heritage Center**
alaskanative.net
8800 Heritage Center Drive
Anchorage, AK
@akheritagecenter
Statewide cultural center with immersive exhibits and programs

**Cheesh-Na Tribal Council**
cheeshna.com
Near Slana and Mentasta Mountains

**Chickaloon Native Village**
chickaloon-nsn.gov
In Matanuska Valley

**Native Village of Chitina**
nativevillageofchitina.com
On Copper River at start of McCarthy Road

**Chugach Alaska Corporation**
chugach.com
Regional Native corporation centered on Prince William Sound and outer coast of Kenai Peninsula

**Cook Inlet Region, Inc.**
ciri.com
@ourciri
@ciri
Regional Native corporation centered on Cook Inlet

**Kenaitze Indian Tribe**
kenaitze.org
Centered along Kenai River on Kenai Peninsula

**Knik Tribal Council**
kniktribe.org
Along Knik Arm (north side) and in Susitna Valley

**Land Acknowledgment Workshops**
melissashaginoff.com/land-acknowledgment-workshop
Alaska Native land acknowledgment workshops and resources from a local artist and activist

**Native Governance Center**
nativegov.org/a-guide-to-indigenous-land-acknowledgment
A guide to Indigenous land acknowledgment from a Native-led nonprofit in the Midwest

**Native Land Digital**
native-land.ca
@nativelandnet
Interactive map that helps answer "Whose land am I on?"; available as a smartphone app

**Native Village of Eklutna**
eklutna-nsn.gov
Along upper Knik Arm (south side) in Anchorage area

**Ninilchik Village Tribe**
ninilchiktribe-nsn.gov
At Ninilchik River on Kenai Peninsula

**Qutekcak Native Tribe**
qutekcak.org
Instagram @qutekcaknativetribe
In Resurrection Bay and Seward area of Kenai Peninsula

**Seldovia Village Tribe**
svt.org
In Kachemak Bay on Kenai Peninsula

**Valdez Native Tribe**
valdeznativetribe.org
In Prince William Sound and Valdez

## LAND MANAGERS

Some entries are listed under the park name or equivalent, with a cross-reference to the parent agency so that readers can more easily match them up with the managing agencies highlighted in the trip write-ups.

**Alaska Division of Mining, Land, and Water**
dnr.alaska.gov/mlw
This office within the Alaska Department of Natural Resources manages state lands outside designated park and recreation areas.
550 W. 7th Avenue, Suite 1360
Anchorage, AK
(907) 269-8400

**Alaska Division of Parks and Outdoor Recreation (Alaska State Parks)**
dnr.alaska.gov/parks
This office within the Alaska Department of Natural Resources manages designated parks, recreation areas, and other special management areas on state land. Search for a park, recreation area, or trail by name. To make cabin and campground reservations, visit alaskastateparks.reserveamerica.com.
550 W. 7th Avenue, Suite 1380
Anchorage, AK
(907) 269-8700
Instagram @akstateparks
Twitter @alaskastparks

**Chugach/Wood-Tikchik Area Office**
Potter Section House
Mile 115 Seward Highway
Anchorage, AK
(907) 345-5014

**Kenai Peninsula Area Office**
Morgan's Landing Campground
Mile 85 Sterling Highway
Sterling, AK
(907) 262-5581
Manages Kachemak Bay State Park, Caines Head State Recreation Area, Kenai Peninsula state campgrounds

**Matanuska-Susitna/Copper Basin Area Office**
Finger Lake State Recreation Site
Mile 0.7 Bogard Road
Wasilla, AK
(907) 745-3975
Covers Denali State Park, Hatcher Pass Management Area, Nancy Lake State Recreation Area, and state campgrounds in Mat-Su, Copper Basin, and Valdez areas

**Anchorage Coastal Wildlife Refuge**
Managed by Alaska Department of Fish and Game
adfg.alaska.gov; search for refuge name
ADF&G Division of Wildlife Conservation
Anchorage, AK
(907) 267-2189

**Anchorage Parks and Recreation**
muni.org/Departments/parks/Pages/default.aspx
General: (907) 343-4355; parks@muni.org
Kincaid Park (Trip 33): (907) 343-6397; kincaid@muni.org
Instagram @anchorageparksandrec
Twitter @ANCParksandRec

**AT&T**
For access to Lion Head (Trip 48), call AT&T's Anchorage office from a place with reliable phone service: (907) 264-8363 or (800) 252-7521.

**Caines Head State Recreation Area**
See Alaska Division of Parks and Outdoor Recreation.

**Chugach National Forest**
fs.usda.gov/chugach

**Forest Supervisor's Office**
161 E. 1st Avenue, Door #8
Anchorage, AK
(907) 743-9500

**Glacier Ranger District**
145 Forest Station Road
Girdwood, AK
(907) 783-3242
Includes Girdwood, Portage, Turnagain Pass, Spencer, and Grandview

**Seward Ranger District**
33599 Ranger Station Spur
Seward Highway mile 23.5, near Seward
(907) 288-3178
Includes Kenai Mountains

**Chugach State Park**
See Alaska Division of Parks and Outdoor Recreation.

**City of Whittier**
whittieralaska.gov
(907) 472-2327

**Cook Inlet Region, Inc.**
ciri.com
On the website, see "Our Lands," then "Permitting."

**Denali State Park**
See Alaska Division of Parks and Outdoor Recreation.

**Hatcher Pass Management Area**
See Alaska Division of Parks and Outdoor Recreation.

**Homer Parks and Recreation**
cityofhomer-ak.gov/recreation
(907) 235-1583
parks@cityofhomer-ak.gov

**Joint Base Elmendorf–Richardson**
jber.isportsman.net
Contact JBER for access to military land for recreation and for information about Arctic Valley Road conditions (Trips 27 and 34).
(907) 552-8609 or (907) 552-9453

**Kachemak Bay State Park**
See Alaska Division of Parks and Outdoor Recreation.

**Kenai Fjords National Park**
nps.gov/kefj/index.htm
1212 4th Avenue
Seward, AK
(907) 422-0500
@kenaifjordsnps
Reservations for Willow Cabin start October 15 for winter.

**Kenai National Wildlife Refuge**
fws.gov/refuge/kenai
For canoe routes, see "Visit," then "Visitor Activities," then "Canoe System." For cabin and campground reservations, go to recreation.gov. Visitor center is at 2139 Ski Hill Road in Soldotna.
(907) 260-2820

**Nancy Lake State Recreation Area**
See Alaska Division of Parks and Outdoor Recreation.

**Palmer Hay Flats State Game Refuge**
Managed by Alaska Department of Fish and Game
adfg.alaska.gov; search for "Palmer Hay Flats"

ADF&G Division of Wildlife Conservation
Palmer, AK
(907) 861-2112

**Seldovia Native Association, Inc.**
snai.com/lands
Contact SNAI for land use information and permits.
(907) 234-7625

**Valdez Parks and Recreation**
valdezak.gov/149/Parks-Recreation
(907) 835-4440

**Wrangell–St. Elias National Park and Preserve**
nps.gov/wrst
(907) 822-5234
@wrangellstenps

**Headquarters and visitor center**
Mile 106.8 Richardson Highway
Copper Center, AK
(907) 822-5234

**Chitina Ranger Station**
Mile 33 Edgerton Highway
Chitina, AK
(907) 823-2205

**Kennecott Visitor Center**
Kennicott, 5 miles north of McCarthy
(907) 205-7106

**Slana Ranger Station**
Mile 0.5 Nabesna Road
Slana, AK
(907) 822-7401

## RESERVATIONS, RENTALS, AND MAP SOURCES

Listings are organized into these categories: cabin, hut, and campground reservations; gear rentals by region; map sources; and transportation.

### Cabin, Hut, and Campground Reservations

**Alaska Division of Parks and Outdoor Recreation**
alaskastateparks.reserveamerica.com
Cabin and campground reservations

**Alaska Huts Association**
alaskahuts.org
Reservations for Manitoba Cabin (Trip 16)
@alaskahuts

**American Alpine Club**
aacbackyard.org/alaskasection
americanalpineclub.org/snowbird-hut
Information about donations for use of Snowbird Hut (Trip 43)
alaska@americanalpineclub.org

**Chugach National Forest**
recreation.gov
Cabin and campground reservations

**Eagle River Nature Center**
ernc.org
Cabin, yurt, and campsite reservations for Trip 25
(907) 694-2108

**Kenai National Wildlife Refuge**
recreation.gov
Cabin reservations

**Mountaineering Club of Alaska (MCA)**
mtnclubak.org
Information on making a donation for use of MCA mountaineering huts (Trip 43)

**State of Alaska cabins and campgrounds**
See Alaska Division of Parks and Outdoor Recreation.

### Gear Rentals

#### *Kenai*

**Alaska Canoe and Campground**
alaskacanoetrips.com
Canoes, shuttle service, mountain bikes, camping equipment
35292 Sterling Highway
Sterling, AK
(907) 262-2331

**Beemuns Bike and Ski Loft**
beemuns.com/bike-and-ski-loft
Fat-bike and auto rack rentals
35277 Kenai Spur Highway Road
Soldotna, AK
(907) 262-1234
@beemunsbikeloft

**Bike Cooper Landing LLC**
bikecooperlandingak.com
Mountain bike rentals
17158 Frontier Circle
Cooper Landing, AK
(907) 231-6793

**Cycle Logical**
cyclelogicalhomer.com
Fat-bike, bikepacking gear, and car rack rentals; shuttle service
302 E. Pioneer Avenue
Homer, AK
(907) 299-7746
@cyclelogicalhomer

**Take Refuge Canoe**
akcanoe.com
Fully supplied canoe trip packages, both guided and unguided. Call for canoe pickup location.
(907) 602-9647

#### *Anchorage*

To rent all kinds of bikes and accessories, search online for "bike rental anchorage." There are several outfitters.

**Alaska Mountaineering and Hiking**
alaskamountaineering.com
Nordic skate and boot, ski and boot, and ice axe rentals
2633 Spenard Road
Anchorage, AK
(907) 272-1811
@alaskamountaineering

**Alaska Outdoor Gear Rental**
alaskaoutdoorgearrental.com
Hiking, camping, and winter gear rentals; bear spray, canisters, and fences; bikes and boats
540 Potter Drive
Anchorage, AK
(907) 830-0232
@alaskaoutdoorgearrental

**Downtown Bicycle Rental**
alaska-bike-rentals.com
All kinds of bike and trailer rentals
333 W. 4th Avenue
Anchorage, AK
(907) 279-5293

**Lifetime Adventures (Eklutna Lake)**
lifetimeadventure.net
Kayak and mountain bike rentals available at Eklutna Lake trailhead
info@lifetimeadventure.net
Phone: (907) 746-4644
Text: (907) 232-9219

**REI**
anchorage.rentals.rei.com
Hiking, camping, winter gear, bikes, and boats rentals
500 E. Northern Lights Blvd.
Anchorage, AK
(907) 272-4565

### Mat-Su

**Backcountry Bike and Ski**
backcountrybikeandski.com
Fat-tire bike and cross-country ski rentals
132 W. Arctic Avenue
Palmer, AK
(907) 746-5018
backcountrybikeandski@gmail.com

**Tippecanoe Canoe Rentals**
Nancy Lake State Recreation Area
Willow, AK
(907) 355-6687
paddleak@mtaonline.net

### Copper Basin

**Larry's Bike Shop and Fat Mermaid Bike Rental**
Rentals: (907) 835-3000
Repairs: (907) 831-0978
Rentals are at Fat Mermaid restaurant, 143 N. Harbor Drive in Valdez.

**Prince William Sound College**
pwsc.alaska.edu
College in Valdez rents cross-country skis short- and long-term. Navigate to the "Health & Fitness Center" menu on website.
(907) 834-1684

**Valdez Stay and Play**
valdezstayandplay.com/rent-a-bike
E-bike and kayak rentals
(907) 835-5515
valdezstayandplay@gmail.com
@valdezstayandplay

## Map Sources

Many businesses that rent gear carry a selection of maps. See the Gear Rentals section.

**CalTopo**
caltopo.com
This online mapper offers free basic access and paid subscriptions. The free version provides a seamless USGS map base. Users can upload GPS tracks and print maps.

**Gaia GPS**
gaiagps.com
Online mapper with free basic access and paid subscriptions

**Ground Truth Alaska Maps**
ground-truth-trekking.square.site
Map of Tutka Backdoor Trail (Trip 1), among others

**US Geological Survey (USGS) Maps**
usgs.gov/products/maps/overview
Visit store.usgs.gov to view, download for free, or purchase hard copies. Visit store.usgs.gov/map-locator to determine which USGS map covers a certain location.

**Winterbear**
winterbear.com
Download the free Bomber Traverse map (Trip 43) or purchase a weatherproof physical copy.

## Transportation

Some bus or van services and water taxis allow people to get on and off at any location in their service area or route. Ask about trailhead stops.

**Alaska Bus Company**
alaskabuscompany.com
Passengers can get off at locations between Homer and Anchorage.
info@alaskabuscompany.com
(907) 299-6806

**Alaska Department of Transportation and Public Facilities**
For a statewide interactive road conditions map, see 511.alaska.gov. For Anton Anderson Memorial Tunnel (a.k.a. Whittier Tunnel for Trips 20 and 22) information, see dot.alaska.gov/creg/whittiertunnel or call (877) 611-2586.

**Alaska Railroad Corporation**
alaskarailroad.com
Access to Trip 15; transportation between Talkeetna, Wasilla, Anchorage, Girdwood, Whittier, and Seward
reservations@akrr.com
(800) 544-0552
@alaskarailroad

**Ashore Water Taxi**
homerwatertaxi.com
4246 Homer Spit Road
Homer, AK
(907) 235-2341
ashorewatertaxi@gmail.com

**Blackburn Heritage Foundation**
Kennicott–McCarthy shuttle van
(425) 351-5021
dtal544@frontier.com

**Copper Spike Transport**
copperspiketransport.com
Van transport between Anchorage, Valdez, or Glennallen and McCarthy
(907) 406-9599
jamie@copperspiketransport.com

**Flattop Mountain Shuttle**
alaska-bike-rentals.com
This once-per-day shuttle from downtown Anchorage to Glen Alps trailhead is run by Downtown Bicycle Rentals.
(907) 279-5293

**Homer Ocean Charters**
homerocean.com
(907) 235-6212
homeroceancharters@gmail.com
@homeroceancharters

**Interior Alaska Bus Line**
interioralaskabusline.com
Transport along the Glenn Highway, Tok–Anchorage (also Tok–Fairbanks). Website includes links to public transit in several communities including Anchorage, Girdwood, Kenai Peninsula, Talkeetna to Trapper Creek to Willow, and Palmer to Wasilla.
(800) 770-6652

**Kennicott Shuttle**
kennicottshuttle.com
Ground shuttle between Glennallen and McCarthy
(907) 822-5292

**Mako's Water Taxi**
makoswatertaxi.com
4308 Homer Spit Road
Homer, AK
(907) 235-9055
mako@xyz.net
@makoswatertaxi

**Millers Landing**
millerslandingak.com
Water taxi for Caines Head and Kenai Fjords National Park
13890 Beach Drive
Seward, AK
(907) 331-3113
reservations@millerslandingak.com
@millerslanding

**Park Connection**
alaskacoach.com
Bus connection between Kenai Fjords National Park and Denali National Park (Anchorage, Denali, Seward, Talkeetna, Whittier)
info@alaskacoach.com
Toll-free: (800) 266-8625

**Seward Bus Line**
sewardbuslines.net
Anchorage, Whittier, Seward
Toll Free: (888) 420-7788
sewardbuslines@acsalaska.net

**Seward Water Taxi**
sewardwatertaxi.com
At Seward Small Boat Harbor
(907) 362-4101
akcoastalsafari@hotmail.com
@sewardwatertaxi

## OTHER HELPFUL RESOURCES

This section covers sources for avalanche safety, wilderness first responder and first-aid courses, trail conditions, and more.

### Avalanche Information and Courses

**Alaska Avalanche Information Center (AAIC)**
alaskasnow.org
(907) 314-0188
info@alaskasnow.org
@avalancheinformationcenter

**Alaska Avalanche School**
alaskaavalanche.org
@akavalancheschool

**Alaska Guide Collective**
alaskaguidecollective.com
@alaskaguidecollective

**Alaska Pacific University**
alaskapacific.edu

**Chugach National Forest Avalanche Information Center (CNFAIC)**
cnfaic.org
(907) 229-9060
staff@chugachavalanche.org
@chugachavy

**Hatcher Pass Avalanche Center (HPAC)**
hpavalanche.org
@h_p_a_c

**Valdez Avalanche Center**
alaskasnow.org/valdez
(907) 255-2241
@valdezavycenter

## First-Aid Education

**Alaska Avalanche School**
alaskaavalanche.org
Navigate to medical courses.

**Alaska Pacific University**
alaskapacific.edu
Search for "outdoor programs" or "WFR."

**National Outdoor Leadership School (NOLS)**
nols.edu
Alaska-specific courses available

**Red Cross**
redcross.org
Navigate to your community.

**Wilderness Emergency Medical Education**
akwildmed.com

## Trail and Snow Conditions

Several Facebook groups and pages offer crowdsourced information: Alaska Backcountry Ski Addiction, AK Hiking Connections, Anchorage Fat Bike, Crow Pass Trail, Crust Ski Alaska, Hiking in Alaska, and NordicSkate-SouthCentral Alaska.

**Cross Country Alaska**
snowio.com
All-modes trail and area reports

**Alaska Backcountry Cross Country Skiing**
crust.outlookalaska.com
Backcountry skate skiing and ski touring areas, conditions, and webcams

## Other Key Information

**Alaska Public Lands Information Center**
Multiagency public lands information for Southcentral Alaska
605 W. 4th Avenue, Suite 105
Anchorage, AK
(907) 644-3680

**Ground Truth Alaska**
groundtruthalaska.org
Resource for Tutka Backdoor Trail (among other Kachemak Bay adventures), trail building, wilderness expeditions, climate change research and resource issues
(907) 399-5530
contact@groundtruthtrekking.org

**Mat-Su Trails and Parks Foundation**
matsutrails.org
(907) 746-8757
info@matsutrails.org

**Public Information Center**
dnr.alaska.gov/commis/pic
Information about state lands in Southcentral Alaska
550 W. 7th Avenue, Suite 1360
Anchorage, AK
(907) 269-8400
TTY: 711 for Alaska Relay, or 800-770-8973
dnr.pic@alaska.gov

# CONSERVATION AND OUTDOOR ORGANIZATIONS

**Alaska Conservation Foundation**
alaskaconservation.org
Raises and distributes funds for conservation; maintains statewide Alaska Conservation Directory
@alaskaconservationfoundation
@AKConservation

**Alaska Quiet Rights Coalition**
Facebook.com/AlaskaQuietRightsCoalition
Advocates for natural quiet and nonmotorized uses of public land

**Alaska Trails**
alaskatrails.org
Advocates for trails statewide; builds trails; advocates for Alaska Long Trail
@alaskatrails

**Chugach Park Fund (at the Alaska Community Foundation)**
alaskacf.org/blog/funds/chugach-park-fund
Raises and distributes funds for park projects

**Chugach State Park Citizen Advisory Board**
dnr.alaska.gov/parks/misc/chugachadviseboard.htm
Advises state park managers about park trails and issues

**The Conservation Fund**
conservationfund.org/where-we-work/alaska
Conserves lands, often through purchase, and creates partnerships

**Great Land Trust**
greatlandtrust.org
Conserves land for habitat and public access typically by conservation easement
@greatlandtrust

**Matanuska-Susitna Borough Parks, Recreation, and Trails Advisory Board**
matsugov.us/boards/parks-trails-board
Advises borough on trail issues

**Mat-Su Ski Club**
matsuski.org
Runs cross-country ski programs and grooms trails
@matsuskiclub

**Mat-Su Trails and Park Foundation**
matsutrails.org
Raises and distributes funds for trails and parks

**Mountaineering Club of Alaska**
mtnclubak.org
Organizes trips and mountaineering skills courses and maintains huts

**Native Conservancy**
nativeconservancy.org
Conserves lands important to Alaska Native lifeways as a land trust
@nativeconservancy

**Nature Conservancy**
nature.org
Conserves lands and advocates for natural systems
@nature_org

**Sierra Club Alaska Chapter**
sierraclub.org/alaska
Advocates for conservation and hosts club events and hikes
@sierraclubak

**Singletrack Advocates**
singletrackadvocates.org
Advocates for and builds trails, with a focus on mountain bikes
@singletrackadvocates

**Valdez Adventure Alliance**
valdezadventurealliance.com
Manages trails, campgrounds, and outdoor festivals near Valdez
@valdezadventurealliance
@AdventureValdez

**Valley Mountain Bikers and Hikers**
vmbah.wildapricot.org
Advocates for trails in Mat-Su region

# Further Reading


Alaska Department of Fish and Game et al. "Know Your . . . Bear Facts: The Essentials for Traveling in Bear Country." Revised July 2013. www.adfg.alaska.gov/static/species/livingwithwildlife/bears/pdfs/know_your_bear_facts_brochure.pdf.

Bearbiology. "Staying Safe in Bear Country." Video, 30:35, March 5, 2021. www.youtube.com/watch?v=s-zkGuh42l4.

Cascio, Julie. *Wild, Edible, and Poisonous Plants of Alaska*. Pub. No. FNH-00028. Fairbanks, AK: Cooperative Extension Service, 2016. http://cespubs.uaf.edu/publications?show=1#1382.

Fredston, Jill A., and Doug Fesler. *Snow Sense: A Guide to Evaluating Snow Avalanche Hazard*. 5th ed. Anchorage, AK: Alaska Mountain Safety Center, 2011.

The Mountaineers. *Mountaineering: The Freedom of the Hills*. 9th ed. Seattle, WA: Mountaineers Books, 2017.

Tremper, Bruce. *Avalanche Essentials: A Step-by-Step System for Safety and Survival*. Seattle, WA: Mountaineers Books, 2013.

Wilkerson, James A., ed. *Medicine for Mountaineering and Other Wilderness Activities*. 6th ed. Seattle, WA: Mountaineers Books, 2010.

# In Recognition

This book that you hold in your hands was inspired by *55 Ways to the Wilderness in Southcentral Alaska*, a book originally published in 1972 and based on a project of the Mountaineering Club of Alaska in partnership with Mountaineers Books.

**The Mountaineering Club of Alaska** is a 501(c)(7) nonprofit corporation, founded in 1958, whose mission is to maintain, promote and perpetuate the association of persons who are interested in promoting, sponsoring, improving, stimulating and contributing to the exercise of skill and safety in the art and science of mountaineering. The club runs Basic Mountaineering School workshops, various training courses, and an annual ice climbing festival. It also sponsors trips and operates a network of public mountaineering huts. Members hold monthly meetings, open to the public, with a variety of outdoor programs. Contact info@mtnclubak.org or visit www.mtnclubak.org to learn more.

# Index

# About the Authors

Lifelong Anchorage resident **John Wolfe Jr.** studied at Middlebury College in Vermont before returning to Alaska. He founded the nonprofit Alaska Mountain and Wilderness Huts Association. He and his wife, Gretchen Nelson, included their daughters in outdoor excursions as they grew up. John became coauthor of this guide with his mother, Helen Nienhueser, starting with the fourth edition. Although he has guided on Denali, John loves the simple peak scrambles of the Chugach Mountains best of all.

Photo by Anne Raup

**Rebecca Wolfe** has been hiking in Southcentral Alaska since childhood. She earned a bachelor's degree from Smith College and a master's of architecture from Montana State University. Becca enjoys finding new ways to experience the Alaska backcountry on skis and by bike, though backpacking in the mountains is when she feels most at home. She splits her time between Mojave, California, and Anchorage, Alaska.

Photo by Gretchen Nelson

Find resources related to this guidebook, including digital maps and photographs, additional trips, and a way to submit changes you find in the field at 55waysalaska.com.

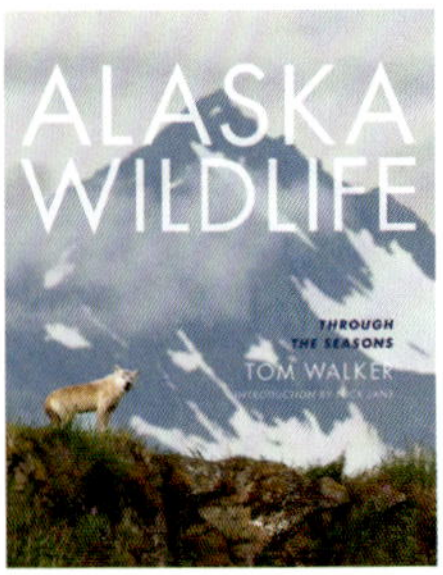
ALASKA WILDLIFE
THROUGH THE SEASONS
TOM WALKER

DENALI
NATIONAL PARK
THE COMPLETE VISITORS GUIDE
BILL SHERWONIT

DAY HIKING
Southcentral Alaska

Wild Shots
TOM WALKER
A Photographer's Life in Alaska

SETH KANTNER
A THOUSAND TRAILS HOME
LIVING WITH CARIBOU